FANTASY LITERATURE

FANTASY LITERATURE

A Core Collection and Reference Guide

Marshall B. Tymn
Kenneth J. Zahorski
and
Robert H. Boyer

R. R. BOWKER COMPANY
New York & London, 1979

To our wives,
Darlene, Marijean, and Barb

Published by R. R. Bowker Company
1180 Avenue of the Americas, New York, N.Y. 10036
Copyright © 1979 by Xerox Corporation
Printed and bound in the United States of America

Library of Congress Cataloging in Publication Data

Tymn, Marshall B   1937–
    Fantasy literature.

    Includes index.
    1. Fantastic fiction, English—Bibliography.
2. Fantastic fiction, American—Bibliography.   3. Fantastic fiction—History and criticism—Addresses, essays,
lectures.   I. Zahorski, Kenneth J., 1939–   joint
author.   II. Boyer, Robert H., 1937–   joint author.
III. Title.
Z2014.F4T9   [PR830.F3]   016.823'0876   79-1533
ISBN 0-8352-1153-3

Contents

Foreword

While art for the sake of art has always been defensible, these days the idea may leave us unsatisfied; especially when dealing with fantasy, a form that deliberately, exuberantly, seems to turn from the real world to one of its own creation. Too much has happened to us. Our problems are not figments of a maniac's imagination, though they often appear to be. They are brutally real. They demand real solutions. Despite the advances we have made in trying to civilize ourselves, events in the span of even one generation have been beyond invention of the wildest fancy. We are entitled to ask for usefulness. We need all the usefulness we can get.

The difficulty lies in our understanding of the word usefulness. Can fantasy, for example, prevent cavities, reduce overweight, or guarantee all of us brilliant careers in real estate? Probably not. No more than honor can set a leg. No one seriously expects it. The proposition is absurd. I wonder if, in essence, what fantasy does is all that different from what we expect of literature in general: that it engage specifically, directly, whatever topics currently preoccupy us. Well, so it should. Sometimes. But it is, I think, rather limiting to validate a work of art only by reference to newspaper headlines. Neither *The Tempest* nor *The Magic Flute* is judged primarily on the basis of its utility. Literal-mindedness is an admirable quality in airline pilots; but not necessarily in writers. Or readers.

Justifiably, we ask for relevance, social awareness, and all similar virtues. Do we always recognize them when we find them? We sometimes mistake trendiness for durable truth. The great works of art, which must include the great works of fantasy, have always spoken to us. We haven't always known how to listen.

Moreover, for many adults (certainly not for children) fantasy is thought to be an indulgence, something to outgrow. This is to equate being mature with being matter-of-fact. Fantasizing is a lifelong activity of the human organism; as natural as breathing; in some ways equally essential.

Imagination may well be one of our survival mechanisms, intrinsic to the brain itself. Researchers such as Robert E. Ornstein, in *The Psychology of Consciousness* and elsewhere, have gathered data that suggest what poets have always known: we are paradoxical beings. The evidence indicates that paradox and polarity are inherent in the very structure of the brain. To oversimplify: one hemisphere is rational, cognitive, analytical;

the other, nonrational, nonverbal, intuitive. One half, an intellectual; the other, a visionary. We need both to maintain equilibrium in this universe within our heads.

There may even be a physiological basis for one of the greatest of human gifts: hope. Lionel Tiger, for example, in *Optimism, the Biology of Hope*, speculates that hope, and a sense that somehow things will work out well, have been bred into us. "While there's life there's hope" may turn out to be sound neurophysiology.

The body, according to current research, produces its own "feel-good" medicine: called "endorphins," they reach receptor sites in the brain and spinal cord, and give us a sense of well-being, even in desperate circumstances. Indeed, desperate circumstances are the times we need those endorphins the most. They encourage us to make an extra effort even when all efforts seem vain; by making that effort, hoping against hope, we automatically increase the odds in our favor. And we've long known the effect of adrenalin, also created by our bodies, in mobilizing physical and mental resources.

To consider that some of our noblest human impulses may be not only culturally conditioned, or learned attitudes, but may also derive from electrochemical transactions, that our imagination has developed along with our cerebral cortex, is to me neither demeaning nor reductive. On the contrary, I find it awe-inspiring and all the more marvelous. I see no cause for indignation in the idea that we are physical entities, whatever else we may be. I also admit I'm a bad Euclidian and believe the whole can be greater than the sum of its parts.

Dreaming—our own private do-it-yourself fantasy—may be another survival mechanism. It helps us keep our sanity. In sensory deprivation experiments, without sound, light, or tactile sensations, without any external stimulation, the subjects did not simply shut down their minds and go to sleep. Instead, they generated spontaneously an elaborate pageant of images, visions, and adventures. Conversely, in other experiments, subjects were awakened whenever their rapid eye movements indicated they were dreaming. They were allowed ample sleep; but, deprived of dreams, they soon began suffering terrible anxieties, physical discomfort—in short, they got very sick.

By the same token, deprived of the waking dream we call art, deprived of the created or re-created dream we call fantasy, we can also suffer an acute kind of psychic malnutrition. We lack a certain dimension of personality. The result is, simply, that we are less than what we might be.

In the long run, however, the testing ground for fantasy is not in the laboratory but on our own nerve endings. Instead of asking "Is it useful?" it may be more profitable to ask "Does it work—and does it work on *us*?"

Yes. If we let it. If we are not afraid to allow ourselves to be deeply moved at levels not often accessible through works of surface realism. Great fantasy has the direct impact of a dream and the strength of a metaphor. Dreaming, indeed, is to consciousness what metaphor is to language. And what metaphor is to language, fantasy is to literature.

By no means would I dispute the "therapeutic" value of fairy tales and myth-based fantasy for the young: in defusing anxieties and resolving emotional conflicts, as Bruno Bettelheim analyzes them in *The Uses of Enchantment.* Even if this were its only function, it would still be a vital one. But, while adults may overcome infantile conflicts, they acquire others no less acute; and, no less than children do we need ways that help us make sense of our inner and outer worlds. Fantasy operates on adults with the same strength as on the young. An adult may respond to fantasy on one level, a child on another. But respond they do. Magic does not discriminate according to age, sex, or ethnic origin.

However, as in all true magic, fantasy declines to reveal its ultimate secret. We may only guess. We recognize its power to refresh, to give new perspectives, to fill us, in Tolkien's words, with "awe and wonder"; and certainly to delight and entertain us—itself no mean feat. Effortlessly, it engages the deepest and most abstract questions of theology, cosmology, metaphysics. Or, for the sheer joy of it, plays like a juggler with ideas, relationships, and possibilities. It can, with equal ease, evoke ancient archetypes and resonances of the Jungian collective unconscious; and simultaneously reflect the most immediate contemporary problems. Its meanings can be both clear and elusive; suggestive yet never fully grasped.

We read fantasy any way that pleases us at a given moment: as mythologists, historians, theologians, psychoanalysts, or social critics. In the end, I must agree with what Elizabeth Cook says about these perspectives in *The Ordinary and the Fabulous:* "None of them are right separately, and all of them are right collectively."

Fantasy Literature is oriented toward high fantasy—works in which the major action takes place in a secondary world. In chapter 1, Robert H. Boyer and Kenneth J. Zahorski give a detailed analysis of the genre, to which I can add only appreciation. Without straying too far, I would note here a certain analogy between high comedy and high fantasy, and between low comedy and low fantasy—terms, as the authors emphasize, which are not value judgments and have nothing to do with high or low quality.

Low comedy, reveling in pratfalls, insane machinery, and related disasters, shows us as physical beings at odds with, and at the mercy of, a world implacably physical. Our self-importance, our most grandiose ambitions, can be set at nought by a banana peel. High comedy deals with the banana peels of human emotions, relationships, and our ideas about them. Underlying it is a poignant, often heartbreaking sense of transiency. Even our best qualities, like our worst, are ephemeral. We will none of us be here very long.

High fantasy and low fantasy stand in a similar relationship. Low fantasy, usually set in a rational, physically familiar world, challenges us with the coexistence of the nonrational. High fantasy, in its secondary world, challenges us to examine the values of our primary world: a play of philosophies, not merely a play of enchanted objects.

Fantasy allows itself to deal in absolutes, a source of both dramatic strength and critical reproach. As for the latter, I would only suggest that writers of fantasy are neither more naive nor simpler-minded than anyone else. The quest for truth ends, if it ends at all, more often in paradox. The more we seek absolutes, the more we find ambiguities. In my opinion, the absolutes of fantasy function as reference points only; benchmarks for surveyors of human attitudes.

In making readers aware of what to me is the richest, most fascinating genre, *Fantasy Literature* does its first service. While the prevailing literary weather today may be hard realism, interest in modes of high imagination continues to grow. *Fantasy Literature* meets a most obvious and immediate need by helping to answer the question: "What shall I read next? I've read such-and-such. What else will I like?"

This is no question to take lightly. Anyone who suggests titles for further reading—librarians, teachers, parents, other readers—assumes a responsibility. Whether we are young or old, a certain book at a certain time can make a difference in our lives.

Drs. Boyer and Zahorski also pay readers (and writers) a high compliment. They believe literary quality is literary quality whether in the form of a child's book or an adult's. While books clearly intended for children are not included in the core list, it does include but does not segregate all-ages books (although some were published originally as juveniles).

Until now, detailed guides to high fantasy have not been all that easily available even to educators and library professionals. *Fantasy Literature*, however, combines in one volume bibliography and annotations that are both evaluations and appreciations, plus a reference section compiled by Marshall B. Tymn.

I hope this volume will reach professionals and nonprofessionals; those who read for practical information and those who read for pleasure and personal interest—these areas are not mutually exclusive.

Finally, I hope it will come into the hands of inveterate realists. Inside every realist I suspect there lurks a fantasist. If this book demonstrates that "true to life" is not always true enough, it will have performed its most commendable service.

Drexel Hill, Pennsylvania   Lloyd Alexander

Preface

Since the mid-1960s there has been a great rise of interest in fantasy literature. The recent but widespread popularity of fantasy is evident in the proliferation of course offerings on the subject in colleges and secondary schools and in the increase in the number of new and reprint titles published every year. More critical works are appearing devoted exclusively to fantasy. Major publishers have supplied the need for research tools by issuing reference works and special texts to meet the demands of the scholar and teacher. Along with this proliferation of fantasy materials, both primary and secondary, has arisen the need for bibliographic control of the literature. It was primarily with this need in mind that the present volume was compiled.

Fantasy Literature is intended to serve a wide audience: as an acquisitions tool for librarians building core fantasy collections; as a guide to the literature for teachers; as a reference handbook for fantasy scholars and researchers; and as a comprehensive introduction to the literature of fantasy and its related activities for interested readers who wish to acquaint themselves with some of the best works in the field.

In several important respects, *Fantasy Literature* is a unique reference tool. The introductory essay "On Fantasy," which opens Part I, analyzes the nature and development of the genre and presents fresh material on the definition of fantasy and its various subgenres. The annotated bibliography that follows is a highly selective core list consisting of more than 240 seminal works of high fantasy as defined in chapter 1. The annotations are more substantive than those in other current fantasy reference texts and will greatly facilitate the task of selection by prospective readers, librarians, and teachers. Part II, Research Aids, provides comprehensive coverage of the various scholarly and fan activities within the field, and includes material that has never before been systematically listed.

In order to make the Core Collection as meaningful as possible, a strict set of criteria has been applied in determining what titles should be included:

1. All selections are works of adult or all-ages high fantasy. No works written exclusively for children are listed, although the all-ages designation encompasses many well-established children's favorites.
2. All selections are works of high-quality prose fiction, judged by the same critical norms applied to any piece of literature.

3. With the one exception of *Undine* by the German author Baron de la Motte Fouqué, all titles were written in English.
4. All selections belong to the period of modern high fantasy, that is, to the period that begins with such eminent Victorian writers as John Ruskin, Lewis Carroll, Jean Ingelow, and most prominently, George MacDonald, whose earliest fantasy, *Phantastes*, appeared in 1854. *Undine*, written earlier in the century, is included as a forerunner from the Continent, mainly because MacDonald used it as the example of the classic faery tale.

No works published after 1978 were considered for inclusion. A relative few of the core list selections are somewhat difficult to locate, but they have been included here in the hope that the increasing interest in the field will encourage publishers to make more readily available long out-of-print works.

The bibliographic citation for each core title specifies author or editor; title, publisher, and year of first English-language edition; and publisher and year of current reprint edition. Variant titles and paperback editions are noted where appropriate. (A list of Core Collection titles currently available in the United Kingdom and a directory of American and British publishers are included as separate sections following Part II.) Sources used to verify first edition and reprint titles were *American Book Publishing Record, Books in Print, British Books in Print, British Museum General Catalogue, Cumulative Book Index, National Union Catalogue, Paperbound Books in Print*, and *Whitaker's Cumulative Book Index*. A number of other specialized checklists and indexes were also consulted and have been included in the annotated list of reference works in chapter 3.

The core list annotations provide the following information: bibliographic data; brief plot summary; critical evaluation, including comments on character delineation, thematic import, narrative structure, and style; subgenre classification, such as myth fantasy, faery-tale fantasy, Gothic fantasy, or science fantasy; and comparable works. Where relevant, the annotations for collections and anthologies include the entire tables of contents.

Fantasy Literature represents the joint efforts of three coauthors, who undertook responsibility for particular sections. Robert H. Boyer and Kenneth J. Zahorski, members of the English faculty of St. Norbert College, DePere, Wisconsin, wrote the introductory essay and compiled and annotated the core collection titles. Marshall B. Tymn of the English Department of Eastern Michigan University, Ypsilanti, Michigan, who originated the idea for the book, compiled and wrote Part II, Research Aids, and verified the bibliographic citations for the core list.

Acknowledgments

We gratefully acknowledge all those who so generously assisted in the preparation of this book, especially Mark Allen, who along with Gina Reinardy and Louanne Crowder assisted in composing the core list annotations; and Roger C. Schlobin, whose expert knowledge of the fantasy field made him an invaluable resource.

We are also indebted to Elizabeth Cummins Cogill for supplying information on library fantasy collections; to John Pennington and Barbara Basche for their research and bibliographical assistance; to Karen Prevetti for her guidance and constructive criticism; and to Peggy Schlapman, Cindy Poss, and Betty Clouthier, who typed and proofread the manuscript. We are grateful, too, to the staffs of the Brown County and St. Norbert College libraries, especially Lori Wieseckel, Don Pieters, and Gene Bunker; to Dean Robert Horn of St. Norbert College for his encouragement and support; and to the many small press publishers and fantasy organizations who responded to requests for information.

Finally, a special thanks must be extended to Lloyd Alexander, who graciously agreed to write the foreword to this volume. His kindness, courtesy, and cooperation will not soon be forgotten.

I
The
Literature

1

On Fantasy

Fantasy: What Is It? Definition and Classification

"When sitting down to write a work of fantasy, does an author define the genre first, and then write accordingly?" This was the response given by a student in a recent course in science fiction and fantasy literature to the question, "Is this book high or low fantasy?" The student's implied objection was quite correct. It is a reminder that the best definitions come after the fact and are a way of organizing a body of knowledge (or in this case a particular branch of literature) that enables readers to more fully appreciate it, discuss it, and make discriminating judgments about it. An author does not ordinarily begin to compose with a given definition or formula in mind. But an avid reader, a teacher, or a student, having read a number of works of a particular sort, tends to want to discuss them, to make comparisons, and to seek out more. Thus one is led into a consideration of definition and distinctions.

Fantasy, as a literary genre, is composed of works in which nonrational phenomena play a significant part. That is, they are works in which events occur, or places or creatures exist, that could not occur or exist according to rational standards or scientific explanations. The nonrational phenomena of fantasy simply do not fall within human experience or accord with natural laws as we know them. Thus history as we know it does not record that someone pulled a sword from a stone, or that someone forged a ring of power to control nine other rings of lesser power in Middle Earth. If such events or places are recorded, we regard the source not as history or as realistic fiction, but as fantasy.

The presence of nonrational phenomena, then, is the principal criterion for distinguishing fantasy from history or from other types of literature. Mainstream literature, of course, deals with life on this (our) world, and in fact puts a premium on verisimilitude—on the appearance of reality and the laws that govern it—as it is perceived by the majority of people. Fantasy, on the other hand, has its own vision of reality and may have its own natural laws, which differ from the generally accepted ones.

The difference between fantasy and mainstream literature is thus readily apparent; less apparent is the difference between fantasy and several other nonmainstream types of literature. Chief among these are dream visions, psychological phantasies, weird tales, lost race adventures, and science fiction. All of these types resemble fantasy in that they present seemingly nonrational phenomena, but in each case there is a rational or scientific explanation for, or rationalization of, the phenomena. Fantasy offers no such scientific explanations.

In the case of the dream vision, a favorite type of story in the Middle Ages, the explanation is simply the nocturnal meanderings of the mind. In psychological phantasies, a concussion suffered in a plane crash, a traumatic wartime experience (*Slaughterhouse Five*), or daydreaming ("The Secret Life of Walter Mitty") explain the unrealities in a fashion that satisfies the most exacting realist. Weird tales frequently present unexpected but perfectly logical explanations for what appear to be nonrational phenomena: A catatonic fit, for instance, explains how a presumably dead girl can come back to life to haunt her brother in Poe's classic "The Fall of the House of Usher." (Weird stories do not always supply such logical explanations, in which case they are fantasy; they will be discussed later as Gothic fantasy.) Lost race adventures present settings and peoples so exotic that they seem impossible. The premise underlying many of these works, however, is that some barrier—usually geographical—has isolated the lost race so completely that its customs have evolved in a unique way, or have not evolved at all. Thus H. Rider Haggard depicts a race of people in Africa in an antique and primitive splendor in *The People of the Mist*. However exotic, this story contains no magic; and however improbable, the situation is possible, even today when unexplored territories have become so few.

Science fiction is the largest of all the nonmainstream categories of literature, and in many ways it is most closely akin to fantasy. It certainly examines worlds that do not correspond to present realities, but implies that such brave new worlds are possible some time in the future, given certain scientific inventions or societal evolutions. Science fantasy, as we shall see later in this discussion, differs from science fiction in that it is basically fantasy that employs science in several rather specific ways.

All of the genres mentioned above are thus related to fantasy in that they describe what seem to be nonrational phenomena, but these phenomena are nonrational in appearance only; the genres are really quite distinct from fantasy. It should be mentioned, however, that in some instances the rational premises of certain works are inconsequential, or are, as C. S. Lewis has said, simply "a sop for the intellect"; such works may readily be classified as fantasy despite a technicality. Thus, *Alice's Adventures in Wonderland* is rightly considered a fantasy despite the "Wake up, Alice dear!" that comes near its conclusion.

The significant use of nonrational phenomena not only enables us to distinguish between fantasy and the various other branches of literature, but also serves as one of the two principal criteria—the other is setting—that guide us in dividing the genre into its two major classifications: high fantasy and low fantasy. These two criteria are interrelated, since setting in fantasy refers to the type of world described, and nonrational phenomena are governed by the laws that prevail in this world. The worlds of high fantasy are secondary worlds, such as the Forest Sauvage, Middle Earth, or Prydain, and they manifest a consistent order that is explainable in terms of the supernatural (i.e., deities) or in terms of the less definable (but still recognizable) magical powers of faërie (e.g., wizards and enchantresses). Hence, *The Once and Future King* (T. H. White) and *The Lord of the Rings* (J. R. R. Tolkien) and *The Black Cauldron* (Lloyd Alexander) are high fantasy.

On the other hand, the world of low fantasy is the primary world—this real world we live in. It too demonstrates a consistent order, but its order is explainable in terms of natural law (which excludes the supernatural and the magical—for the most part). The gods and faeries no longer, alas, walk here. Consequently, when something nonrational occurs, as it does in low fantasies such as Peter S. Beagle's *Lila the Werewolf* and Oscar Wilde's *Portrait of Dorian Gray*, there are no explanations, rational or nonrational. The causes simply are not forthcoming; they are inexplicable. In a high fantasy secondary world, the metamorphosis of a young lady into a wolf or the aging of the portrait of Dorian Gray would be explained by some magical or supernatural agency that would be accepted in that world.

The secondary world, wherein nonrational causality operates, is clearly central to an understanding of high fantasy and its distinctness from low fantasy. Writers of high fantasy have dealt with the secondary world as related to the primary world in three different ways. Some simply ignore the primary world completely, introducing readers to the other world from the first page. Thus, Ursula K. Le Guin's Earthsea has no connection with our world; there is no portal through which one may pass from one to the other. The primary world does not exist—physically or geographically, that is. Spiritually, certainly, the two worlds are related, since Le Guin lives in the primary world and writes, as do all authors, from her human imagination and experience. Other writers find it useful to set their secondary worlds in some sort of more direct relationship to the primary world, enabling them to further define their secondary worlds by comparison with this one. Lord Dunsany does this in *The King of Elfland's Daughter*, and readers discover such contrasts as the radically different pace at which time progresses in the secondary world, where a few moments may be equal to years in this world. C. S. Lewis achieves the same effect in his Chronicles of Narnia.

One of the fascinating aspects of the relationship of secondary to primary worlds is, as in Lewis's books, the nature and variety of portals through which one passes to and fro, portals quite unlike the spaceships that transport people to other worlds in science fiction, but no less complex and much more mysterious. In some fantasies—Jane Langton's *Diamond in the Window* is a good example—the portal becomes the focus for the entire work. Some recent writers, such as Joyce Gregorian in *The Broken Citadel* and Ruth Nichols in *The Marrow of the World*, have introduced the startling device of a story that starts out in this world with a character who is actually from the other world, but who doesn't realize her true origin and identity until she passes through the portal to that other world. It is apparent that the rich possibilities stemming from the juxtaposition of the two worlds are many.

Finally, there are the writers who use the world-within-a-world technique. There are no portals; the secondary world is simply a particular location within the primary world. It is usually marked off by physical boundaries within which events transpire that do not occur elsewhere, that is, within which a different set of laws pertains. This may be a secret garden like the medieval gardens of love, or it might be a portion of consecrated ground sacred to some divinity, as in John Buchan's "The Grove of Ashtaroth." One of the best examples of this type is Peter S. Beagle's *A Fine and Private Place,* where the walls of the Yorkchester Cemetery mark it off as a secondary world surrounded by New York City. Inside these walls, if you are like Jonathan Rebek, you can commune with ghosts, or, if you are a ghost, you can think yourself anywhere—except beyond the gates of the cemetery where your body lies. In the case of Beagle's novel, two ghosts circumvent this law by having their bodies exhumed and transferred to another place. In all three cases, whether the authors appear to ignore the primary world, or create a portal between it and the secondary world, or place the secondary world within the primary, they have their eyes on the primary world and offer readers fresh perspectives on it.

The secondary world, then, with its discernible though nonrational causality, is what characterizes high fantasy. Low fantasy, on the contrary, features nonrational happenings that are without causality or explanation because they occur in the rational world where such things are not supposed to occur. This aspect of low fantasy is what accounts for its ability to shock or surprise the reader into horror or laughter. Weird tales of the low fantasy variety, like Wilde's *Portrait of Dorian Gray*, are so chilling because what happens in them is very far out of the ordinary, yet very nearby, in an otherwise ordinary world. Farces, such as those written by the young Aldous Huxley or John Collier or Max Beerbohm, are so bizarre because their events intrude upon and violate the norms of the workaday world. And beast fables, such as Aesop wrote, or as George Orwell has more recently written in *Animal Farm,* draw our attention to their lessons—not because the lessons are themselves so different from what we are used to hearing, but because we are surprised and charmed by animals that can talk in our world. This charm, as well as the spell of a well-told tale, is what has made Richard Adams's low fantasy *Watership Down* so popular. (*Watership Down* is a special case, since two of its chapters contain myth-based stories. The rest of the book, however, features no nonrational causality or secondary world setting.)

However entertaining weird tales, farces, or animal fables may be, we are not concerned in this volume with the horrors or laughter or learning of low fantasy; rather, we are intent upon experiencing the "awe and wonder" (Tolkien's terms) afforded by high fantasy. And it is the secondary world with its supernatural (myth fantasy) or magical (faery-tale fantasy) causality that chiefly evokes this sense of "awe and wonder." Chiefly—but not solely, by any means. The setting and causality are reinforced in this task by three other closely related characteristics of high fantasy: noble characters, archetypes, and elevated style.

High fantasy characters are diverse, yet similar in that they are of an elevated stature. So diverse and numerous are they that they defy any but the most general classification, the principal groups being gods, faeries, and humans. The gods and goddesses dwell apart in their empyrean homes, Wyddfa or Norgaard or Olympus, but they have their favorite places in our world where they frequently visit to commune with humans. Faery is the generic term for an inhabitant, other than human, of the realm of faërie, and this includes everyone and everything from dragons to dwarfs. Humans are sometimes natives of the other world, or they sometimes wander into it—or are summoned thither—from the primary world. Despite their diversity, a generous percentage of creatures in high fantasy are of elevated stature. Gods and goddesses surely are. And most faeries—dragons especially, frequently symbols of royalty in our world—seem to trace their lineage almost endlessly. They are mostly regal folk. Humans in high fantasy are generally lower in the hierarchy than gods or faeries, being far younger than these creatures, but they are most often also of high or noble estate. Epics and romances, two of the older kinds of high fantasy, confined themselves exclusively to humans of noble birth. Happily, modern writers, with whom we are concerned here, have made a place—sometimes a prominent one—for us common folk.

The hero in high fantasy is usually a human or humanlike being and is almost always a representative type, an Everyman character. We read in

Evangeline Walton's *Prince of Annwn* of Arawn, the Grey Prince of the dead, and of Rhiannon, a goddess of love and life, and we are fascinated; it is, nonetheless, the human Pwyll who most firmly gains our sympathies and our allegiance. Or we are held spellbound by Beagle's description of the regal unicorn in *The Last Unicorn,* but ultimately we are more concerned with the fate of the inept magician Schmendrick, even though—or perhaps because—he is such a dolt. Both Pwyll and Schmendrick are Everyman types, recognizable characters who represent all of us on our journeys. Their conflicts, their quests, their flaws, and their virtues are those we all share, and these universal aspects take precedence over their individual personality traits.

Before leaving the hero, mention should be made of two types of heroes that have made their appearance in modern high fantasy, the commoner-hero and the morally ambivalent hero (we will deal with the barbarian hero in a later section on sword and sorcery). The commoner-hero has been with us ever since George MacDonald's Curdie, the son of a miner, saved the princess from the goblins. And J. R. R. Tolkien has the wise Elvenking Elrond comment at the Great Council in Rivendell that it is the time of the halflings to come to the fore as heroes—so Frodo and his gardener Samwise become the ringbearers. More recently still, Ursula K. Le Guin details Ged's rise from shepherd to the exalted position of Archmage of Earthsea. And Carol Kendall makes a special point of showing us that minnipins can be heroes when they must. In all of these cases, the hero is reluctant, but once the task is undertaken, the commoner-hero discovers hitherto unsuspected qualities of nobility: courage, generosity, loyalty to the right.

The appearance of the morally ambivalent hero should better be termed reappearance. Robin Hood is, of course, the prototype. Two modern writers who make extensive use of this type of hero are E. R. Eddison and Fritz Leiber. Eddison's Lord Groh in *The Worm Ouroboros,* though not the protagonist, steals our attention because his complex motives cause him to change sides more than once; his changing of sides even throws some mild doubt on which side is good and which evil. Leiber's two roguish heroes, Fafhrd and Gray Mouser, also offer interesting studies and similarly challenge the traditional good-versus-evil motif of high fantasy. Though basically good, their commitment is not to the good but to their own independence and individuality. But, whether a commoner-hero or a morally ambivalent one, or even the more traditional noble sort, the hero of high fantasy remains an Everyman.

The Everyman character of the hero is an example of the next aspect of high fantasy to be considered, the archetype. Archetypes are important in all types of literature in varying degrees, but nowhere are they as plentiful or as prominent as in the myth-based tales or faery tales of high fantasy. These types of fantasy draw directly from the most ancient well of stories, the very source of archetypes; while mainstream literature, even when it draws from the same well, adulterates the pure water with so many new and particularizing details that it becomes murky. It is not our purpose here to delve into the psychological or literary complexities of the archetype. C. G. Jung, and later his pupil Maud Bodkin, as well as many others, have devoted volumes to the study. Suffice it to say that high fantasy presents the archetypal characters, situations, settings, language, and themes in bold relief to readers to elicit from them recognition and deep instinctual responses, whether of wonderment and joy or of fear and repulsion. Thus, in Tolkien's *Hobbit*, readers recognize and shudder at the utter isolation and negativism of hell when they discover Gollum peering with pale eyes from his island habitat deep underneath the mountain, surrounded by dank water and impenetrable darkness. Readers respond with joy rather than repugnance, however, when they read in Kenneth Morris's *Book of the Three Dragons* of the death and rebirth of Pwyll in the life-giving Cauldron of Ceridwen and of the successful achievement of his long quest for immortality. Finally, few readers can remain unmoved by the sensuous beauty and the nobility of the Green Lady, the Eve of her world, in C. S. Lewis's *Perelandra*. In these examples, we recognize (whether we label them as such or not) the outcast (Gollum), the hero (Pwyll), and the mother (Green Lady) archetypes. These characters are furthermore reinforced by additional archetypes—underground darkness, the pattern of death and rebirth, the life-color green.

The elevated stature of the characters, the Everyman quality of the heroes, and the evocative archetypes blend nicely with the supernatural or magical causality and the secondary world of high fantasy. But the final ingredient, and perhaps the greatest challenge to the writer, is a style that can support these elements and clothe them in appropriate language. The dialogue must befit the stature of the speakers; descriptive passages must be in an elevated style that necessarily works through imagery and comparison to create the imaginary worlds.

Few, if any, critics have considered the style of description found in high fantasy in general, but Ursula K. Le Guin has written an excellent essay on dialogue, and we can do no better than to refer here to her *From Elfland to Poughkeepsie* (Portland, OR: Pendragon Press, 1973): "The Lords of Elfland are true lords, the only true lords, the kind that do not exist on this earth; their lordship is the outward sign or symbol of real inward greatness. And greatness of soul shows when a man speaks" (p. 11). When high fantasy characters speak, their accents should be those of Elfland, not of Poughkeepsie. Le Guin then quotes from three master stylists of the genre—E. R. Eddison, Kenneth Morris, and J. R. R. Tolkien—to illustrate dialogue that is authentic Elfland, but with differences, showing that there is no absolute formula. Eddison uses the archaic speech of the sixteenth century, Morris a high comic mode, and Tolkien a style characterized by dignified simplicity. To these masters and to others who Le Guin mentions, such as Lord Dunsany, Evangeline Walton, and James Branch Cabell, one might add Le Guin's own name, as well as that of Peter S. Beagle. In *The Last Unicorn* Beagle uses the low and high styles of speech to show the change of Prince Lir from an ordinary person to a Lord of Elfland. When Lir first meets the Lady Amalthea, he says, "Hi. . . . Glad to meet you." After his spirit is refined under the influence of this noble lady, Lir greets her at day's end with "Give you good evening, my lady." The first statement sounds like Poughkeepsie, this world of ours, the second like Elfland, clearly elsewhere.

To illustrate the appropriate descriptive style of high fantasy we need once again simply to examine some of the masters and observe their technique. Lord Dunsany is rightly regarded as one of the matchless stylists of modern fantasy—or of modern literature for that matter, which explains why the many attempts to imitate him have for the most part been failures. Here is a fairly typical sample of his descriptive prose, taken from *The King of Elfland's Daughter* (New York: Ballantine Books, 1973):

> No sooner had Lirazel read the rune on the scroll than fancies from Elfland began to pour over the border. Some came that would make a clerk in the City to-day leave his desk at once to dance on the sea-shore; and some would have driven all the men in a bank to leave doors and coffers open and wander away till they came to green open land and heathery hills; and some would have made a poet of a man, all of a sudden as he sat at his business. (pp. 61–62)

What one immediately notices is the highly stylized, poetic nature of the second sentence. It is a long, rolling sentence with the rhythm of successive ocean waves moving onto the beach. The careful parallelism of the successive clauses, their balanced length, and the felt but unobtrusive alliteration contribute to the spell-casting effect of the passage—and this is precisely what the scroll does to Lirazel, the King of Elfland's daughter.

While Dunsany operates primarily through his highly stylized and sonorous sentences, C. S. Lewis finds the simile most helpful to describe the marvelous settings of his Outer Space trilogy. In the following passage, Ransom, the hero, gets his first view of the Isle of Meldilorn in *Out of the Silent Planet* (New York: Macmillan, 1973):

> Amidst the lake there rose like a low and gently sloping pyramid, or like a woman's breast, an island of pale red, smooth to the summit, and on the summit a grove of such trees as man had never seen. Their smooth columns had the gentle swell of the noblest beech-trees; but these were taller than a cathedral spire on earth, and at their tops, they broke rather into flower than foliage; into golden flower bright as tulip, still as rock, and huge as summer cloud. (p. 105)

Notice also the rich, sensuous visual and tactile imagery of the passage.

A third master stylist, one largely forgotten until people like Ursula K. Le Guin discovered his books on dust-covered shelves, is Kenneth Morris. Morris's descriptive style makes one wish to have been raised in Wales. His prose, which at first seems elaborate and ornamental, is actually a prose of eloquent simplicity. In the excerpt presented here, Pwyll (now Manawyddan) has arrived at the home of the enchantress Ewinwen in *Book of the Three Dragons* (New York: Arno Press, 1978):

> It was a garden in a valley, the loveliest in the world; and a population bluebell-slender, daffodil-beautiful, wandering in it, and at their games and diversions. They came about him when he appeared, all graceful, gracious and friendly; and greeted him with birdlike voices. . . . (p. 58)

This is a prose that one somehow expects from an ancient Welsh tale, a folk-tale prose of common words and numerous but simple descriptive adjectives. Note that the only two similes are compressed into the compound adjectives "bluebell-slender" and "daffodil-beautiful." Such compounds, a favorite device of Morris's, evoke the antique nature of his source, the *Mabinogion*.

The passages presented here should make it clear why Dunsany, Lewis, and Morris are so often praised (Lewis not so much as the others) for their style. The style of each is unique and quite distinct from the others; all, however, are elevated and appropriate to their subjects and, taken together, exhibit many of the most prominent stylistic techniques of high fantasy.

When it comes to verbal humor, another important technique in fantasy, George MacDonald is the model, and his "Light Princess" is his masterpiece. The princess is "light" because she has been deprived of her "gravity" by a witch. MacDonald has a good deal of fun playing with these two terms, and others as well, throughout his story, and he does so—here is the challenge of using humor in high fantasy—without diminishing the beauty and gravity of his faery tale.

In concluding this discussion of style, it is fitting to comment on the most important selection of words an author makes in a work, the choice of names. There is, in the traditional faery tale, magic in names; in giving their real names, characters show complete trust by revealing their true identities. Ursula K. Le Guin describes this nicely in her Earthsea-related short story "The Rule of Names." In this story, a wizard rashly judges that he has obtained power over another by discovering his foe's real name. Indeed, he has required his foe to reveal himself by giving his name; unfortunately for the rash wizard, however, when he utters the name, his foe takes his true shape—that of the dragon Yevaud! Proper names, properly chosen, express the nature of the character, which is why many heroes do not use, or even receive, their names until they have proved their worth.

Place names and generic names have much the same effect of suggesting the real nature of the place or thing named. One of the chief defects, for instance, of E. R. Eddison's *The Worm Ouroboros* is the author's selection of names for the princely countries of his secondary world. Pixyland, Witchland, and Demonland are not apt names for places inhabited by such heroes as his. On the other hand, Tolkien, recognizing that as a "Sub-creator" (his term) his first task is the selection of appropriate names, makes meticulous and unerring selection of the nomenclature of his Middle Earth. One need but page through Tolkien's books to recognize the expressiveness of his names. On one hand, the reader encounters Morgoth, Mordor, Nazgul, and Mirkwood; on the other he is introduced to Elrond, Rivendell, Dunedain, and Lorien. Even out of context these titles bespeak the allegiance in the good-evil conflict of those named. In all of Tolkien's works, the name that is perhaps the most mellifluous and describes one of the most noble of his characters is Lúthien Tinúviel. Fittingly, Tolkien made a gift of this name to his wife.

As mentioned at the outset of this brief discussion of style, the style must support the other elements of high fantasy, but if it is not equal to the task, the entire work will collapse. As Le Guin puts it, "The style, of course, is the book" (*From Elfland to Poughkeepsie,* p. 25). Poor style is the surest giveaway of a second-rate fantasy, just as an effective style is the first indicator of authentic fantasy.

MYTH AND FAERY-TALE FANTASY

We have said a good deal about the way in which the presence of nonrational phenomena distinguishes fantasy from other types of literature, and how the nonrational causality—supernatural or magical—that is part of the order in the secondary world sets high fantasy apart from low fantasy. We have also mentioned that the two classes of high fantasy, based on the type of nonrational causality present, are myth fantasy (supernatural causality) and faery-tale fantasy (magical causality). It is time we examined these two types of high fantasy in greater detail.

Myth fantasy consists of those stories that posit supernatural causality. This definition thus includes such works as Hesiod's *Theogeny,* Ovid's *Metamorphoses,* the *Elder Edda,* the *Mabinogion,* the Koran, and the Bible. Some might object to our calling these last two myth, especially myth fantasy. Yet such they are since they posit divine causality, a causality that is not reducible to rational or scientific explanation. That does not mean that divine causality is opposed to, or by, reason or science. It is in fact reasonable to accept divine causality, even direct divine intervention in the lives of men and women, but reason cannot explain such causality any more than it can explain the nature of divinity. Thus, to call a story that in some way embodies currently held religious beliefs or faith a myth or myth fantasy is not to deny the underlying truth, or even the literal truth, of that story. One might note here, however, that many modern scripture scholars regard the Biblical narratives as stories that demonstrate a deep faith in particular aspects of divine providence rather than as stories that must be taken as literally true. In this sense many, if not all, myths are true in that they express humanity's various beliefs about the gods. Many of these myths are admittedly less noble, or perhaps less enlightened, than are the Biblical myths. It also follows, by the way, that faery tales, insofar as they embody humanity's beliefs about its own nature, are true, a fact that anthropologists and psychologists have come to recognize.

In any case, however, we are dealing here with modern high fantasy, not with the Bible or the other early repositories of myth. Consequently, we are concerned with three types of myth fantasy: retellings, modern adaptations, and new inventions. These categories are borrowed, with thanks, from Elizabeth Cook, who discusses the appearance of myth in modern literature in *The Ordinary and the Fabulous* (New York: Cambridge University Press, 1976). The first category, the retellings, includes three types: the rationalized, the literal, and the interpreted rehearsal of the myth. The rationalized myth, like Mary Renault's excellent version of the Theseus myth in *The King Must Die* and *The Bull from the Sea,* is actually a demythologized version that takes away supernatural causality, and therefore is not fantasy at all. The literal retelling is a modern, often simplified, translation of the original source, and thus does not fall within our present study, since we are not discussing the early texts. The interpreted retelling, however, which fills in gaps or supplies motivations not in the sources or makes explicit what is implied in the originals, does concern us as modern myth fantasy. Celtic mythology, as contained in the *Mabinogion,* is the principal bene-ficiary of such modern interpreted retellings. Kenneth Morris has given us his *Fates of the Princes of Dyfed* and *Book of the Three Dragons.* Evangeline Walton has similarly refashioned the *Mabinogion* in her four novels: *The Prince of Annwn, The Children of Llyr, The Song of Rhiannon,* and *The Island of the Mighty.* The *Mabinogion* has attracted this kind of interpretive retelling because it is fascinatingly enigmatic. It was not written down until the thirteenth century, at a time when the writers recognized its powerful origins but had forgotten many of the details.

The second category of myth fantasy, the modern adaptations, includes a much greater number of works than the interpretive retellings. One of the finest practitioners of this subgenre is C. S. Lewis, who has written an adaptation of the Cupid and Psyche myth in *Till We Have Faces,* an adapta-tion of the Adam and Eve myth in *Perelandra,* and an adaptation of the redemption myth in *The Lion, the Witch and the Wardrobe,* to name only a few of his myth adaptations. E. R. Eddison elected to adapt the Greek myths in his Zimiamvian triology. And Lloyd Alexander draws his inspira-tion and some of his events and characters from the *Mabinogion* in his Chronicles of Prydain. The difference between Alexander's adaptation and Morris's and Walton's interpretive retellings is that Alexander simply uses names, settings, and events to create his own story, while the other two retain but amplify the story as told in the original source.

The final category, new inventions, consists of tales that might be analogous to traditional myths, but tell of completely different gods and events. Lord Dunsany's *Gods of Pegana* is an early example. Following him, H. P. Lovecraft fashioned his bizarre Cthulhu mythos. But the supreme achievement in this category is Tolkien's *Silmarillion.* Although *The Silmarillion* parallels the creation myths, especially the Judeo-Christian version, it is unusually carefully detailed, and uniquely Tolkien's. In providing explanations for the existence of angellike beings, the Ainur, and for the creation by Ilúvatar (God) through the Ainur of the physical world and of elves, dwarfs, men, and hobbits, Tolkien subcreates a whole universe. One of the added fascinations of this universe is that it is the one in which *The Lord of the Rings* and *The Hobbit* are set.

Faery tales are closely related to myth. Tolkien uses the terms "high myth" for myth proper and "low myth" for faery tales. The latter are in fact descended directly from the former. The difference is that in the faery tale the gods have faded as supernatural forces, but their powers remain in the form of magic. In a sense, the gods welcome their oblivion and allow other selected, but lesser, beings to take their place and, at their own peril, to learn something of the divine powers of shape changing (a favorite pastime of many of the gods) or of controlling the laws of nature. The wizard or sorcerer or magician of the proper disposition could acquire at least a partial knowledge (herein lay the peril) of these powers and, according to his or her disposition, use them for good (white magic) or ill (black magic). And, as we know, some of the divine powers were themselves renegades or abusers of their prerogatives, and thus, in another way, magic is white or black.

In any case, the supernatural powers of the deities of myth become, in faery tales, the unstable forces of magic, which are difficult to control by the lesser beings who make the attempt. Magic, in the most successful of modern faery tales, continues to be this once-divine power now in the hands of beings of lesser strength and understanding. It should be noted that the surrogates of the gods still sometimes appear in the guise of fays or faery queens or faery godmothers, but for the most part the manipulators of magic are humans—wizards and sorceresses and the like—and the supernatural powers have accordingly become enfeebled, often effecting little more than illusion.

A cursory glance at works by Tolkien, Le Guin, Roger Zelazny, Beagle, and Jane Yolen illustrates these properties of magic. In Tolkien's Middle Earth, both Saruman and Sauron have become corrupted and controlled by the Ring of Power that they had sought to control, even though their motives were noble (at least Saruman's was, at the start). In Le Guin's Earthsea trilogy, the magician Ged works a dangerous spell before he is ready to control its effects, and then must devote himself to undoing the powers he has so carelessly loosed. The same is true of the hero in Zelazny's Amber series. Beagle's magician in *The Last Unicorn* learns that he can only work true magic when he empties himself and becomes a vessel for a power far superior to and much wiser than himself. And Yolen's hero in *The Magic Three of Solatia* learns that for every act of magic there is an unforeseen consequence, often detrimental even to the best-intentioned, that must be accepted. It is clear from these examples that magic is a derivative of supernatural power, and that the faery tale is the offspring of myth.

There are, of course, faery-tale elements written down in the epics and romances of the Middle Ages, in *Beowulf* and in *Sir Gawain and the Green Knight*. These are the earliest literary faery tales, in which the gods have already passed their twilight. And there is the oral tradition of the faery tale, exemplified by the stories assiduously collected in the last century by the Brothers Grimm. But what we are concerned with in this volume is, as in the case of myth, the modern literary descendants of the genre—works that recapture the magic of that immortal secondary world of faërie.

GOTHIC FANTASY

Earlier in this introduction we spoke of weird tales, tales that are not fantasy when they offer rational explanations for weird phenomena; we also pointed out that if the stories eschew such rationalizations, they are fantasy—Gothic fantasy. Gothic fantasy, as the designation implies, is fantasy that features Gothic elements. The term "Gothic," of course, can mean different things to different readers. When we use the term, we are not concerned so much with the particular literary characteristics of a formal genre, such as the Gothic novel, as with what we consider to be the very essence of Gothicism—that is, humankind's archetypal fascination with, and fear of, the unknown and the unnatural. It is this profound sense of dread that is at the very heart of the genuine Gothic tale, and only if the author can imbue the reader with the same feelings of dread and apprehension that are felt by the characters themselves has he or she passed the test.

There are many ways in which an author can convey this sense of dread, but the key to success is the creation of an effective ambience. As H. P. Lovecraft states in his classic work *Supernatural Horror in Literature* (New York: Dover Publications, 1973), an appropriate atmosphere is absolutely essential to the Gothic mode. If the author hopes to produce the desired sensations, he or she must create a convincing milieu of mystery, or awful fear, or evil foreshadowing, or some combination thereof. Highly connotational words, evocative images and descriptions, mysterious settings that produce strong feelings of awe and wonder, subtle characterizations that hint at the darker facets of personality, and carefully structured plots that produce suspense and tension—these are some of the techniques used to create an authentic Gothic ambience. In addition, authors will use many of the more specific Gothic devices and paraphernalia, such as forbidden books of black magic, evil potions and spells, moldering skeletons, dark and forbidding castles replete with fearful torture chambers and gloomy subterranean chambers, and a fascinating assortment of inhuman* agents, including ghosts, demons, gryphons, vampires, sylphs, trolls, and werewolves. It is this unique ambience with its resultant suspense and emotional impact that characterizes the true Gothic tale, and it is this fundamental element that must be present in order for a work of literature to be categorized as Gothic fantasy.

Just as fantasy literature in general can be divided into high and low fantasy, so too can Gothic fantasy be divided by the same primary differentiating criteria of causality and setting. In addition to these broader distinctions (high and low), there are other more subtle differences between Gothic high and Gothic low fantasy. To begin with, the effect of the Gothic is more startling in low fantasy. This, of course, is because the nonrational element occurs in an otherwise realistic context. To encounter a horrific troll in a Lapland hotel in an age of electric trains (as we do in one of T. H. White's short stories, "The Troll") is far more bizarre and incongruous than to encounter a similar creature in a subterranean cavern in faërie, as we do in Poul Anderson's *Three Hearts and Three Lions*. When the reader follows the author into a magical realm, such encounters are to be expected, and the reader can be content with the assurance that they cannot happen here. The reader of White's story, however, is much more likely to decide not to visit such outposts of civilization as the Arctic Circle. By placing nonrational events or creatures in a secondary world, the author gives them a distance that they lack in the primary world.

Still another noteworthy difference of the Gothic in the two types of fantasy is its function in relation to theme. In high fantasy, the Gothic motif more often plays a role subordinate to a theme that it reinforces. Thus, in a story like George MacDonald's "Cross Purposes," the themes of mutual trust and courage emerge when the protagonists, two children, overcome their fear in passing through the maze of darkness, a journey that is also a rite of passage through the uncertainties of adolescence into adulthood. On the other hand, in low fantasy, largely because of the immediacy of the effect of the Gothic elements, the fear itself is dominant and the theme, if one appears at all, is secondary. Perhaps no better example can be given than the Gothic low fantasy short stories of Algernon Blackwood and H. P. Lovecraft.

Both fantasy and Gothic literature are intriguing and venerable forms that have fascinated scores of noteworthy authors over the centuries. It should not be surprising, then, that many have enthusiastically accepted the challenge of combining the two types. The list of Gothic fantasy practitioners is impressive indeed. In the realm of Gothic low fantasy are writers

---

*The term "supernatural" is reserved here for gods and goddesses, while ghosts and their kin are referred to as "inhuman." Although good precedent exists for using supernatural in the much broader sense (to include all nonrational phenomena), it is preferable to limit the meaning of the word in order to avoid its recent usage as a blanket term.

such as Arthur Conan Doyle, Algernon Blackwood, H. Rider Haggard, William Hope Hodgson, H. P. Lovecraft, M. R. James, T. H. White, Ray Bradbury, and Peter S. Beagle; authors of Gothic high fantasy include George MacDonald, A. Merritt, Robert E. Howard, C. L. Moore, Clark Ashton Smith, Fritz Leiber, Poul Anderson, and Ursula K. Le Guin. There seems little question that just as Gothic fantasy has attracted authors of note in the past, so too will it continue to attract writers of equally fine talent in the future. And as long as humankind continues to be fascinated by the mysterious and the dreadful, their works will continue to find an enthusiastic audience.

SCIENCE FANTASY

In the term science fantasy, science is the adjective, fantasy the noun; it is not science/fantasy or science-fantasy. Science fantasy is a type of high fantasy that offers scientific explanation for the existence of the secondary world and, usually, for the portal by which one can pass from the primary to the secondary world. Once in this secondary world, which is the principal setting of the work, magical causality takes the spotlight, and this remains nonrational, unexplained by the science. In science fantasy the major focus is on the magical secondary world; in most, but not all cases, science and the primary world are soon forgotten. This volume mentions a small number of writers of science fantasy, but the list is impressive. A brief examination of the works of some of these authors will further clarify the definition of science fantasy.

C. S. Lewis is the oldest member of the group. In *Out of the Silent Planet*, the first book in Lewis's Outer Space trilogy, Ransom, the hero, is transported to Malacandra (Mars) in a spaceship that is every bit as plausible as, if not considerably more plausible than, H. G. Wells's seemingly scientific travel machines. But once on Malacandra, Ransom encounters a theocratic system, with an angellike creature called an Eldil presiding over three equal, nonhuman but rational species in the name of Maleldil, son of the creator of the universe. Lewis has written a myth fantasy in which he employs a spaceship to transport his hero into a secondary world where supernatural causality reigns.

Poul Anderson, in two of his books, *Three Hearts and Three Lions* and *A Midsummer Tempest*, employs the device of parallel universes to explain the existence of the secondary worlds of faërie in which the books are mainly set. The idea of the parallel universe is that more than one universe exists simultaneously in the same place, but they occupy different dimensions. Many parallels exist between the two universes because they have evolved from a common universe, which at a certain point in history split into two quite different ones. In Anderson's science fantasy the key difference is that magical causality operates in one of the universes while in the other (ours) it does not, or at least has not for some time. Thus, in *Three Hearts and Three*

Lions, Holger Carlsen moves from our world into a medieval world—Carolingian—in which the magic that we regard as a fanciful invention of the romance writers is real. The Forest of Faërie and Morgan Le Fay really exist. Anderson does not supply a particular portal in *Three Hearts and Three Lions*. In his other science fantasy, *A Midsummer Tempest*, the premise is that a parallel world exists in which Shakespeare's plays are not fiction, but historical accounts. The faery court of Oberon and Titania and the magic book and staff of Prospero are still to be found. No portal is needed because the hero, Prince Rupert, belongs to the Shakespearean world, but at one point he enters the Old Phoenix Tavern where a girl from the United States explains to him the parallel universe concept. One can go into a variety of these universes by choosing from among the different doors by which to leave the tavern.

Clifford Simak also uses the parallel universe device, and provides considerably more detail concerning it, in his *Enchanted Pilgrimage*. The principal setting is the Wasteland, a medieval, twelfth-century sort of world, but the date is 1975. Into this world have come characters from two other parallel universes. Alexander Jones comes from our dimension, while Mary has been born in the Wasteland, in Witch House, but of parents who come from a third dimension. Jones's is, of course, a technological, rational world; Mary's is apparently a world of humanism. They join ranks with Mark Cornwall in his world, the Wasteland, a world of magic and of all sorts of beings—trolls, unicorns, witches, and many others—that are simply parts of legends out of the pasts of their worlds. Jones uses some undefined machine as a portal and by this means moves between worlds several times in the story. Simak's science fantasy is unique in terms of the amount of attention given to the parallel universes, and also because he introduces flying saucers, a robot (Bucket), and a character (the Caretaker) from a completely different planet. And for a good portion of the book he mingles these science fiction devices and recognizable technology (Jones rides a motorcycle) with the magic of the Wasteland. Still, the setting and principal focus is the Wasteland, its creatures, and its magic. Interestingly, it is this world that the Caretaker has chosen for his experiment—to join technology, humanism, and magic (the respective contributions of the three parallel universes) to form an ideal world.

The two other science fantasy writers included in this book are Andre Norton and C. J. Cherryh. Both use the device of alternate worlds. These alternate worlds differ slightly from parallel universes in that they are not simply different or parallel dimensions of one world, but are other worlds entirely that exist simultaneously with one another. Both writers employ specific place or time-warp portals for transportation. In *Witch World,* Norton uses the Siege Perilous of Arthurian vintage to transfer her hero from our world to the Witch World, a matriarchal world where witches use magic to defend themselves from their superstitious but warlike neighbors. C. J.

Cherryh, in *Gate of Ivrel,* uses the Gates between Worlds as portals "into elsewhen as well as elsewhere," where one encounters the fascinating witch-woman, Morgaine.

The factors that unite the above works under the heading of science fantasy stand out in fairly bold relief. First, in each case, science—in the form of astronomy or paraphysics or paratemporal mathematics (the last two are Anderson's terms)—explains the existence of the secondary world in which magic is a reality; but, significantly, science is unable to explain the magic. Second, the primary focus of these books is on the magic and its operation in the secondary world. Third, and most important, the effect of employing a rational scientific explanation for the existence of a magical world is to convince readers of the reality of the nonrational causality of magic. In Lewis's case, science persuades us of the truth of myth, both Christian and pre-Christian. Science and magic in these works are thus integrated in an effective, functional manner. Science fantasy is a relatively new direction in high fantasy, an attractive one that should continue to expand and enhance the genre in the future.

SWORD AND SORCERY FANTASY AND HEROIC FANTASY

"Sword and sorcery" and "heroic fantasy" are two of the most popular and frequently used descriptive terms in the fantasy field today. They are also two of the most abused and misused appellations. There are two primary reasons for this unfortunate situation. First of all, over the years the terms have come to mean different things to different people, and as a result they now lack commonly accepted definitions. Second, while the two terms are used interchangeably by some authors, critics, and enthusiasts, others treat them as dissimilar designations. A few examples should prove instructive.

Lin Carter, in his introduction to L. Sprague de Camp's *Literary Swordsmen and Sorcerers: The Makers of Heroic Fantasy* (Sauk City, WI: Arkham House, 1976), defines the sword and sorcery subgenre in the following terms:

> "Sword and Sorcery" is the term by which *aficionados* affectionately refer to that school of fantastic fiction wherein the heroes are pretty much heroic, the villains thoroughly villainous, and action of the derring-do variety takes the place of sober social commentary or serious psychological introspection. . . . In a word, then, Sword & Sorcery is written primarily to *entertain:* a motive generally suspect and largely obsolete in modern letters. (p. xi)

A somewhat different definition is given by Diana Waggoner in her full-length bibliographical study of fantasy literature, *The Hills of Faraway: A Guide to Fantasy* (New York: Atheneum, 1978):

> As a re-creation of the medieval epic and romance forms, heroic fantasy lends itself to the creation of wholly different geographies, but it is not confined to them. Heroic behavior is possible in any setting and is the real criterion of this type.

It means that physical courage and exciting events are not enough; every action must have a serious purpose. Adventure fantasy is an unambitious form of heroic fantasy, with the heroism left out. The reader identifies with the hero not because he is good, but because he is strong, clever, and resourceful. His conflicts with his opponents are interesting only as action; he does not necessarily deserve to win. . . . Most adventure fantasy remains what it has always been—escapist trash. (p. 36)

Still another perspective on the subgenre is provided by Hans Joachim Alpers in "Loincloth, Double Ax, and Magic: 'Heroic Fantasy' and Related Genres" (*Science-Fiction Studies,* March 1978, pp. 19–32). Alpers, who is from West Germany, sees heroic fantasy as embodying the following primary traits:

"Plausibility and reality are not as important as all that. What matters is, rather, the adventure, the free flow of the imagination, and characters of flesh and blood that allow us to empathize." . . . A second characteristic of HF is a specific attitude to violence, i.e., to oppressing and killing human beings: it is practiced not only by villains, but primarily by the heroes. . . . The third mark of HF is fatalism, coupled with the static character of the Fantasy worlds, at least in the serials. . . . The fourth characteristic is an uncompromising commitment to the ideology of the power of man over man. . . . The ideologies thereby propagated are: magic-mystic understanding of the world, i.e., mystification of relationships that could be grasped by the intellect; right of the stronger as the principle of societal organization; glorification of violence, particularly killing; oppression of women; emphasis on the racial superiority of the Nordic (Aryan) type; fatalism toward hierarchic structures and their consequences, such as wars; the *fuehrer* principle: the greatest butcher of them all shall determine our fate; imperialistic policy; and anti-intellectualism. (pp. 30–31)

A few observations on the above definitions should serve to point out some of the difficulties created by the manner in which the two terms are currently being used. (1) Carter and Alpers seem to be describing two very different subgenres, since one uses the designation "sword and sorcery" and the other "heroic fantasy," and since one presents a very positive view and the other an extremely negative outlook. This is not the case, however. They are both describing the same subgenre of literature. (2) Even though Waggoner and Alpers are using the same descriptive designation—"heroic fantasy"—they are not talking about the same thing. As far as Waggoner is concerned, only those writers who truly attempt to recreate the medieval epic and romance forms, and who feature in their works heroic action motivated by serious purpose, are bona fide members of the school of heroic fantasy (as distinct from adventure fantasy, which has "the heroism left out"). And who are these writers? She restricts her list to major fantasists such as William Morris, Lord Dunsany, E. R. Eddison, T. H. White, and J. R. R. Tolkien. When Alpers talks about "hardcore heroic fantasy," on the other hand, he focuses on authors such as Robert E. Howard, Lin Carter,

L. Sprague de Camp, and John Jakes—the creators of barbarian super-heroes such as Conan the Cimmerian, Thongor of Lemuria, and Brak the Barbarian. It is true, however, that Waggoner's conception of adventure fantasy is in certain respects similar to Alpers's conception of hardcore heroic fantasy. (3) Waggoner not only uses a different term (adventure fantasy) when referring to that school of fantasy Carter calls "sword and sorcery," she also exhibits a strikingly different attitude toward it. Carter defends it as good entertainment, while Waggoner states that "most adventure fantasy remains what it has always been—escapist trash."

Confusing? Yes, indeed. And remember that the confusion here has been kept to a minimum by using only three of the many variant definitions. The misunderstanding and confusion grow proportionately as additional definitions and terminologies enter the picture.

As mentioned earlier, a real problem exists here. If we are to clear up some of the fuzzy and misleading genre and subgenre designations and definitions that currently plague the fantasy field, we must begin with such indefinite terms as sword and sorcery and heroic fantasy. The present use of these terms is not only confusing to teachers, librarians, students, and casual readers of the genre, but is also unjust to fantasists who are indiscriminately thrust into pigeonholes in which they do not belong. This problem is compounded because in many quarters the term sword and sorcery is synonymous with literature of poor quality. Given this feeling that sword and sorcery is escape literature with little redeeming literary value, it seems unfair to classify superb writers like William Morris, Lord Dunsany, E. R. Eddison, T. H. White, J. R. R. Tolkien, and Lloyd Alexander as sword and sorcery fantasists. And this type of classification does take place on a fairly wide-spread basis. For that matter, given the view of heroic fantasy that Alpers articulates in his article, it also seems unjust to place any of these writers in the heroic fantasy category.

This problem of imprecise genre definition manifests itself most clearly in bibliographical studies such as that published in the January 1972 issue of *The English Journal* (Vol. 61, pp. 43–51). Don Adrian Davidson's "Sword and Sorcery Fiction: An Annotated Book List" is historically significant in that it is one of the first articles about sword and sorcery fantasy to be directed at an academic audience. It is a thoughtful article that served the very valuable function of alerting academicians to fantasy literature when most were still unaware of the riches to be found in this area of literary endeavor. It does, however, pose some interesting problems of genre definition. Under the general heading of "Sword and Sorcery Fiction," Davidson includes works by Poul Anderson, Edgar Rice Burroughs, Lin Carter, L. Sprague de Camp, Lord Dunsany, E. R. Eddison, Jane Gaskell, Robert Heinlein, Robert E. Howard, Katherine Kurtz, Fritz Leiber, Talbot Mundy, Mervyn Peake, Fletcher Pratt, J. R. R. Tolkien, Henry Treece, and Manly Wade Wellman. Some of the works Davidson lists pretty clearly fall into the sword and sorcery subgenre as defined by Lin Carter (e.g., the works of Carter himself, de Camp, and Howard). Others, however, just as clearly belong in the heroic fantasy category as defined by Waggoner (e.g., Dunsany, Eddison, and Tolkien). To complicate matters, pure Gothic fiction (Mervyn Peake's Gormenghast trilogy) is also included. More precision in definition and categorization is sorely needed in the field, but it will be difficult to achieve if we continue to use terms that lack commonly accepted meanings.

It is, of course, easier to identify problems than to solve them. And the problem of genre definition that we are dealing with here has been exacerbated because of its longevity. Over the decades, it has had an opportunity to become deep seated; the misunderstandings have had more than ample time to take seed, grow, and spread. Can anything be done to ameliorate the situation? Although there are certainly other possible solutions, the following two proposals seem to be the most feasible.

One approach would be to apply the term heroic fantasy only to those works that meet the rather strict criteria set forth in Diana Waggoner's definition. A highly restrictive use of the term would, indeed, be a step in the right direction. Furthermore, by observing the distinction Waggoner makes between heroic fantasy and adventure fantasy, we could categorize those works similar to heroic fantasy, but which have "the heroism left out." That is, we could separate works of heroic fantasy from works of sword and sorcery. This approach is not without its drawbacks, however. They are twofold. First of all, the descriptive term adventure fantasy is imprecise. Like sword and sorcery and heroic fantasy, adventure fantasy means different things to different readers. Second, the retention of the heroic fantasy designation would continue to create confusion unless we effected a widespread clarification of the new restrictive meaning of the term. Such a comprehensively broad indoctrination seems highly unlikely.

The second and ultimately more satisfactory solution would be to replace heroic fantasy and sword and sorcery with more precise descriptive terms. But what designations could be used? Actually, the use of the term high fantasy would take care of many of the problems we have discussed. To begin with, most of the fantasy works of the writers Waggoner places in the heroic fantasy category fit quite naturally and logically into the general category of high fantasy. Placement here has the advantage of allowing for a more precise categorization of the works as either myth or faery-tale fantasy. Furthermore, the designation high fantasy would not carry with it the unfavorable connotations currently associated with sword and sorcery.

However, not all of the works currently classified as sword and sorcery should be placed in the high fantasy category. There is a well-defined group of novels and short stories that demands a separate subgenre. These are the works featuring primitive superheroes such as Conan the Conqueror and Brak the Barbarian. (These kinds of works Waggoner would classify as adventure fantasy, Alpers as hardcore heroic fantasy.) Most of these fantasies display certain characteristics that give them a distinct identity. What are some of the common traits?

First of all, the central figure, the barbarian superhero, is the focal point: the raison d'être of the novel or short story. He (or she—there are female counterparts to barbarians like Conan, C. L. Moore's Jirel of Joiry, for example) is a fierce, sometimes foolhardy, warrior who hacks his way through battle after battle, leaving piles of mangled bodies in his bloody wake. With unbounded stamina and astounding resilience, he fights his way out of the most dangerous situations imaginable, and exacts terrible revenge upon those who try to capture or kill him. He has a kind of primitive charisma that some women find attractive, and thus he is often accompanied by a voluptuous, scantily clothed female companion. Of course, this kind of hero also feels free to take whatever woman he wants, whether she wants him or not. In sum, he is tough, determined, violent, and not given to heavy thinking. There are some interesting exceptions, of course. Michael Moorcock's Elric of Melniboné, for example, is basically a peace-loving, contemplative soul who is forced into a more violent life-style by extenuating circumstances. Most of the barbarian superheroes, however, are not nearly as psychologically complex as Elric the melancholy albino, and this shallowness of character delineation usually extends to the other characters as well. Thus, flat characterization is a hallmark of what we shall call the "sword and sinew" novel. There is little, if any, psychological probing; motivations are the most fundamental.

A second identifying trait of the sword and sinew work is its emphasis upon action. The reader is irresistibly catapulted along by the swift progression of action-packed episodes. Indeed, the fast-paced narrative is perhaps the greatest strength of this subgenre. The reader can expect few dull moments. Neither can one expect, however, a great deal of sophistication in the structural technique employed. The linear development of these highly episodic works is usually simple and painfully repetitive.

A third distinguishing feature is the lack of thematic substance. In the sword and sinew novel or short story the reader finds action for action's sake, and is rarely intellectually challenged. This is not a literature of ideas. And it is this intellectual and thematic hollowness that most distresses readers used to thoughtful high fantasy works like Le Guin's Earthsea trilogy, Beagle's *Last Unicorn,* and Natalie Babbitt's *Tuck Everlasting.*

A fourth identifying trait is the employment of a rather simple, pedestrian, and colloquial literary style. Distinctly absent is the "elevated style" that characterizes most works of high fantasy. Although there are some exceptions, to be sure, most writings of the sword and sinew school do not reach the stylistic heights of works such as Dunsany's *King of Elfland's Daughter,* Eddison's *The Worm Ouroboros,* Le Guin's *Wizard of Earthsea,* Walton's *Prince of Annwn*, Beagle's *Last Unicorn*, and Patricia McKillip's *Riddle-*

Master of Hed. It is difficult, for example, to find passages in Lin Carter's Thongor of Lemuria series, or John Jakes's Brak the Barbarian books, or Robert E. Howard's Conan stories that match the verbal beauty of Dunsany's description of the glamorous "lawns of Elfland," or Walton's vivid portrayal of the meeting of Pwyll and Arawn, the Grey Man of Death, or Beagle's poignant initial description of the last unicorn, who lives in a "lilac wood" and is "no longer the careless color of sea foam, but rather the color of snow falling on a moonlit night." The style of the sword and sinew work, like its rawboned superhero, is frequently muscular, energetic, and hard-driving, but seldom is it elevated, sophisticated, or brilliantly polished.

Finally, the novels of this subgenre are characterized by an extreme emphasis upon gratuitous and sensational violence. Of all the traits mentioned here, this is perhaps the most characteristic, and the most disturbing. Killings and maimings of the most brutal and sadistic sort can be found in these works, and it is this feature that has been in large part responsible for the bad press sword and sinew (i.e., sword and sorcery) works have received. (At this juncture it is appropriate to remind the reader of the other negative traits listed in Alpers's article.)

Whether sword and sinew is the best identifying term for this fantasy subgenre is certainly open to question. Less questionable, however, is the need to put the barbarian superhero work in a separate subgenre. This, along with the use of the high fantasy designation, might clear up some of the genre/subgenre definition problems described above. The problems created by the use of sword and sorcery and heroic fantasy as descriptive designations pose a real challenge to students and practitioners of fantasy literature. This challenge must be met and successfully dealt with in the near future. Perhaps this discussion can serve as the first step in that direction.

ALL-AGES HIGH FANTASY

We suggest the use of the term "all ages" to resolve a number of problems that have adversely affected many readers and writers of high fantasy. This type of fantasy has traditionally posed a problem of categorization. Until recently, it has generally been assumed, especially in the United States, that high fantasy is for children. Only children, so adults condescendingly reasoned, were uncritical and gullible enough to enjoy literature about faeries or magic. But since the paperback edition of the works of Tolkien was published in 1965, adults have begun to learn what children instinctively knew —that high fantasy, when written well, is both entertaining and serious literature. Old fallacies die hard, however, as authors have discovered to their dismay when they have found their works placed on the children's literature shelf although they hadn't thought they had written for children, or at least exclusively for children. Vera Chapman's English publisher, for example, issued three of her titles as children's books when she never intended them as such. Fortunately, her American publisher, Avon Books, has remedied this situation. But Chapman's case is only one of many examples of the still-lingering assumption that if it's fantasy, it is probably for children. This situation is, of course, unfair to the writer, whose audience is thereby limited, and to the adult readers who miss out on some fine literary fare as a consequence.

Ironically, the increasingly wider audience for high fantasy created by adult recognition and appreciation of the genre has brought with it problems of categorization. Now that high fantasy is being written for and read by people of all ages, it is being classified, like realistic literature, as "children's," "juvenile," or "adult," with the adverse effect that the latter two groups are again missing out on good reading. Without getting into the troubled waters of classifying literature by age groups, it should be made clear that high fantasy differs from mainstream literature in ways that defy the standard classifications. First, the protagonists in high fantasy need not be children for the book to appeal to children, whereas in realistic literature they generally are. *Gulliver's Travels* is the classic example, but there are others. Cnite Caerles, in Patricia McKillip's *Throme of the Erril of Sherill,* is a grownup, though with the childlike capacity for being receptive to new and unexplainable occurrences. The same is true of the protagonists, familiar to children, in Howard Pyle's Arthur stories.

On the other hand, children are frequently the protagonists in fantasy, but this doesn't mean that the books are intended exclusively for children. The child protagonist in high fantasy, when met with the challenges of the secondary world, often acts much like an adult. This is clearly the case with the Pevensie children when they enter Narnia, there to become kings and queens. It is also true of the protagonists in many other works. Joyce Gregorian, for example, makes a special point of this phenomenon in *The Broken Citadel,* in which her young heroine is herself surprised by her deepened level of maturity when those around her expect it. The point is that in high fantasy children can somehow identify with older protagonists and older readers can identify with the child protagonists; whereas in realistic literature the protagonists usually are of an age consonant with the intended readers.

A second difference between high fantasy and realistic literature with regard to categorization is that high fantasy, being outside of our world and thus far from our more immediate and personal concerns, more readily avoids personal and topical themes in favor of more universal ones. Thus Edmund in Lewis's *The Lion, the Witch and the Wardrobe* learns that the petty sibling rivalries in which he engaged with his sister in our world can have far-reaching and ominous consequences for the entire world in Narnia. In the high fantasy secondary world, the chief concerns are not with such problems as a teenager's first date or how someone is dressed or is teased by his or her peers. Such concerns may be present, but are put into perspective when the characters find themselves confronted with more profound issues, issues that relate to people regardless of age. In short, fantasy is a universalizing element in literature because magic and the gods possess a high seriousness. This is why so much high fantasy has something to attract readers of all ages. To classify such works as children's or juvenile or adult is too prescriptive and places unfortunate limitations on the potential audience, and is thus unfair to writer and reader alike.

It will be interesting at this point to hear from some of the writers of what is usually classified as children's high fantasy regarding the category into which their books are placed. C. S. Lewis, describing the genesis of his own faery tales in *Of Other Worlds* (New York: Harcourt Brace Jovanovich, 1975, p. 37), comments that his stories began with visual images such as "a fawn carrying an umbrella." Later, the idea of Christianity entered and only later still did the appropriate form suggest itself: "I wrote fairy tales because the Fairy Tale seemed the ideal Form for the stuff I had to say." In a further comment about intended audience, he states, "I was therefore writing 'for children' only in the sense that I excluded what I thought they would not like or understand; not in the sense of writing what I intended to be below adult attention" (pp. 37–38). What Lewis wrote in the Chronicles of Narnia is by no means "below adult attention," yet these books are classified as children's literature. Speaking on the same subject of audience, Lloyd Alexander, in a recent interview with us, suggested that many authors, including himself, are like Lewis in that they write fantasy, not exclusively for children, but simply as the best way of saying what they want to say. "In the case of Tolkien who was writing for his children or Stevenson writing for Lloyd Osborne or what have you, I still think this was a great pretext to do what they really wanted to be doing." Commenting about his own experience, Alexander said that writing what for want of a better term are called children's books (his Prydain books and his more recent *The First Two Lives of Lukas-Kasha*) "has been for me personally the greatest creative experience that I have known. . . . For example, *Lukas-Kasha*. . . . I suppose at rock bottom it has a speculation on the nature of God." It is clear, then, that works such as those by Lewis and Alexander are not solely for the amusement of children, but for the reading pleasure and edification of all.

The foregoing discussion does not state or imply that all high fantasy is necessarily for all ages. Some books are primarily, if not exclusively, for either adults or children, the two extremes of the spectrum of readers, and these works do not qualify as all-ages fantasy. Beagle's *Last Unicorn* or Tolkien's *Silmarillion* are adult books, though we should not rule out the possibility of at least some children responding to them. At the other extreme are children's picture books or books that are slightly more advanced because they have fewer pictures and more (but still elementary) words, and little if any additional substance. It is important to note, however, that such books should be able to hold an adult's attention at least while he or she is reading them to children. If they don't hold any attraction for adults, they probably won't for children either. The two classes of books that do not fit into the all-ages category are, accordingly, adult books in which the fantasy appeal would be smothered for most children by the difficulties of language or idea, and children's books that, while possessing some attractions, would not usually be sought out for leisure reading by an older reader.

All-ages fantasy, then, consists of those works that can be read with equal (though different) appreciation by the child, the adolescent, and the adult. The classic examples of works that fall within this group are those of the two eminent Victorian writers George MacDonald (the Curdie books) and Lewis Carroll (the Alice books). MacDonald influenced not only Carroll, but also the modern writers of all-ages fantasy, J. R. R. Tolkien (*The Hobbit*) and C. S. Lewis (the Chronicles of Narnia). Among contemporary writers, all-ages fantasy boasts a large number of authors, among them some of the finest writers of fantasy at the present time: Joan Aiken, Lloyd Alexander, Ursula K. Le Guin, and Patricia McKillip. This, of course, is only a selection of the many writers of all-ages fantasy included in this book.

The works of the writers just cited display certain common characteristics, an examination of which should help to make firm our definition of the term all-ages. All-ages fantasy displays the characteristics of high fantasy generally (thereby fundamentally relating it to an adult readership), but it handles these characteristics in a way that is also attractive to children and young adults. All-ages books treat causality and setting in a sophisticated fashion, examining, for instance, the ramifications and implications of magic and the responsibility of the magician, as Jane Yolen does in *The Magic Three of Solatia*. In this work, it is only when magic is used as a last resort and without any selfish aims that the user can handle it without somehow being undermined by it. In children's literature, magic frequently comes in large doses and without any side effects. Also, the setting in all-ages fantasy most often describes a secondary world of many sizable—but clearly chartered— lands, as witness the elaborate topography of Le Guin's Earthsea, while the children's variety takes the simpler form of "In a far-off land. . . ."

The characters in all-ages fantasy are handled in a similarly sophisticated manner; there is a marked emphasis on character development. Action waits upon character rather than the reverse. Often a character is in doubt about the right course to take. Thus, Taran doesn't know where to begin to find his true identity in Alexander's *Taran Wanderer*. Then, too, characters in the all-ages group are often less than perfect in rather serious ways. Taran's quest, just mentioned, is selfishly motivated by the hope that he is of noble birth. Most important, the characters in all-ages works, in addition to being developed as individuals, are representatives of types of human beings, regardless of age—rather than representatives of a particular age group. Taran on his quest, for example, acquires the name of Wanderer; despite his youthful appearance he becomes an Everyman character representing all of us in our search for our true identity, a search that ends only with the grave.

Interestingly, it is in the use of archetypes that all-ages fantasy most clearly demonstrates its universal appeal, and this is appropriate. By their nature, archetypes evoke an unlearned and instinctive response such as can be elicited from perhaps the youngest of humans beyond the cradle. A dark enclosed place is repellent to everyone, just as sunlight attracts us all. Such archetypes are, naturally, considerably refined or detailed in all-ages works, such as Le Guin's *Tombs of Atuan*, in which Ged wanders at length through the stifling and lightless caverns of Atuan. Even a description of this archetype by a less talented and powerful author than Le Guin could elicit essentially the same response in a child, most probably because children are more open and sensitive than adults in their response to archetypes.

Of all the characteristics of high fantasy, the one that most clearly distinguishes all-ages works is style. And the writer who immediately comes to mind in this context is George MacDonald, one of the most successful and durable of all-ages writers. In *At the Back of the North Wind*, in the two Curdie books, and in his short fantasies—all works incorrectly categorized as children's—MacDonald delights his readers, regardless of age, with his style. He doesn't apologize for using big words like "enigmatical" that would send many an adult in search of the dictionary. Nor does he miss an opportunity for a pun for those interested or alert enough to notice. Nor does he eschew the use of rich descriptive passages that please any reader with an eye to fine style. In "The Light Princess," anthologized in Boyer and Zahorski's *The Fantastic Imagination* (New York: Avon Books, 1977), MacDonald describes the rebirth of the countryside this way:

> And a rain came on, such as had never been seen in that country. The sun shone all the time, and the great drops, which fell straight to the earth, shone likewise. The palace was in the heart of a rainbow. It was a rain of rubies, and sapphires, and emeralds, and topazes. The torrents poured from the mountains like molten gold; and if it had not been for its subterraneous outlet, the lake would have overflowed and inundated the country. (pp. 95–96)

If, as mentioned earlier in this introduction, "poor style is the surest giveaway of a second-rate fantasy," the absence of a sufficiently elevated style is one of the first indicators that a book does not warrant all-ages status.

In addition to the manner in which it treats the characteristics of high fantasy, all-ages fantasy possesses another important dimension that sets it apart from children's fantasy and makes it appealing to children, juveniles, and adults: this dimension is its strata of appeals, or levels of meaning. This dimension also distinguishes all-ages from adult fantasy, since adult fantasy is more limited in that its levels of meaning or appeal exclude children. Asked for his view of what it is in a fantasy work that appeals to readers from the ages of 9 or 10 to 85, Lloyd Alexander replied, "It seems to me that in a funny kind of way it has to do with substructures and subtexts and attitudes and feelings below the surface of the work itself." "Subtexts" is a good word to describe the multiple levels of meaning and appeal that characterize an all-ages fantasy. It is precisely this trait that gives works such as Lewis's Chronicles of Narnia enduring all-ages appeal. On one level these books are meaningful examples of the effects of one's behavior on others; on another they are Christian allegory; on another they are still more universal and archetypal stories of humanity's origins and destiny. Another example is Natalie Babbitt's *Tuck Everlasting.* On one level, this novel is a fascinating description of perpetual youth; on another, it offers a profound commentary on the nature of time and the problems of living outside of time.

One of the outstanding traits of good all-ages fantasy is that children, though they do not consciously grasp the various subtexts as adults do, will intuitively perceive some of these deeper layers of meaning and store them up for future recall. In *Taran Wanderer,* for instance, we read in one scene of how Taran finds the magic spring from which he hopes to learn his true identity. When he peers into the waters he sees only his own reflection, but for him this is an awakening; it is a numinous moment, the realization of a profound truth—that he or any person is noble, not because of his blood, but because of his deeds, self-image, or self-worth. The youthful reader senses Taran's new awareness and the symbolism of the spring that conveys it, but on a less conscious level than the adult. The scene is one that is likely to remain with the child and to be remembered with deeper appreciation in later years.

We are not so sanguine as to believe that our use of the term all-ages will solve the problems that have plagued writers and readers of fantasy for a number of years. Bookstore managers and librarians are not likely to hasten to rearrange their shelving systems to make separate space for all-ages fantasy—though this would be nice, and perhaps would even increase sales or circulation as well as benefit the reader. We hope, however, that we have at least increased readers' awareness of the sizable number of fantasy works they may have missed because as adults they haven't recently wandered into the so-called children's or juvenile sections, or because as children they were intimidated by the labels juvenile or adult.

Current Developments and Trends in Fantasy

Since the appearance in paperback of J. R. R. Tolkien's *The Lord of the Rings* in 1965, there has been a remarkable resurgence of interest in fantasy literature. As might be expected, this has manifested itself in a number of noteworthy developments and trends, one of the most auspicious of which is the high priority American publishing houses are currently giving fantasy literature. Publishers are now printing new works with increasing frequency, reissuing many of those long out of print, and introducing handsome reprint and facsimile editions of fantasy classics. The Ballantine Adult Fantasy series, under the editorship of Lin Carter, represented one of the first large-scale attempts to provide readers with inexpensive paperback editions of fantasy classics. Launched in 1969 with a reprinting of Fletcher Pratt's *Blue Star,* the series was discontinued in 1975, after Ballantine had printed scores of high-quality fantasy works. The demise of the series was a disappointing setback, but the addition of fantasy titles under the imprints of a growing number of publishing houses (e.g., Newcastle, Avon, Arno, Atheneum, Dell, Dover, Ace, DAW, Signet, Del Rey) has helped keep the bookshelves well stocked with a wide variety of fantasy works. Although publishing trends are notoriously unpredictable, there seems to be good reason for optimism about the future of this genre.

The current vogue of fantasy has not affected the publishing world alone; it has also exerted a powerful influence upon the realm of academe. The widespread popularity of the genre among students and faculty has resulted in the creation of many fantasy literature units and courses, on both secondary and college levels. With this renewed pedagogical interest has come deserved critical attention. In the past 10 years more book-length treatments of fantasy have appeared than in any other decade of the period of modern fantasy. Some of the most noteworthy of these studies are Lin Carter's *Imaginary Worlds: The Art of Fantasy* (1973); Tzvetan Todorov's *The Fantastic: A Structural Approach to a Literary Genre* (1973); C. N. Manlove's *Modern Fantasy: Five Studies* (1975); L. Sprague de Camp's *Literary Swordsmen and Sorcerers: The Makers of Heroic Fantasy* (1976); Eric S. Rabkin's *The Fantastic in Literature* (1976); W. R. Irwin's *The Game of the Impossible: A Rhetoric of Fantasy* (1976); and Diana Waggoner's *The Hills of Faraway: A Guide to Fantasy* (1978). Many fine critical essays have also been written, and, at long last, some basic reference tools are being prepared by scholars who possess the necessary expertise and training. Much work, however, remains to be done. High-quality reference works devoted *exclusively* to fantasy (most deal with both fantasy *and* science fiction) are still scarce; the problem of genre definition has not yet been satisfactorily solved (fantasy and science fiction, fantasy and horror literature, and fantasy and lost-race novels are still often lumped together under a single descriptive designation); and there is still a profound need for adequate bibliographic control. Many of these concerns are now being addressed, however, and the research in this field promises to be some of the most exciting and rewarding of the century.

Perhaps the most encouraging development for American fantasy enthusiasts is the emergence of a strong contingent of home-grown fantasists. It is hardly a secret that the era of modern fantasy has been dominated by the British. From the mid-nineteenth century to the 1960s, Americans have had to look across the Atlantic for their fantasy fare. George MacDonald, William Morris, Lord Dunsany, David Lindsay, E. R. Eddison, C. S. Lewis, J. R. R. Tolkien—all hailed from the British Isles. True, there were a few noteworthy expeditions into fantastic realms on this side of the water: for example, Frank R. Stockton's delightfully witty and satiric fantasy short stories; L. Frank Baum's immensely popular, and uniquely American, Oz books; James Branch Cabell's impressive Poictesme cycle; and Kenneth Morris's splendid retellings of the tales of the *Mabinogion*. And to this list can be added the names of a few other American notables such as Clark Ashton Smith, A. Merritt, and David H. Keller, but even then the American inventory pales by comparison with the list of British fantasy luminaries.

In the last decade and a half, however, there has been a heartening turn of events. A surprisingly large number of talented fantasists have appeared on the American literary scene. Bolstering the ranks of veteran authors such as C. L. Moore, Andre Norton, Poul Anderson, L. Sprague de Camp, Fritz Leiber, and Evangeline Walton are newcomers such as Ursula K. Le Guin, Lloyd Alexander, Peter S. Beagle, Patricia McKillip, Susan Cooper, Carol Kendall, Jane Langton, Sanders Anne Laubenthal, Nancy Bond, Katherine Kurtz, C. J. Cherryh, and Stephen R. Donaldson. Most of these writers began their careers in the field of fantasy in the sixties, and some as recently as the seventies. American fantasy has finally come into its own, and American writers are now exerting an influence on the genre similar to that exercised by the British prior to 1960.

The preceding list of American authors reveals still another major development in the realm of fantasy literature: an increasingly large number of contemporary fantasists are women. This has not always been the case. Until quite recently, fantasy, like science fiction, has been a male-dominated genre. Although it is difficult to determine exactly why the number of women fantasists has increased so dramatically of late, the fact itself is indisputable. Besides the American women mentioned above, we must add British authors such as Sylvia Townsend Warner, Joan Aiken, Mary Stewart, Vera Chapman, Joy Chant, Tanith Lee, and Pat McIntosh. This predominance of women in the field must be considered a major development and, seemingly, a major trend in contemporary fantasy.

Another noteworthy development has been the rediscovery of neglected major talents in the field. Three of the most striking examples are Kenneth Morris, Barry Pain, and James Branch Cabell. Kenneth Morris (1879–1937) is one of the finest but least known of contemporary American fantasists. (Although born in Wales, Morris spent most of his adult life in the United States, and it is here that he seems to have been most productive in terms of his writing.) An inspiring teacher and brilliant intellect, Morris wrote a number of works of history, literary criticism, poetry, and fiction. The three of his books of most interest to fantasy readers are *The Fates of the Princes of Dyfed* (1913), *Book of the Three Dragons* (1930), and *The Secret Mountain and Other Tales* (1926). The first two volumes are close retellings of certain tales from the *Mabinogion*, while the latter is a fine collection of myth-based stories. In her instructive essay on style,

From Elfland to Poughkeepsie, Ursula K. Le Guin includes Morris as one of three "master stylists" of modern fantasy, along with E. R. Eddison and J. R. R. Tolkien. The praise is well deserved; not so well deserved, however, has been Morris's obscurity. Fortunately, there are now healthy signs of resurgence. Both *Princes of Dyfed* and *Three Dragons* have recently come out in handsome reprint editions (see annotations), and at least two of his *Secret Mountain* stories have been anthologized.

Barry Pain (1865–1928) is being mentioned more frequently in critical studies of fantasy, and his short fantasy fiction now and then finds its way into anthologies. A talented writer who during his lifetime was read primarily for his skills as a humorist and parodist, Pain is now being looked to by many contemporary readers for his highly polished, psychologically oriented short stories. Many of these stories are high fantasy, and top-notch high fantasy at that. A collection containing some of his finest fantasies, including the remarkable "The Glass of Supreme Moments," is *Collected Tales: Volume One* (1916). Rarely does one find fantasy stories that exhibit the deep psychological insight and the unique whimsy and sardonic wit that Pain brought to his. It is to be hoped that even more consideration will be given to this talented but neglected craftsman.

James Branch Cabell (1879–1958) is also beginning to receive more attention from scholars and publishers. This important but rather neglected American fantasist has always had a small, devoted coterie of enthusiasts; now, however, interest in his fantasy novels appears to be more widespread. Three of his Poictesme works, *The Silver Stallion* (1926), *The Cream of the Jest* (1917), and *Jurgen* (1919), have already been reprinted, and "The Music from behind the Moon," a delightful segment from *The Witch Woman,* has been included in the anthology *The Fantastic Imagination.*

Far more dramatic is the phenomenal revival of interest in a few American writers of Gothic and sword and sinew fantasy. The best known of the Gothic fantasy authors is H. P. Lovecraft (1890–1937). After being saved from possible literary obscurity by August Derleth and Donald Wandrei in 1939 (the date of the Arkham House publication of *The Outsider and Others,* the first collection of Lovecraft's short fiction), Lovecraft has now become one of the hottest literary properties on the market. Almost all of his works have been reprinted in paperback, and the enthusiastic reception they are receiving is sure to keep them in print for some time. Two other Gothic fantasists receiving good reprint consideration are Clark Ashton Smith (1893–1961) and A. Merritt (1884–1943); both are gifted, if uneven, writers who deserve the attention they are now getting. Tremendously popular are the works of Robert E. Howard (1906–1936), one of America's most prolific writers of sword and sinew fantasy. Although his career was brief (he committed suicide at the age of thirty), his output was prodigious, and most of his works are now readily available in both American and English paperback editions.

Also appearing on the bookshelves are a number of reprint editions of the fantasy novels and short fiction of George MacDonald (1824–1905), William Morris (1834–1896), H. Rider Haggard (1856–1925), William Hope Hodgson (1875–1918), David Lindsay (1876–1945), Lord Dunsany (1878–1957), and E. R. Eddison (1882–1945). Especially popular are the Haggard works. Paperback reprint editions of a number of his high fantasy and borderline fantasy works are appearing with surprising regularity.

The interest in Morris, Dunsany, and MacDonald started a bit earlier than the interest in Haggard, and it is still active and enthusiastic. Morris's appeal is generally limited to adults. MacDonald's Curdie books and his other faery tales, on the other hand, appeal to readers of all ages, and will probably always be more widely read and popular than Morris's lengthy and stylistically somewhat heavy prose romances. Within the past six years two fine collections of MacDonald's stories have been published: *The Gifts of the Child Christ: Fairy Tales and Stories for the Childlike,* a two-volume collection of the entire corpus of MacDonald's stories edited by Glenn Edward Sadler; and *The Complete Fairy Tales of George MacDonald,* a collection of eight of MacDonald's most delightful fantasies, edited by Roger Lancelyn Green. Dunsany's appeal is also to readers of all ages, with an inclination toward the adult reader. Although his high fantasy classic *The King of Elfland's Daughter* is readily accessible in paperback, his short stories, unfortunately, are in and out of print. *Gods, Men and Ghosts,* edited by E. F. Bleiler, is perhaps the finest and most accessible anthology of his fantasy stories on the market. Lin Carter edited some good Dunsany samplers for the Ballantine Adult Fantasy series, but these have been out of print for some time. More attention needs to be paid to this master of fantasy. As for Hodgson, his sea stories have always been fairly accessible, but now fantasy enthusiasts can also obtain in paperback *The House on the Borderland,* one of the most unique and bizzare Gothic fantasies ever written.

The renewed interest in the fantasy works of the talented authors listed above undoubtedly constitutes one of the most satisfying and rewarding developments of the past decade. Further explorations of the glamorous realms of faërie, however, should result in still other exciting discoveries. In some instances these discoveries will be of little-known fantasy tales written by well-known mainstream authors. Cases in point are some of the short stories of H. E. Bates, John Buchan, Alexander Grin, Mark Van Doren, William Hope Hodgson, Selma Lagerlöf, and Jorge Luis Borges. In other instances, American readers will discover British fantasists who are fairly well known in their native land but not so widely recognized here—writers such as Erik Linklater, Vera Chapman, and Sylvia Townsend Warner. Perhaps the most pleasant discoveries, however, will be made by adults who finally recognize that many writers who have been relegated to the nursery and the children's sections of libraries have something to say to them as well—all-ages fantasists such as Frank R. Stockton, Lloyd Alexander,

Joan Aiken, Alan Garner, Natalie Babbitt, Nancy Bond, Joyce Gregorian, and C. S. Lewis.

One of the most intriguing developments in fantasy is the current popularity of cinema and television adaptations of fantasy works. Although television producers have shown interest in fantasy programming (especially Gothic) for some time now, as evidenced by the "Twilight Zone" series of the late fifties and early sixties (and its close relative "Night Gallery" of the early seventies), only recently have they undertaken full-scale productions of fantasy classics.

The 90-minute television version of Tolkien's *Hobbit,* aired in the fall of 1977, signaled the beginning of a new era in fantasy programming. Reactions to the Arthur Rankin, Jr.–Jules Bass production were strong— and mixed. The Romeo Muller script was generally true to the novel, and the Rankin animation (based on the style of Arthur Rackham) was competent. But even the most conscientious of adaptations is sure to disappoint those with preconceived mental pictures of the characters and settings of Middle Earth. After all, how can any animated version of a character like Gollum hope to match the vision conjured up by the magic of Tolkien's vivid description? Be that as it may, millions of Tolkien enthusiasts were afforded the rare opportunity of seeing their favorite work dramatized in a new medium, and, perhaps even more important, millions of viewers not familiar with Tolkien's masterpiece were introduced to it.

The overall success of the television version of *The Hobbit* did not go unnoticed. A fantasy special based on C. S. Lewis's *The Lion, the Witch and the Wardrobe* was broadcast this spring and a one-hour animated special showcasing Wil Huygen and Rien Poortvliet's delightfully quaint and lovable *Gnomes* (Ray Bradbury will write the script) is scheduled to be aired later this year. Whether or not the medium of television can effectively and convincingly depict the unique imaginary world of the fantasist is still open to question. What is clear is that for better or for worse fantasy enthusiasts can expect to see many of their favorite works on television in the next few years.

Appearing with even more regularity are cinema adaptations of fantasy works. Fantasy in motion pictures is not unique, of course, to the seventies. In 1937, Walt Disney Studios released the full-length animated fantasy feature *Snow White and the Seven Dwarfs,* and two years later L. Frank Baum's *Wonderful Wizard of Oz* made its debut on the silver screen. Then, in 1940, the Disney people gave us *Fantasia,* a bona fide cinema fantasy classic. The innovative techniques and imaginative flair of this production inspire awe and admiration to this day. After this tour de force, the Disney animators went on to create a number of other fine feature-length films based on fantasy works, including *Cinderella* (1950), *Alice in Wonderland* (1951), *Peter Pan* (1953), and *Sleeping Beauty* (1959). During the fifties and sixties the Disney studios gave greater attention to live-action films than to animated features and to subjects other than fantasy. With the current revival of interest in fantasy and animation, however, the Disney organization is rebuilding its staff of animators and is currently engaged in an elaborate production of Lloyd Alexander's *Black Cauldron,* the second book in his magnificent Chronicles of Prydain. According to a recent *Newsweek* article by David Ansen and Stryker McGuire, *Cauldron* is scheduled for a 1984 release ("Disney's New Cauldron," *Newsweek,* Nov. 20, 1978, p. 81).

Perhaps the most important producer of fantasy films today is Ralph Bakshi. After experimenting with a number of innovative animation techniques in *Wizards,* he decided to accept the ultimate challenge: a cinema adaptation of Tolkien's *The Lord of the Rings.* He did it knowing full well that other accomplished filmmakers such as Walt Disney, Stanley Kubrick, and John Boorman had failed in their attempts to adapt the epic work. Like the television version of *The Hobbit,* Bakshi's production of the first half of *The Lord of the Rings* has evoked some praise and much criticism. Many viewers and critics feel that Bakshi has deceived moviegoers by entitling his movie *The Lord of the Rings* without clearly indicating that only half of Tolkien's narrative is recounted (a sequel, of course, is planned). Others, especially those unfamiliar with Tolkien's novel, complain of difficulty in following the action, and in keeping straight the identities of the various characters. These criticisms are justified to an extent. However, looking at the other side of the ledger, it seems clear that Bakshi has made an honest and conscientious attempt to preserve the integrity of the Tolkien work. The delineation of main characters such as Frodo, Samwise, Gandalf, Aragorn, and Gollum is essentially accurate, and the script by Chris Conkling and Peter S. Beagle is crisp, lively, and literate. Although Bakshi's animation technique, which uses an interesting combination of live action and animation, sometimes results in rather jarring juxtapositions, it also creates some strikingly vivid and memorable screen images—especially in the chase and battle scenes. In balance, Bakshi's film, like any other, has its own particular strengths and weaknesses. It is far from being flawless, but it does succeed in setting a respectable standard for future fantasy adaptations.

Fantasy works other than Tolkien's are also receiving the attention of today's filmmakers. Most notable is the full-length animated version of Richard Adams's *Watership Down.* As a matter of fact, some critics see this film as being significantly better than Bakshi's *The Lord of the Rings,* and insist that producer-writer-director Martin Rosen has set the standard by which future fantasy films will be judged. David Ansen, for example, in a recent critical review of *The Lord of the Rings* and *Watership Down* ("Hobbits and Rabbits," *Newsweek,* Nov. 20, 1978, pp. 79–81) concludes: "Long after the Hobbits and elves of *The Lord of the Rings* have faded from memory, this bird [the seagull Kehaar] and these rabbits will linger in the mind like the classic Disney characters who preceded them." Perhaps Rosen's most noteworthy accomplishment is his creation of psychologically complex and believable characters. This careful delineation of character, a script that preserves the integrity of the Adams novel, and solid animation combine in a film that appeals strongly to moviegoers of all ages. There is nothing cute or saccharine about the Rosen production; the scenes that portray cruelty and death in the novel, and there are several, are treated with candor and convincing authenticity in the film.

Fantasy enthusiasts desiring visual presentations of their favorite fantasy settings and characters need not rely solely upon television and the cinema, however. At no other time in history have the works of fantasy artists both old and new been so readily available and accessible. This unprecedented accessibility constitutes a major, and extremely healthy, development in the field.

Never before have we had at our fingertips so many high-quality fantasy art books, and at such reasonable prices (many are in large-format paperback editions). Although some very handsome collections have been marketed by a number of publishing houses in the past few years, Bantam's Peacock Press fantasy art series, under the general editorial direction of Ian and Betty Ballantine, deserves special mention. Carefully edited (most by David Larkin) and aesthetically pleasing, they are printed in large-format paperback, thus putting them within the budgets of most buyers. The Peacock Press titles not only include some of the old masters of fantasy art, such as Kay Nielsen, Edmund Dulac, and Arthur Rackham, but some of the most recent as well. As a matter fact, the striking collection entitled *Once upon a Time: Some Contemporary Illustrators of Fantasy* (1976) serves as a kind of "Who's Who among Contemporary Fantasy Artists." Included in the volume are works by Chris McEwan, Wayne Anderson, Tony Meeuwissen, Frank Bellamy, Nicola Bayley, Peter Le Vasseur, Pauline Ellison, Brian Froud, Alan Lee, Ian Miller, Reg Cartwright, James Marsh, Peter Barrett, Owen Wood, and Ken Laidlaw. The very length of this listing offers convincing proof of the healthy state of contemporary fantasy art. And to this list ought to be added the names of David Johnston (his cover for the Ballantine paperback edition of Evangeline Walton's *Children of Llyr* was featured in the November 4, 1972, issue of *Saturday Review*); Frank Frazetta (especially known for the covers he has done for E. R. Burroughs's novels); Gail Garraty (illustrator of the Bantam paperback edition of Le Guin's Earthsea trilogy); and Tim Kirk and the Brothers Hildebrandt, popular fantasy illustrators who are probably best known for their artistic conceptualizations in the annual Tolkien calendars published by Ballantine.

Although the Peacock Press series is currently leading the field, other publishing houses are also making their presence felt. Harry N. Abrams, Inc., is a case in point. Published in the fall of 1977, *Gnomes,* a hardcover book priced at $17.50, was on the national best-seller lists just three weeks after it hit the bookstands. It has already sold more than 700,000 copies, and has created a kind of gnomomania that shows little sign of waning. Abrams has followed this phenomenally popular work with one that promises similar success—*Faeries*, edited by David Larkin and illustrated by Brian Froud and Alan Lee. Both Froud and Lee are exceptionally talented English fantasy artists whose styles nicely complement each other. Froud, of course, has already established himself as a sort of cult hero ("Proud of Froud" buttons are popping up everywhere) through Peacock Press collections like *The Land of Froud* (1977). He is a prolific and versatile artist whose fantasy creations are as imaginative and freshly original as any in the field. He seems destined to become one of our century's most popular fantasy artists.

Although the art book is the most obvious manifestation of the new emphasis on visual fantasy, another very recent development that deserves careful watching is the publication of illustrated novels, collections, and anthologies. It will be interesting to see how heavily illustrated large-format novels like Larry Niven's *The Magic Goes Away* (illustrated by Esteban Moroto) will fare in the marketplace. An example of an anthology making rather heavy use of illustrations is Boyer and Zahorski's *Dark Imaginings: A Collection of Gothic Fantasy,* which contains 17 original pen-and-ink drawings by James Cagle. The bookmakers have made their move; they are now waiting for readers to make theirs.

One other contemporary development ought to be given another mention here: the increasing interest in fantasy among adult readers. Patrick Merla may not have been the first to notice this curious phenomenon, but he was undoubtedly the first to bring it to the attention of thousands of readers. In an enlightening article in the November 4, 1972, issue of *Saturday Review,* Merla points out: "Children are forsaking innocence in their reading habits to peruse stark realities, while adults, paradoxically, are wandering more and more into fictional never-never lands" (p. 43). The paradoxical trend that Merla recognized in the early seventies persists today. This is not to say, of course, that young readers have completely forsaken the fantasy genre. Actually, it is still, as it always has been, extremely popular among readers of all ages. What is surprising, though, is the extremely high level of interest in the adult sector. This, of course, bodes well for fantasy. And there seems little doubt that the current popularity of fantasy among readers of all ages will be with us for some time to come.

But what is the source of this vitality? We have mentioned two of the appeals of fantasy in this introduction—the perspective it provides on our world by viewing it at a distance from the secondary world, and the sense of awe and wonder it elicits. This sense of awe and wonder is related to perspective. On one hand, awe and wonder derive from the otherness of the secondary world, the "arresting strangeness," as C. S. Lewis terms it, that springs from creatures, landscapes, and the magical and supernatural causality of the secondary world. And on the other hand, awe and wonder derive from our recognition of elements within the other world that remind us of similar elements in our own world that we tend to forget—universal situations and Everyman characters (archetypes), values and standards, and even the creatures and settings. Tolkien, in his essay "On Fairy-Stories," reprinted in *The Tolkien Reader* (New York: Ballantine Books, 1966), refers to such recognition as "recovery," "a regaining of a clear view" or "seeing things as we are (or were) meant to see them" (p. 57). Thus, Tolkien suggests, we cannot read in fantasy of Pegasus without then viewing a horse in a new, fresh light. Chesterton states the same idea in somewhat different words in "A Fairy Tale," from the collection *Lunacy and Letters* (New York: Arno Press, 1958): "Fundamental to the fairy tale is the fact we forget that we have forgotten."

In addition to awe and wonder and the fresh perspective they offer, high fantasy (again according to Tolkien) generates a "piercing glimpse of joy" (p. 70). What he means by this—he uses the term "eucatastrophe" for it—is that though sorrow and death occur, they are not the end for humankind, or, if they are, they are also the source of human greatness. Thus, in Tolkien's own works, the elves of Lorien knowingly sacrifice their power and their home to contribute to the downfall of the evil of Mordor; their departure from Middle Earth, along with that of other heroes of the great battle, is one of the saddest but noblest episodes in their long history.

High fantasy, however, has always produced these effects of perspective, awe and wonder, and joy. Why is it only in recent years that it has been discovered—or rediscovered? The answer is apparent. Ours is a frenetic age; today, perhaps more than ever before, people have a deeply felt need to escape for a time in order to restore their sense of awe and wonder and to regain a fresh perspective on this world. It is our hope that the present volume will serve as a helpful guide to those readers who wish to explore the restorative realms of fantasy—guiding them not only to the magic portals themselves, but also through the wondrous lands that lie beyond.

2

Core Collection

Novels and Short Story Collections

Aiken, Joan. *A Harp of Fishbones and Other Stories.* London: Cape, 1972. New York: Puffin, 1975 (paper).

Joan Aiken is generally classified as a writer of children's fiction. Like the fantasy stories of most accomplished writers, however, her sprightly and richly imaginative tales are entertaining and satisfying to readers of all ages. "For readers ten and over" is the claim made for the stories contained in the Puffin edition—and the claim is valid. The volume includes "A Harp of Fishbones," "The Boy with a Wolf's Foot," "Mrs. Nutti's Fireplace," "Hope," "The Lost Five Minutes," "The Rose of Puddle Fratrum," "A Jar of Cobblestones," "A Long Day without Water," "The Prince of Darkness," "Two Tales of Burnt Porridge," "Humblepuppy," "The River Boy," "The Gift Pig," and "The Dark Streets of Kimball's Green." Not all of these stories are fantasy in the strictest sense of the term. The majority are, however, and they will serve to give the reader a good sampling of Aiken's brand of fantasy. Especially fine is the title story, a delightful faery tale that vividly exhibits Aiken's consummate craftsmanship. The characters are carefully delineated; the narrative is fast paced and strongly unified; the secondary world is convincingly described; and the prose style is energetic and polished. The story is moving, full of poignant episodes; especially memorable is the segment describing Nerryn's successful breaking of the mountain goddess's spell (some readers will be reminded of similar scenes in Lewis's Narnian chronicles). Readers who find this fantasy fare to their liking will want to turn to other Aiken collections such as *All You've Ever Wanted* (1953), *A Small Pinch of Weather* (1969), *The Green Flash* (1971), and *A Bundle of Nerves* (1976). Illustrated by Pat Marriott.

Alexander, Lloyd. *The Book of Three.* New York: Holt, 1964.

Lloyd Alexander ranks as one of the best writers of high fantasy to emerge since Tolkien, and his five novels comprising the Chronicles of Prydain are true classics of the genre. *The Book of Three* introduces the series and, like the books that follow, draws much of its material from the Welsh *Mabinogion,* thus relating Alexander to Evangeline Walton and Kenneth Morris. Alexander, however, unlike Walton or Morris, alters his source considerably. In fact, Alexander uses his ancient source as a guide or a jumping-off point for his own invention, though much of the original still shows through concretely in places and imbues the spirit of Alexander's work throughout. In *The Book of Three,* the kingdom of Prydain is being threatened by the ominous and evil Arawn, Prince of Annuvin, a god of the underworld. His advances have long been checked by the House of Don, now led by Gwydion. But Arawn has acquired a new warlord, the Horned King. Both sides, however, seek some answer from the oracular pig, Hen Wen, who is kept by the wise old enchanter, Dollben. Yet none of these grand people is the hero of the work. This unsuspected honor comes to Taran, Dollben's Assistant Pig-Keeper, a young foundling. It is he who accompanies Gwydion in search of Hen Wen, who has run away in a panic. When Gwydion disappears, Taran finds himself the leader of a small band that must warn the House of Don of the approach of the Horned King. The events which transpire throughout the story hold the reader's attention, as Taran escapes from an enchanted castle, discovers the ancient sword Dyrnwyn, and visits the pre-fall valley of Medwyn and the underground kingdom of the Fair Folk. Interesting as these adventures are, Alexander's memorable characters are by far his greatest achievement: Princess Eilonwy, garrulous and engaging; Fflewdder Fflam, a comically inept minstrel; Gurgi, perhaps best described as an apelike creature who speaks in rhymes and is generally so covered with leaves and twigs that he looks like "a walking beaver dam." These characters all reappear in the next books, which like *The Book of Three*, are characterized by magic, humor, and warmth. Although the chronicles can be read separately or in any order, it is best to read *The Book of Three* first and *The High King* last.

Alexander, Lloyd. *The Black Cauldron.* New York: Holt, 1965. New York: Dell, 1969 (paper).

In his introduction to this second of the Chronicles of Prydain, Alexander comments that his intention is to add to the series and to deepen it. He accomplishes this in several ways. In *The Book of Three* there was hardship, but the conflict was resolved with the side of good and its protagonist Taran emerging relatively unscathed. There is more at stake in *The Black Cauldron*. The quest here is to destroy the Cauldron, through which Arawn, prince of the underworld, enslaves men after their death, depriving them of their final rest of both body and, presumably, soul. In accomplishing this objective, two of Taran's company knowingly sacrifice their lives and their dreams. These are Adaon, the bard and son of Taliesen, and Prince Ellidyr, a basically noble warrior, but one torn and tormented by a distorted vision of heroism. Also, Taran's own desire for heroic achievement and recognition comes to the fore, paralleled somewhat by Ellidyr's. Taran must also sacrifice his dream and he does so before it corrupts him, unselfishly giving up the magical brooch, which had given him so much stature among his companions, in order to obtain the Cauldron. But while *The Black Cauldron* adds a definite dimension of tragedy to the chronicles, it retains the humor and ingenious character creation of the first book. Fflewddor Fflam is there, breaking harpstrings when he exaggerates the truth. And so are Princess Eilonwy and the engaging Gurgi. To his gallery of unique creations Alexander adds Gwystyl, one of the Fair Folk, who keeps watch at an underground outpost and is terribly put out when forced to give sanctuary to Taran and his companions. And Alexander provides the delightful but somehow daunting portraits of Orddu, Orwen, and Orgoch, the Welsh equivalent of the three fates. Alexander creates in *The Black Cauldron* a successful blend of tragedy and comedy with a resultant wisdom. Taran and the readers come to recognize that one can never come to terms with evil without being corrupted.

Alexander, Lloyd. *The Castle of Llyr.* New York: Holt, 1966. New York: Dell, 1969 (paper).

In *The Castle of Llyr,* the third of the Chronicles of Prydain, Alexander develops two plots that seem at first to be little connected. The book begins with Taran and Gurgi accompanying Princess Eilonwy to a small kingdom on the Isle of Mona where she is to live at court and learn to be a lady. Shortly after their arrival, however, Eilonwy is kidnapped by the treacherous Chief Steward Magg who is in the employ of Achren the sorceress. At this point the plot shifts to another action entirely. Taran, while seeking for Eilonwy and accompanied by Prince Rhun, Fflewddor Fflam, and Gurgi, is chased by a giant cat called Llyan, and becomes trapped in a cave with the cowardly and mean giant, Glew. They do escape, but these adventures have only incidental relationship to what happens later in the story. To devote half a book to these adventures, interesting though they are, seems to distract from what ought to have been the major plot, the search for Eilonwy and the clash with Achren—happenings which do occur, but why postpone them so? The answer is the theme. The subject of the book is the desire for power or recognition, which indeed is the major subject throughout the Chronicles of Prydain. In the first plot of *The Castle of Llyr* readers meet the small-minded giant Glew, who took a potion to achieve his bigness, but got himself imprisoned in a cave as a consequence. One of his earlier experiments had resulted in a cat becoming the enormous Llyan, but Llyan retained his basic good nature. In the second plot Achren seeks power (another form of bigness) by using Eilonwy, who, as a daughter of the House of Llyr, can read the book of spells. Eilonwy herself is tempted, but chooses instead to destroy the potentially evil book of power. And finally there is Taran, the Assistant Pig-Keeper, who dreams of nobility. In this book Taran must take an oath to help keep the bumbling Prince Rhun safe. The irony is that Taran acts nobly, but is not a prince, while Rhun, who of course is a prince, acts like a clown. It is certainly clear by this, the third chronicle, how consciously Alexander has substantively integrated the series through the theme that the desire for greatness, if not controlled, can lead one astray. And Llyan, Glew, and Rhun demonstrate yet again Alexander's genius at creating characters.

Alexander, Lloyd. *Taran Wanderer.* New York: Holt, 1967. New York: Dell, 1969 (paper).
Taran Wanderer, the fourth of the Chronicles of Prydain, records Taran's continuing quest to perform heroic deeds and to discover the identity of his parents, who he intensely hopes will be of noble blood. The significant difference in this fourth chronicle is that Taran is entering manhood, and the book takes on a more serious tone. Indeed, it becomes a classic quest tale, a rite of passage into manhood; like all serious quests it is, or at least includes, the journey of self-discovery. Significantly, Taran gives up even his title of Assistant Pig-Keeper for the less specific one of Wanderer. *Taran Wanderer* continues the progressive deepening of the chronicles, but without sacrificing the warm humor and excitement of the earlier books. Taran aids King Smoit to settle a potential civil war through a very Solomon-like judgment; he confronts the wraithlike sorcerer Morda; he learns humility when he accepts what he believes to be his base-born father Craddoc; and he finally peers into the Mirror of Llunet. In most of these adventures, Taran is sorely tempted in one way or another to become ignoble. He passes these trials and acquires wisdom and humility through which he finally realizes that nobility is manifested in the way one acts rather than in the color of one's blood. Alexander's humor ripples through the book and is even more refreshing than in the earlier works, flowing as it now does through a more serious Prydain. Alexander also has nicely modulated Taran's speech, suiting it to his increased wisdom and nobility. One misses Eilonwy in *Taran Wanderer,* but self-discovery is, after all, a solitary undertaking. Only Gurgi keeps his master company.

Alexander, Lloyd. *The High King.* New York: Holt, 1968.
If writing a good ending to a single book is a challenge, then doing so for a closely integrated series such as the Chronicles of Prydain is doubly challenging. No one succeeds better at this than Lloyd Alexander in *The High King*, fifth and last of the chronicles and a winner of the Newbery award. Those who have read the previous books will enjoy a reunion, not only with the regulars such as Princess Eilonwy, Gurgi, and Fflewdder Fflam, but in many cases with those who appeared only once before but played parts of some importance, like Prince Rhun, or farmer Aeddan, or Medwyn of the peaceful valley. The meeting is one of mingled joy and sadness, since it is the call to the final battle against Arawn that draws everyone together. This final winner-take-all confrontation with Arawn is the central action of the book, and it is described in an outstanding narrative that is moving and absorbing. The readers, whether or not they have made previous acquaintance with the characters in the earlier chronicles, cannot help but be moved by their deeds: Ffewdder Fflam burning his beloved harp to provide warmth for his companions, or Princess Eilonwy illuminating the valley with her magic bauble to discover the ghostly but fierce Cauldron-Born warriors of Annuvin. Nor can the readers fail to become engrossed in Taran's ingenious guerrilla tactics as he delays the Cauldron-Born from reinforcing Arawn's besieged stronghold by engineering a great flood. The most poignant part of the book, however, comes after the battle is won by Gwydion with Taran's help. This is when the friends part company. Taran and Eilonwy forego the gift of the happy-ever-after Summer Country in order to remain in Prydain to help set things in order. And "thus did an Assistant Pig-Keeper become High King of Prydain." The more difficult sacrifice for Taran and Eilonwy, however, is separation from their companions, for Gurgi, Fflewdder Fflam, Dollben, and all the others have no choice but to depart; their part in the history of this world is ended. And with their departure comes the closing of all the entries to the land of the Fair Folk; thus ends the age of magic and enchantment for men—at least, for now. It is clear by now to readers familiar with Tolkien's *The Lord of the Rings* how much Alexander's conclusion resembles Tolkien's—the last all-out battle and the departure for a mystical realm. In one major respect, at least, Alexander improves on Tolkien. Whereas Tolkien rarely describes conflicts between large forces in any great length or detail, Alexander does and does it well, thereby more closely involving the reader in so important an action as the decisive last battle. And he does so with finesse, avoiding the gruesome butchery detailed in many works of sword and sinew. Indeed, the conclusion points out that winning the battle is the easy part; ruling the people will be considerably more demanding. This theme is a variation on the idea that integrates the five chronicles—that greatness is not a matter of birth or even of bold deeds, but of wisdom and humility and responsible choice.

Alexander, Lloyd. *The Foundling and Other Tales of Prydain.* New York: Holt, 1973.

A companion volume to the Chronicles of Prydain, containing six brief but delightful short stories: "The Foundling," "The Stone," "The True Enchanter," "The Rascal Crow," "The Sword," and "The Smith, the Weaver, and the Harper." All tell of happenings before the time of Taran, Assistant Pig-Keeper, and feature some of the characters first introduced in the chronicles. The title story, "The Foundling," for example, provides a fascinating and enlightening account of the childhood and youth of Dollben the enchanter. The reader, however, doesn't have to possess a knowledge of the chronicles in order to enjoy and profit from these finely wrought tales of fantasy. Although Alexander's works, including those in this volume, are often classified as juvenile fantasy, it will not take the open-minded and discerning adult reader long to find that his fantasy works appeal to readers of all ages. Like Lewis's Narnian tales, the Prydain stories are both entertaining and substantive. A case in point is "The Smith, the Weaver, and the Harper," which not only effectively satirizes human greed, but also subtly articulates the profound importance of integrity and pride in one's craft. All the stories in this fine collection display the lucid style, instructive satire, and sly wit for which Alexander is noted. Illustrations by Margot Zemach.

Anderson, Poul. *The Broken Sword.* New York: Abelard-Schuman, 1954.

"Whatever can die is beautiful—more beautiful than a unicorn, who lives forever." This quotation from Beagle's *Last Unicorn* makes an important observation pertinent to Anderson's *Broken Sword.* Skafloc, the hero of this fine Norse epic, is a changeling, a human stolen at birth and raised by the elf-earl Imric as his own fosterling. The differences between Skafloc and the elves nicely define the characteristics of each race; they point out the tragedy, but likewise the beauty, of being human and mortal. The plot, typical of the epic (one is reminded of *Beowulf* as well as of the Icelandic Eddas and sagas), is episodic. Trollheim attacks Alfheim (Elfinkind). Skafloc emerges as the hero for the elves—unlike them he can wear and wield iron. As warrior, lover, and wanderer he encounters gods, humans, demons, and a variety of creatures from the realm of faërie. Yet the plot is not exaggerated; characters are well drawn, their motives and behavior convincing. Battle scenes seem authentic, while the love scenes are poignant rather than melodramatic. It is interesting that, in his foreword to the 1971 edition, Anderson compares his treatment of elves to Tolkien's. Tolkien's elves are kind and courteous, whereas his own, belonging to an earlier tradition, are indifferent or even inimical to man. However, now that Tolkien's *Silmarillion* has been published, depicting the first age of Middle Earth, the two writers seem to agree more closely in their treatment of elves. Another parallel between the works of these two authors is the northern (Norse) notion of tragedy as the basis for human greatness.

Anderson, Poul. *Three Hearts and Three Lions.* Garden City, NY: Doubleday, 1961. New York: Berkley, 1978 (paper).
Holger Carlsen, known in legend as Holger Danske or Ogier le Danois, is
"The Defender" and the Continental equivalent of Arthur of Britain,
returning in time of grave need. In this story, Holger has forgotten his
identity due to the machinations of Morgan Le Fay. Holger's quest thus
starts as a personal one, to solve the mystery of his identity. This quest leads
him to the magical sword, Cortana, and to the realization that he is the
leader of the forces of law in their struggle against Morgan Le Fay and the
powers of chaos. Along the way Holger gathers some unusual companions:
the dwarf, Hugi; the swan-may, Alianora; and the Christianized Saracen,
Carahue. Opposing Holger are an array of creatures from the Middle World
(faërie), including elves, a fire drake, a giant, a werewolf, a nixie, a troll,
cannibals, a hell horse, and, most prominently, Morgan herself. The setting
is a medieval Europe not long after the time of Charlemagne, which borders
on the Middle World of faërie. This setting does not, however, belong to
our world, but to a parallel world. The connection between this parallel universe and our own is explained in the introduction and conclusion that
frame the story. The time setting for these framing chapters is World War II,
thus relating our world to the conflict of chaos versus law examined in the
parallel universe otherworld. Anderson's strengths are his colorful descriptions of Holger's adventures and his use of courtly speech and several dialects
to create a suitably archaic tone and to help delineate character. In its min-
gling of humor and seriousness, *Three Hearts and Three Lions,* even though
it was written before *The Broken Sword,* is more akin to Anderson's later
fantasy work, *A Midsummer Tempest.*

Anderson, Poul. *A Midsummer Tempest.* Garden City, NY: Doubleday,
1974. New York: Del Rey, 1978 (paper).
Anderson is one of a growing number of science fiction writers (and possibly
the best of them) who has successfully established a relatively new subgenre
of fantasy by blending science and fantasy. Other outstanding practitioners of
science fantasy are Clifford Simak (*Enchanted Pilgrimage*) and Andre
Norton (the Witch World series). All three use the technique of the parallel
universe, or something akin to it, to cross over into the otherworld realm of
fantasy. Of the three, Anderson places least stress on science, and he also
emphasizes the elements of faery-tale romance more than those of sword
and sinew. This is especially true of the spritely novel *A Midsummer Tempest.*
The book posits a parallel universe in which Shakespeare is recognized as
"the great Historian." Thus Oberon, Titania, Puck, Ariel, Prospero, and
Caliban are—or were—historical figures. The time setting is the English
Civil War between the Puritans and the Royalists—in our universe, the first
half of the seventeenth century. The only other major difference between
this universe and ours is the presence of the steam-engine locomotive, the

symbol of practical Puritan progress at the expense of nature—particularly of the forests that the faeries inhabit. This is why Oberon and Titania (and Puck) decide to help Prince Rupert of the Rhine, nephew of Charles I and leader of his troops. The war is going badly for the English king; the Faery King and Queen, however, advise Rupert to travel to Prospero's island to acquire Prospero's discarded wand and book of magic. Rupert does in fact eventually recover Prospero's magical possessions with the help of Ariel and Caliban (and his sweetheart Jennifer Alayne) and returns just in time for the last desperate stand of King Charles's army. Charles has chosen to make his stand at Glastonbury Tor. Will Fairweather, the prince's English yeoman, with Prospero's book and wand as talismans, awakes the sleeping powers of the land, including the dead resting under Glastonbury Tor. The Royalists join with these natural and not-so-natural forces to defeat Cromwell and his Puritans. *A Midsummer Tempest* is much more lighthearted than Anderson's earlier fantasies. Indeed, it is something of a stylistic tour de force. Anderson's handling of style is brilliant, courtly, colloquial, or archaic, as the character and situation demand. Had the style been ineffectual, such a book (which inevitably invites comparison with Shakespeare's style) would have been merely ludicrous. In addition to his stylistic gymnastics, Anderson also creates several intensely moving magical scenes, particularly the final battle scene. Of Anderson's three fantasy novels, one, *The Broken Sword*, is pure high fantasy. The other two—*A Midsummer Tempest* and *Three Hearts and Three Lions*—are classified as science fantasy. Some of Anderson's other works employ the parallel universe device (*Operation Chaos*, for example) but they emphasize science almost to the exclusion of fantasy.

Anthony, Piers. *A Spell for Chameleon.* New York: Ballantine, 1977 (paper). Voted the best fantasy novel of the year (1977) by the British Fantasy Society, *Chameleon* is a long, highly detailed novel that is reminiscent in its inventiveness and imaginative power of Jack Vance's *Dying Earth* stories. The setting is the exotic, magical land of Xanth, where "no nonmagical person [can] remain beyond his quarter-century mark." This rule prompts Bink, the seemingly "nonmagical" protagonist, to "go to see the Good Magician Humfrey and learn what his own magic talent [is]." Humfrey verifies that Bink does indeed possess some powerful, albeit unidentifiable, magic, but when Bink fails to demonstrate his talent before the king he is exiled. While he is in exile in Mundania (a nonmagical land similar to our own primary world), Bink, with the help of the evil magician Trent and Chameleon (a girl who undergoes a monthly cycle of change that ranges "from ugly intelligence to lovely idiocy"), discovers his unique magical talent—he cannot be harmed by magic. This is a highly entertaining novel. Anthony, like T. H. White in *The Sword in the Stone* and C. S. Lewis in the Narnian chronicles, proves that it is possible to inject humor into a fantasy novel without necessarily destroying the seriousness or credibility of its magic. As a matter of fact, one of the strong points of the novel is its exploration of the nature and uses of magic, although the reader should be warned that Anthony has a tendency to overuse magical paraphernalia. The novel contains enough spells (spells of "aversion," "ignorance," "illusion," "repulsion," "self-preservation," "truth"), for example, to place all of its characters in a state of perpetual enchantment. This magic overkill extends into other areas as well. All in all, though, this is an action-packed, witty, and smoothly written novel that is deserving of the recognition it has received from the British Fantasy Society.

Arnason, Eleanor. *The Sword Smith.* New York: Condor, 1978 (paper).
Although not in the same class as Peter S. Beagle's *Last Unicorn,* Patricia McKillip's Riddle-Master books, or Ursula K. Le Guin's Earthsea trilogy, Arnason's *Sword Smith* is a charming and unpretentious high fantasy that exhibits the marks of a promising talent. Using a spare and somewhat tele-graphic style, Arnason recounts the many adventures of Holrin Limper, master smith of Eshgorin, and his rather unusual traveling companion, Nargri, a young dragon small enough to fit comfortably in a saddlebag. Limper, too, is unusual, not only in his inimitable skill as a smith, but also in the fact that he was reared by a dragon. It was while with the dragons that he learned his craft—dragons are, we discover, extraordinarily fine smiths—and met Nargri, who asked to accompany him on his travels so that she could learn more about life on the earth's surface (most dragons have underground dwellings). Her traveling companion is now a fugitive, however. Fed up with trying to satisfy the whimsical demands of the King of Eshgorin, Limper shelves his hammer and flees the country—only to find that a man with a price on his head cannot enjoy life very much how-ever far he might wander. After narrowly escaping from a number of would-be captors, including a greedy caravan master, a cannibalistic moun-tain dweller, Enrin Silvershield (captain of the palace guard at Eshgorin), and assorted dragons and trolls, Limper is still unsure of his place in life at the novel's conclusion. It seems clear, however, that he must somehow practice his craft if he is to fulfill his destiny and give his life meaning. Arnason's style is not particularly polished, and she fails to imbue her work with the kind of magic one expects to find in a work of fantasy, but she does make her characters come to life and manages to create a secondary world that is both believable and interesting. Especially fascinating is her treatment of dragons. While humanlike in form and nature, they are por-trayed in a refreshingly original fashion—for this reason alone the novel is worth reading. Noteworthy, too, are her detailed descriptions of the black-smith's work, an element absolutely essential in this fantasy novel, which poignantly illustrates the causal relationship between one's craft and one's happiness.

Babbitt, Natalie. *Tuck Everlasting*. New York: Farrar, 1975. New York: Bantam, 1976 (paper).

Although usually classified as a children's book, *Tuck Everlasting* is a beautifully written fantasy novel that will appeal to readers of all ages. The narrative focuses upon the relationship between 10-year-old Winnie Foster and the Tuck family, four mortals who unwittingly acquired everlasting life by drinking the water of a magic spring. Through a series of poignant and thought-provoking episodes, both the blessings and drawbacks of life without death or change are revealed. Perhaps the most memorable statements about the plight of the immortal living in a world of constant change are made by "Tuck," the father, who tells Winnie: "But dying's part of the wheel, right there next to being born. You can't pick out the pieces you like and leave the rest. Being part of the whole thing, that's the blessing. But it's passing us by, us Tucks. Living's heavy work, but off to one side, the way *we* are, it's useless, too. It don't make sense. If I knowed how to climb back on the wheel, I'd do it in a minute. You can't have living without dying. So you can't call it living, what we got. We just *are*, we just *be*, like rocks beside the road." Thematic substance, however, is not the only thing that *Tuck* offers the reader. Babbitt has the rare ability to delineate characters who truly come to life; characters who are colorful and interesting; characters with whom it is possible to identify. She puts this talent to fine use in *Tuck*. How easy it is to empathize with Winnie's mixed feelings of anxiety and joy, confusion and amazement, as she eats her first meal with the Tucks; with Mae's happiness as she is freed from her jail cell; and with Jesse's exuberant optimism about life and the future. Add to this Babbitt's skillful handling of characterization, her careful plotting, her ability to create tone and atmosphere, and her lucid and seemingly effortless prose style, and you have one of those all too rare literary phenomena—an almost flawless piece of fiction. An American Library Association Notable Children's Book, *Tuck* was selected by the *New York Times* as "one of the best books of the year [1975] for children."

Bates, H[erbert] E. *Seven Tales and Alexander*. London: Scholastic Press, 1929.

Besides the lengthy title story, "Alexander," this handsome volume contains "The Barber," "The Child," "A Comic Actor," "The Peach Tree: A Fantasy," "A Tinker's Donkey," "The King Who Lived on Air: A Child's Tale," and "Lanko's White Mare." Only two of these stories—"Peach Tree" and "Air"—are fantasies, but both are of high literary quality. "Peach Tree," as a matter of fact, is one of the most polished and thoughtful stories in the collection. Especially noteworthy are Bates's soft, exotic, and loving descriptions of the peach tree and the mysterious garden at the end of the wall. Like the rare perfumes of the wondrous garden, an atmosphere of tender melancholy hangs over the story. But there is thematic substance as well. Through his careful handling of tone, setting, and character delineation Bates has made "Peach Tree" a splendid vehicle for an exploration of the intriguing concept of appearance versus reality. The final effect is not unlike that of Shakespeare's *Midsummer Night's Dream;* the reader is left wondering where illusion ends and reality begins, and whether our entire concept of reality is somehow deficient. Although not nearly so sophisticated in terms of literary technique, "Air" is a delightfully whimsical faery tale about a rather silly king (at least he is at the beginning of the story) whose "favourite pastime had been to shoot ripe pomegranate seeds into the left ear of his chancellor kneeling ten yards away." In Bates's capable hands, however, even this droll tale takes on serious thematic implications as the heretofore insensitive king undergoes an epiphany after seeing "the wan, narrow faces of the people who were starving" as the result of a terrible famine. It is a pity that this superb literary craftsman did not write more fantasy short stories, but we must be thankful for the few he has shared with us.

Baum, L. Frank. *The Wonderful Wizard of Oz.* Chicago: Hill, 1900. Reprinted as *The Wizard of Oz.* New York: Barnes & Noble, 1976 (paper). Dorothy's journey to Oz is one of the most remarkable and memorable journeys to an otherworld in all of fantasy. It has, of course, been immortalized in film and has come to be known as one of the truly American popular classics—our equivalent of *Alice in Wonderland.* Unlike *Alice,* though, *The Wizard* is usually left to the film critics and, unfortunately, to the nursery. Its simple style has apparently obscured its imaginative power, and the film version has certainly distorted our notion of the tale's plot. Indeed, only half of the tale is represented in the film—and not necessarily the best half. We can see the Munchkins in the film, but we can read about the Winkies, the Quadlings, and the absurd Hammer-heads. We see the Winged Monkeys serve the Wicked Witch, but we can read how they later serve both Dorothy and Glinda. Most important, perhaps, Baum, unlike MGM, saw no need to rationalize Dorothy's adventures as a dream; pure and simple, she visited Oz, a land of magic. There is a significant sense of geography in the book, the geography of Oz in opposition to gray and plain Kansas. Likewise the characters of Oz are a good deal more lively than Aunt Em or Uncle Henry (the only Kansans in the work besides Dorothy). The Wizard's charming humbuggery is a function of the contrast between the two worlds, and its impact is a refreshing form of satire. He is, after all, "'a very good man, but . . . a very bad wizard.'" There is much here that is of interest to the fantasist besides the magic of the witches and the parade of Dorothy's companions. Tolkien's Shelob may owe something to the great spider that the Cowardly Lion defeats, and the Queen of the Field Mice who saves the troupe from the poppy field is a remarkable example of the communion between human and animal that we all subconsciously desire (see Tolkien's "On Fairy-Stories"). The land of Oz, happily, is not confined to the pages of *The Wizard*. In all, some 40 book-length tales of Oz have been told, 14 by Baum and the rest by Ruth Plumly Thompson, John R. Neill, Jack Snow, and Rachel Cosgrove. None of the others enjoys the popularity of *The Wizard*, but each has something to offer. Each discovers some new corner on the map of Oz or investigates more closely some familiar one.

Beagle, Peter S. *A Fine and Private Place*. New York: Viking, 1960. New York: Ballantine, 1976 (paper).

A graveyard flanked by a New York City expressway is the setting for this novel. Jonathan Rebek has lived for the past 19 years in the Yorkchester Cemetery, attended only by a cantankerous raven who brings him food and news from the outside world. Mr. Rebek can see and communicate with his ghostly neighbors, although most of them forget about him a few weeks after their arrival—one of the characteristics of death is forgetfulness to the point of oblivion. Michael Morgan, however, proves the exception, forcing himself to remember how it was to be alive; in the process Michael makes some startling discoveries about what he was truly like when alive. He also persuades a lady ghost, Laura Durand, to join him in combatting forgetful oblivion. Their relationship is both humorous and touching. Their actions prompt Mr. Rebek to reevaluate his own situation, and when the middle-aged widow, Gertrude Clapper, discovers him, his self-examination reaches a crisis point. *A Fine and Private Place* is an exceptional novel in a number of ways. The main characters are memorable, but so are the support characters, such as the cynical but altruistic raven and the saturnine cemetery attendant, Campos. The delightful humor of the book, as is typical in Beagle's writing, springs largely from the speech and mannerisms of the characters. Yet characters retain their deeper sides, as does the book as a whole. Then, of course, there is Beagle's style, truly a thing of beauty. Beagle always hits the right note, whether recording a dialogue between a raven and a squirrel or describing a scene of tender emotion between Michael and Laura. Another of Beagle's traits is his ability to structure his works to a dramatic climax. Few readers will forget the powerful conclusion to *A Fine and Private Place*. Another fine book by Beagle is *Lila the Werewolf*. It, however, is low fantasy, taking place in Manhattan. Of course, *A Fine and Private Place* also has New York City for its setting, but the difference is that the Yorkchester Cemetery becomes a secondary world with its own nonrational laws, right in the midst of one of the world's largest cities.

Beagle, Peter S. *The Last Unicorn*. New York: Viking, 1968. New York: Ballantine, 1976 (paper).

We observe unicorns from time to time in works of fantasy, but only Peter

Beagle has succeeded in letting us observe ourselves from the perspective of the unicorn. In this splendid novel, the unicorn, becoming aware one day that she is indeed alone—the last of her kind—undertakes a quest to restore her kindred to their proper place as guardians of natural beauty and goodness (not of naive innocence). Only those who are pure (in spirit) or those who are quite wicked recognize the unicorn; most people mistake her for a horse. The pure who join the unicorn are Schmendrick, the bungling magician, and Molly Grue, the slatternly mistress of an inept highwayman. Chief among the wicked are the Red Bull and King Haggard, who have some connection with the missing unicorns. Prince Lir, the king's heir, enters the book somewhat later, but not too late to become the human hero of the work. The story itself, set in a medieval secondary world, is based on the journey–quest motif, and offers a delightful series of adventures, including a magical metamorphosis that is unique even in fantasy literature. The superb story is only one of the achievements of *The Last Unicorn*. It effectively parodies some of the stock-in-trade of medieval romance; it examines the nature of magic and of magicians; it combines humor with serious fantasy as successfully as the works of such masters as George MacDonald and C. S. Lewis; it penetrates both the reader's intellect and deepest imagination through allegory and symbolism. And its author does this in a style that moves, decorously, from courtly eloquence to earthy slapstick. If there were a "ten best" list of modern fantasy, *The Last Unicorn* would certainly be on it.

Bellairs, John. *The Face in the Frost.* New York: Macmillan, 1969. New York: Ace, 1978 (paper).

The jacket of the 1978 Ace Books paperback edition of this book quotes Ursula K. Le Guin's comment about *The Face in the Frost:* "This is authentic fantasy by a writer who knows what wizardry is all about." The book is, in fact, a compendium of magical properties and events, with the emphasis on the Gothic varieties: books of spells, tarot cards, prophetic globes, wraiths, ancient curses, shape shiftings, magical keys, travel through mirrors, and much more. The plot on which all of these details hang is the conflict between the congenial wizards Prospero and Roger Bacon and the power-mad Melichus. Until near the conclusion, however, the plot is more that of a detective story than of wizardly combat, since Prospero and Roger must trace numerous clues to discover who and then where their opponent is and how he is trying to use the most powerful of all the books of wizardry. Melichus, almost distractedly, throws in all varieties of Gothic creatures to scare Prospero and Roger, who are very human and susceptible wizards, somewhat akin to T. H. White's absentminded Merlin. They are, nonetheless, equal to the challenge and successfully thwart Melichus. The book is genuinely frightening at times and quite serious about its magic, but a playfully humorous tone is rarely absent. Occasionally, in fact, one suspects the author of writing a parody of fantasy. Few fantasy motifs seem to have been omitted. There is even a pumpkin turned into a carriage, since Prospero cannot ride a horse. In the end, however, the reader is satisfied and pleased that Bellairs has been making fun with magic, and not at it. The book is not a theme book but an impressive display of magical fireworks. It is aptly illustrated by Marilyn Fitscher.

Blackwood, Algernon. *The Dance of Death and Other Tales.* New York: Dial, 1928.

This fine collection contains "The Dance of Death," "A Psychical Invasion," "The Old Man of Visions," "The South Wind," "The Touch of Pan," and "The Valley of the Beasts." Only one story, "The South Wind," is not a fantasy; the other four consist of both high and low fantasy. "A Psychical Invasion," featuring the occult investigator John Silence (one of Blackwood's most popular characters), is the longest and perhaps most substantive of the selections. "The Dance of Death" goes well beyond the psychic phenomena of "Invasion" in that it actually describes the protagonist's encounter with Death (in the guise of a beautiful young woman he meets at a dance). In most Gothic works, Browne's rendezvous would be treated as a horrific event, but here it is described as a pleasant release from anxiety and depression. (For a similar treatment see Peter S. Beagle's "Come Lady Death.") "The Touch of Pan" and "The Valley of the Beasts" are both myth fantasies. Besides the vividly described scenes of woodland revelry, "Pan" offers a convincing thematic statement on the sterility, hypocrisy, and artificiality of certain segments of society. In "Valley" the reader follows the choleric and insensitive protagonist, Grimwood, into the deep and mysterious Canadian forests, where, in his pursuit of "the biggest moose in the world," he encounters the great Indian god Ishtot. Grimwood barely escapes from the fabled Valley of the Beasts, but when he finally returns to civilization he is a "quiet, easy-tempered, almost gentle sort of fellow." The experience has been harrowing indeed, but cathartic and enlightening as well. This collection serves as an excellent sampler of Blackwood's superb brand of Gothic fantasy.

Blish, James. *Black Easter; or, Faust Aleph-Null.* Garden City, NY: Doubleday, 1968.

In an author's note Blish writes: "Whatever other merits this book may have, it neither romanticizes magic nor treats it as a game." Indeed, it is Blish's concrete, explicit, and serious treatment of black magic that helps make this work so unique and memorable. Although the events of the novel have cosmic implications, the plot line is rather simple. Baines, a fabulously wealthy industrialist, engages the services of Theron Ware, Doctor of Theology and Black Sorcerer, whose specialty is "crimes of violence." Hinting at a major commission yet to come, Baines asks Ware to end the lives of Rogan, the governor of California, and Dr. Albert Stockhausen, a brilliant scientist close to discovering a "scholium" currently possessed only by Baines's company. With the help of his demons, Ware quickly dispatches his first two victims. Baines, admitting that he is a man who takes "pleasure in the controlled production of chaos and destruction," now presents Ware with his major commission: "I would like to let all the major demons out of Hell for one night, turn them loose in the world with no orders and no restrictions—except, of course, that they go back by dawn or some other sensible time—and see what they would do if they were left on their own hooks like that." Ware, at first, is stunned by the audacity of the request, but then feels the challenge of the great "experiment," and agrees to attempt the conjuration on Easter night (Black Easter). The demons are unleashed and chaos reigns. Even Brother Domenico Garelli, an adept practitioner of white magic who has been monitoring Ware's actions, is unable to neutralize the black powers. Armageddon has come, but with a horrific twist— the forces of evil, not good, prevail. God is dead. Few works of fantasy contain such remarkably explicit descriptions of ceremonial black magic. Especially vivid is the final section, "The Last Conjuration," where Blish achieves an extremely high level of immediacy and authenticity. Although set in southern Italy, this work can be classified as high fantasy because of the secondary-world nature of the Grand Circle where Ware practices his hellish arts. Readers will want to peruse *The Day after Judgment,* the sequel to *Black Easter.*

Blish, James. *The Day after Judgment.* Garden City, NY: Doubleday, 1971. There has been some confusion among bibliographers about which books actually make up the After Such Knowledge trilogy, and what their relationship is. Blish nicely clarifies this matter in an author's afterword to *The Day after Judgment:* "This novel [*Judgment*], though it is intended to be able to stand as an independent entity, is a sequel to another with nearly the same cast of characters, called *Black Easter.* . . . These two books, considered as a unit, in turn make up the second volume of a trilogy under the overall title of *After Such Knowledge.* The first volume is a historical novel called *Doctor Mirabilis* . . . ; the last, a science-fiction novel called *A Case of Conscience.* . . . These two volumes are independent of each other and of *Black Easter* and *The Day after Judgment,* except for subject matter. . . ." *Judgment* is a worthy sequel to *Black Easter.* It is a tightly structured, energetic novel featuring the same kind of intriguing philosophical concerns that make its successor so distinctive. The action begins on the "sullen full morning of the day after Armageddon"; the earth is horribly pockmarked with H-bomb craters, fires race across devastated cities and the surrounding countryside, and the anguished cries of the survivors pierce the poisoned air. The stench of death hangs over all. The earth has become not only a figurative hell, but a literal one—for the city of Dis, "the fortress surrounding Nether Hell," actually exists in Death Valley, California. The forces of darkness indeed appear to have won the battle to end all battles. It is in this earthly hell that Father Domenico, Baines, Theron Ware, and Jack Ginsberg continue to play out their particular roles. The four naturally gravitate toward the demonic city of Dis, finally enter through its hellish portals, and there have an audience with "that archetypal dropout, the Lie that knows no End, the primeval Parent-sponsored Rebel, the Eternal Enemy, the Great Nothing itself SATAN MEKRATRIG." His words astonish the four, and will no doubt be equally astonishing to readers of the novel. From beginning to end, Blish supplies us with surprises and plenty of food for thought. *Judgment* is the kind of novel that cries out for, and deserves, more than one reading.

Bond, Nancy. *A String in the Harp.* New York: Atheneum, 1976.
Another of the increasing number of books using the distinctive enchantment of Wales, *A String in the Harp* is every bit as good as the superb Welsh-related works of Susan Cooper (The Dark Is Rising series) or Alan Garner (the Alderley books). In Bond's story, a 12-year-old boy, Peter, finds the harp key of Taliessen, the sixth-century Welsh bard. Peter's father is a professor on leave from his university in the United States to teach and study in Wales, and the family has settled in a place near Aberstwyth on the northwest coast, the area in which Taliessen lived much of his life. The harp key is magical. It hums or sings to Peter, enabling him to see with an inner eye events from Taliessen's life. The power of the key increases as the story progresses, at times actually superimposing events from the sixth century on those of the present, with other people as well as Peter seeing these events. But in one sense the key has found Peter rather than the other way around, and it has a mission for him that he must discover. Paralleling this plot are the events related to Peter's family, the Morgans. Peter's mother has died only the year before and the whole family, including Peter's older and younger sisters, Jen and Becky, and his father, David, is having a difficult period of adjustment. At first the wet, cold climate and barren landscape of Wales further depress everyone except the resilient nine-year-old Becky. Only when the family begins to perceive the different beauties and to appreciate the traditions of the country do they begin to resolve their personal problems. And the magical harp key becomes the catalyst for awakening them to these enchantments of Wales, thus interrelating the two plot lines. The interweaving of the family and the Taliessen plots is not the only excellent achievement of the book. Bond, who has lived in Wales, gives the reader an accurate depiction of, and a genuine appreciation for, the country, without glossing over its less attractive features. She handles the colorful Welsh dialect particularly well. She draws upon Welsh history and legend and most importantly upon the Welsh mythology of the *Mabinogion* in relating scenes from the life of Taliessen.

Brooks, Terry. *The Sword of Shannara.* New York: Random, 1977. New York: Del Rey, 1978 (paper).

In characterization and theme this book is throughout a close imitation of Tolkien's *The Lord of the Rings.* Here is the core of the plot: Shea Ohmsford is informed by the druid Allanon that Shea is heir to the House of Shannara, in fact, the only known heir. Shea is, therefore, the only one who can wield the legendary Sword of Shannara against Brona, the Warlock Lord. Accompanied by a Fellowship that includes warrior princes, two elves (one named Durin), a mighty dwarf, Shea's home-loving adopted brother, and the wizard Allanon, Shea sets out to try to find the sword and defeat the Warlock Lord and his Skull Bearers (wraiths), trolls, and gnomes. If this plot sounds familiar, that's because you have read Tolkien's *LOTR* or seen the movie. Brooks's major themes are also, as one might expect, the same as Tolkien's: knowledge must be accompanied by responsibility; isolationism is pointless. Most of the critics have accused Brooks of being too imitative in their strongly negative reviews. On the other hand, the book is basically well written, despite being too long (prepare to do some skimming if you opt to read this one). Before accepting the accusation that the book is too imitative, however, one should ask the question: Does Brooks offer any worthwhile additions to Tolkien's construct? He does, but whether these additions justify the work as a whole is hard to determine. One of the features unique to *Sword* is the time setting—some hundreds of years after the "Great Wars," clearly nuclear holocausts. One of the consequences of the atomic devastation is the appearance of races other than man: dwarves, trolls, gnomes. Elves, on the other hand, always existed but never had much commerce with humanity. This is an interesting plausibility device. The entertaining con artist, Panamon Creel, a type familiar in high fantasy, is another Brooks addition. Perhaps the most important difference between Tolkien and Brooks is the latter's use of an unexpected ending springing from the nature of the sword. *The Sword of Shannara* is a problem book, but it is a book and a problem that some will certainly want to consider.

Brunner, John. *The Traveler in Black.* New York: Ace, 1971 (paper).

The breezy style here, with its occasional nod to the grotesque, is absurd in light of the seriousness of the issues raised—and the contrast produces a delightful book. Indeed, this work smacks of the ironic distance of Cabell at his best, matter-of-factly asserting that consistency has its own inconsistency, order its own chaos. It records a continuing battle between order and chaos, where the traveler (who "had many names, but one nature") strives finally to establish order. Armed with his single nature—he is unchanging and unchangeable—and his staff of light, he battles such hobgoblins as Laprivan of the Yellow Eyes, Lacrovas-Pellidin-Agshad-Agshad, and Lady Luck. Yet he must also contend with pigheaded peasants and numbskull scriveners, for all forms of enchantment, luck, and irrationality are chaotic. The fantasy of the work is little more than a cosmetic for Brunner's musings about order and chaos, yet it is applied with such bravado that one cannot help but enjoy the final product. We get touches of Twain's *Connecticut Yankee in King Arthur's Court* when a twentieth-century Londoner becomes a god for a day—in another time and place—dispelling the superstitions of some villagers. We also find touches of Goldman's *Princess Bride* in the traveler's obsessive (and irrational) dogging of the irrational. However, this work is serious in a way that the other two are incapable of: while making fun of fantasy (a chaotic genre in this case), it demonstrates that chaos can be useful. Chaos has, like order, its own proper sphere, and unlike order that is too strict it can be a great deal of fun.

Buchan, John. *The Watcher by the Threshold and Other Tales.* Edinburgh and London: Blackwood, 1902. St. Clair Shores, MI: Scholarly Press, 1971.

Of the five longish short stories that make up this Buchan collection, three are fantasies: "The Far Islands," "The Watcher by the Threshold," and "The Outgoing of the Tide." The latter two are similar in that they both treat supernatural visitation, while "The Far Islands" revives the Celtic legend of the Isle of the Apple-Trees. All of these tales are typical of Buchan's fantasies: brilliant style, fascination with arcane myths and legends. and interest in human psychology. "The Far Islands" is, perhaps, most typical, tracing the genealogy of the Irish god Bran through many generations to a modern descendant, Colin. Colin is at once the hero and the tragic victim of the tale since his legacy gives him many talents as well as a brooding desire to visit beyond the "Rim of the Mist." Beyond the rim lies the Isle of the Apple-Trees and Colin's reaching the isle is both psychologically interesting and fantastic. Here, as in the other two tales, psychology and fantasy are closely intertwined, and it is this mixture that is Buchan's trademark. In fact, each of these fantasies could be seen as a tale of psychology if Buchan were not careful to corroborate apparent illusion with factual detail. An example might serve: When Ladlaw of "The Watcher" is possessed by the spirit of the Roman Justinian, the cause of his fear and near madness is confirmed by the double shadow that he casts and the tongues that he speaks. The narrator of the tale witnesses these phenomena, creating a strong sense of an otherworld.

Buchan, John. *The Moon Endureth: Tales and Fancies.* Edinburgh and London: Blackwood, 1912.

This collection contains nine stories and several poems that feature a variety of historical and mythical settings and a notable preoccupation with the Scottish Highlands. Three of the stories qualify as fantasy, although nearly all of them have elements that are fantastic. The first, and perhaps the best of the three, is the intriguing "The Grove of Ashtaroth." It is a tale of Africa that discovers the reality of myth in the obsession of an English sportsman,

Lawson, who builds himself a domain in an enchanted grove and there re-kindles the worship of the ancient nemesis of the Hebrews, Ashtaroth. The presence of Ashtaroth is in some way dependent on the grove, and Lawson's spiritual frenzies here all but consume the man. What makes the story such a superior piece is the delicate balance that is established between illusion and reality. Lawson's apparent madness and the subsequent confirmation of his sanity force us to question our own assessment of what is real. The other two fantasies, "The Green Glen" and "The Rime of True Thomas," are more earthy. They are set in Scotland and benefit from strong touches of local color. The glen is the focal point for the enactment of an ancient Scottish love legend; the rime is the vehicle for a vision of the Scottish Elysium. The latter tale includes a charming conversation between the major character and a Respectable Whaup (curlew), a talkative, wise, and somewhat condescending bird. All of the tales have very strong settings that allow, by contrast, for a clear portrait of a world within a world. Notable, too, as in all of Buchan's work, is his evocative style.

Cabell, James Branch. The Biography of Manuel. *The Works of James Branch Cabell.* Storisende Edition. 18 vols. New York: McBride, 1927–1930.

Cabell is a realist who writes romance. He delights in clever erudition and fantastic plots and settings, but his major characters remain distinctly human in their aspirations and frustrations. These characters are as appropriate to the magic isle of Sargyll as they are to historical Provence or twentieth-century America—and this enormous work shows us corners of all these worlds. The protagonists proceed in their own fashions—swaggering, stumbling, or simply surviving—regardless of how or where they are transported. Their only common denominators are their poignant humanity and their ties to Dom Manuel, count of Poictesme. For this is the tale of Dom Manuel and his descendants; it ranges over seven centuries and through a variety of worlds. Manuel is a thirteenth-century count (a former swineherd) whose exploits gain him status as a Redeemer. His descendants (less famous, and no more noteworthy) gradually fade into the mainstream of Western history. The fantasy of the series manifests itself in at least two ways. In a broad sense, the assumption of the entire series is fantastic: Cabell rewrites Western history, geography, and mythology, sketching and populating heaven, hell, earth, and a variety of sorcerous realms. Yet, in a more narrow sense, most of the individual volumes only assume this backdrop and proceed to record in "realistic" fashion the lives of one or another of Manuel's lineage. Six of the individual volumes, however, are genuine fantasies (see annotations following); they are the only ones in which the otherworld and magic are primary concerns. Even in these, though, Cabell's technique is primarily ironic. His romance characters and fabulous creatures speak and act very much like human beings, even when their contexts are wholly otherworldly. Only one character seems to transcend the entire series: Horvendile the poet. His appearance signals the fantastic, and he inevitably directs the other characters to their quests. Most of these characters lead empty lives that find happiness only in the pursuit of the dubious ideals of chivalry, gallantry, and poetry. Yet, however dubious when viewed realistically, these ideals can be fulfilling, and this is the final advice of the series: If life is viewed from the vantage point of romance and through the glass of magic, it can be fulfilling and indeed wonderful.

Figures of Earth. Storisende Edition, Vol. II. New York: Del Rey, 1979 (paper).

This is the story of Manuel's rise from swineherd to royalty, of his successful attempt to "make a figure in the world." His early tries at fulfilling this task find him fashioning mud figures next to a swine wallow. Yet his vigorous following "after [his] own thinking and [his] own desires" (his pigheadedness) gain him a victory over the famed magician, Miramon Lluagor. So begin his adventures, varied as they are. He succeeds in animating one of his mud figures through the power of the black stone, Schamir, held by the sorceress, Freydis, queen of Audela. Later, he raises his plain and somewhat shrewish wife from death. In his old age (he ages very quickly while serving the head of Misery—a nearly allegorical character), Manuel must give up his adventures, but finds a surrogate in the magical window of Ageus—an enchanted portal to an undefined realm. Finally, like all heroes, he must submit to Grandfather Death. His death, like all his accomplishments, is viewed in a peculiar way by his court, and he is acclaimed a Redeemer.

The Silver Stallion. Storisende Edition, Vol. III. New York: Del Rey, 1979 (paper).

The silver stallion was Dom Manuel's heraldic device and this is the tale of his closest followers. In fact, eight interlocking accounts are presented here, one about Manuel's wife and the others about seven of his lieutenants. As a composite, the volume deals with the rise and fall of Manuel's reputation as a Redeemer. Indeed, by the end of the work, only Donander still believes in Manuel—and Donander himself has become a god who should know better. The adventures here are uproarious, yet touching—especially those of Coth, Manuel's most belligerent retainer. Coth sets out to prove that Manuel still lives and learns from Manuel's own mouth (in the Place of the Dead) that "man alone of animals plays the ape to his dreams." In most cases, the adventures of Manuel's retainers manifest this aphorism.

Jurgen. Storisende Edition, Vol. VI. New York: Dover, 1978 (paper).

This is Cabell's best-known work—perhaps because it was suppressed by the courts for nearly two years, or perhaps because it is his best work. It is, no doubt, bawdy, but it is hardly pornographic. It is the tale of Coth's son (see *The Silver Stallion*), who was the only eyewitness to Manuel's death. Jurgen has matured and become a well-to-do pawnbroker who, for a kindness rendered and a slip of the tongue, must rescue his wife from a mystical realm. He is aided along the way by Nessus the Centaur and meets (and has sexual relations with) a variety of legendary and mythological women. The book is full of remarkable portals and worlds within worlds. Jurgen chases the sun and enters the garden between dawn and sunrise; he visits heaven and meets his father in hell. Finally, he faces Koshchei—he "who made things the way they are." Jurgen does rescue his wife and returns to his mundane existence, fearing to return home without the butter he had promised Dame Lisa. He who "had faced sorcerers and gods and devils intrepidly" is thoroughly intimidated by the wife he has rescued.

Something about Eve. Storisende Edition, Vol. X.
Gerald Musgrave is the hero of this tale—an early nineteenth-century poet of very moderate success and a distant descendant of Dom Manuel. He is visited by a Sylan, Glaum of the Haunting Eyes, and is offered a spiritual existence in exchange for the loan of his body. Musgrave agrees, since he thinks the trade will gain him access to the "great and best words of the Master Philologist." The success of Musgrave's venture depends largely on his perseverance, and he must pass through the lands of Lytreia, Turoine, Mispec Moor, and others. These lands, populated by fox-spirits and sphinxes, wear down the poet's inner strength, and he retires to his former existence without the great and best words. The tale is like Cabell's others in its exorbitant plot and wry irony. More noticeable, though, is an allegorical level of meaning: names are obviously anagrammatic and Musgrave's journey is blatantly that of Everyman. Yet there is much of this sort of writing in all of Cabell's works, and its self-consciousness here is, if anything, more humorous than bothersome.

The Cream of the Jest. Storisende Edition, Vol. XVI. New York: College & Univ. Press, 1973.
The levels of narration in this work are involved. Cabell writes a story in which a character, Richard Fentnor Harrowby, records the story of his friend Felix Kennaston. Kennaston's tale is of his dream-state pursuit of his ideal woman, Ettarre (see *The Witch Woman*). In his dream, Kennaston is Horvendile, the elusive figure who pirouettes in and out of the entire Biography of Manuel. A talisman of power, the sigil of Scoteia, is the means whereby Kennaston enters his dream state. There he courts Ettarre, but the slightest physical contact sends Kennaston/Horvendile back into the mundane world of the twentieth century. Kennaston's dream visions place him in a variety of fantastic contexts, some mythic, some historical, but Ettarre is in them all. The ironic twist of the story is that Kennaston's talisman is only one half of the cover of a jar of cold cream (pun, no doubt, intended). Yet on the outermost layer of narration the sigil is much more. Its apparent scribble can be decoded, and its text summarizes Cabell's per-

spective on Kennaston's life—and on the lives of Manuel and all his descendants. For the pursuit of Ettarre by Horvendile is, in a number of ways, the beginning, middle, and end of the Biography of Manuel. As Kennaston astutely observes, "the comedy of the life of Manuel . . . does not ever vary."

Cabell, James Branch. *The Witch Woman: A Trilogy about Her.* New York: Farrar, 1948.
These three tales properly belong to the Biography of Manuel because they are all about Ettarre, Manuel's third daughter. The first of the tales, and perhaps the best, "The Music from behind the Moon," appears in Volume IV of the Storisende edition of the biography, but the others are later additions. All appear here in forms that differ slightly from their originals. "The Music" is the tale of Madoc's rescue of Ettarre from behind the moon. His weapon of conquest is a quill from the wing of the Father of All Lies, and he cheats the Norns (fates) by an ingeniously simple mathematical device. He is a poet, pursuing the "skirling" music of Ettarre's beauty, and he can be seen as that same Horvendile who haunts the entire biography. In the other tales, Ettarre is pursued by the chivalrous Alfgar ("The Way of Ecben") and by the werewolf, Odo ("The White Robe"). This third story is not particularly effective, but the other two are among the very best of Cabell's shorter pieces.

Carroll, Lewis [pseud. of Charles Lutwidge Dodgson]. *Alice's Adventures in Wonderland.* London: Macmillan, 1866. Reprinted as *Alice in Wonderland.* New York: Crown, 1974 (paper).
If most fantasy relies on plot and description to create a sense of an otherworld, *Alice* uses plot and linguistic distortion. We find, of course, many fantastic occurrences—the fall down the rabbit hole, the conversation with the Caterpillar, the disappearance of the Cheshire Cat—things impossible in this world that draw us into Wonderland. However, we also find twists of logic and language that challenge Wonderland in some ways. Puns, parodies, and fallacies jar the flow of our vision by attracting our attention and countering our expectations. As a result, the very stuff of the story—language—becomes unreliable; Carroll satirizes his own vehicle. Yet satire is not the only effect of linguistic play; like any other type of play, it posits its own rules, and it delights. Alice, while in Wonderland, expects "nothing but out of the way things" because inconsistency has its own consistency; *in*consistency becomes *inner* consistency. Likewise, the persistent language distortion produces delight—in the same way any riddle, puzzle, or anecdote does. Turns of wit not only establish their own laws, but by freeing us from *our* own, they provide us with a fresh perspective, the essence of delight. The many contributions of *Alice* to the history of fantasy, too, should be noticed. It is surely the best-known example of a work that uses dream as a portal. The frame of the dream allows for an associative plot; perhaps only Lindsay

(Voyage to Arcturus) uses the technique better. Also, if Carroll wasn't the first to send a child into an otherworld, he certainly was the great popularizer of the notion, paving the way for many works of children's literature that qualify as fantasy. In Wonderland, animals talk (however much like adult humans), Alice becomes a giant, and a deck of cards is animate. These and many other aspects of the work make it a model for later attempts. Unfortunately, the entire work is cast as a dream. After following Alice down the rabbit hole and through Wonderland, the reader is told that Alice has been dreaming, that the adventure was not true. The parallel dream of Alice's sister mitigates the disappointment somewhat, but it is still acute. Wonderland's credibility is challenged.

Carroll, Lewis. *Through the Looking-Glass and What Alice Found There.* London: Macmillan, 1872. New York: St. Martin's, 1977 (paper).
This work is even more filled with puzzles, anagrams, and puns than *Alice in Wonderland.* Its action, as is well known, dramatizes the moves of a game of chess: Alice, as a white pawn, moves until she is "queened"; she then captures the Red Queen, while checkmating the Red King. The device does not hamper the action of the work, although it makes for an episodic plot; it is little more than a clothesline for Alice's adventures in her various squares. Along the way from Q2 to Q8, she visits the Garden of Live Flowers, Tweedledum and Tweedledee (or is it Tweedledee and Tweedledum?), Humpty Dumpty, the White Knight, and others. As in Wonderland, there is a distinct sense of dream here, for this, too, is a dream vision—of sorts. Where the dream of Wonderland is unquestionably Alice's, here we are not sure whether the dream is hers or the Red King's; we are not sure whether the dreamer is the main character or a removed narrator. The same technique is used by Dunsany in some of his tales. The double possibility is typical of the entire work. Since the portal within the dream is a mirror (the rabbit hole in Wonderland), Carroll carefully sets doubles before us, challenging us to find differences or to resolve puzzles. Yet, as in *Alice in Wonderland,* the dream device damages the work while serving the plot. For as the logic of the work is dreamlike, so the wonder may well be just the product of a little girl's mind.

Chant, Joy. *Red Moon and Black Mountain: The End of the House of Kendreth.* London: Allen & Unwin, 1970. New York: Dutton, 1976. New York: Del Rey, 1978 (paper).
Joy Chant's first novel is a successful blend of myth and faery tale for adults. Three English children are enchanted into the world of Vandarei while cycling on a country road in Essex. Oliver, in his mid-teens, finds himself with a nomadic tribe of horsemen called the Hurnei, or the Khentors (centaurs), where his name takes the form of O'li'vanh or Crowned Victor. He is greeted as one sent by the gods, a point that is reinforced when a divine horse, actually a unicorn called Dur'chai, arrives miraculously to be his com-

panion. Nicholas and Penelope, Oliver's younger brother and sister, appear in a different part of this world, among a noble people called the Harani who dwell in Kendrinh, the Starlit Land, and are ruled by the Star Enchanters. These two peoples form an alliance against the Black Enchanter Fendarl, a Star Enchanter who has been corrupted by a knowledge beyond his power to control. Actually, Fendarl is the victim of a higher power, one which, like Satan in the Christian myth, had earlier rebelled against his master and had been cast out by his peers. Each of the three children has a specific task to perform, but the chief burden falls upon Oliver, who must meet Fendarl in mortal combat. After this ordeal he finds he must make a further sacrifice, one even greater than risking his life, for his warring has released Vir'Vachel, the Mother, an earth-goddess figure whose powers cannot be controlled by man or, apparently, the other higher powers. The scenes in which this primal deity appears and works her fearful magic are charged with an archetypal forcefulness. The plot is effectively handled throughout. The book nicely balances the Oliver and the Nicholas–Penelope plots, maintaining an equal interest in both. Chant skillfully makes appropriate and effective use of the high style, both in describing the action and in the dialogue. She devises personal and place names with the care and logic of a philologist. There are perhaps too many characters and too many different names for the same character, a common difficulty in myth-based fantasy, but the Star Enchantress In'serinna, and the English boy Oliver (O'li'vanh) emerge through their internal conflicts as memorable figures. The mythic hierarchy of powers, though not the center of focus as in Tolkien, is certainly reminiscent of *The Silmarillion,* a comparison that is all the more interesting because *Red Moon and Black Mountain* appeared six years before Tolkien's compendium of the mythology of Middle Earth.

Chant, Joy. *The Grey Mane of Morning.* London: Allen & Unwin, 1977.
In 1970, Joy Chant made her literary debut with *Red Moon and Black Mountain,* a finely crafted novel that seems destined to become a fantasy classic. Readers had to wait seven long years for the publication of her next book, *The Grey Mane of Morning,* but it was well worth the wait. Like *Mountain,* its secondary world setting is the land of Vandarei, but unlike its predecessor it has no primary world framework. *Mountain*'s narrative begins and ends in the quiet English countryside; in *Morning,* there is no movement between primary and secondary worlds—Vandarei is the only world involved. While the physical settings of both novels are similar, the chronological settings are not. *Morning* recounts events in the very early history of Vandarei, events predating those of *Mountain.* Thus, just as Tolkien's *Silmarillion* serves as a "prequel" to *The Lord of the Rings, Morning* serves as a prequel to *Mountain,* providing background information that gives the reader greater insight into the situations and events described there. In essence, *Morning* is the story of the nomadic Khentors' rebellion against the Kalnat, the town-dwelling "Golden Ones." After refusing to pay their

usual tribute to the Kalnat, the Khentors do battle with them, scoring a decisive victory. Their triumph marks the beginning of a new age for the Horse People, the people of the plains. The leader of the Khentors, and central figure of the novel, is the courageous young warrior Mor'anh. We witness his development as a man, priest, warrior, and tribal leader; his love affairs with Runi and Manui; his close friendship with his sister Nai, and his spear-brother, Hran; and his epic journey to the land of The Cities. Mor'anh, like the other main characters of the novel, is remarkably well delineated. In most regards, *Morning* is as fine a novel as *Mountain:* both works are intricately plotted and suspenseful; both are set in a richly detailed and imaginatively conceived secondary world; and both feature characters who are interesting and believable. *Morning,* however, does not manage to evoke the sense of awe and wonder that is so strongly felt in Chant's first work. This is primarily due to the fact that *Mountain* has more magic. Although nicely handled, the supernatural element in *Morning*—Mor'anh's communication with Kem'nanh, god of the Khentors—does not have the powerful effect of the magic of *Mountain*. Unfortunately, *Morning* does not have any episodes comparable to the Battle of the Eagles or the final confrontation between Li'vanh (Oliver Powell) and the evil sorcerer Fendarl. One hopes Chant's next novel will contain more of the glamour and enchantment that made her first work so memorable.

Chapman, Vera. *The King's Damosel.* London: Collings, 1976. New York: Avon, 1978 (paper).

The story is principally about the Lady Lynett, the same damosel who figures so prominently in the "Gareth" section of Malory's *Morte d'Arthur.* But in Chapman's book, Lynett becomes a vibrant and sympathetic young woman, much more human and individuated than Malory's shadowy figure. We first meet her on her wedding day. She is to marry the crude Gaheris, while her sister Leonie weds the noble Gareth, a situation that seems completely unfair to Lynett. Through a series of flashbacks we become acquainted with the events leading up to the present, some tragic, some humorous. The flashbacks end with the actual wedding night, which is no normal first night of marriage. Hereafter the story proceeds chronologically. King Arthur, guided by Merlin, appoints Lynett his damosel or royal messenger to his vassal knights. So begins Lynett's twofold quest, to be Arthur's messenger and the sign of his desire for loyalty rather than grudging submission, and to seek revenge for a personal wrong—and later to seek expiation for her great sin. One cannot begin to illustrate in any detail the sort of adventures that Lynett, accompanied by several of the most famous of Arthur's knights, experiences. They range from martial encounters to mystical journeys of the mind, the next one always more surprising and fascinating than the one before it. Chapman's book is a bold adaptation of the "Gareth" and "Grail" sections from Malory and of the Grail literature from the earlier French sources. She handles these materials, particularly the Grail literature, authoritatively and imaginatively, successfully creating a work with archetypal depth and significance. She furthermore interweaves the Arthurian materials with the mythology of the Celtic Mother Goddess. And the author brings to bear all of this wealth of literary and religious tradition on the personal life of the Lady Lynett. This focus not only personalizes the sources, but gives the book a substantial unity that the medieval sources often lack. Those who enjoy this work will be delighted to know that it is the first of a loosely connected trilogy, and they will want to proceed to *The Green Knight* and *King Arthur's Daughter*.

Chapman, Vera. *The Green Knight.* London: Collings, 1975. New York: Avon, 1978 (paper).
Fifteen-year-old Vivian's convent education comes to a halt when her Aunt Morgan (Le Fay) takes her to the Castle of Haut-Desert, the castle of the Green Knight, to introduce her to the art of witchcraft. Eighteen-year-old "little" Gawain, the son of Gareth and the Lady of Lyonesse, also the nephew of "great" Gawain of Orkney and King Arthur's Court, goes to Arthur's court to be initiated into the order of knighthood. It is this Gawain who accepts the challenge of the Green Knight, and it is Vivian who reluctantly, under pressure from Lady Morgan Le Fay, tests Gawain's chastity. It is a brilliant retelling of the medieval poem "Sir Gawain and the Green Knight," using Malory's *Morte d'Arthur* and Celtic mythology for supplementary background. As is the case with the best of its type, this retelling adds perceptive insights into the older tales and legends without changing any of the essentials. The handling of the mythic and magical elements is subtle and deeply moving. The story itself successfully blends childish pranks, sinister magic, and profound myth as it describes the maturing of the two young protagonists in the face of evil and deception. The plot is suspenseful and reaches a powerfully dramatic climax. But the most memorable aspect of the book is the shifting, first-person narrative point of view. The first four sections are told alternately by Vivian and Gareth; the fifth is told by young Melior, a disciple of Merlin, who guides his aging master to answer a mysterious summons to Stonehenge. Chapman handles these difficult points of view with great skill; as a result, we form deep personal ties with the narrators, especially the two protagonists. And we also see them as they see each other, and as Melior—and Merlin—see them. It is altogether a delightful exercise in perspective. Finally, those who have read Chapman's *King's Damosel* will welcome the brief glimpse they get in *The Green Knight* of the Lady Lynett.

Chapman, Vera. *King Arthur's Daughter.* London: Collings, 1976. New York: Avon, 1978 (paper).
Ursulet ("Little Bear") is the daughter of Arthur and Guinevere and the rightful heir to the throne of Arthur's kingdom. She is the third of the young

heroines in Vera Chapman's fine trilogy The Three Damosels. Like the first two books, *King Arthur's Daughter* extrapolates from several Arthurian sources, in this case from Geoffrey of Monmouth and, as in all three, from Sir Thomas Malory. In this book, Arthur, just a few years before the dissolution of his kingdom, proclaims Ursulet his heir. But in the chaos following the defeat of Arthur and the breaking up of the Round Table, Ursulet hides first in a convent and later as a servant to the increasingly strong Germanic invaders. From this point on, the Lady Lynett, heroine of *The King's Damosel,* assumes a central position as she attempts to have Ursulet proclaimed queen of the Britons. The principal antagonists are Mordred (who survived Arthur's last battle) and the temptress Morgan Le Fay. Chapman's use of the time leap is an effective technique for covering the 20 years prior to the main action. We briefly see Ursulet as a small child in Arthur's waning years, as a 14-year-old girl in the convent after the breakup of the kingdom, and as a serving girl among the invaders before she becomes queen. In developing her characters, Chapman once again invests them with a personality far beyond anything found in the sources. This is particularly true of the Lady Lynett, clearly Chapman's favorite, and the central figure of the trilogy. But it is in theme that *King Arthur's Daughter* makes its greatest impact and its boldest but legitimate extension of the Arthurian sources. In the book's conclusion, the Kingdom of Arthur becomes a metaphor for the Kingdom of the Lord, a spiritual rather than a temporal realm. Thus Arthur's promise that he will come again takes on messianic significance. Chapman doesn't quite succeed in effecting the transformation from temporal to spiritual boundaries, but the attempt is fascinating and is reminiscent of the portrayal of Logres by C. S. Lewis *(That Hideous Strength)* and Charles Williams *(Taliessen through Logres).* Finally, one of the pleasures in reading *King Arthur's Daughter* is that it hearkens back in a number of ways to the first two works. Thus it is best to read it last, while the first two works can be read in any order or completely separately from the trilogy.

Cherryh, C. J. *Gate of Ivrel.* New York: DAW, 1976 (paper).
Cherryh is a very promising new writer of fantasy and science fiction whose fine talents have already won for her the prestigious John W. Campbell Award for the best new writer of the year. Although *Ivrel* does not consistently display the polish and craftsmanship of works like Ursula K. Le Guin's *Wizard of Earthsea* and Patricia McKillip's *Forgotten Beasts of Eld,* it is an energetic, intricately plotted, and highly detailed novel that deserves a careful reading. It is a science fantasy novel, but in it there is more of the latter than of the former. As a matter of fact, if the prologue, with its scientific explanation of the "Gates between Worlds," were removed, pure high fantasy would be the end result. In essence, *Ivrel* is a quest novel. The primary focus is Nhi Vanye's quest to find honor after being banished from his homeland for the killing of his half-brother, Nhi Kandrys. Also sharing

center stage, however, is the mysterious witchwoman, Morgaine, whose quest is to seal the gates, those ancient passageways that lead "into elsewhen as well as elsewhere. . . ." Their quests merge when Morgaine, as a "lord," claims Vanye as her servant ("ilin") for the period of a year ("He must fight her enemies, tend her hearth—whatever things she required of him until a year had passed from the day of his oath"). After an arduous and dangerous journey, Vanye and his "liyo," his lady-lord, reach the fabled Gate of Ivrel, and there confront their foes Thiye and Liell; the former is killed, but Liell, through magic, escapes in the body of Chya Roh, a cousin to Vanye. Although Cherryh does many things well in *Ivrel,* her most impressive accomplishment is breathing life into Morgaine and Vanye. In episode after episode we see not only a concrete delineation of their characters, but an equally detailed and believable development of their relationship. Thus when Vanye takes the awful plunge through the Gate of Ivrel in pursuit of his "liyo" with the resultant tearful reunion of the two, the reader is able to empathize in a heartfelt way only possible when a fine literary craftsman has created truly flesh-and-blood characters. *Well of Shiuan* continues the exploits of this intriguing pair of adventurers.

Cherryh, C. J. *Well of Shiuan.* New York: DAW, 1978 (paper).
A highly imaginative and skillfully plotted novel that continues the adventures of Vanye, the outcast, and his lady-lord, Morgaine. *Shiuan* is set in a dying world, a world slowly but surely being destroyed by flood and earthquake. Its inhabitants have only one slim hope for survival—to somehow pass through one of the "Wells" (Stonehenge-like gateways) that lead to other times and other worlds. Whether or not these portals can be used as escape routes, however, depends upon who controls them. Two otherworld figures contend for possession: Morgaine, who, as in *Gate of Ivrel,* is attempting to seal the gates, and her nemesis, Liell, who, in the form of Chya Roh, is attempting to gain power through the possession of the portals. A terrific series of struggles between the two take place, but the main Well of Abarais remains open long enough for thousands of inhabitants of the drowning planet to pass through. Even Morgaine and Vanye make their escape through the portal into a new "land of grass and plenty." Cherryh's attempt at creating a high style (in large part through the periodic use of archaic language by Morgaine) is not entirely successful, but in general she handles her dialogue deftly and convincingly and manages through her vivid and carefully detailed descriptions to create believable characters and settings. As in *Ivrel,* her finest accomplishment is the thoughtful and sensitive treatment of the complex relationship between Vanye and Morgaine. Less effective is the delineation of Jhirun, a young woman whose story serves as the framework plot of the novel. All in all, a very readable and interesting work of science fantasy.

Colum, Padraic. *The Boy Apprenticed to an Enchanter.* New York: Macmillan, 1920.

First published in 1920, Colum's short novel is without question one of the most delightful all-ages fantasies of the century. The crisp and energetic narrative focuses on the relationship between a young apprentice named Eean and his master, Zabulun the Enchanter. Apprenticed to the awesome sorcerer against his will, Eean spends three years in his charge before he is able to make his escape. While in the exotic city of Babylon, where Zabulun hopes "to steal the Magic Mirror of the Babylonians," Eean is saved from a grisly death by a young girl named Bird-of-Gold. The two flee from Babylon with Zabulun in pursuit. The remainder of the narrative recounts their desperate attempts to stay one step ahead of the evil Enchanter. The final confrontation between Eean and Zabulun takes place on the Island of the White Tower, the home of Merlin the Enchanter. For a while, the struggle is largely between Merlin (he has agreed to help Eean) and Zabulun, who put on an awesome display of magical powers. The shape-shifting scenes here are powerful and unique. Zabulun is finally defeated, not by Merlin, however, but by the apprentice himself, who physically overpowers his master and works from him a promise of freedom. To add even more joy and satisfaction to the conclusion of this magical fantasy, Colum brings to full flower the relationship between Eean and Bird-of-Gold by having the two married by an "old blind sage . . . by the rays of the rising sun." Although Colum does most things well in *Enchanter,* perhaps the most noteworthy aspect of the work is its elevated style. The description of Merlin's infatuation with the beautiful Vivien in the concluding section of the book is especially well done. In short, Colum gives us enduring proof that the best entertainment devised by man remains the tale well told.

Cooper, Susan. *Over Sea, under Stone.* New York: Harcourt, 1966.

In this, the first volume of Susan Cooper's fantasy sequence The Dark Is Rising, we meet some of the major characters of the series, and the groundwork is laid for a fascinating chronicle. The story opens with the arrival of the Drew family at Trewissick, a small fishing village in South Cornwall, where they are to spend their summer vacation in the company of their Great-Uncle Merriman. The children, Simon, Jane, and Barney, playing indoors on a rainy afternoon, find an ancient manuscript in the hidden attic of the Grey House where they are staying. At first they are intrigued by a maplike drawing on the paper and determine to spend their time searching for the treasure to which they are sure it leads. But slowly at first and then more rapidly events take place that convince them that there is more at stake than a mere treasure and that they themselves face very real danger in their quest. At the center of everything stands Great-Uncle Merry, and the children realize that though he is on their side, even he is not always what he seems. Baffled by the obscure clues and pursued closely by the mysterious

Mr. Withers, his supposed "sister" Polly, and the terrifying Mr. Hastings, the Drews finally unravel the meaning of the phrase "over sea, under stone" and find the golden chalice and its contents. At their moment of triumph, however, the enemy appears, and only the timely arrival of Great-Uncle Merry thwarts the forces of darkness for the time being. While one part of the treasure, a small lead case containing a second manuscript, is lost to the watery depths of the sea, the grail is saved and placed in a museum. Only Merriman and the three children are aware of the origins of the golden cup and the important role it plays in the battle between the Light (good) and the Dark (evil). Cooper handles this age-old theme in an inventive and entertaining fashion. The characterizations, especially of the youngest child, Barney, are meticulous and believable, down to the petty squabbles of the children. The adult figures are less detailed and somewhat one-dimensional, with the exception of Great-Uncle Merry, whose role is less clearly defined but at the same time pivotal to the story. Without him, it becomes a tale of the adventures of three British children on holiday. South Cornwall and the little fishing village are beautifully depicted and it is not difficult to picture the story's setting. Readers should not be too upset by the sometimes juvenile tone. And while the author only hints at a deeper, more powerful theme in this volume, readers should be encouraged to go on to the other four books of the series, which develop and expand that undertone.

Cooper, Susan. *The Dark Is Rising.* New York: Atheneum, 1973. New York: Aladdin, 1976 (paper).

The second book of Susan Cooper's fantasy series by the same name, The Dark Is Rising, is the story of Will Stanton. On the eve of his eleventh birthday and only a few days before Christmas, young Will becomes aware of many disturbing changes that are taking place in his life. Not the least of these changes is Will's realization that he is no ordinary small boy, but the last of the Old Ones, a race of people born to battle the forces of the Dark. More than that, Will is a special Old One, for he is the Sign-Seeker and it is his destiny to find and join the six signs. Only then can the Dark be turned back. Aided by Merriman Lyon, the first of the Old Ones, Will is able to complete his quest, but not before the Dark has used every available weapon against him. He has several terrifying encounters with the Rider, one of the agents of the Dark and as powerful as an Old One in his way. Will is also hindered in his search for the signs by the Walker, an old and decrepit man whose background mysteriously covers a span of centuries. Will's own family, unaware of this mortal conflict taking place, is threatened by the Dark time and again. However, on the twelfth night of Christmas, sur-rounded by a raging flood brought on by the powers of the Dark, Will faces the worst challenge of all and is forced by the Rider to choose between the life of his sister and the relinquishing of the signs to the Dark. But, strengthened by his friend Merriman and others of the Old Ones, Will makes the right decision and, with the help of the Hunter and his Hell Hounds, the Light forces the Dark to the ends of the earth. In a ritual that is witnessed by Old Ones from every corner of the world, the signs of bronze, wood, iron, stone, water, and fire are joined and returned to Will. He then learns that they are only the second of the four Things of Power that the Light will need to have any hope of overcoming the Dark on its day of final rising. Powerfully written, this 1974 Newbery Honor Book is an exciting and timeless work of fantasy. As she does in her first book, Cooper makes her characters come alive in a way not often managed. Perhaps the most touching and beautifully done characterization is that of Hawkins, sometimes known as the Walker. We first encounter him as Merriman Lyon's young liege man; the bond between them is as strong as between father and son. But he is swayed by promises of power from those of the Dark and eventually betrays his master, and, in doing so, betrays the Light. This action condemns him to centuries of fearful living and running as the Walker, never knowing peace or contentment. Cast aside by the Dark after his usefulness is ended, he is finally released from his own private hell. Cooper makes much more use of symbolism in this book than in *Over Sea, under Stone,* bringing in old traditions such as the power in holly berries to ward off evil and the immunity of running water to magic. She interweaves these phenomena with her own symbols of the six signs, the Book of Gramarye, and the haunting, bell-like music Will hears. The resulting creation is a beautiful blend of symbols that balance perfectly. Overall, the combination of reality and fantasy compares favorably with such works as C. S. Lewis's Chronicles of Narnia and Alan Garner's Alderley books.

Cooper, Susan. *Greenwitch.* New York: Atheneum, 1974. New York: Aladdin, 1977 (paper).

In this book we witness the coming together of the major characters from the two previous volumes of the fantasy sequence The Dark Is Rising, as they collaborate on the quest to regain a golden chalice that has been stolen by an agent of the Dark. Simon, Jane, and Barney Drew, the three children who found the grail the first time, share this adventure with Will Stanton, an 11-year-old schoolboy who is also one of the Old Ones (masters of the Light), and who possesses powers beyond imagining. The action takes place once again in the peaceful fishing village of Trewissick in South Cornwall at the time of the annual spring rite of the making of the Greenwitch. The Greenwitch, a huge image of branches and leaves, is fashioned by the women of the village and flung into the sea for good luck in fishing and harvesting. Jane, who is invited to watch the ancient ceremony, senses a deep sadness in the Greenwitch, and when given an opportunity to wish for something, wishes that the Greenwitch be happy. This seemingly insignificant gesture plays a major role in the recovery of the grail and the subsequent revelation of its secret message. Simon and Barney have a chilling encounter with the man from the Dark who is posing as a wild-eyed painter. Due to his untimely calling up of the Greenwitch, her wild magic is loosed and runs rampant throughout the village. When her magic is finally banished by the Old Ones, it takes with it the careless painter; and the forces of the Light, armed with the knowledge found in the grail's inscription, prepare themselves for the last rising of the Dark. Written on a slightly more superficial level than the second book of the series, this story is still capable of spellbinding any reader. It almost seems that when writing about the Drew children, Cooper finds it necessary to avoid the deeper levels the sequence otherwise plumbs and to maintain a strict, though colorful, recounting of what actually happens. There is not as much symbolism either, except for the obvious, such as the Greenwitch. Jane is developed more fully here, and of the three Drews she is the most thoughtful and sensitive. Perhaps it is even desirable that the emotional pace established in the second book be slowed down, giving the series a chance to build it up again in the final two books, *The Grey King* and *Silver on the Tree*.

Cooper, Susan. *The Grey King*. New York: Atheneum, 1975. New York: Aladdin, 1978 (paper).

Set in Wales, a country rich in folklore and ancient traditions, the fourth volume of Cooper's fantasy series continues and heightens the otherworldly atmosphere of the other stories. Will Stanton, a young British schoolboy, is again one of the central characters, but he is joined in his adventures by another young boy named Bran Davies. Bran is a strange and lonely child, his white dog Cafall his only companion. Will has been sick for a long time at the outset of the story and it is not until he meets Bran that he regains his memory of being one of the Old Ones and of the conflict between the Light and the Dark. There are certain tasks that Will must perform to aid the Light in the struggle and he needs the help of Bran and Cafall. They are hindered in their quest by the Grey King, one of the High Lords of the Dark who uses an embittered man as his agent. After several terrifying experiences, including a ravaging fire and the inexplicable slaying of several sheep, the boys are finally successful in their attempts to attain the golden harp and to awaken the six Sleepers who will be needed in the final battle. In a spellbinding climax, Bran is revealed to be the Pendragon, Arthur's son brought forward in time to be present when the Light would most need him. Indeed, the influence of the Arthurian legend is most strongly felt in this book and adds an interesting dimension. A finely developed aspect of this story is the portrayal of Will and Bran's relationship, which proceeds on dual levels. They become friends as any two young boys with similar interests, but their relationship as an Old One and the Pendragon simultaneously develops. Perhaps the most touching episode involves the unjust slaying of Cafall and Bran's immediate reaction, which is to reject both the Light and the Dark and to wish to be left alone. This incident also emphasizes the theme that without cruel and bitter people the Dark would never have a chance to rise. The one feeling that everyone will share after reading this winner of the John Newbery Medal will be one of impatience to read the final book of the series, *Silver on the Tree.*

Cooper, Susan. *Silver on the Tree.* New York: Atheneum, 1977.
The final volume of Cooper's outstanding fantasy series The Dark Is Rising more than lives up to the expectations that have been building since the first volume. The setting once again is Wales, though parts of the story take place in other times and places outside of this world. Will Stanton and Bran Davies are joined by the three Drews, Simon, Jane, and Barney, at the time of Midsummer. Together they discover the secret of the singing mountains, and then Will and Bran must go on their own quest in the Lost Land, a timeless yet doomed country that holds the final Thing of Power needed to stay the Dark in its rising. We also go back in time with Will and Merriman to witness the first pushing back of the Dark by Arthur and his knights. But that resistance was not to last, and it is necessary for Bran, as Arthur's son, to vanquish the Dark forever. After many setbacks, he and Will manage to locate the crystal sword, and the stage is now ready for the final confrontation at the Midsummer Tree. There, the Drews, Will, Merriman, and Bran find that their success depends upon the actions of a mortal man who wants nothing more than to be left alone. His decision to help the Light, which is based on his love for Bran, makes the ultimate victory of the Light a reality. Then Bran himself is faced with the choice of joining his famous father and claiming his birthright or staying on earth and relinquishing all claims to immortality. He chooses to remain, because he feels that by doing so he can continue to keep the Dark from ever coming to power again. This book is by far the most complex of the series, and although it can certainly be enjoyed for the story line alone, an understanding and appreciation of the deeper theme make it even more compelling. The image of the Dark as the embodiment of all the mindless prejudice, cruelty, and petty hatreds found in humanity everywhere is not new, but it is most strongly stressed in this final volume. Also, there are more elements of high fantasy found here, particularly in the section that deals with the Lost Land. Once again, Cooper's best work is done in her characterizations. From book to book she has slowly added dimensions and colored the five children and Merriman to make them the very real people they are at the end. *Silver on the Tree* is the most mature of the books in the series and is a fitting finale to a marvelous sequence.

Davidson, Avram. *The Phoenix and the Mirror.* Garden City, NY: Doubleday, 1969. New York: Ace, 1978 (paper).
Fantasy writers since William Morris have successfully used medieval legends as inspiration. In this work Davidson rediscovers another old

tradition and puts it to good use: the tradition of Vergil Magus. Since the twelfth century, necromancy has been associated with *The Aeneid,* and it is as a magician, not as an author, that we find Aeneus here. He and his apprentices are commissioned to produce a virgin speculum, a magical mirror with the power of far-sight. The materials necessary to the mirror are rare in the Roman world and Vergil must travel far afield to acquire them. In his travels, he encounters a dazzling array of legendary beasts: the manticore and the cockadrill, the gargoyle and the magnificent phoenix. But Vergil himself is something of a wonder. Although his magic is white, he conjures with a mandrake and his house is guarded by a Brazen Head. He has fire at his fingertips and prescient dreams. Yet, with all the wonders of this world, there is a strong sense of history—that combination of history and legend found in the fantasies of Mary Stewart and T. H. White. Although Davidson is not the stylist that Stewart and White are, he does balance comedy and seriousness nearly as well as White, and his treatment of magic is far less tentative than Stewart's. His world is peopled with real sailors and soldiers as well as real alchemists and magi. It is a world that tantalizes and satisfies, capitalizing on familiarity with medieval accounts and reflecting a firm knowledge of the first century B.C.

de la Mare, Walter. *Broomsticks and Other Tales.* London: Constable, 1925.
This fine collection contains 12 of de la Mare's best short stories: "Pigtails, Ltd.," "The Dutch Cheese," "Miss Jemima," "The Thief," "Broomsticks," "Lucy," "A Nose," "The Three Sleeping Boys of Warwickshire," "The Lovely Myfanwy," "Alice's Godmother," "Maria-Fly," and "Visitors." All of the selections except two—"A Nose" and "Visitors"—are fantasy, and of the remaining 10 the majority are low rather than high fantasy because they are set in the primary rather than a secondary world. Two high fantasies that deserve special mention are "The Dutch Cheese" and "The Lovely Myfanwy." Both are charming and sprightly faery tales that nicely display de la Mare's delightful wit and his smooth and polished prose style. "Cheese" describes, in a whimsical and lighthearted fashion, the skirmishes that take place between a rather sullen and stubborn young farmer and a tribe of faery folk that is "striving to charm [his] dear sister Griselda away." In his attempts to thwart the mischievous faeries he does "nothing but fret himself," and in the end he learns, the hard way, that these sprightly creatures can be formidable foes indeed. "Myfanwy" is a longer and more substantive tale that tells of a Welsh nobleman's stubborn efforts to keep all suitors away from his beautiful daughter Myfanwy: "Lovely indeed was she. Her hair red as red gold hung in plaits to her knees. When she laughed it was like bells in a far-away steeple. When she sang, Echo forgot to reply. And her spirit would sit gently looking out of her blue eyes like cushats out of their nest in an ivy bush." True love finally prevails, however. Myfanwy marries a hand-

some and clever young prince, and her father sees how truly selfish and unjust he has been—but only after he has been turned into an ass by eating a magic apple that possesses the "sole virtue . . . of making any human who tasted it more like himself than ever." In sum, this is a collection of remarkably even quality that deserves a place in any fantasy collection. The handsome woodcut designs are by Bold. See also de la Mare's *Penny a Day* (Alfred A. Knopf: New York, 1960), a delightful collection of faery tales that includes three of the stories featured in *Broomsticks* ("The Three Sleeping Boys of Warwickshire," The Lovely Myfanwy," and "The Dutch Cheese") plus three others: "A Penny a Day," "Dick and the Beanstalk," and "The Lord Fish." This latter collection is illustrated by Paul Kennedy.

Dickson, Gordon R. *The Dragon and the George.* New York: Ballantine, 1976 (paper). Garden City, NY: Nelson Doubleday (Science Fiction Book Club), 1976.

A thoroughly delightful tale of chivalry, brave deeds, and fierce dragons, *The Dragon and the George* will be enjoyed and appreciated by all who read it. The dragon is Jim Eckert, a history professor at Riveroak College. He and his fiancée, Angie Farrell, have been astrally projected into another time and place, and Jim into another body, that of a young dragon named Gorbash. ("George" is simply a dragon's term for any human.) Their adventures in this mystical land lead them from dragon caves to a magician's hut, through marshes and forests, and finally to the Loathly Tower. Jim (or Gorbash) makes many friends along the way, most notably Sir Brian Neville-Smythe, a fine example of knighthood in flower, and Aragh, a fierce and courageous wolf. They are joined in their travels by a Robin Hood-like outlaw named Giles o' the Wold, his men, and his daughter, Danielle. Different though all these personages are, they form a congenial group and fight together for each other's causes. The final battle takes place at the Loathly Tower where all the evil and dark forces are concentrated, and it takes the combined courage and strength of all our heroes to overcome the enemy. This tale is extremely readable and the author has successfully combined humor with an exciting and suspenseful narrative. Readers who are familiar with C. S. Lewis's *Voyage of the "Dawn Treader"* from the Chronicles of Narnia will note the similarities between Edmund's dilemma as a dragon and the problems that Jim encounters. But overall Dickson's characters are most reminiscent of those found in T. H. White's *Once and Future King.* They are endowed with a sense of reality and a certain spirit of lightheartedness. This combination serves to make them very endearing and memorable. The author also maintains a skillful weaving of twentieth-century symbols such as Social Security numbers with the trappings of a culture of knighthood and magic. Most, if not all, readers will applaud Jim and Angie's decision to remain in this primitive but exciting land with their new friends.

Donaldson, Stephen R. *Lord Foul's Bane.* New York: Holt, 1977. New
York: Del Rey, 1978 (paper).

Donaldson's first work, a fantasy trilogy called the Chronicles of Thomas
Covenant the Unbeliever, brings the excitement of the discovery of a major
new talent. The character of Thomas Covenant is a stunning, multidimen-
sional creation, to which Donaldson has brought considerable skill as a
writer and a personal knowledge of Covenant's disease. Covenant, a successful author, loses two fingers of his right hand to leprosy before he discovers
and arrests the disease. Frightened by his experience at the leprosarium,
where he witnesses the deterioration of lepers who relax their guard, he
determines not to become one of them. Shunned by the townspeople and
deserted by his wife and child, Covenant tries to give his white gold wedding
ring to a beggar, who refuses it. Shortly after, a police car strikes him and
he awakes in the Land. Summoned by Drool Rockworm, an evil Cavewight,
Covenant faces Lord Foul, who tells him to take a message of doom to the
Lords in Revelstone. Lena, daughter of Atiaran and Trell, discovers him
and soothes his wounds with hurtloam, the Land's healing mud. Covenant
finds his leprosy healed, and in the rush of feeling caused by the regeneration
of his nerves, rapes Lena. Lena hides the outrage from her parents, as
Atiaran has agreed to guide Covenant to Revelstone. Atiaran tells Covenant
of the "wild magic" of his ring's white gold, unknown in the Land.
Frustrated by the fabled power of white gold, over which he has no mastery
and about which even the Lords know little, Covenant feels impotent and
confused, calling himself the Unbeliever. He refuses to believe in either the
Land or his returning feelings. The Lords recognize Covenant's worth and,
hearing his tale of Foul's plans for the Land's destruction, convince him
against his will to help them in their quest for the Staff of Law, which Drool
had used to bring Covenant to the Land. All the inhabitants of the Land—
the Ranyhyn, great unfettered horses served by the Ramen, their human
friends; the Bloodguard, ageless men who guard the Lords with their lives;
the Lords; and Lord Foul himself—recognize and respect Covenant for the
white gold he possesses. To the end Covenant remains the antihero, helping
in spite of himself to recover the Staff of Law. Donaldson has created an
enthralling adult fantasy. This is not a Tolkien-like fantasy with a great
hero eager to do service for a troubled land. Donaldson's antihero is a
stubborn, unbelieving man whose first act in the Land is rape, and whose
overall goal is self-preservation. The complexities of Covenant's motivations, the carefully delineated Land, along with Donaldson's steady-paced,
crisp writing, combine to form a compelling tale much greater than the sum
of its parts.

Donaldson, Stephen R. *The Illearth War.* New York: Holt, 1977. New York:
Del Rey, 1978 (paper).

This is Volume II of the Chronicles of Thomas Covenant the Unbeliever.
After regaining the Staff of Law, Thomas Covenant mysteriously returns

to his own land, where leprosy still figures as the central part of his life. Badgered by his neighbors, Covenant tries to sort out his experience in the Land. His useless wedding ring and maimed hand, which had made him a hero there, are ordinary again. Covenant fights the temptation to view the Land and its approaching destruction by Lord Foul as real. Answering a telephone call from his wife, he cuts his head on a table. Reality blurs, and he is again in the Land. Forty years have passed there. His former friends have aged; Foul has gained strength; and Elena, Covenant's daughter by Lena, has become the new High Lord. Another outlander, Hile Troy, has been accidentally summoned from earth to aid the Land. Born without eyes, Troy can see in the Land, healed in the same way Covenant had been. Troy's expertise in war strategy gives the Lords sorely needed hope, for Covenant is the Unbeliever still. Foul's most deadly servants, the Ravers, have taken over the bodies of three giants, formerly the most trusted friends of the Land. Again Covenant's white gold is needed, but he still has no mastery over it. Troy's careful plans, destroyed when Foul's army marches early, have to be given over to a desperate attempt to stop Foul in a dangerous forest. Caerroil Wildwood, a powerful Forestal, guards the last of the ancient trees in Garroting Deep, which have never forgiven men for killing their fellows and clearing the Land. Wildwood saves Troy's army by hanging a Giant-Raver and demanding that Troy be turned into a tree and become an apprentice Forestal. Covenant goes with Elena—guided by Amok, a servant of the Land's almost legendary Old Lord Kevin—to the mysterious Melenkurion Skyweir, a mountain near Garroting Deep. Elena drinks of the water Amok warns her against and gains the Power of Command. She forgets her history and summons Kevin, who desecrated the Land in his last battle with Foul, to demand that he now destroy Foul. Foul's power defeats Kevin again, killing Elena and causing the Staff of Law to be lost. Blaming himself for Elena's death, Covenant fades from the Land, finding himself in his own world. All is as it was before: he suffers from a head injury, his leprosy again ravages his body, his wife has long since hung up the telephone. He faces the knowledge that Foul could destroy the Land easily with its army nearly beaten, its High Lord dead, and the Staff of Law gone. Donaldson manages not only to sustain but to enhance the promise he brought to *Lord Foul's Bane,* the first volume of the trilogy. He has lost none of his power or imagination; indeed, he adds greater depth and complexity both to his main character and to the two worlds that claim him. Covenant's story should have an honored place among the great works of fantasy literature.

Donaldson, Stephen R. *The Power That Preserves.* New York: Holt, 1977.
   New York: Del Rey, 1979 (paper).
This is the third and final volume of the Chronicles of Thomas Covenant the Unbeliever. Regaining consciousness in his own world, Thomas Covenant, leper and best-selling author, must sort out the ill feelings left by his

refusal to help the Land and its beleaguered inhabitants. Determined to help someone, he risks bodily injury and the crippling infection it can bring to a leper to aid a small child lost in the woods near his country home. As he runs toward her, hoping to save her from the bite of a rattler, he stumbles and strikes his head against a rock. Once again he feels the now-familiar pull of the Land. The girl's danger fills his mind, however, and he fights the summons. But the pull is too strong and he awakes in the Land, seven years after High Lord Elena's attempt to battle Lord Foul with the spirit of Kevin Landwaster. He pleads with High Lord Mhoram to send him back to save the child, but Mhoram reasons that the Land's need is greater. Three of the Bloodguard, ageless men sworn to protect the Lords with their lives, are trying to bring a piece of the Illearth Stone to Revelstone. They become enthralled by the stone's power and bring it instead to Foul's Creche, the seat of his power. Foul sends the three to attack Revelstone, after maiming their hands to resemble Covenant's. Still the girl fills Covenant's mind, and Mhoram sends him back to his world. He saves the child, but the snake bites him. Wearily, knowing he is dying, he gently asks Mhoram to bring him back to the Land. Revelstone is under siege by Foul's army, led by the second Giant-Raver, Satansfist, but Covenant isn't in Revelstone. He has been summoned by Triok, the lover of Lena, and Saltheart Foamfollower, Covenant's giant friend. The need in Mithil Stonedown, Lena's town, is also great. Covenant again undergoes trials that would have killed him in his own world, facing anew the miracle of his nerve regeneration. When his magical white gold wedding ring is lost, Foul recovers it and places it in the hand of High Lord Elena, reborn to do Foul's bidding. Covenant fights Foul through her, regaining the ring and freeing Elena from her undead service. With the ring and the Staff of Law, Covenant finally does battle with the one he had so long avoided, Lord Foul. After the battle, Covenent returns to his world. Hospitalized, half-dead from the snake bite, he hears the voice of the Land's creator, the beggar who had refused his gift of the wedding ring in Volume I. The beggar/creator offers him life in the Land, which he can make real for Covenant, or life in this world, by stilling Covenant's allergic reaction to the antivenin. Guided as always by his survival instincts, Covenant chooses. This last book in Donaldson's trilogy is no less powerful than the first two. Donaldson's skill as a writer, along with the knowledge of leprosy he gained through his father (an orthopedic surgeon who worked extensively with lepers), combine with Donaldson's thoroughly imaginative creativity to produce a polished and convincing work of adult fantasy. One may or may not like Covenant, but his compelling story should be read.

Dunsany, Lord [Edward John Moreton Drax Plunkett]. *The Gods of Pegana.* London: Matthews, 1905.
Lord Dunsany's place in fantasy literature is easily located: he is among those at the top. If MacDonald and Tolkien have had a profound effect on the field, Dunsany has had a pervasive effect. His talent for exotic names and places

and his visions of bizarre worlds have been emulated by writers of all types of fantastic literature—high, low, Gothic, mythic, weird. Yet few of Dunsany's emulators have duplicated his heights of imagination, and none has achieved his dexterous style. For style is Dunsany's strength; his can roll with all the sonorous majesty of the Bible or it can trot off wry wit. At his best, Dunsany can evoke an otherworld without ever leaving this one. His London is no less capable of mystery than the river Yann, simply because it is described in language that conjures rather than states. His diction is rich, his snytax flexible, and his cadences are superbly timed. All a reader must do is submit. *The Gods of Pegana* is one of Dunsany's most significant contributions to fantasy. This is a collection of short sketches that are mythopoeic in the fullest sense. In an ornate fashion it records the creation of the gods by Māna-Yood-Sushāī and the drumming of Skarl that measures time. The work is, in a sense, a bible, since it poses a genesis and an apocalypse. It has a strong Eastern flavor; its pure originality is its most startling quality.

Dunsany, Lord. *Time and the Gods.* London: Heinemann, 1906. New York: Arno, 1972.

In many ways this is a continuation of *The Gods of Pegana.* The ornate Eastern style and the mythopoeic content are the same, yet the tales are concerned with man and his reaction to the gods instead of the actions of the gods themselves. The cosmology of Pegana is expanded slightly, and the powers of fate and chance play a great role. As a result, the work has a semi-allegorical tinge.

Dunsany, Lord. *The Sword of Welleran and Other Stories.* London: Allen, 1908.

The two heroic tales, the title story and "The Fortress Unvanquishable Save the Sacnoth," are the best of this collection. Both benefit from an exotic atmosphere and the deft use of a narrator. The other tales range from visions of afterlife to semi-allegorical dialogues. In each case, however, there is a sense of wonder provoked by Dunsany's intentionally archaic style.

Dunsany, Lord. *A Dreamer's Tales.* London: Allen, 1910. Philadelphia: Owlswick, 1979.

The majority of the stories here are dream visions, but the dreamworld they pose is as real as the waking world. The teller of the tales is the dreamer, and he leads us through exotic places with even more exotic names, such as Astahahn, "where Time is manacled and fettered . . . who would otherwise slay the gods." The atmosphere is rich, even luxurious; the tone is languid, perhaps sonorous. The work anticipates the dream tales of H. P. Lovecraft and C. A. Smith. This work and "The Sword of Welleran" are both included in a collection called *A Dreamer's Tales and Other Stories* (Norwood, PA: Norwood Editions, 1978).

Dunsany, Lord. *The Book of Wonder.* London: Heinemann, 1912. New
York: Arno, 1976.
Wry wit and irony are prevalent here. The tales turn on unexpected actions
and reactions, gently satirizing human fears and dreams. Famous thieves
pursue exotic prizes and heroes assault fortresses. The stuff of romance is
here, but in one way or another the romance is turned inside out. The work
is similar in many ways to the works of Richard Garnett and James Branch
Cabell.

Dunsany, Lord. *Fifty-One Tales.* London: Matthews, 1915. Reprinted as
The Food of Death: Fifty-One Tales. N. Hollywood, CA: Newcastle,
1974.
A collection of very short and very serious sketches, allusive and semi-
allegorical. We find here Charon's last trip over the river Styx and a
vision of the tomb of Pan. Some of the vignettes are without an otherworld,
yet most are fully fantastic. There is little development in any of the sketches;
each seems to exist for a single delicate effect.

Dunsany, Lord. *Tales of Wonder.* London: Matthews, 1916.
Perhaps Dunsany's least successful volume of short fantasy, this is primarily
a collection of low fantasy, alcohol tales, and semi-allegorical visions of
London. Yet there are occasional examples of high fantasy, notably "The
Long Porter's Tale" and "How Plash-Goo Came to the Land of None's
Desire." Many of the stories are posed in a tale-within-a-tale frame, where
the narrator listens to—and challenges—the extravagant or fantastic tales of
others. It is these challenges that damage the stories, qualifying and apologizing for the fantasy.

Dunsany, Lord. *Tales of Three Hemispheres.* Boston: Luce, 1919. Philadelphia: Owlswick, 1976.
This collection is divided into two sections—the title section and "Beyond
the Fields We Know." The former is composed of short tales of the power
of various gods in various lands. The second section includes a reprint of
"Idle Days on the Yann" (from *A Dreamer's Tales*) and two continuations
of this story. The three tales combine as one of Dunsany's best sustained
narratives—the efforts of a dreamer to visit and revisit a desirable vision.

Dunsany, Lord. *The King of Elfland's Daughter.* New York and London:
Putnam, 1924. New York: Ballantine, 1969 (paper).
In this fantasy classic, the men of the Parliament of Erl, bored with their
quiet life, approach their king and voice a rather extraordinary request:
"We would be ruled by a magic lord." The king responds by sending his son
Alveric to Fairyland to seek the hand of Princess Lirazel, the king of Elf-
land's daughter. Armed with a sword of "thunderbolt iron" magically forged

by the witch Ziroonderel, Alveric passes over the magic boundary into Elfland and, after many perilous adventures, returns with the princess. They are wed, have a son, Orion, and seem destined to lead a happy life in the land of Erl. Then the king of Elfland, through the power of a magic rune, causes his daughter to drift (literally) back into his domain. The remainder of the novel describes Orion's growth into manhood and sadly recounts Alveric's frustrating 12-year attempt to recross the border into Fairyland and regain his beloved wife. Finally, the three are reunited when the king of Elfland, with the aid of another rune, causes the boundary separating the two worlds to advance and subsume the kingdom of Erl. This is a remarkably polished novel full of splendid descriptions. Dunsany is a true master of the high style that characterizes the best of fantasy works. Consider, for example, this description of Alveric's first glimpse of Lirazel: "She walked dazzling to the lawns without seeing Alveric. Her feet brushed through the dew and the heavy air and gently pressed for an instant the emerald grass, which bent and rose, as our harebells when blue butterflies light and leave them, roaming care-free along the hills of chalk." Although essentially a delicately romantic and sentimental piece, there are sprinklings of zesty humor. Many of the lighter moments are created by the words and antics of Lurulu, one of the most capricious and highly acrobatic trolls of all faërie.

Dunsany, Lord. *The Charwoman's Shadow.* New York and London: Putnam, 1926. New York: Del Rey, 1977 (paper).

When a youth apprentices himself to a magician to learn the black arts, he places his soul in grave danger. Yet Ramon Alanzo Matthew-Mark-Luke-John of the Tower and Rocky Forest avoids the danger of eternal damnation through his inherent altruism, his courage, and a good dose of dumb luck. He wields these weapons against his teacher, the Magician, a stern taskmaster whose respect for knowledge is thoroughly warped by his disdain of ignorance. It is, of course, knowledge that Ramon seeks: initially, the alchemical means to fill his sister Mirandolla's dowry box; later, the knowledge to mix a love potion for the same Mirandolla; and finally, the wherewithal to regain his shadow and that of the Magician's kindly Charwoman. For Ramon, like the Charwoman, had to give his shadow in payment to the Magician, who uses them for his conjurings, sending them out into the "chill of Space." As must be apparent by now, this tale represents a remarkable blend of bumbling and high magic, of country bumpkins and master sorcerers. It produces some gentle satire and some tough-minded philosophizing as well. For Dunsany refuses to tell a story simply; he sketches a portrait of the Golden Age of Spain, when daughters were sold into marriage, and where priests chased imps screaming from their woodland hideouts. The sketch is solidly critical of ignorance and social injustice, yet it extols belief and praises nobility, and qualifies as great fantasy on the strength of its inherent morality. Still, Dunsany's genius is not limited to this. He has been justifiably called the greatest stylist of fantasy and there are passages in this volume to prove it. His plot is never dry and frequently its turns are quite effective. The journey of the shadows into the "chill of Space" and, later, Ramon's dance with his shadow are two truly remarkable scenes. In many ways this volume alone justifies Dunsany's important place in the history of fantasy.

Dunsany, Lord. *The Sword of Welleran and Other Tales of Enchantment.* New York: Devin-Adair, 1954.

Appearing in a brief publisher's note to this treasure trove of Dunsany stories is the following explanation: "The sixteen stories in this book were selected by Lord Dunsany, with the assistance of Lady Dunsany, from various of his books which have long been out of print. They are the stories by which the author most wished to be remembered, and they reflect his gift of fancy most entertainingly." An examination of the collection offers no reason to doubt the legitimacy of these claims. Contained in this handsome volume are "The Sword of Welleran," "The Kith of the Elf-Folk," "The Distressing Tale of Thangobrind the Jeweller," "The Three Sailors' Gambit," "A Story of Land and Sea," "The Wonderful Window," "Idle Days on the Yann," "The Widow Flynn's Apple Tree," "The Exiles' Club," "East and West," "The Assignation," "The Hen," "The Bride of the Man-Horse," "Bethmoora," "Poltarnees, Beholder of Ocean," and "The Return." Worthy of special mention are "The Sword of Welleran" and "The Kith of the Elf-Folk," two of his most popular and substantive fantasy tales. "Sword" is an excellent example of Dunsany's distinct brand of heroic fantasy. He handles his subject with such authority that the reader is immediately drawn into the imaginary kingdom in which the action takes place. Especially noteworthy is his use of evocative names such as Cyresian, Soorenard, Mommolek, Rollory, Akanax, Iraine, Rold, Sajar-Ho, and Seejar. "Elf-Folk," a moving tale of a wild thing's search for a soul, nicely exhibits Dunsany's love and understanding of nature, the Biblical cadence of his poetic prose, and his remarkable ability to delineate, in a sensitive, delicate, and believable fashion, the creatures of faërie. Attractive line drawings by Robert Barrell.

Dunsany, Lord. *At the Edge of the World.* Ed. Lin Carter. New York: Ballantine, 1970 (paper).

This is the first of three Dunsany collections Lin Carter compiled for the Ballantine Adult Fantasy series; the subsequent volumes, *Beyond the Fields We Know* and *Over the Hills and Far Away,* are also included in the core listing. Collectively, these competently edited works provide readers with many of Dunsany's finest short stories, and a few of his most popular poems and dramas. Unfortunately, these inexpensive paperbacks have been out of print for the past few years. *At the Edge of the World* contains (1) eight stories from *Time and the Gods* (1906)—"The Cave of Kai," "Of the Gods of Averon," "Mlideen," "The King That Was Not," "The Men of Yarnith," "In the Land of Time," "Time and the Gods," and "The Opulence of Yann"; (2) one tale from *The Sword of Welleran and Other Stories* (1908) —"The Fortress Unvanquishable Save the Sacnoth"; (3) seven selections from *A Dreamer's Tales* (1910)—"Poltarnees, Beholder of Ocean," "The Idle City," "Bethmoora," "Idle Days on the Yann," "The Hashish Man," "Carcassonne," and "In Zaccarath"; (4) seven stories from *The Book of Wonder* (1912)—"The Dream of King Karna-Vootra," "How the Enemy Came to Thlūnrāna," "The Distressing Tale of Thangobrind the Jeweller, and of the Doom That Befell Him," "A Shop in Go-by Street," "The Avenger of Perdóndaris," "How the Dwarfs Rose Up in War," and "The Probable Adventure of the Three Literary Men"; (5) two stories from *Fifty-One Tales* (1915)—"The Loot of Bombasharna" and "The Injudicious Prayers of Pombo the Idolater"; (6) two tales from *Tales of Wonder* (1916)—"The Bride of the Man-Horse" and "The Quest of the Queen's Tears"; (7) and, finally, three stories from *Tales of Three Hemispheres* (1919)—"How One Came, as Was Foretold, to the City of Never," "A Day at the Edge of the World," and "Erlathdronion." Also included in the volume are a brief introduction and an even briefer afterword. All main sections are preceded by headnotes containing helpful background information. These 30 stories provide a good representative sampling of Dunsany's inimitable brand of short fantasy. The only major Dunsany short story collection not drawn from is *The Gods of Pegana* (1905); editor Carter does, however, include the complete text of *Pegana* in *Beyond the Fields We Know*.

Dunsany, Lord. *Beyond the Fields We Know.* Ed. Lin Carter. New York: Ballantine, 1972 (paper).

This is Carter's second Dunsany collection, bearing the imprint of the Ballantine Adult Fantasy series. It contains (1) the complete text of *The Gods of Pegana* (1905), Lord Dunsany's first book; (2) 10 stories from *Time and the Gods* (1906)—"How Slid Made War against the Gods," "The Vengeance of Men," "When the Gods Slept," "For the Honour of the Gods," "The Wisdom of Ord," "Night and Morning," "The Secret of the Gods," "The Relenting of Sarnidac," "The Jest of the Gods," and "The Dreams of a Prophet"; (3) *King Argimenes and the Unknown Warrior,* a short two-act play written in 1911; (4) 10 poems from his first collection *Fifty Poems* (1929)—"In the Sahara," "Songs from an Evil Wood," "The Riders," "The Watchers," "The Enchanted People," "The Happy Isles," "A Word in Season," and "The Quest"; (5) a final section called "Other Tales" that includes "The Kith of the Elf-Folk" and "The Sword of Welleran" from *The Sword of Welleran and Other Stories* (1908); "The Madness of Andelsprutz" and "The Sword and the Idol" from *A Dreamer's Tales* (1910); and four stories from *The Book of Wonder* (1912)—"Miss Cubbidge and the Dragon of Romance," "Chu-bu and Sheemish," "How Nuth Would Have Practised His Art upon the Gnoles," and "A Story of Land and Sea." Carter chooses his selections with care, and begins each section with a brief commentary containing helpful background information. Also included in the volume is an afterword by Carter that briefly explores "Dunsany's impact on the writers who arose after him through their use of invented names. . . ." Some contemporary fantasists whom Carter lists as having been influenced by Dunsany are H. P. Lovecraft, Clark Ashton Smith, Robert E. Howard, Fritz Leiber, L. Sprague de Camp, Jack Vance, Michael Moorcock, and John Jakes. All in all, this second collection, like the first *(At the Edge of the World)*, serves as a good sampler of Dunsany's fantasy literature.

Dunsany, Lord. *Over the Hills and Far Away.* Ed. Lin Carter. New York: Ballantine, 1974 (paper).

The third and final Dunsany collection Lin Carter edited for the Ballantine Adult Fantasy series is divided into four main sections: (1) "Tales of the World's Edge" contains "The Journey of the King," a novella taken from *Time and the Gods* (1906); three short stories—"The Fall of Babbulkund," "The Bird of the Difficult Eye," and "The Secret of the Sea"; and a short one-act play called *The Compromise of the King of the Golden Isles.* (2) "Tales of Far Away" contains 12 very short tales—"The House of the Sphinx," "Blagdaross," "The Lonely Idol," "An Archive of the Older Mysteries," "The Loot of Loma," "The Last Dream of Bwona Khubla," "How Plash-Goo Came to the Land of None's Desire," "The Prayer of Boob Aheera," "East and West," "How the Gods Avenged Meoul Ki Ning," "The Man with the Golden Ear-Rings," and "Poor Old Bill"; and another short one-act play entitled *The Queen's Enemies.* (3) "Tales of Near at Hand" contains 14 short stories exhibiting "familiar settings of the Waking World"—"The Bad Old Woman in Black," "The Field," "Where the Tides Ebb and Flow," "The Little City," "The Highwayman," "In the Twilight," "The Ghosts," "The Doom of La Traviata," "A Narrow Escape," "The Lord of Cities," "The Unhappy Body," "The Gifts of the Gods," "On the Dry Land," and "The Unpasturable Fields." (4) "Tales Jorkens Told" contains four tales told by Mr. Joseph Jorkens at his favorite haunt, the Billiards Club—"The Curse of the Witch," "Hunting the Unicorn," "The Pale-Green Image," and "The Sacred City of Krakovlitz." The volume concludes with an apt, and very poignant, short poem by Dunsany entitled "At Sunset." Like the preceding two collections, each section begins with a brief but interesting and useful headnote, and the entire body of selections is preceded by an introduction that provides readers with a brief biographical sketch of Dunsany. As Carter points out in his introductory comments, this volume "spans more than forty years of Dunsany's life" (1906–1948); for this and similar reasons it, like its two predecessors, is a good sampler of Dunsanian fantasy. One hopes these three volumes will soon be reprinted so that readers can have ready access to them.

Dunsany, Lord. *Gods, Men and Ghosts: The Best Supernatural Fiction of Lord Dunsany.* Ed. E. F. Bleiler. New York: Dover, 1972 (paper).

This excellent sampler of some of Dunsany's finest short fiction includes a great many of his most memorable fantasies. Bleiler, who has done a commendable job of selecting the 34 writings (most of them quite short), divides the book into four distinct sections. The first section, "Men," contains 10 stories that recount various bizarre and eldritch happenings: "The Three Sailors' Gambit," "The Three Infernal Jokes," "The Exiles' Club," "Thirteen at Table," "The Wonderful Window," "The Bureau d'Exchange de Maux," "The Ghosts," "The Probable Adventure of the Three Literary Men," "The Coronation of Mr. Thomas Shap," and "Poor Old Bill." Bleiler singles out "Sailors' Gambit" for special praise, calling it "the best chess story ever written." It certainly deserves this attention, but the story that probably best characterizes this first section is "The Three Infernal Jokes," the story of a man who sells his soul for three jokes "which shall make all who hear them simply die of laughter." Dunsany's marvelously effective juxtaposition of the comic and the tragic in this clever tale reflects the rare wit and ingenuity displayed in all the others. The second section, "Heroes and Wonders," is of special interest to fantasy enthusiasts since it contains such classics as "The Hoard of the Gibbelins" (with its marvelous opening line, "The Gibbelins eat, as is well known, nothing less good than man"); "How Nuth Would Have Practised His Art upon the Gnoles," "The Distressing Tale of Thangobrind the Jeweller, and of the Doom That Befell Him" (these three form a kind of trilogy dealing with the exploits of some of fantasy literature's most interesting burglars); "The Sword of Welleran" (one of Dunsany's very best stories of heroism); "The Fortress Unvanquishable Save the Sacnoth"; and "Idle Days on the Yann" (a remarkable exercise in evocative description). These works, and the other seven included here, combine to make this section the backbone of the volume. This section alone is worth the book's purchase price. The third section, "Jorkens," contains six tall tales of Jorkens, that most delightful and masterful liar of the Billiards Club: "The Sign," "The Neapolitan Ice," "Jorkens Consults a Prophet," "The Walk to Lingham," "How Ryan Got Out of Russia," and "A Mystery of the East." No subject is beyond the reach of Jorkens, and in these stories he holds forth on matters as diverse as transmigration, free will and destiny, and Eastern magic. Those new to the Jorken stories can get a good idea of their flair and style by reading the short "Neapolitan Ice," where we see Jorkens explore the Arctic in his imagination, through the liberating effects of the liqueurs in a Neapolitan Ice. Delightful. The fourth and final section, "Gods," features several short pieces from *The Gods of Pegana,* and four stories from *Time and the Gods:* "Time and the Gods," "The Coming of the Sea," "The Secret of the Gods," and "In the Land of Time." Here we see Dunsany the mythmaker at his very best. These stories, exhibiting the rich Biblical cadences of his inimitable prose style, are some of the most richly imaginative of the volume. In sum, this handsome collection is probably the best on the market today. The final touch is added by a liberal salting of twenty of Sidney H. Sime's delicate and delightful illustrations.

Eddison, E. R. *The Worm Ouroboros.* London: Cape, 1922. New York: Del Rey, 1977 (paper).
This is the earliest and easily the most popular of Eddison's grandiose romances, first published in 1922. It is fitting that the catalyst for its recently renewed popularity should be the interest in fantasy kindled by the works of J. R. R. Tolkien, for Tolkien had read Eddison and very likely drew some of his inspiration from him. The many heroic and magical adventures of this tale begin in a rather unusual fashion. An English gentleman is conveyed to Mercury by a small talking bird, a martlet, and allowed to observe, undetected, the royal court of Demonland. Eddison fortunately soon drops this awkward device and simply tells the tale. The story is principally about the conflict between Demonland and Witchland, with Witchland clearly the aggressor. King Gorice XII of Witchland is a powerful wizard and enchants the Demon Champion, Goldry Blusco, to a distant mountaintop. He then invades Demonland when its lord, Brandoch Daha, goes in quest of Goldry. Eddison clearly enjoys describing the heroic deeds of battle, but the book's real interest lies in Brandoch Daha's quest. This Demon Lord overcomes numerous physical and mental trials, including scaling a glacier, freeing a demigoddess, and overcoming despair, before finding Goldry and releasing him from the spell. Eddison creates an entire world with its own mythology whose divinities and demigods resemble those of both Northern and Mediterranean myths. He describes his divinities and aristocratic characters in a style whose elegance is unmatched even by Dunsany. His use of names, for some reason, lacks the polish of his style generally. Two of the lesser kingdoms are Pixyland and Goblinland, names completely unsuited to the sophistication of the story. Eddison's characterization is also sophisticated, avoiding the good versus evil oversimplification. Lord Gro, a character who changes allegiances three times and dies ignobly, is yet a sympathetic and even noble character of considerable complexity. Despite a few minor weaknesses, *The Worm Ouroboros* richly deserves its renewed status as a fantasy classic.

Eddison, E. R. *Mistress of Mistresses.* London: Faber, 1935. New York: Del Rey, 1978 (paper).
This is the first book Eddison wrote in his Zimiamvian trilogy. When it appeared in 1935, it pleased but puzzled many readers, so Eddison wrote the other two books, *A Fish Dinner in Memison* and *The Mezentian Gate,* to clarify his world of Zimiamvia. Present readers thus have a distinct advantage over Eddison's contemporaries in being able to read the later books first. *Mistress of Mistresses* has a strong plot line, involving the struggle of various

factions for power over the three kingdoms of Zimiamvia after the death of King Mezentius. The king's son is rightful heir, but he is a weakling and is soon disposed of. Contenders now include Mezentius's bastard son, Duke Barganax; his legitimate daughter, Antiope; his vicar, Horius Parry; and various lesser nobles. Lord Lessingham, the epitome of nobility, allies himself for some inexplicable reason with the capable but treacherous Lord Parry. This plot is straightforward, but it is not the only, or even the major, focus of the book. Enchantments, visions, shape shiftings, and various other semi-divine occurrences (generally under the direction of the rather long-winded philosopher, Dr. Vandermast) entertain the reader but interrupt the proceedings. The really puzzling aspect of the book, however, is the question of who Lessingham is. He seems to have inhabited a different world, our earth perhaps, until he died. He also seems to recognize Queen Antiope of Zimiamvia as someone named Mary to whom he had been married in his other existence. This puzzle is intriguing but is never solved satisfactorily, unless one reads—or preferably has already read—the other two books of the trilogy. The book has many riches such as plot and style and especially the sensuous portrait of Fiorinda–Aphrodite, but it has flaws as well. The frequently mystical, dreamlike ambience of many of the chapters is enjoyable, but has little to do with the plot; the lengthy philosophical passages are ponderous and largely superfluous. *Mistress of Mistresses* is, nonetheless, a rewarding experience, especially if read in conjunction with the other two books, or at least as a companion to *A Fish Dinner in Memison.*

Eddison, E. R. *A Fish Dinner in Memison.* New York: Dutton, 1941. New York: Del Rey, 1978 (paper).
This middle book of Eddison's Zimiamvian trilogy was originally published in 1941. Of the three books it strikes the best balance between action and philosophizing, between the dramatic and the discursive. It also makes clear the relationship between Zimiamvia and our world. The action shifts back and forth between these two worlds, creating numerous parallels of personal, social, and political behavior. The time setting on earth, which includes the years of World War I, contrasts with the peace and unity established by the divine King Mezentius in the three kingdoms of Zimiamvia. The most interesting parallel, however, is that of Lady Mary Lessingham on earth to her Zimiamvian counterpart, Lady Fiorinda. Both are clearly types of the goddess Aphrodite, but in different ways. Lady Mary is the faithful wife of Lessingham, while Fiorinda becomes the mistress of Duke Barganax, refusing marriage because, in line with the medieval courtly love tradition, marriage deadens love. Interestingly, Mary and Lessingham pretend not to be married when they travel. In presenting both worlds, Eddison is concerned almost exclusively with the upper class, displaying his obviously aristocratic and conservative tendencies. It is in the climactic scene, "The Fish Dinner: Symposium," that Eddison reveals the precise and astounding relationship

between the two worlds. At a dinner in Memison, King Mezentius offers the following question: "If we were Gods, able to make worlds and unmake 'em as we list, what world would we have?" Everyone says he or she would be satisfied with the present world, until Fiorinda (Aphrodite) dictates the nature of a different world (earth) and King Mezentius (Cronus or Zeus) actually makes it. Mezentius and his mistress, Amalia, enter this world where they live as Lessingham and Lady Mary, returning after their earthly deaths, at different times. The dramatic and philosophical impact of this climactic scene is completely absorbing, especially within the context of the entire book. And the concluding chapters are no letdown, as Fiorinda disposes of earth. Despite the fact that the creation of earth follows an established mythic pattern, its presentation in *A Fish Dinner in Memison* appears as one of the most unusual inventions in fantasy literature. If readers wish to sample but one work of Eddison's Zimiamvian trilogy, it should be this one.

Eddison, E. R. *The Mezentian Gate.* London: Elek, 1958. New York: Del Rey, 1978 (paper).
Eddison died in 1945 and left this book in manuscript form. The first third and the conclusion are complete. In between are a few complete chapters and what the author called "Arguments with Dates," which are actually fairly detailed synopses of the projected chapters. Thus the book works quite well as a totality. It is also a blueprint for the entire Zimiamvian trilogy, shedding a good deal of light on the incidents and, more importantly, on the supernatural causality in the other two books, *A Fish Dinner in Memison* and *Mistress of Mistresses.* In writing this book, Eddison clearly wanted to clarify the world of Zimiamvia; thus it is the most direct and easiest to read of the three works. And, although the books can be read independently, or in any order, readers will probably find the trilogy most intelligible if they start with *The Mezentian Gate,* even though it was the last to be written. Before going any further, it should be mentioned that the entire trilogy will appeal most to readers who like their fantasy to contain a mixture of adventure and philosophy, with the philosophy appearing in lengthy stretches of dialogue. And readers who tend to skip over such discussions are likely to miss the mythic foundations of the trilogy. Those who are willing, however, to take the time to read the philosophical discussions will be amply rewarded with some amazing concepts in which myth and reality become one. One helpful way of viewing Eddison's trilogy is as a paean of praise to woman in her capacities as mother, wife, and lover. For Eddison all three are contained in the different guises of Aphrodite, and all three are present in each book. Yet one can discern different emphases. In *The Mezentian Gate,* Queen Stateira is primarily the Mother-Aphrodite. Her son, King Mezentius, is the greatest of rulers, uniting the kingdoms of Rerek, Fingiswolde, and Meszria in a peaceful federation. This book, and the trilogy as a whole, is

also an examination of the nature of divinity. Queen Stateira is clearly a mother goddess, but never realizes her divinity. Fiorinda, the Lover-Aphrodite, awakens to the realization of her divinity in one of the most powerful and effective scenes in the book. While resting in the forest, she is literally transfigured and is worshiped by forest creatures, including the dryad Anthea, who attends her. As in all of his books, Eddison's style here is equal to the enormous task he imposes on it: elegant, polished, sensuous.

Gardner, John. *Grendel.* New York: Knopf, 1971. New York: Ballantine, 1975 (paper).

An absorbing and thoughtful retelling of the Beowulf legend from the monster's point of view, Gardner's version incorporates, in one form or another, most of the major episodes found in the first part of the Anglo-Saxon original: Hrothgar, the leader of a powerful tribe of Danes, builds the magnificent meadhall of Heorot; Grendel, a troll-like monster who lives in an underwater cavern with his mother, makes deadly nighttime raids on the hall for 12 long years; Beowulf, nephew of Hygelac, King of the Geats, hears of Hrothgar's troubles and, with a small band of warriors, sails to Denmark to help destroy the marauding monster; Beowulf and Grendel engage in a fierce hand-to-hand struggle in which the latter is fatally wounded. All of these familiar events, however, are seen through Grendel's eyes, and thus the reader is given a completely fresh perspective on them. Through the author's deft handling of the stream-of-consciousness technique the inner-most thoughts and feelings of Grendel are laid bare. The picture that finally emerges is not of a malevolent, bloodthirsty monster, but rather of a con-templative, misunderstood, and terribly lonely creature. The reader is slowly coaxed into sympathizing with this tormented soul who turns upon man, not because of any inherent love of death and destruction, but because man has forced him into this role—has literally taught him to be a savage killer. Ironically enough, Grendel is more cerebral and philosophical (he professes a kind of atheistic existentialism) than the humans who revile him. Gardner captures some of the stylistic flavor of his original model through the use of kennings ("shadow-shooter," "earth-rim-roamer"), songs, and an episodic/digressive structural format. In addition, he emphasizes some of the same thematic concerns contained in the eighth-century poem. Especially well handled is the exploration of the nature of heroism (see the Unferth/Grendel confrontations). *Grendel* is a highly imaginative, ingenious, and witty work of high fantasy that will prove stimulating to all readers, but especially to those familiar with the work on which it is based. Illustrated by Emil Antonucci.

Garner, Alan. *The Weirdstone of Brisingamen.* London: Collins, 1960. Cleveland: Collins-World, 1979.

The first, and probably the best, of Garner's Alderley books, *Weirdstone* seems destined to become a fantasy classic. Set in the ruggedly beautiful Peak District of North Central England, the novel describes in an energetic and suspenseful manner an awesome struggle between good and evil. The central characters in this struggle are two youngsters, Susan and her brother Colin, who, while their parents travel abroad, are spending six months on the farm of Bess and Gowther Mossock. Shortly after their arrival, Susan discovers that the crystal tear-shaped stone set in her bracelet (an ancient heirloom) is really Firestone, the magical Weirdstone of Brisingamen. It is an ancient spellstone of great power, and both the forces of light, led by the wizard Cadellin Silverbrow, and the forces of darkness, led by Nastrond, vie for possession of it. After changing hands a few times, Firestone finally ends up with its rightful owner, Silverbrow. One of Garner's primary strengths as a fantasist is his remarkable ability to vividly and believably delineate creatures of faërie. This he does beautifully in *Weirdstone*. Here the reader will encounter the Morrigan, a treacherous shape-shifting witch, the horrific blind hounds of the Morrigan, giant troll-women called the mara, hideous goblinlike creatures called svarts, the wolf Managarm, and a pair of extraordinarily courageous and resourceful dwarfs, Durathror and Fenodyree. There seem to be some echoes of Tolkien in Garner's book; for example, the flight of the children and their dwarf companions through the tunnels of West Mine and the Earldelving while hotly pursued by the svarts is reminiscent of the goblins' pursuit of Bilbo and the dwarfs in chapter 4 of *The Hobbit*. Garner's episode, however, is much longer than Tolkien's and in many respects is more vivid and horrific. Readers with claustrophobic tendencies might do well to pass over chapter 14, "The Earldelving." Garner's works seem to be quite popular in England, but are not so well known on this side of the Atlantic. 'Tis a pity.

Garner, Alan. *The Moon of Gomrath.* London: Collins, 1963. Cleveland: Collins-World, 1979.

Garner's second novel, *Gomrath,* carries on the Alderley story begun in *The Weirdstone of Brisingamen.* Most of the *Weirdstone* cast is here: the wizard, Cadellin Silverbrow; his nemesis the Morrigan, an evil shape-shifting witch; the good farm couple, Bess and Gowther Mossock; and of course the central characters, Susan and Colin. The action begins with the appearance of the elf-lord, Atlendor, who is in search of the evil force responsible for the disappearance of many of his people. Once again, Susan and Colin are drawn into the action because of a magic bracelet worn by the former. This bracelet, the Mark of Fohla, possesses strong magic, and Susan decides to use its power to help Atlendor. As she gets caught up in the struggle she nearly loses her very soul and identity to the forces of the Old Magic. The Mark of Fohla protects her, though, and with her aid the forces of good finally prevail, defeating not only the Morrigan, but also the Brollachan, a shapeless cloud of evil reminiscent of the abominable emanations that appear in Lovecraft's

Cthulhu stories. This action-packed novel is almost as good as its predecessor, but it suffers somewhat from a rather heavy dose of expository material in the beginning chapters, and also from the introduction of too many characters throughout the course of the narrative. The reader begins to feel like a stranger at a cocktail party who is introduced to a dozen or so guests and is then expected to remember not only their names but also something about their backgrounds. This is especially true when the Einheriar of the Herlathing appear on the scene about midway through the book. The narrative proper is followed by an extremely interesting and informative author's note, in which Garner explains, "Most of the elements and entities in the book are to be seen, in one shape or another, in traditional folklore. All I have done is to adapt them to my own view."

Garner, Alan. *Elidor*. London: Collins, 1965. Cleveland: Collins-World, 1979.
Bored and listless while on a free day in Manchester, England, the four Watson children—Nicholas, Helen, David, and Roland—wander into a slum clearance area, and there, after encountering a mysterious fiddler, discover a crumbling church that encloses a magic portal leading into the secondary world of Elidor, the "Green Isle of the Shadow of the Stars." After passing through the portal they find that the fiddler is really Maleborn of Elidor, a resolute warrior who is attempting to bring light back to his land. Years ago there was light and happiness in all of Elidor, but now night reigns in all but one of its four main castles, because the powers of darkness slowly gained control while the folk of Elidor lived in "ease" and "did not mark the signs." Garner's fast-paced narrative recounts the trials and adventures the Watson children encounter both in Elidor and their own world as they aid Maleborn in his attempt to beat back the forces of darkness. Most of the action takes place in the primary world, and although it is appropriate that the main emphasis is on the Watson family, it seems a shame that the reader doesn't get to know Maleborn, Findhorn (a unicorn), and the fascinating world of Elidor a little better. Like Garner's other novels, *Elidor* is smooth and polished, and is especially noteworthy for its vivid descriptions of the various crossings from the primary to the secondary world and back again.

Garner, Alan. *The Owl Service*. New York: Walck, 1967.
Set in a Welsh river valley not far from Aberystwyth, this intriguing novel has as its foundation one of the many stories of the *Mabinogion,* that wonderful repository of Welsh myth and legend. Alison, her stepbrother Roger, and their parents are spending some time in the house that had once belonged to Alison's dead father. One day Alison hears something scratching in the loft above her bed and asks Gwyn, the housekeeper's son, to investigate. He climbs into the loft and in its darkest corner finds a complete dinner

service decorated with what appears to be an owl design. Alison, Roger, and Gwyn soon discover that the possession of this mysterious owl service represents the first stage in their partial reenactment of the tragic legend of Blodeuwedd, the woman made out of flowers by the famous wizard, Gwydion. Garner does a superb job of breathing new life into this old story of love, treachery, and resultant death. Well done, too, is his delineation of the three teenagers; their aspirations, feelings, and rather complex inter-relationships are sensitively studied. Much of the work consists of dialogue, which Garner handles with deftness and confidence. Also worthy of mention is the author's creation of sustained suspense and an atmosphere of fore-boding and mystery.

Garner, Alan. *Red Shift.* New York: Macmillan, 1973.
From the standpoint of plot pattern and character delineation this is prob-ably the most complex and innovative of Garner's novels. Moving back and forth in time, the narrative recounts some of the most important and critical events in the lives of three young Englishmen: Tom, a sensitive, emotional, and highly intelligent scholar of the twentieth century; Macey, a second-century Briton caught up in the tribal warfare of his age; and Thomas, a seventeenth-century youth who becomes an unwilling participant in the brutal struggles of the Civil War between Royalist and Roundhead. Although separated by huge blocks of time, each youth seems to affect, unknowingly, the actions and destinies of the two others, primarily through the agency of an ancient votive ax with which all three have come in contact. The precise nature of the ax's power is never explained, but its ultimate effect is a dissolution of the barriers of time. This is a very ambitious novel, and well worth the reading, but as fantasy it is probably not as effective as the earlier works in which the author made heavier use of magic and mythology. The main plot, which examines Tom's relationship with his narrow-minded parents and his girl friend, Jan, is both poignant and powerful, but the other two parallel plots are not nearly as well conceived or convincingly handled. The story of Macey is especially difficult to follow, primarily because of the dialect used and the fragmentary nature of its segments. Gar-ner is to be commended for his bold literary experimentation and for his attempts to dramatically show how the preternatural and mundane merge in everyday life. One can only hope, however, that he hasn't thrown away the mold from which the delightful Alderley novels were cast. *The Weird-stone of Brisingamen* remains the best pure fantasy he has created.

Garnett, Richard. *The Twilight of the Gods and Other Tales.* London: T. Fisher Unwin, 1888; enl. ed. London: Lane, 1903. Darby, PA: Darby Books (n.d.).
This is a curiosity among collections of fantasy. Of the 28 tales included, nearly half are fantasy; among the rest are examples of original fables, meta-

morphoses, historical tales, and dream visions. The quality of the fantasy here is elusive. It ranges from gentle satire in "The Demon Pope" to wry moralizing in "The Dumb Oracle." In each tale, the distance achieved through exotic setting is turned back on this world and used to display human foibles. For even though the tales are peopled with demons, magicians, and gods, the quality of the works is primarily anecdotal. Yet Garnett's astonishing erudition and his rolling style can capture readers time after time, leading them into his otherworlds only to pull the rug out once again. Myth and historical fantasy prevail, allowing free play for Garnett's learning as well as his imagination. He shows us the Olympian view of the rise of Christianity ("The Twilight of the Gods") and Satan as a hen-pecked husband ("Madame Lucifer"). In "Ananda the Miracle-Worker," Buddha and one of his monks are used to satirize religion, while the descent of Apollo accounts for the mixed styles of the poet in "The Poet of Panopolis." In all of the tales, especially the fantasies, Garnett's wit shines. He is as ready a hand with magic rings as with bishop's crosiers, and if he treats both lightly at times, he is rarely disrespectful toward either.

Goldman, William. *The Princess Bride.* New York: Harcourt, 1973. New
    York: Ballantine, 1977 (paper).
William Goldman has written an exceptionally witty and sometimes grotesque parody of heroic fantasy. What is also exceptional about this book is that while it makes fun of the excesses of the genre, it tells a good tale and presents a worthwhile idea in a different way. In the preface the author speaks to us in his own person, the man who wrote the stories for the films *Butch Cassidy and the Sundance Kid* and *The Stepford Wives.* He tells us that he has written an abridged version, basically cutting out unexciting parts of "S. Morgenstern's satiric history of his country," so that it would read like the children's book he thought it was when his father read it to him years ago. After this explanation, Goldman gives us his abridgement, breaking in periodically to explain what he has omitted. The story itself takes place in the kingdom of Florin (Guilder is the enemy country), which is somewhere between Sweden and Germany, some time "before Europe." The central plot involves the attempts of Westley to reclaim his beloved Buttercup from the wicked Prince Humperdink. But one of the subplots steals the show. This concerns the quest of Inigo Montoya to avenge the death of his father, who was killed by a man with six fingers—a man who turns out to be Prince Humperdink's sadistic lieutenant. Despite the mock heroics that occur throughout—or perhaps because of them—we become attached to Westley and Buttercup and Inigo. What elicits our sympathy is that, despite their exploits, the heroes fail, or almost fail. And the ultimate theme of the work is that life is not fair, a reversal of the usual conclusion to a faery tale—or, more accurately, a reversal of what is generally assumed to be the conclusion to a faery tale.

Gregorian, Joyce Ballou. *The Broken Citadel.* New York: Atheneum, 1975.
Here is a book with archetypal and mythic foundations reminiscent of
McKillip's *Forgotten Beasts of Eld* or even more closely of Le Guin's *Tombs
of Atuan.* The Broken Citadel is different from these, however, in many
particulars, but most notably in the hugeness of its scope. It provides a
complete pantheon, basically Middle Eastern in flavor, but with echoes of
most other major mythologies. Within the main plot, which encompasses a
one-year odyssey, it recounts the ancient and recent history of a people
through ballads, tales, and chronicles. The final effect is impressive, albeit
at times confusing. One of the more interesting aspects of the mythology is
the ancient feud between the Great Mother and the First Father, and their
subsequent male versus female, god versus goddess feud, a major element
in mythologies. As in these other mythologies, the primacy of the male
divinity has not been a clear or unmixed blessing. But even the gods and
goddesses are subordinate to a higher power, which is—or is symbolized
by—the Kermyrag, a phoenixlike creature whose agents are the Yinry (akin
to fate or destiny). But this is not what the book is principally about; it is
simply the mythological background. The major plot centers around three
characters. Sibby (the name is significant both as Sib and Sibyl) Barron is
an 11-year-old twentieth-century girl from West Newton, Massachusetts.
Leron is prince of Tredana, heir to its throne. Semirimia (a conscious echo
of the name of Semiramis, the fabled Assyrian queen) is a seductive goddess and the Deathless Queen of Treclere. Unfolding the mystery of how
these three relate to each other, and what they do to each other, occupies
most of the book. Gregorian succeeds in keeping the relationship well disguised until the climax, yet gives the reader generous clues all along. And
while this mystery is unfolding, readers are entertained by a colorful array
of characters, a series of exotic landscapes, and the implied comparison
between this Arabian Nights otherworld and our own world where a sense
of the supernatural has been smothered by mundane pursuits. The book
has defects. It is unnecessarily detailed in places, needlessly obscure in
others; and Sibby, the main character, is not consistently drawn. Despite
these defects, however, and despite the book's bulk (373 pages), readers
will find it difficult to put this one down until the last page.

Haggard, H[enry] Rider. *She: A History of Adventure.* New York: Lovell,
   1887. New York: Del Rey, 1978 (paper).
A work near the border of fantasy, *She* belongs, perhaps, to the genre of
the adventure story, but its setting, its atmosphere, and the characterization of She qualify it for consideration here. Its style and depth of thought
earn it a place among the finer pieces of fantasy. The tale is set primarily in
Africa, but a lost Africa, a hidden world that predates the Pyramids—a
world that worships and serves *She-who-must-be-obeyed.* For She has
counted two thousand years, waiting for the return of her lover Kallicrates.

Her power derives from her bath in the Fire of Life, an undying volcano, and from the knowledge of Kôr, a civilization old even by her standards. She has a mirror of vision and can kill with a glance. She is awesome in her beauty and terrible in her patience. When Leo Vincey and Horace Holly discover She's lost land, they discover too that Vincey is the reincarnation of her lover. Yet this is more Holly's story than Vincey's, for Holly tells it; through him, we consider She and the promise of longevity. Her beauty compels his love as well as Vincey's, but Holly's English tough-mindedness balks at the notion of approximate immortality. There is much that is Gothic here: corpses used as torches and vast sepulchral caverns. Yet Holly's narrative challenges the horror at all fronts, speculating rather than fearing. This speculative quality is important. Magic is presented as knowledge of natural law rather than mere conjuring; death is considered both as a terminus and as a grand undertaking. In effect, the work is similar to John Buchan's: controlled thought blending with high adventure and intrigue. The story is anticipated in two works—*Wisdom's Daughter* and *She and Allan.* The first is the tale of She's empowering, while the second introduces Allan Quatermain, Haggard's familiar adventure hero. The series is completed in *Ayesha: The Return of She,* where Vincey and She meet again in Tibet.

Haggard, H. Rider, and Andrew Lang. *The World's Desire.* London: Longmans, 1890. New York: Del Rey, 1977 (paper).
This work combines an entertaining adventure story based on myths related to Odysseus and Helen with a complex psychological-theological theme. One concludes that the former must come from Haggard and the latter from Lang, though this is an oversimplification that does neither one justice. The story begins with Odysseus's supposed second return to Ithaca. He finds his house and kingdom ruined, his family dead, his people dispersed. Aphrodite, who has a grudge against Odysseus because he has never come completely under her sway, directs him to his final journey, the quest to obtain his "Heart's Desire"—Helen of Troy, who is now in Egypt. Odysseus arrives, disguised, in the midst of the Biblical plagues of Egypt shortly before the Jewish Exodus. He is distracted in his quest by Meriamun, Pharaoh Meneptah's queen, who is a beautiful wizard in league with the "Ancient Evil." Meneptah casts a spell on Odysseus (he has forgotten a warning about this from Aphrodite), which causes him to only partially achieve his "Heart's Desire." Helen, whose symbol is a star, is aligned with the benevolent goddess of love, Aphrodite. Meriamun, on the other hand, is allied with some sort of evil god or devil; her symbol is the snake. Again, there are clear Biblical echoes with Meriamun (Eve) and the serpent tempting man from pure good (Helen—love). The reincarnation motif enters here in a striking but bewildering manner. Odysseus, Helen, and Meriamun are apparently all reincarnated from a previous life in which the three had ac-

tually been two beings joined in a uniting love. But some evil occurred (more Biblical echoes) that created disunity and strife. Reading this book is definitely an entertaining and mind-stretching experience, even though the reader feels at times trapped in a maze for which the authors never fashioned a proper key.

Haggard, H. Rider. *Eric Brighteyes.* London: Longmans, 1891. New York: Zebra, 1978 (paper).

Icelandic sagas lie behind many works of fantasy, but few works employ these ancient tales to such an extent as this one. The setting is medieval Iceland, where berserkers haunt the untraveled ways, and outlaws, fair game for anyone, go a-viking to pass their time of exile. The sea and the hearth are the two centers of culture, and the sword or the ax is the final test of a man's mettle. The atmosphere of a historic saga permeates this work, allowing for prophecy, magic swords, and witchcraft. Eric, son of a yeoman, aspires to the hand of Gudruda the Fair, daughter of Asmund the Priest. Gudruda agrees, but her half-sister, Swanhild, daughter of Groa the Witch, contrives to separate the two. The witch-daughter's devices are effective and Eric's path to Gudruda's hand is heroic and bloody. Swanhild, too, loves Eric and she is fully willing to shame both of them for his love. Indeed, Swanhild does not stop at murder, treachery, or the black arts in her pursuit of Eric's affection. But his love of Gudruda and his stalwart honor serve him well. However, this is a saga, not a romance, and neither Eric nor Gudruda is fated to have a happy life. Eric and his faithful thrall, Skallagrim the Baresark, pursue fame and happiness in their viking expeditions, but they find little of the latter. Swanhild's conjurings place friends as well as enemies before their potent blades. Gudruda, too, is beset by Swanhild's machinations. She is nearly forced to marry the terrible Ospaker Blacktooth, Eric's mortal enemy. The tale benefits from a superb atmosphere—a nice combination of heroic adventure and prophetic irony. Its battle scenes are brilliant, and its touches from the dark side of witchcraft thoroughly effective. If it is possible to capture the true flavor of a saga in modern narrative, this one does so.

Hales, E. E. Y. *Chariot of Fire.* Garden City, NY: Doubleday, 1977. New York: Avon, 1978 (paper).

This is a witty and entertaining story based, with a fair amount of accuracy, on Dante's *Inferno* and Milton's *Paradise Lost.* The hero, Henry Brock, a middle-aged employee of British Rail, dies suddenly and is assigned to the Second Circle of Hell, that of Passionate Lovers (or, as Dante expressed it, the Lascivious). Here Henry meets the likes of Tristan, Dido, Helen of Troy, and, most prominently, Antony and Cleopatra. He also makes the rather startling discovery that hell has a railroad, the Limbo Line, connecting Limbo with upper and lower hell. Brock, being rather brash in a good-natured way, and a railwayman by trade, becomes the key figure in infernal plots and heavenly counterplots (this is where Milton figures prominently). But the story itself, however ingenious, is merely a vehicle for Hales's imagination, which creates a good deal of fun by extrapolating from Dante's and Milton's descriptions of hell. We are introduced to a fascinating gallery of historical figures, primarily from the Second Circle but also from Limbo, such as Caesar, Virgil, Aeneas, Amazon queens, and even the Biblical Samaritan Woman, who plays an important part in the conclusion of the story. Fortunately, one does not have to remember Dante or Milton or the Bible too clearly in order to enjoy the book—but it helps. In addition to its entertainment value, *Chariot* also offers some interesting insights into the concept of hell. These are not necessarily new or particularly profound ideas, but they do provoke thought. As fantasy, *Chariot of Fire* belongs to a relatively small category. It is myth fantasy, but it is so close to what many people believe is literal that some might object to the term "myth." While it lacks their depth, it is perhaps most closely related to the theological fantasies of Charles Williams (*War in Heaven*) or C. S. Lewis (*Perelandra*).

Hancock, Neil. Circle of Light series. 4 vols. *Greyfax Grimwald; Faragon Fairingay; Calix Stay; Squaring the Circle.* New York: Popular Library, 1977 (paper).
Tolkien fans will be more than a bit gratified with this series—and more than a bit upset. For like so many other works of recent fantasy, the Circle of Light series draws a great deal from *The Lord of the Rings* in the form of inspiration, and compliments Tolkien in doing so, but it never quite achieves the same level of success. We have the epic sweep of Tolkien and the interest in the quiet side of life, the vast, magical powers, and the simple affection for homemade meals. Unlike *The Lord of the Rings,* however, here we have touches of the beast fable—where an otter and a bear join a dwarf as the major figures of the work. The animals speak more like Rat and Badger from *The Wind in the Willows* than like any of Tolkien's creations, yet they do seem to fit with their companion Broco, a typical good-natured but crotchety dwarf. On the other hand, neither the animals nor the dwarf seem quite appropriate to a war of infantry and rifles—or maybe the war is inappropriate to them. Whatever the case, there is a subtle incongruity behind this work, one that is evident in the style as well as the plot. For a wizard who gets "miffed" is no less disconcerting than a bear with a semiautomatic. Yet, problems aside, the series benefits from an engaging sequence of events and some truly fine scenes. The companions are called to Atlanton Earth and are involved in the battle between light and dark, between Lorini and Dorini. On the side of light, we have the wizards of Greyfax Grimwald and Faragon Fairingay, Cephus Starkeeper, and our three companions. Darkness leads Fire-slayer and Sun-eater, Cakgor the wolf, and the terrible Doraki. The role of the companions is apparently

small, yet like Frodo's it hides great purpose. Their inherent morality, also like Frodo's, is their trump. Their task is to carry the Arkenchest, the vessel of the Five Secrets that Dorini needs to assure her grip on Atlanton Earth. With them, darkness can control. Yet the work is not limited to the battle for Atlanton Earth, for it ranges throughout the universe called Windameir. We travel to the stars and to the land after death, occasionally catching glimpses of the Last Home. We see that the actions of Bear, Otter, and Dwarf, however heroic, imitate larger actions occurring in Cypher, the palace of light. But the actions in Cypher are hardly final. After defeat here, the forces of light meet those of darkness again—beyond Calix Stay—beyond death. Even on this level, the conflict is not absolute; the war does not end in victory or defeat, but in resolution and continuation. Behind all this is the undefined movement of fate, which is, frankly, a bit confusing. We are never quite sure what is the place of willful action in this network. Nevertheless, the sweep of these works allows for a considerable play of imagination. Hancock invents a few fascinating races, notable among them the Roots. Like Tolkien's Ents, they are from the dawn of time, but they are animate rocks rather than trees. Then, too, the use of magic is successful, including shape shifting; far-seeing; mystical doorways; and many other forms of enchantment. Two weaknesses of the works, however, must be noted: a tendency to repeat certain descriptive patterns and a cosmology that is not quite solid.

Hodgson, William Hope. *The Boats of the "Glen Carrig."* London: Chapman & Hall, 1907. Westport, CT: Hyperion, 1976 (paper).
This novel is one of the most distinctive and imaginative Gothic fantasies of the twentieth century. The fast-paced, highly episodic narrative recounts the adventures of John Winterstraw and his fellow survivors of the wrecked *Glen Carrig,* from the time they leave their foundering ship in lifeboats to their happy return to the port of London aboard the *Seabird,* a derelict ship they have rescued from the "weed-choked sea." Before the *Seabird* carries them safely home, however, they have a harrowing encounter with the half-human trees of the eerie land of Lonesomeness; are nearly dashed to bits by the preternatural fury of a great storm; sail through the "cemetery of the oceans," a seaweed-choked body of water sprinkled with rotting hulks and inhabited by monstrous crabs and "devilfish"; and do battle with the weed men, hideous creatures with "great eyes as big as crown pieces," beaklike noses, and "slug-like," undulating, "white and slimy" bodies. Hodgson is a gifted writer with remarkably fine artistic instincts. His use, for example, of the first person point of view gives his narrative an immediacy and realism that strengthen its ability to evoke feelings of horror and dread. Then, too, he makes excellent use of the foil technique by juxtaposing the unrelieved horror of the first three-quarters of the book with the light and sometimes even farcical concluding scenes involving the "buxom woman," Mis-

tress Mary Madison, and the narrator. Perhaps most noteworthy, however, is Hodgson's creation of his own secondary world, the mythic world of the Sargasso Sea. It is one of the most memorable and unusual otherworlds ever created, and most surely one that will spellbind readers for years to come.

Hodgson, William Hope. *The House on the Borderland.* London: Chapman & Hall, 1908. Westport, CT: Hyperion, 1976 (paper).

While on a fishing expedition in an isolated part of western Ireland, the narrator and his friend Tonnison discover a "crumpled and dilapidated" manuscript in the debris of a mysterious ruin. Back in his tent, the narrator reads the macabre tale of "The House on the Borderland." Written by the man who once lived in the house now reduced to ruins, the diary vividly describes his dreamlike travels through space and time and his fearful struggles with grotesque swine-creatures who repeatedly attack his home. A master at portraying the unnatural and the malevolent, Hodgson is in top form in *Borderland.* From the discovery of the manuscript to the last anguished entry of the diary, when "somethi——" crawls out of the "great, oak trap" in the basement, pads up the steps, and confronts the writer, causing him to break off his writing in midsentence, Hodgson manages to sustain an atmosphere of suspense and evil foreboding. Readers familiar with H. G. Wells's *Time Machine* will discover some fascinating parallels between it and *Borderland.* Perhaps most noteworthy are the similarities between the voyages of the Time Traveller and those of Hodgson's diarist; both, interestingly enough, depict destruction on a cosmic scale. Similar too is the framework device used by the two authors. There even seem to be echoes of Wells's malign Morlocks in Hodgson's depictions of the swine-creatures who live in a vast subterranean pit near the ancient house. For years after his tragic death in World War I, Hodgson's works were largely neglected, but there has been an encouraging revival of interest in them since 1946, when August Derleth published his four novels in an omnibus edition. *Borderland,* the novel most critics consider his finest, provides convincing proof that the attention presently being paid to Hodgson and his writings is well deserved.

Hoffmann, E. T. A. *The Best Tales of Hoffmann.* Ed. E. F. Bleiler. New York: Dover, 1967 (paper).

Of the seven faery tales, or märchen, that Hoffmann wrote in his lifetime, three are translated here: "The Golden Flower Pot," "Nutcracker and the King of Mice," and "The King's Betrothed." The rest of the stories in the collection can be variously categorized (Gothic, romance, adventure), but the three märchen are clearly fantasies—beautiful ones at that. Each of the three employs a world-within-a-world pattern to great effect. In "The King's Betrothed," the gnome Daucus Carota is the king of a vegetable realm that exists in the garden of Fräulein Aennchen and her astrologer father. In "Nutcracker," Christmas gifts come to life—a familiar motif, but one that benefits from Hoffmann's sense of drama and attention to detail. Indeed, both of these tales are so close to traditional faery stories (*volksmärchen*), that it is difficult to tell where tradition ends and Hoffmann begins. Not so with "The Golden Pot." This tale is, in many ways, the best of the fantasies of the German Romantic movement. It fictionalizes a search for paradise, and in doing so represents a conflict between the ideal and the real. Anselmus, an insignificant poet, is employed by Archivarius Lindhorst, a fire-spirit who has descended to the earthly realm. The poet falls in love with the spirit's daughter, Serpentina, but is seduced by a former girl friend who is aided by black magic. Ornate description, startling magic, and a careful balance between two worlds typify the work. Anselmus's laborious transcription of manuscripts allows him access to Serpentina, but his single copying error lands him in a bottle on the shelf. His unwillingness to accept the otherworld and divorce himself completely from the mundane is his difficulty—the thematic focus of the work. The settings of Hoffmann's tales, unlike Tieck's or Fouqué's, are contemporary with the author, yet like these other romanticists (who were friends of his), Hoffmann argues that nature is animate and wonder is available to all who care to look for it. Like these others as well—maybe more than these others—Hoffmann's impact on MacDonald, Morris, and the development of fantasy is worthy of note.

Ingelow, Jean. *Mopsa the Fairy.* London: Longmans, 1869. New York: Garland, 1976.

Mopsa the Fairy is a remarkable mid-Victorian work that merits a place on the fantasy shelf alongside the works of Ingelow's much better remembered contemporaries George MacDonald and Lewis Carroll. It first appeared three years after Carroll's first Alice book and three years before Mac-Donald's first Curdie book. *Mopsa* differs from the Alice and Curdie books in the straightforward simplicity of the story, which does not attempt the mathematical or religious complexities of these other works. Yet the narrative is richly imaginative and quite as original in its way as the works of MacDonald and Carroll. The narrative style is fittingly simple and unobtrusive. Jack enters the otherworld of faërie through the hollow of a tree, where he finds four tiny faeries in a bird's nest. He pockets the faeries and, at their insistence, begins to whistle, whereupon he is lifted from the hollow tree by an albatross and flown to Fairyland. Jack's task is to escort the four faeries—he favors the one called Mopsa—to an unknown destination by sailing down a river in a boat that responds to his commands. He becomes something of a Huck Finn, encountering all sorts of adventures when necessity or curiosity draws him to the river banks to explore the different countries within Fairyland. The quest becomes gradually more concrete when Jack recognizes that Mopsa is growing daily and is, in fact, a faery queen. Together, however, they resist the fate set for Mopsa, that is, to rule over her appointed land after releasing it from enchantment. Mopsa cannot, of course, escape her fate, nor Jack his. And thus the story conveys, dramatically and with barely a trace of preachiness, the favorite Victorian theme of duty and responsibility. In addition to the magical adventures of Jack in Fairyland, readers will enjoy the author's portrayal of the different races of faeries and their alluring, but potentially dangerous, attractiveness for humans. The depiction of the faery races in *Mopsa* is reminiscent of *The Kingdoms of Elfin,* the work of another woman fantasist, Sylvia Townsend Warner, who wrote one hundred years after Ingelow.

Kendall, Carol. *The Gammage Cup.* New York: Harcourt, 1959. New York: Voyager, 1966 (paper).

The Gammage Cup is the sort of book that brings a wide smile to the lips of readers whenever they recall it. The book is a gentle but firm satire on conformity. Slipper-on-the-Water is one of twelve villages inhabited by the Minnipins, or Small Ones (about the size of Tolkien's hobbits), whose ancestors fled from the aggressive Mushrooms, or Hairless Ones, to the Land Between the Mountains some 880 years before. The Minnipins not only don't visit the world outside, they practically never even visit the other villages. Consequently, the Minnipins of Slipper have become extremely provincial in their beliefs and customs. For example, any paintings that do not conform to the one in the museum are considered "blobs." And it turns out that the painting in the museum is a diagram of a family tree that someone in years past had mistakenly labeled a family portrait. One of the more ominous objects of the satire is the family of hereditary political leaders— fittingly, their name is Period—who control public opinion almost absolutely. Fortunately for all, there are five Minnipins who are not cowed by these silly or potentially disastrous narrow views. Predictably, these include an artist (a blobber) and a poet. Less predictably, however, the group includes a historian, a museum keeper, and the town treasurer, thus avoiding the usual stereotype of the nonconformist. Also gratifying is the fact that the story avoids oversimplifying the conflict between the majority of the Minnipins and the "Oh, Thems." When the "Oh, Thems" accept exile to the Sunset Mountains, the villagers provide them with boats and supplies. And when the Minnipins' ancient enemies, the Mushrooms, plan an attack on Slipper, the exiles warn the villagers just in time. The Period family then acknowledges their stubborn tunnel vision and humbly put themselves under the command of Muggles, the girl who has become the leader of the exiles. Nonconformity is an age-old subject, but it receives a fresh depiction in *The Gammage Cup.* The story itself is well plotted, though sometimes Kendall slows the pace too much by including relatively insignificant detail, such as the construction of a house. Most of the characters are flat, except for the shy Muggles who is the point-of-view character and who develops believably into a firm, sensible leader. The main magic in the book is the device, very familiar since Tolkien, of the sword that gleams when the enemy is about; it becomes "bright when the cause is right." Mainly a theme book, there is much to enjoy and laugh at along the way in *The Gammage Cup.*

Kendall, Carol. *The Whisper of Glocken.* New York: Harcourt, 1965.
Readers who enjoyed Kendall's *Gammage Cup* had to wait over five years for this second book about the Minnipins, but the wait was amply rewarded. As in the earlier book, the setting for *The Whisper of Glocken* is the Land Between the Mountains. The time is just a few years, apparently, after the events of the first book. We once again meet Muggles and the other Outlaw-Heroes of Slipper-on-the-Water, but, though these Old Heroes help, this new adventure is for a set of unsuspecting and unlikely New Heroes, including Glocken, the bellringer. These New Heroes must journey beyond their valley to find out what has caused the Watercress River to overflow and reverse its course. Not only is this creating a flood, but an old Minnipin adage warns that the valley will remain safe only as long as the Watercress flows in its accustomed way. The New Heroes journey through mountains and across deserts, encountering numerous challenges to their abilities and courage, qualities they only now discover, until they are finally captured by the Hulks (large people), who have dammed up the Watercress to mine its channel of valuable minerals. The New Heroes escape and seek shelter in a cave where Glocken discovers the truth about one of the old Pretend stories of "then." The Whisper of Glocken is a small, high-pitched bell, which one of Glocken's ancestors had used to form the underground channel for the Watercress. Glocken finds the Whisper in the cave and knows what to do because he has always paid attention to the Pretend stories. The dam is destroyed and the Watercress restored to its proper course. *The Whisper of Glocken* is a richly meaningful all-ages book. It undermines the stereotyped view of the hero and constructs a more realistic picture of courageous little people who are broad-minded or imaginative enough to accomplish what has to be done. There is also a definite echo in this book of T. H. White's theme *(Mistress Masham's Repose)* that bigger is not better. Kendall's characters in *The Whisper of Glocken* are generally better developed and individuated than in her earlier book, but the single most important improvement in terms of characters is the addition of the Diggers. The Diggers are three-legged desert creatures, smaller than Minnipins, who are equipped with sharp claws. They are somewhat dull-witted and communicate in squeaks, but fortunately for the New Heroes, they are generous and helpful. They are also laughable, since whole groups of them will imitate a Minnipin action, such as slapping someone on the back, while making a contented humming sound. The Diggers are one of the reasons that *The Whisper of Glocken* is a superior all-ages fantasy.

Kurtz, Katherine. *Deryni Rising.* New York: Ballantine, 1970 (paper).
Deryni Rising is the first volume in Kurtz's high fantasy series the Chronicles of the Deryni. It is the story of Kelson Haldane, the young king of Gwynned, and his friends and protectors, Duke Alaric Morgan and Father Duncan MacLain. Morgan and Duncan are Deryni, members of an ancient race of sorcerers who have long been persecuted in the Eleven Kingdoms. When King Brion is slain by Charissa, another Deryni, those people in Gwynned who hate and fear the Deryni rise up in rebellion against Kelson in view of his Deryni sympathies. At the same time, Charissa threatens not only his kingship but his very life. Morgan and Duncan have many harrowing and dangerous experiences as they work to help Kelson overcome the rebellious factions and avenge his father's death. At the coronation ceremony, all things come to a head as Kelson is revealed to be Deryni himself and Charissa challenges him to an arcane duel. Even though he is inexperienced in Deryni ways, with the help of Morgan and Duncan he manages to vanquish the wicked sorceress and is at last crowned king of Gwynned. This is an exciting tale with an intricate plot peopled with fascinating and likeable characters. Though some elements are familiar to us, such as the Church and its various rituals and traditions, the book can definitely be considered high fantasy. The setting is an imaginary land and the Deryni possess such qualities as mind-reading, healing by touch, and self-transportation in an instant. The Eleven Kingdoms and many of the characters are described in such rich and vivid detail that they would immediately be recognizable. It is also interesting to note that Kurtz has given the Deryni a history that is frequently referred to and that gives the story credence. Since there are many issues left unresolved at the end, it is unlikely that any reader would not want to continue with *Deryni Checkmate* and *High Deryni*.

Kurtz, Katherine. *Deryni Checkmate.* New York: Ballantine, 1972 (paper).
This continuation of the saga of King Kelson of Gwynned and the Deryni's fight for survival flows smoothly from the end of the first volume, *Deryni Rising*. The priests and a rabble of peasants grow in strength, and their opposition to those of Deryni heritage is now a fierce and mindless hatred focused on total destruction. Kelson's closest friends and advisors, Duke Alaric Morgan and Father Duncan MacLain, are relentlessly pursued by the Church and rebels alike as they strive to halt the mounting disquiet and prove that human and Deryni can live peacefully side by side. For Gwynned is also threatened with invasion by Wencil of Torenth, and unless the country can stand against him undivided by internal strife, it will surely be taken. A personal crisis for Duncan arises when he must reveal his Deryni powers in order to save Morgan from certain death. As priest and Deryni—states of being generally assumed to be irreconcilable—he is tortured by feelings of guilt. Finally, a council of bishops votes to excommunicate the two Deryni,

and Kelson is faced with choosing between his country and his dearest friends. But, as this volume ends, he decides to ignore the excommunication order, and he, Duncan, and Morgan join forces in a last attempt to save their country. Kurtz has no problems maintaining the pace and excitement she established in *Deryni Rising*. She has the ability to introduce new characters and make them very interesting and real in a few short sentences. Such is the case with Kevin MacLain, his fiancée, Bronwyn Morgan, and the architect Rimmel, who harbors a secret passion for Bronwyn. Their tragic story is not essential to the main theme, but its inclusion further illustrates that the Deryni heritage is truly a two-edged sword. And the tragedy would not have the impact it does if the characters had not been developed as fully and carefully as any destined to live out the series. The persecution of the Deryni is an example of the continual struggle between good and evil often found in fantasy literature. But Kurtz adds a twist by not making all the Deryni good and all the humans evil. The evil is that some people hate and fear other people merely for what they are, and that there are always those who will take advantage of that prejudice. The third volume, *High Deryni*, will be next on the reading list of those who enjoyed the first two.

Kurtz, Katherine. *High Deryni.* New York: Ballantine, 1973 (paper).
In this third volume of the Chronicles of the Deryni, the leader of the rebel faction is finally persuaded to join forces with the king of Gwynned against the invading troops of Wencil of Torenth. King Kelson, little more than a boy in years, is once again aided in this task by his close friends Duke Alaric Morgan and Father Duncan MacLain. The three young Deryni are able to halt the growing wave of persecution against those of their heritage so the country can unite to face a truly evil enemy, who also happens to be Deryni. For although a corrupt Deryni has powers at his disposal that enable him to inflict more pain and torture than his human counterpart, like humans Deryni can be either good or bad. It is an individual choice that we observe many characters making throughout this story. As the two armies come face to face for the final battle, the Camberian Council makes a ruling that the victory will be decided by a duel arcane. It is to be fought with Deryni weapons by four from each side. But the ending has a twist that will surprise even the most perceptive reader. One of Wencil's trusted friends reveals his true identity and the duel is never fought. In the guise of Rhydon of Eastmarch, Stefan Coram is able to poison his supposed comrades and win the battle for Kelson and his supporters. It seems impossible, but *High Deryni* is even more exciting and spellbinding than its two predecessors. Perhaps the most interesting departure from the other books is the development of a love relationship between Morgan and the beautiful Richenda, countess of Marley. It does not play a major role in the story line, but among other things it does give us some new insights into Morgan as a man. Richenda is

a vibrant and welcome addition to a cast of characters that is dominated by males. She does for this book what Eowynn did for Tolkien's *Return of the King*. Some of the other major characters also continue to develop and grow. Kelson and Duncan come to terms with, respectively, their kingship and priesthood, and are able to reconcile these offices with their Deryni natures. Sean Lord Derry undergoes much personal pain and suffering at the hands of Wencil and emerges a stronger person. There are four appendixes to help the reader sort out the various characters and places, a time line for the history of the Eleven Kingdoms, and an essay on the genetic basis for Deryni inheritance. The end of the story is not altogether happy, but this only serves to make *High Deryni* a very real tale.

Kurtz, Katherine. *Camber of Culdi.* New York: Ballantine, 1976 (paper). New York: Del Rey, 1979.
This book is sometimes called Volume IV in the Chronicles of the Deryni and sometimes Volume I in the Chronicles of Camber. The events in it take place some two hundred years prior to those in the first three Deryni chronicles. It is the story of Camber MacRorie and the part he and his family play in the restoration of the Haldane line to the throne of Gwynned. Although Camber and his family are of Deryni blood and possess certain extrasensory powers, they are dismayed and angered by the actions of the current Deryni ruler. When they learn of the existence of a direct descendant of the previous human rulers, Camber, his son Joram, and their close friend Rhys Thuryn work to place Cinhil Haldane on the throne. They are hampered in their efforts not only by agents of Imre, the Deryni king, but also by the heir himself. For Cinhil has lived the better part of his adult life as a cloistered monk and is unwilling to abandon that role for one of a layman, let alone a king. As their treasonous deeds become more difficult to conceal, Camber and his family are forced to take the reluctant Cinhil into hiding, where they prepare for the day of final reckoning. Cinhil becomes resigned to his royal heritage, but it is not until the death of his infant son at the hands of one of Imre's men that he becomes wholeheartedly involved in the effort to overthrow the Festillic ruler. This is accomplished with the death of Imre and the disappearance of his sister. *Camber of Culdi* is carefully written to correspond with any reference made to this earlier time period in the other Deryni chronicles. The characters are thoughtfully developed, from the despicable Imre to the wise Camber. But the most fascinating character is the elusive Cinhil Haldane. His struggle against his heritage, which changes to passive resistance and finally to willing acceptance, is skillfully portrayed and very believable. This story is also probably Kurtz's most somber. Her depiction of Cathan MacRorie's anguish and of Imre's despair after Cathan's murder is real enough to pierce the reader's soul. There are five helpful appendixes: an index of characters, an index to place names, and three lineage charts.

Kurtz, Katherine. *Saint Camber.* New York: Del Rey, 1978.

Volume II in the Chronicles of Camber, *Saint Camber* is the continuation of the story that revolves around Camber MacRorie, his family, friends, and foes. The action picks up almost immediately from the end of *Camber of Culdi.* The kingdom of Gwynned has been reclaimed by the rightful human heir, Cinhil Haldane, with the aid of Camber and other supporters. But many problems still face the Deryni lord. Ariella, sister of the deposed ruler and mother of his child, has fled to nearby Torenth where she plots with foreign Deryni powers to march against Gwynned. At a time when Camber's advice and counsel is most needed by the immature king, Cinhil turns his back, blaming Camber for his lost priesthood and the deformities of his infant sons. He becomes progressively more bitter and Camber is at a loss as how to regain the king's trust. But the story takes a bizarre twist when Alister Cullen, a close friend and Vicar General of the Michaelian Order, is slain in a battle with Ariella. Camber and his son Joram find Alister and Ariella both dead, and Camber comes to a startling decision. Alister had the trust and confidence of the king, and Camber realizes that the only way for him again to have a close relationship with Cinhil is to assume the shape of Alister and let it be Camber MacRorie who has died. The shape-changing spell is difficult to work and maintain, but Camber manages to do it. As it becomes necessary to let more people in on the secret, Camber/Alister is increasingly apprehensive about the result if Cinhil or others should discover the truth. But a new problem arises when rumors about miracles supposedly performed by the dead Camber begin to circulate. Efforts on the part of Camber's family to stop the stories backfire, and the entire affair culminates in the petition of a new order of priests for the canonization of Camber. Horror-struck by this turn of events, Camber/Alister and Joram try unsuccessfully to halt the canonization procedure. As each new piece of evidence is presented, the hierarchy of the Church becomes more convinced that Camber truly deserves sainthood. Even Cinhil is a witness to one of Camber's "miracles," and his unwilling testimony is the final proof needed to make St. Camber a reality. The pace of the Deryni chronicles is continued without a falter in this tale. But more gripping than the action and battles that take place is the deeper story of one man's sacrifice of his own identity to be able as someone else to help his kind and his country. Kurtz has used this theme before in *High Deryni,* when Stefan Coram reveals that he has been masquerading as Rhydon of Eastmarch for several years. Again, this is for a noble purpose and provides an interesting twist to the plot. One of the finest characterizations is that of Cinhil Haldane, the priest-king, whose struggle to be at peace with himself is a thought-provoking aspect of the story. As in the other books, the appendixes help the reader sort out names, places, and lineage. The conclusion of Camber's story, Volume III, *Camber the Heretic,* is in progress.

Kuttner, Henry. *The Mask of Circe.* New York: Ace, 1948 (paper).
This novel, perhaps Kuttner's best, is a curious blend of fantasy and science fiction. Sitting across the campfire from his friend Talbot, Jay Seward ("seaward") recounts an amazing tale of space-time travel in which he relived some of the adventures of his legendary ancestor Jason. Like Jason, Seward sailed upon the *Argo*, encountered Hecate and the Circe of Aeaea, and gained possession of the fabled Golden Fleece. Since Seward was both Jason and himself, however, he engaged in new exploits as well, thus adding interesting twists to the old legend. His final act in this parallel world was to fulfill the prophecy that "when Jason came again, he would be as a sword against Apollo in Hecate's hand." After relating his mind-boggling tale to Talbot, the men retire, but before the night is over Seward has once again answered the siren call of the voices from the "strange half-world of legend" and has returned to the "mist-shrouded" ship that will undoubtedly carry him to further epic adventures. In many ways *Circe* echoes the style and approach of A. Merritt in *The Ship of Ishtar*. Unlike Merritt, however, Kuttner attempts to explain much of what happens in his narrative through logic and science. Seward's space-time journey, for example, is supposedly made possible through "narco-synthesis" (i.e., "under a hypnotic the patient is forced to look back on his own crises, things buried in his unconscious mind . . ."), and both the Fleece and Apollo are explained away as "machines." Kuttner's attempts at explaining myth and the supernatural in scientific terms are fascinating but not entirely effective or convincing. Illustrated by Alicia Austin.

La Motte Fouqué, Baron de. *Undine.* London: Bell & Daldy, 1859. Westport, CT: Hyperion, 1978.
George MacDonald maintained that if he were asked what a faery tale was, he would reply: "Read *Undine*." Not that this is the only faery tale; rather, according to MacDonald, it is the most beautiful. It is indeed a beautiful tale, the love of a water sprite, Undine, for an undeserving knight, Huldbrand. The knight finds the creature in a secluded and mysterious forest, tended by her foster parents and protected by her real uncle, Kühleborn, a fearsome water wight. Undine, in effect, woos the knight and captures his affection, only to lose it when they return to his castle. Importantly, though, Huldbrand's love for Undine endows her with a soul, changing her from a thoughtless and carefree maiden to a responsible wife. MacDonald's own tale, "The Light Princess," may have been influenced by this one, for it has a similar transformation. *Undine* is a superb example of the German Märchen, relying as it does on archetypes and expressing an animistic view of nature. Undine and her relatives are presented as the inhabitants of nature and the causes of natural phenomena. Kühleborn, in particular, raises storms and swells streams. At one point, he shows Huldbrand a vision of

inner earth, disclosing all manner of gnomes and goblins. But MacDonald's observation on the tale's beauty should be the final word. The emotion of the work is tender without insipidity and the descriptions are charming without affectation. This *is* a beautiful work and is important as a representative of the German romantic school.

Langton, Jane. *The Diamond in the Window.* New York: Harper, 1962. New
    York: Trophy, 1973 (paper).

In *The Diamond in the Window,* Jane Langton shows that one can write a successful work of high fantasy using a specifically American heritage as basis. Her setting, which plays an important part in the book, is Concord, Massachusetts, some time in the first half of the twentieth century. Two children, Edward and Eleanor Hall, live with their Aunt Lily and her slightly crazed brother Fred in an old and rambling Victorian house on Walden Street. One day they discover an attic room, furnished for two children about their own age, with a large, stained-glass, keyhole-shaped window with an enormous diamond set in the middle. Their aunt, who had hoped they would never find this room, tells them that their other aunt and uncle, Ned and Nell, after whom they are named, had lived in the attic room until they suddenly disappeared some years before. Prince Krishna, who was visiting from India to study transcendentalism with Uncle Fred before he became crazed by Ned and Nell's disappearance, also vanished. Edward and Eleanor discover a series of riddles in a poem scratched into one of the facets of the keyhole-shaped window. The poem includes clues to nine treasures. The children move into the attic room, which, when light comes through the key-window at the proper angle, acts as a portal to various secondary worlds. The children enter these worlds as though in dreams, but they aren't dreams because one can get trapped in them, especially if one cannot solve the riddles; for each dream presents the children with one of the nine riddles from the poem. Here is where Langton is at her best. With unusual ingenuity and imagination, she employs quotations and events from the two great Concord transcendentalists, Emerson and Thoreau, and from another Concord writer, Louisa May Alcott, in several of the clues and treasures hinted at in the riddle-game verses. The rich creativity and fine style which Langton employs in these scenes make it difficult to describe them in synopsis form. These scenes, and the book as a whole, operate on various literary, historical, and philosophical levels, and this is what makes *The Diamond in the Window* a unique and highly successful all-ages fantasy. Jane Langton has written two other books involving Edward and Eleanor and the magical games of Prince Krishna: *The Swing in the Summerhouse* (1967) and *The Astonishing Stereoscope* (1971). Both are fine books of all-ages fantasy, but though they contain some scenes of magic as good as any in the first book, they do not sustain the high level of literary excellence and ingenuity that *The Diamond in the Window* does.

Laubenthal, Sanders Anne. *Excalibur.* New York: Ballantine, 1973 (paper).
Excalibur is one of the increasing number of works of high fantasy written
in recent years that draws its inspiration and material from Arthurian legend.
With the appearance of this novel, Laubenthal deservedly joins the ranks of
Arthurian fantasists such as Charles Williams, C. S. Lewis, T. H. White,
Mary Stewart, and most recently Vera Chapman. *Excalibur* is not a retelling of any particular Arthurian source, but rather an extrapolation from
most of the best known ones (most prominently from the *Morte d'Arthur*
and the *Mabinogion*). Laubenthal clearly is indebted to C. S. Lewis and
still more to Charles Williams, a debt she readily acknowledges (see Lin
Carter's introduction). She borrows the idea of an unbroken succession of
Pendragons from Lewis *(That Hideous Strength);* from Williams she also
borrows the notion of transference, or the voluntary acceptance by one individual of another's burden. To this richness of sources and teachers, Laubenthal brings her own considerable talents. Her unique contribution to the
expanding Arthurian map is to bring both the Grail and Excalibur to Mobile,
Alabama, in the mid-twentieth century. To accomplish this extraordinary
improbability, she draws upon the legend of the twelfth-century voyage of
the Welshman Madoc (a possible descendant of Arthur) to the New World,
specifically to the Gulf Coast. And Madoc brought the Arthurian treasures
with him. Thus the stage is set for another encounter between good and evil,
or Logres and Britain, as Laubenthal (after Lewis and Williams) designates
it. But Laubenthal is too original and too good a writer to use the legendary
materials simply as stage sets for a battle. She continues extrapolating and
interpreting, and, in fact, contributing to the myth. Her portrait of Morgan
Le Fay as an ambivalent but ultimately heroic character is one convincing
example. The entire work elicits the reader's admiration and arouses the
sense of wonder, but the slow-motion climax accomplishes these feats best.
This is one of those books that expands the imagination and leaves the
reader breathless but delighted from the effort.

Lee, Tanith. *The Winter Players.* New York: St. Martin, 1976.
In this first-rate high fantasy novella, Oaive, 17-year-old priestess of the
House of the Bone, is visited by a mysterious young man with wolflike features who calls himself Grey. When Oaive refuses to grant his request for a
fragment of bone, one of the shrine's three miraculous relics, he steals it.
She pursues him, and during the first of a number of confrontations, he
reveals his true name (Cyrdin), and cryptically states that she is now a part
of a "strange game" in which there is a "third player also." From this point
on the quest alters for Oaive. Cyrdin "become[s] the quest, and the Relic
of Bone merely a symbol." What game is she involved in? Who is Cyrdin,
and why has he entrusted her with his true name? Who is the mysterious third
player? All these questions are soon answered by the third player himself—
the evil priest-lord, Niwus, who "cursed" Cyrdin's entire family, turning

them into wolves, and has used the young man as a pawn in his quest to gain control of the magical relic. The game now becomes deadlier, but Niwus is finally destroyed, and after some intriguing space/time journeys Cyrdin and Oaive begin a new life together. This is one of Lee's finest fantasies: the narrative is smooth, unified, and energetic; the characters are memorable and richly delineated; and the prose style is as sleek as the coat of a well-groomed cat. *Players* is brief but substantive. The reader discovers, along with Oaive, that the real wellsprings of power and wisdom reside in one's own heart and soul, and that only after the acquisition of self-trust and confidence can these wellsprings be tapped.

Lee, Tanith. *Companions on the Road.* New York: St. Martin, 1977. New
    York: Bantam, 1979 (paper).
This is a powerful and substantive high fantasy novella. On the eve of the battle of Avillis a young soldier, Lukon, asks the protagonist, Havor of Taon, to deliver his modest savings to his family if he should die in combat. Avillis is taken, and Lukon is, indeed, killed in battle. Havor is about to set out on his promised mission when Kachil, a "snatchpurse," shows him and a roguish fellow soldier, Feluce, a secret chamber where the evil Lord of Avillis, his son, and his daughter (all killed in the siege) once "conjured up the powers of the Dark, and made their offerings to hell." There they find an exquisite jewel-encrusted golden chalice—the fabled Cup of Avillis. After making an oath to split the prize evenly, the three set off with it. They soon discover that they are being pursued by three "undead" (the hellish Avillis trio mentioned above), and first Kachil and then Feluce are mysteriously murdered in their sleep. Havor knows he is destined to become the next "dream" victim, so he tries to ward off sleep with a herbalist's potion. The potion helps for awhile, but he is finally too exhausted to do battle with the powers of darkness. All seems lost, but Silsi, Lukon's sister, helps save him. The conclusion shows him rid of the chalice and the fearful undead and beginning a new life with Silsi. This is a polished and thoughtful work that contains some of the most intriguing and effective surrealistic dream sequences in contemporary fantasy. Especially memorable is Feluce's fatal dream, in which a beautiful young woman with skin as "pale and smooth as vellum" first entices him and then—in her true horrific form—drowns him in a pool of water. This is a carefully cut and polished fantasy gem that deserves more attention than it has received.

Lee, Tanith. *Volkhavaar.* New York: DAW, 1977 (paper).
One of the hallmarks of a high-quality work of fantasy is its ability to evoke in the reader a sense of "awe and wonder." *Volkhavaar* bears this hallmark. Lee's fast-moving, colorful novel focuses upon four characters: Shaina, a proud and beautiful young slave girl who finally breaks free from her bondage and becomes a sorceress; Barbayat, a witch who teaches Shaina the craft

of sorcery and becomes like a mother to her; Kernik Volk Volkhavaar, "Master of Illusion, Shape-Changer, Deceiver of Minds," who achieves great power as a disciple of the black god Takerna, but loses all of it when Shaina challenges his evil magic with love and goodness; and Dasyel Parvelson, a handsome young actor with whom Shaina falls in love. All of these characters, but especially Shaina and Volkhavaar, are more carefully delineated than the personae of most fantasy novels. Few fantasy works are as permeated with magic and witchcraft as is *Volkhavaar*. Especially impressive and memorable are those passages describing Volkhavaar's illusions. Those he creates at the Arkev Spring Fair, for example, are spectacular indeed. Lee is undoubtedly one of the most promising young fantasy writers on the contemporary scene. Although her sword and sinew novels are better than average, her real talent shows through in high fantasy works such as *Companions on the Road, The Winter Players,* and *Volkhavaar*.

Lee, Tanith. *East of Midnight.* New York: St. Martin, 1978.
This fascinating myth-based novel gives further proof of Lee's considerable talent as a writer of high fantasy. The focus of the narrative is on Dekteon, a proud and fiery young slave. After discovering that his master, Lord Fren, plans to send him to the copper mines—a virtual death sentence—Dekteon makes his escape. With Fren's search party in hot pursuit, the runaway hides under a granite slab that forms part of a mysterious circle of stones. His real adventures—and the real complications of the narrative—begin here. Although quite ordinary in appearance, the hole beneath the slab is actually a Vortex Gate (a bridge between parallel worlds) created by Zaister, Dekteon's "twin," a kind of Sun King who lives in an exotic and highly superstitious parallel world—a world ruled by women. Zaister is the consort of Izvire, the woman-king, the Daughter of Night, and like all consorts before him he is destined to die after completing his five-year reign. It is this knowledge of impending ritual death (the Sun King is killed "in order that the sun remain ever young and vital"), and his knowledge—acquired through sorcery—that his twin exists in a parallel world, that prompt him to create the Vortex Gate. In essence, it is a trap to capture an unwitting, look-alike scapegoat (Dekteon) who will live out the Sun King's reign and die in his place. The bulk of the novel recounts the adventures of the two men as they try to cope with the challenges of their new worlds: Dekteon has taken Zaister's place, and Zaister Dekteon's. Dekteon, using the potent sorcery Zaister used to effect the initial role switch, finally succeeds in re-reversing their roles. The conclusion is a happy one; Zaister is reunited with Izvire and his daughter Versain, and Dekteon begins a new life as a free man. Although fairly short, Lee's novel exhibits a number of interesting characters and concepts; especially intriguing is the depiction of a female-oriented and female-ruled society. Also worthy of mention are the Pallids—white, hairless androids—who act as servants to the royalty of Zaister's world. Lee's

Companions on the Road and *Winter Players* may contain descriptive passages more evocative and rich in imagery than those in *Midnight,* but the reader will not be disappointed with the vivid descriptions of the world ruled by the Moon Priestesses. Perhaps the novel's most distinctive feature is its fast pace; Lee ushers the reader from Zaister's world to Dekteon's, and to the shadow world in between, with a deft and confident hand. Also deftly handled is the multiple point of view; Lee's technique of switching perspectives (the reader sees both through Dekteon's and Zaister's eyes) provides interesting and illuminating insights into both characters and the worlds they inhabit. Readers familiar with Philip Jose Farmer's *Flesh* will see interesting parallels between it and *East of Midnight.*

Le Guin, Ursula K. *A Wizard of Earthsea.* Berkeley: Parnassus, 1968. New
    York: Bantam, 1975 (paper).
The first book of the popular and critically acclaimed Earthsea trilogy (see also *The Tombs of Atuan* and *The Farthest Shore*) is set in Earthsea, a secondary world of countless islands and vast oceans. It recounts the early life of a "man called Sparrowhawk, who in his day became both dragonlord and Archmage." Born in the lonely village of Ten Alders, Sparrowhawk comes under the tutelage of his dead mother's sister, who quickly teaches her adept pupil the rudimentary skills of magic. Perceiving his promise, Ogion, great Mage of Re Albi, gives Sparrowhawk his "real name," Ged, and then takes him on as apprentice. Ged serves well, and at Ogion's suggestion departs for Roke Island, "where all high arts are taught." Ged studies at Roke for five years, excels in the magical arts, and departs a bona fide wizard. He leaves the island, however, with an uninvited guest, a dread Shadow that attached itself to Ged when he engaged in a foolish and forbidden duel in sorcery. It is Ged's quest for the meaning of this fearsome Shadow that generates most of the action in the remainder of the novel. After a soul-wrenching struggle Ged frees himself and becomes a whole man when he recognizes, and names, "the shadow of his death with his own name." Although some works of fantasy exhibit rather shallow character delineation, such is not the case with *Wizard.* Ged's delineation is rich and deep, and the reader is readily able to identify and empathize with him. This novel is entertaining and suspenseful, but above all it is a substantive psychological and philosophical work that explores the realm of magic, human responsibility, self-identity, and the concepts of balance and equilibrium. Like Ged, the reader leaves the work convinced that "you must not change one thing, one pebble, one grain of sand, until you know what good and evil will follow on that act." Winner of the *Boston Globe-Horn Book* award for juvenile fiction. Also an American Library Association Notable Children's Book and chosen for inclusion on the *Horn Book* Honor List. Drawings by Ruth Robbins.

Le Guin, Ursula K. *The Tombs of Atuan.* New York: Atheneum, 1971. New York: Bantam, 1975 (paper).

This fine work of high fantasy, the second volume of the Earthsea trilogy, reintroduces Ged, the protagonist of *A Wizard of Earthsea,* but the central character is really Tenar, a courageous and determined young woman of Atuan. Taken from her parents at a tender age by the priestesses of Atuan, Tenar's life is dedicated to the service of the Powers of the Earth. The early chapters trace her arduous training in the rites of this religious cult. At the age of six she is renamed Arah, the Eaten One, and by the time she is 15 she has "come into her full powers as the One Priestess of the Tombs of Atuan, highest of all high priestesses of the Kargad Lands, one whom not even the Godking himself might command." One day, while making her way through her dark domain, the complex Labyrinth, she discovers an intruder and traps him. The intruder is our old friend Ged, in search of the Amulet of Erreth-Akbe, a charm of great power. At first Tenar is both repelled and attracted by the young wizard, but finally a kind of mutual sympathy and understanding grows between them, and with the aid of the Ring of Erreth-Akbe they escape the religious complex and make their way to Havnor where a new life of freedom awaits Tenar. As in most of Le Guin's works the mythic foundations of *Tombs* are rich and substantive. Above all, though, this is a work about the quest for self-identity. For this reason it is a fine complement to *Wizard.* In that work the reader witnesses the painful maturation of the male protagonist, Ged; in this novel we see the female protagonist undergo the same process. Le Guin handles these explorations of the growth of the human personality with sensitivity and understanding. The combination of rich thematic import, sound character delineation, and strong narrative structure has put the novel on the *Horn Book* Honor List and has made it an American Library Association Notable Children's Book and a Newbery Honor Book. Illustrated by Gail Garraty.

Le Guin, Ursula K. *The Farthest Shore.* New York: Atheneum, 1972. New York: Bantam, 1975 (paper).

This is the final and perhaps most powerful and substantive book of the Earthsea trilogy. Ged is now in middle age and has attained the lofty position of Lord Archmage at the Isle of Roke; he is "the greatest wizard of all Earthsea" and "the only living Dragonlord." His mind is troubled, however, by persistent reports that throughout Earthsea "the springs of wizardry have run dry." Thus, when the Prince of Enlad sends his son Arren to him with an urgent request for aid and counsel, he decides that the time has now come for immediate action. Determined to get at the heart of the mystery, Ged asks Arren to accompany him on a quest to seek out the evil that is destroying the arts of wizardry. Disguised, they set out in Ged's fabled boat, *Lookfar,* and search far and wide throughout the island world of Earthsea before discovering the evil they seek in the form of Cob, one of the living dead and Lord of the Two Lands (i.e., life and death). Cob has found what no other man has—"the way back from death." He has "opened the door that had been shut since the beginning of time," and only after Ged succeeds in closing this portal between the world of the living and the world of the dead does balance and equilibrium return to the world. The quest is thus successfully completed, but only at the cost of all of Ged's strength and magical powers. The narrative concludes with his retirement to the land he loves most—the mountain isle of Gont. It would be unfortunate, however, to think of *Shore* as the story of one man, for in reality it is as much the story of Arren as of Ged. The young prince learns from the Archmage and from the trials of the quest; as he grows in strength, wisdom, and courage, he naturally fills the vacuum created by Ged's loss of power. Kalessin, the mighty dragon of Pendor, probably puts it best when he says, after flying Ged and Arren back to Roke, "I have brought the young king to his kingdom, and the old man to his home." As in the two preceding novels, Le Guin uses every opportunity to articulate the central themes of balance and equilibrium. However, the philosophical import does not become overbearing, precisely because Le Guin practices what she preaches: by deftly balancing theme and action, she gives her novel a stable structural equilibrium. The closing chapters of the novel describing Ged's and Arren's passage through the Dragonrun, with the resultant encounters with Orm Embar and the other awesome dragons, are perhaps the most exciting, action-packed segments to be found in contemporary fantasy. The National Book Award winner for Children's Books in 1973 and a Junior Literary Guild selection. Illustrated by Gail Garraty.

Le Guin, Ursula K. *The Wind's Twelve Quarters.* New York: Harper, 1975. New York: Bantam, 1976 (paper).
This is an excellent collection of Le Guin's short fiction, including science fiction and fantasy stories and what the author calls "psychomyths" (i.e., parables or allegories of the mind). Although all 17 stories are well worth reading, the fantasy enthusiast will be especially interested in "April in Paris," "Darkness Box," "The Word of Unbinding," and "The Rule of Names." As Le Guin explains in her headnote to "April," this is the first story she ever got paid for and the second story she ever published. Both "Unbinding" and "Names" are also important landmark works, representing Le Guin's first explorations of the secondary world of Earthsea. "Darkness Box" is a finely wrought tale of high fantasy that further exhibits Le Guin's remarkable ability to create memorable secondary worlds. In addition to the stories, this volume contains interesting headnotes that provide valuable information on both the genesis of the stories and their place in the author's literary career. Le Guin explains the intent of this collection in a brief foreword: "This collection is what painters call a retrospective; it gives a

roughly chronological survey of my short stories during the first ten years after I broke into print, belated but undaunted, at the age of thirty-two. They appear here very roughly in the order in which they were written, so that the development of the artist may become part of the interest of the book." The book accomplishes this, and provides the reader with some fine entertainment as well.

Leiber, Fritz. *Swords and Devjltry.* New York: Ace, 1970 (paper). Boston: Gregg, 1977.
In the author's foreword to this first of six (at present) volumes of stories about his two rogue-heroes, Leiber explains the writing and publication history of the Fafhrd and the Gray Mouser saga. He wrote the first tale in 1936 and has been adding episodes to the saga now for over forty years. In the late sixties Leiber was asked to collect the stories and arrange them for publication in book form. The 1977 Gregg Press hardback edition, in six volumes, contains 32 stories (ranging in length from a few pages to novelette size) and one full-length novel. Leiber is currently at work on Volume VII. He has done an excellent job of editing his work. In arranging his earlier stories, he has seen the advantage in writing new stories that deal with similar material in order to more closely join the existing tales to each other and to other new stories, and to provide more background on his heroes and other important characters. He has also arranged the stories according to their logical or internal chronology, rather than by publication or composition dates. As a consequence, the nultivolume saga has smooth coherence, consistency of characters, and a fine overall episodic unity. *Swords and Devilry* contains an "Induction" and three fairly long short stories. The "Induction" introduces the reader to Leiber's secondary world of Nehwon (nowhen), a world that is smaller than ours but possesses every possible sort of terrain suitable for adventure: mountains, seas, deserts, frozen wilds, and cities of all types, all roughly akin to our medieval ones. The first short story, "The Snow Women," introduces Fafhrd as an 18-year-old member of a barbarian tribe inhabiting the Cold Waste. This is the story of his initiation into manhood as he breaks his ties with his tribe and his domineering mother by ski-jumping over a deep, wide chasm, a feat that his father had attempted and failed. The reader learns important characteristics of Fafhrd, traits that he later develops: a love of wine, women, and adventure; a thirst for culture; an ability to chant poetry (he had trained as a skald); a good sense of humor; and a bearish sort of good nature. In the second short story, "The Unholy Grail," Leiber describes the coming of age of the young Gray Mouser, or Mouse as he was originally called. Having returned from a trip to find that his sorcerer-tutor has been murdered, Mouse turns to black magic through hatred and a desire for revenge. He had always been torn between black and white magic. Now, after gaining his revenge, though he relinquishes the practice of either kind of magic, he becomes the Gray

Mouser, morally in-between or largely amoral and cynical, but happily possessed of a wry sense of humor. "Ill Met in Lankhmar," the third story, brings Fafhrd and the Gray Mouser together in an alliance that will prove indissoluble. As described in the previous stories, the two are opposites in personality, but they are superior duellists, thieves, and adventurers—best described as Robin Hood types. *Swords and Deviltry* introduces the main ingredients of the recipe that remains constant, with endless savory variations, throughout the series. This recipe includes humor, eroticism, Gothic settings and macabre happenings, and of course much swordplay and magic. The literary merits include an excellent use of language for a variety of functions from puns to ghastly descriptions of death, and tightly knit plots with a good deal of suspense and foreshadowing. *Swords and Deviltry* manifests considerable thematic substance and in-depth character development, but these qualities are relatively rare in subsequent volumes.

Leiber, Fritz. *Two Sought Adventure.* New York: Gnome, 1957. Reprinted as *Swords against Death.* New York: Ace, 1970 (paper). Boston: Gregg, 1977.

In his foreword to Volume II of the Fafhrd and the Gray Mouser saga, Leiber explains that the stories were composed at various dates from 1940 ("The Jewels in the Forest" was the first Fafhrd-Gray Mouser story to be published) to the early seventies. Despite the different dates of composition of the stories, the volume has excellent coherence. As the title of this collection indicates, the unifying motif is death, and at least half the stories deal with the long-dead. However, the first story, "The Circle Curse," does not focus so much on death or the dead. It introduces Sheelba of the Eyeless Face (Sheel) and Ningauble of the Seven Eyes (Ning), the sorcerer-patrons of the Gray Mouser and Fafhrd respectively. Leiber includes this recent story to supply background and balance, since this volume concludes with two stories involving the sorcerers and their champions: "The Price of Pain Ease" and "Bazaar of the Bizarre." The seven stories in between include "The Jewels in the Forest," "Thieves' House," "The Bleak Shore," "The Howling Tower," "The Sunken Land," and "Claws from the Night." Most of these stories, especially the very early "Jewels in the Forest" (published in 1940 in *Unknown* magazine as "Two Sought Adventure"), are extremely Gothic and Lovecraftian, featuring creeping fungi, ghoulish odors, and oozing essences. The concluding tale, "Bazaar of the Bizarre," is perhaps the most memorable of the volume. It lightens the tone to one of considerable humor, even slapstick, and displays a complete bazaar of magics.

Leiber, Fritz. *Swords in the Mist.* New York: Ace, 1968 (paper). Boston: Gregg, 1977.

In the author's foreword to Volume III of the Fafhrd and the Gray Mouser saga, Leiber informs readers that "Adept's Gambit," included in this volume, was the first Fafhrd-Gray Mouser story to be written, though it wasn't published until 1947. The rest of the volume, Leiber says, contains three stories of 1960s vintage and two recent transitional pieces. The most interesting parts of the foreword are Leiber's discussion of his relationship to H. P. Lovecraft and an excerpt from one of Lovecraft's letters in which he comments favorably on "Adept's Gambit." Indeed, the lengthy (87 pages) "Adept's Gambit" is one of Leiber's most memorable pieces, demonstrating that his strongest form is the novelette. Since "Gambit" is set not in Nehwon but on earth during the Hellenic era, Leiber has written a transitional story, "The Wrong Branch," in which the author cleverly transports the heroes out of their own time and universe. "Gambit" itself is replete with humor, suspense, and an eerie black magic. It also employs the theme of surrendering one's will and independence in return for dark knowledge. Of the other four pieces in *Swords in the Mist,* "Their Mistress the Sea" is a transitional work, leading into the undersea adventure story "When the Sea-King's Away"; "The Cloud of Hate" opens the volume on the note of black magic, with a killing mist or cloud; and "Lean Times in Lankhmar," which has little to do with mist or with black magic, is a delightfully humorous tale about the gods *in* Lankhmar and the gods *of* Lankhmar, and how Fafhrd and the Gray Mouser serve them.

Leiber, Fritz. *Swords against Wizardry.* New York: Ace, 1968 (paper). Boston: Gregg, 1977.
This is Volume IV of the Fafhrd and the Gray Mouser saga. In his brief author's foreword, Leiber comments that the two heroes have been comrades now for 10 years, although he has been writing about them for more like 25. Apparently, Leiber does not want to make them middle-aged, and besides, who is to say that time in Nehwon is the same as it is in our world? The four stories in this volume date from the late sixties, and their connecting plot line suggests that the author consciously built one upon the other or that one episode suggested the next. "In the Witch's Tent" has Fafhrd and the Gray Mouser consulting a witch before embarking on a search for some fabled jewels atop a mountain. "Stardock" is the name of the next story and of the mountain they scale in search of the treasure. Only Fafhrd and the Gray Mouser could have the good fortune to be rescued from a frozen death by two presumably beautiful demigoddesses (they are invisible) with whom they go to bed—to insure the continuation of the royal line. They even get the jewels, but discover to their chagrin that in the light of day the jewels, like their mountain ladies, are invisible. The title of the next story, "The Two Best Thieves in Lankhmar," is ironic. Fafhrd and the Gray Mouser are conned out of the night jewels by two women thieves who have a market for just such unusual gems as the two former best thieves brought back from Stardock. Broke because of their loss of the jewels and without each other's knowledge, the two accept positions as bodyguards for two princes, brothers who are feuding over the successor to the kingdom of Quarmall. Thus begins the longest and most substantial story (ac-

tually a novelette) of the volume, "The Lords of Quarmall." Quarmall itself is unusual in being an underground kingdom divided into two levels, each ruled by one of the brother princes. Contests of wits and magic lead up to a startling and ghastly climax. This volume, particularly this last story, again exhibits the overall amoral tone of the saga. Fafhrd and the Mouser are a cut above most of the story's characters, though theirs is an instinctive and selective morality.

Leiber, Fritz. *The Swords of Lankhmar.* New York: Ace, 1968 (paper). Boston: Gregg, 1977.

In Volume V of the Fafhrd and the Gray Mouser saga, Leiber once again offers some interesting observations in the author's foreword, this time about his two heroes, and he makes some specific comparisons. Fafhrd and the Mouser are, he says, the opposite of Tolkien's heroes in being more nearly human—more like some of E. R. Eddison's ambivalent characters, but not so possessed by evil—rather more like Robin Hoods. The novel itself is excellent, demonstrating once again that the longer form is Leiber's forte. The book, though not divided as such, consists of two closely linked novelettes. In the first part, Fafhrd and the Mouser have hired out as guards on grain ships sent by the overlord of Lankhmar, Glipkerio Kistomerces, to an ally to insure Lankhmar's safety from sea invasion. Both heroes become enamored of the Demoiselle Hisvet, who is making the trip, and thus become blind to her sinister plot to destroy the grain fleet with her white rats. It turns out that she is part human, part rat, and that the rat underkingdom is planning to take over Lankhmar. Fafhrd and the Mouser finally realize what is happening, and with the help of Karl Trenkerz, a comical traveler from another time and universe (Karl speaks German), they thwart the rats' attempt to sink the fleet. In the second part Hisvet and her white rats, who have escaped from their failure with the grain fleet, stage a more direct attack on Lankhmar. They nearly succeed, but Mouser takes a magic potion that reduces his size and enables him to infiltrate the underground rat kingdom. Meanwhile, Fafhrd acquires a magic whistle that summons 13 great cats, and together they vanquish the rats. The novel is fascinating for a variety of reasons. The concept of rats becoming rational beings is repulsive, but presents a truly unique perspective on humankind. The vivid description of a race of ghouls whose flesh is transparent is effective, and presents a new dimension in eroticism (with which the book is filled) when Fafhrd makes love to a female ghoul. And Leiber's talent for developing plots with excellent foreshadowing and high suspense finds full play in this longer work.

Leiber, Fritz. *Swords and Ice Magic.* New York: Ace, 1977 (paper). Boston: Gregg, 1977.

This, Volume VI of the Fafhrd and Gray Mouser saga, is the first volume that contains no author's foreword, so one must assume that Leiber has

divulged all pertinent information in the forewords to the previous five volumes. All eight stories are from the seventies, the last having been composed in 1977. The first four stories concern Death's attempts to finally capture the aging Fafhrd and the Gray Mouser. These include "The Sadness
of the Executioner," "Beauty and the Beasts," "Trapped in Shadowland,"
and "The Bait." Fortunately, Death is unsuccessful, albeit unworried about
final victory. The fifth offering, "Under the Thumbs of the Gods," is one
of Leiber's most humorous tales. The gods, upset because Fafhrd and the
Mouser have forgotten them, decide to punish the ingrates by reintroduc-
ing them to all their former loves and then thwarting their aroused erotic
desires. This story thus recapitulates many of the previous tales, since the
heroes have led such active love lives. The conclusion presents a humorous,
ironic twist that satisfies all parties. The sixth story, "Trapped in the Sea of
Stars," finds Fafhrd and the Mouser sailing across the seas of Nehwon and
contemplating the cosmos in a rather new and philosophical vein. Having
thus examined the nature of the Nehwon universe, Leiber expands his
world of Nehwon by introducing a new island continent in the last two
stories, "The Frost Monstreme" and "Rime Isle," which together form a
fine novelette. In the first of these two stories Cif and Afreyt, two beautiful
inhabitants of the legendary Rime Isle, hire Fafhrd and the Mouser to engage two galleons of fighting men to help Rime Isle repulse an anticipated
invasion by Mingol fleets. The two heroes do so, and the second story describes the struggle between the Islanders and the Mingols. This second
story is perhaps the most ingenious and substantive of the entire saga. Cif
and Afreyt, the two females who hired Fafhrd and the Mouser, have each
found an outlander god on their shores. These turn out to be Loki and
Odin, both of whom have been forgotten in their own world. The Mouser,
inspired by the cunning Loki, and Fafhrd, allied with the farseeing Odin,
rally the Islanders to the defense against the invaders. But at the last minute both heroes, realizing that they are being controlled by unreasoning
and belligerent gods, stop the incipient carnage and chaos and effect a
peaceful settlement. This is a humane solution and a unique turn of events
in a type of fantasy popularly termed sword and sorcery. Readers may
sense here something of a new direction for Leiber and his monumental
saga, a shift that is also a deepening, that will fuel their anticipation for the
next promised episodes in the Fafhrd and the Gray Mouser saga.

Leiber, Fritz. *Our Lady of Darkness.* New York: Berkley, 1977 (paper).
"One of these days, some creditable arbiter with his wits about him is going
to realize that Leiber is a giant. Not just another talented fellow with a
pleasant manner and a willingness to take fannish awards for work done to
fannish standards. Not just another coterie hero, but a . . . figure of stature
in 20th century literature, never mind any smaller compass." Although
some might consider this assessment by Algis Budrys (*The Magazine of
Fantasy and Science Fiction,* Sept. 1978) a trifle hyperbolic, it is in essence

correct, and *Our Lady of Darkness* provides convincing evidence of Leiber's ability to create substantive and compelling Gothic fantasy. Set in modern San Francisco, this chilling novel describes Franz Westen's encounter with "Mater Tenebrarum—Our Lady of Darkness." In many ways it is reminiscent of "The Haunter of the Dark," the H. P. Lovecraft classic that is actually referred to in Leiber's narrative. Like Robert Blake of "Haunter," Westen first becomes aware of the presence of a malignant force through his fascination with a brooding city landmark. In Blake's case it is the "spectral hump" of Federal Hill; in Westen's it is the "humped spine" of Corona Heights. Both protagonists manage, through shrewd and dangerous detective work, to discover the identity of the evil presence; Blake, however, does not survive the experience, while Westen does, though barely. Perhaps the most remarkable aspect of Leiber's study in horror and suspense is his exploration of the fascinating realm of paramental phenomena and, in particular, his examination of Thibaut de Castries's "new science" of "Megapolisomancy." Noteworthy too is his vivid description of the final horrific confrontation between Westen and the Lady of Darkness, whose "thin, wide-shouldered body was . . . formed solely of shredded and tightly compacted paper. . . ." This is the surrealistic stuff from which recurrent nightmares are made. Fantasy buffs should be pleased and intrigued with all of Leiber's references to fellow Gothic fantasy authors, such as H. P. Lovecraft, M. R. James, L. Sprague de Camp, and especially Clark Ashton Smith, who actually plays an important role in the novel. This work was the recipient of the 1978 World Fantasy Award (Best Novel), and along with Piers Anthony's *Spell for Chameleon* and Andrew Offutt's *My Lord Barbarian*, received the British Fantasy Award for 1977. *Lady* first appeared in two installments in the January and February 1977 issues of *The Magazine of Fantasy and Science Fiction*. For more of Leiber's Gothic fantasy (mostly low Gothic) see *Night's Black Agents*, a collection containing 12 of his best horror stories.

Lewis, C[live] S[taples]. *Out of the Silent Planet.* London: Lane, 1938. New York: Collier, 1965 (paper).

The initial volume of the acclaimed Outer Space trilogy and a superior work of science fantasy, this is a tale of a journey to another planet and encounters with other races. To this extent Lewis owes (and admits) a debt to H. G. Wells, for there is much here that is reminiscent of him: pseudoscientific explanation, sociological concerns, and many more specific details. Yet Lewis uses the trappings of science fiction for his own purposes—moralistic fantasy. The aliens of the work are highly moral; indeed, one of them is an archangel. The work identifies moral hierarchy as the cause of social harmony. The four distinct races of Malacandra (Mars) live in social harmony because they willingly accept their places in a moral universe, not striving beyond their destinies. By contrast, the humans of the work appear distorted; they are ignorant of their moral freedoms and limitations. Weston, the scientist, is motivated by an inflated ethnocentricity; Devine, the entrepreneur, is simply greedy; and Ransom, the hero, must live through a palpable fear before gaining an understanding of moral order. Once Ransom arrives on Malacandra, he escapes from Weston and Devine and falls in with a group of hrossa, one of the races of the planet. He learns their ways, but more importantly he learns the truth of many myths, both Greek and Christian. Prepared by this knowledge, Ransom meets the intelligence that rules the planet—a fascinating combination of the Greek god Mars and Michael the Archangel. Ransom is offered sanctuary on Malacandra, but he recognizes the necessity of returning to earth. Lewis's presentation of the races of Malacandra is one of the high points of the work; the hrossa, the seroni, and the pfifltriggi all have their unique characteristics. Yet it is the eldila, the angelic, ethereal creatures, that define the atmosphere of the book. They are always present, lending the work a solemn cast; but it is the solemnity of joy rather than sorrow.

Lewis, C. S. *Perelandra.* London: Lane, 1943. New York: Collier, 1968 (paper).

Volume II of the Outer Space trilogy can be readily understood without *Out of the Silent Planet.* The two books are strikingly different: the second one does not resemble science fantasy at all, ignoring scientific mythology in favor of spiritual, and presenting morality as a matter of will rather than order. Ransom is literally spirited to a second planet, Perelandra (Venus), where he discovers an Edenic world of untouched beauty. Its only apparent inhabitant is the Green Lady, who is remarkable in her simplicity and innocence. Weston arrives in his spaceship, but he is a man possessed—a means for the Evil One to enter into this paradise. The Un-man seeks to lead the Lady away from Maleldil much as Satan sought to lead Eve, but the situation is different. Ransom is present, and as a representative of redeemed humanity, he engages the Un-man in debate, and finally in mortal combat. A world is saved, and yet this is primarily the story of one man's responsibility and struggle. Ransom's actions are heroic, but in an unusual sense. He battles a horrible enemy, but his most important weapon is not his strength or courage; it is his unflagging will. The power of the work has much to do with the contrast between Ransom and the Un-man—between thoughtful morality and benighted immorality. Nevertheless, there is much here that is simply beautiful. The early descriptions of Perelandra, with its golden sky and floating islands, are among the very best first impressions of an otherworld in fantasy. The final scene, an apocalyptic vision, is less tactile but stunning anyway. The work discusses free will, femininity and masculinity, vanity, cruelty, and a host of other significant issues. Each of these is woven successfully into the fabric of the action, presenting a work of religious fantasy that is unparalleled in its scope and poignancy.

Lewis, C. S. *That Hideous Strength: A Modern Fairy-Tale for Grown-Ups.*
London: Lane, 1945. New York: Collier, 1968 (paper).

Where the other two works of the Outer Space trilogy are set on distant
planets, the setting here is twentieth-century England. Ransom has returned
from his travels, wounded but unaging, and quietly prepares for the on-
slaught of the Dark Archon. The effects of this Enemy can be seen in humanity's technological advances, which are merely a facade for creeping
immorality and dehumanization. On the surface this technology has the
appearance of "progress," represented by the National Institute of Co-
ordinated Experiments (N.I.C.E.). Ransom's task is to serve as a bulwark
against the Enemy, and since N.I.C.E. has gone beyond the bounds of morality, to strike when the opportunity is available. The opportunity comes
when the ancient magician of Bracton Wood, Merlin, wakens from a cen-
turies-old trance and is infused with the power of angels. Merlin's intervention confounds the servants of the Enemy, reestablishing the balance between good and evil and confirming again the heavenly promise that
humanity shall not be abandoned. The fantasy here is primarily mythological and theological, alluding to Arthurian, Greek, and Christian sources.
Lewis reanimates these accounts by combining and synthesizing them.
Christian providence is manifested in angels that are reminiscent of Greek
gods. Merlin confronts the servants of darkness, but he does so at the direction of the angels. Working with (and against) these vast powers are some
very human characters whose presence adds another dimension to the tale.
Christian mythology is realized in human action and ancient tales are lent
a new significance. The reader becomes aware that these tales—sacred and
profane—carry very basic truths. Characterization is excellent throughout
the book, but the figure of Merlin is a master stroke. His meetings with
Ransom, although they are primarily in dialogue form, lend depth to the
entire work. His recognition that he will be consumed by the powers he
wields is both noble and awesome.

Lewis, C. S. *The Lion, the Witch and the Wardrobe.* London: Bles, 1950.
New York: Collier, 1970 (paper).

This is the first of the seven volumes of the remarkably popular and critically acclaimed Chronicles of Narnia. Because of the dangers posed by
World War II air raids, the four Pevensie children—Peter, Susan, Edmund,
and Lucy—are sent away from their London home to the sprawling country
house of Professor Digory Kirke. While exploring its ancient rooms Lucy
discovers that an old walk-in wardrobe is actually a magic portal leading to
another world called Narnia. On her first visit to Narnia she befriends Tum-
nus the Faun, who reveals that his country is an unhappy place indeed, since
Jadis the White Witch "has got all Narnia under her thumb," and "it's she
that makes it always winter . . . and never Christmas." Lucy returns to Earth
and tries to convince the others that Narnia exists, but they don't believe

her. To complicate matters, Edmund accidentally passes through the portal, falls under the spell of Jadis, and returns with all sorts of ambitious thoughts about becoming king of Narnia. Finally, all four children make the trip to Narnia together and ultimately become key figures in the conflict between Jadis (with her horrible crew of Ghouls, Boggles, Ogres, Minotaurs, and Hags) and Aslan the Great Lion, leader of the forces of good. Edmund, with Aslan's help, finally frees himself from the witch's spell. Since he has been a "traitor," however, the old laws of Deep Magic give Jadis the right to take his life. Aslan sadly agrees that her claim is legitimate, and offers his own life in place of Edmund's. Jadis gleefully accepts the substitution and the noble lion is sacrificed on the Stone Table. Aslan, however, miraculously comes back to life, destroys the White Witch, restores life to all the creatures Jadis had turned into stone during her cruel reign, and crowns the Pevensie children kings and queens of Narnia. They govern Narnia long and well before they return to the primary world where, miraculously, only a few minutes have elapsed. This is a powerful novel that contains some of the most poignant and moving episodes in contemporary fantasy. Especially memorable are the descriptions of the return of spring to Narnia and the death and resurrection of Aslan. Like most high-quality fiction, *Lion* offers the reader more than one level of meaning. It is certainly a good, well-told adventure story, and can be read as such, but it is much more. Lewis, unlike his friend and fellow fantasist Tolkien, was perfectly at ease writing fantasy that made explicit use of Christian myth and doctrine, and he infused *Lion* with plenty of both. The parallels between Aslan and Christ and the Emperor-Beyond-the-Sea and God are only two examples of the many Christian references that appear in the novel. It is this Christian dimension that gives the narrative a depth and substance that make it unique. Although each of the chronicles stands separately (they can be read in any order), this initial volume does introduce material that is very important to the other books in the series. Father Christmas's gifts to Peter (a sword and shield), Susan ("a quiver full of arrows and a little ivory horn"), and Lucy (a dagger and a cordial with healing powers), for example, play significant roles in subsequent novels. Perhaps most important, though, is Lewis's careful delineation of Aslan and his deft handling of the novel's Christian construct. Pictures adapted from illustrations by Pauline Baynes.

Lewis, C. S. *Prince Caspian.* London: Bles, 1951. New York: Collier, 1970 (paper).
Book II in the Chronicles of Narnia begins as the four Pevensies are sitting in a railway station, gloomily awaiting their school-bound trains. Suddenly they experience a "frightful pulling" sensation—something, or someone, is calling them back to Narnia. They return and find that Cair Paravel is now in ruins. Although only a year of Earth time has transpired since their last visit to Narnia, hundreds of years of Narnian time have passed, and

they soon learn from a conversation with Trumpkin the Dwarf that their reign during the Golden Age of Narnia is now discredited as mere make-believe by all except the Old Narnians. Trumpkin also reveals that a struggle for control of Narnia is now taking place between King Miraz (the usurping Telmarine who refuses to believe in, or talk about, Aslan and a "time when animals could talk") and his nephew, Prince Caspian (the legal heir to the throne, who longs for a return to the Golden Age). The Pevensies (and later on Aslan) enter the struggle on the side of Caspian and his Old Narnians (it was Caspian's signal on Susan's magic horn that had pulled the children into Narnia), and after many battles, including a dramatic hand-to-hand combat between Peter and Miraz, Caspian's forces achieve victory and he takes his rightful place as king of Narnia. The Pevensies return to their own world with the sad knowledge that only Edmund and Lucy can ever go back to Narnia, because Peter and Susan are getting too old. Although not quite as powerful and enthralling as the first volume, this book is still excellent fantasy. As in the first book, the highlights are the episodes involving Aslan, but also noteworthy are the comic scenes involving the gallant, swash-buckling mouse Reepicheep and the good-hearted but not overly intelligent giant Wimbleweather. Pictures adapted from illustrations by Pauline Baynes.

Lewis, C. S. *The Voyage of the "Dawn Treader."* London: Bles, 1952. New York: Collier, 1970 (paper).

In Book III of the Chronicles of Narnia, Edmund and Lucy Pevensie and their disagreeable cousin, Eustace Clarence Scrubb, are looking at a picture of a ship, when it suddenly comes to life. They rush toward it, momentarily stand on its frame, and then find themselves actually swimming beside the ship. After being hoisted aboard they discover that it is Caspian's ship, the *Dawn Treader,* and that he is on a quest to find seven Telmarine lords who disappeared after treacherous King Miraz sent them off to "explore the unknown Eastern Seas beyond the Lone Islands." Also on board is the Pevensies' old friend Reepicheep, who is on his own quest to determine the meaning of a seemingly prophetic verse: "Where sky and water meet,/ Where the waves grow sweet,/ Doubt not, Reepicheep,/ To find all you seek,/ There is the utter East." The three newcomers stay on for the voyage and after many amazing adventures (they are captured by slave traders, Eustace is turned into a dragon, a sea serpent attacks the ship, and they are nearly turned to gold) they account for all the missing lords. When the *Dawn Treader* finally reaches the end of the world, Caspian and his crew turn back, but Reepicheep enters "Aslan's country" and the Pevensies and Eustace return to Earth. The return is especially sad for Lucy and Edmund because they are told by Aslan that, like Peter and Susan, they are now too old to return to Narnia. This is in many respects the richest of the Narnia books. The *Odyssey*-like sea voyage is sprinkled not only with lively adventures, but with many exquisite descriptive passages (note especially those in chapter 15, "The Wonders of the Last Sea"). Lewis is a superb literary craftsman who does many things well, but he is especially successful in juxtaposing the serious and the comic. This he does beautifully through chapters 10 and 11, where we first witness Lucy's poignant and joyful reunion with Aslan, with all of its serious spiritual overtones, and then are treated to the hilarious antics of the unforgettable dufflepuds—those bouncy monopods who are constantly doing silly things like "planting boiled potatoes to save cooking when . . . dug up." Readers will also appreciate Lewis's perfectly marvelous delineation of Eustace Scrubb. Pictures adapted from illustrations by Pauline Baynes.

Lewis, C. S. *The Silver Chair*. London: Bles, 1953. New York: Collier, 1970 (paper).
This is Book IV of the Chronicles of Narnia. Depressed both by the gloomy autumn weather and the bullying they've encountered at school, Eustace Scrubb and Jill Pole attempt to gain passage into Narnia by calling Aslan's name. Although not immediately successful, they finally do gain entrance to Aslan's Mountain through a magical door in an old stone wall. Aslan gives Jill a task: she is to go in search of Prince Rilian, the long-lost son of King Caspian. Before the Great Lion literally "blows" Jill into Narnia (Eustace has already been conveyed there in this manner), he provides her with four Signs (instructions) by which she will be guided in her quest. Once in Narnia Jill and Eustace get some help and counsel from Glimfeather and his fellow owls (the Parliament of Owls episode is delightful), and then, with Puddleglum the Marsh-wiggle, they set out on their perilous mission. After a narrow escape from the Giants of Harfang, who planned to eat the trio at their autumn feast, the adventurers are once again taken captive—this time by the doleful Earthmen of Underworld. Their captors take them before a handsome young man who is under the enchantment of an evil sorceress, the Queen of the Deep Realm. Under the enchantment the young man's sanity and remembrance of the past return only at night, and each night the queen makes certain that he is bound to a silver chair so that no one can hear his anguished cries for help. Eustace, Jill, and Puddleglum do hear, however, and discover that the young man is none other than Rilian. Once freed, the prince destroys the silver chair and the wicked queen, and then with his rescuers escapes the Underworld via a tunnel the queen had ordered excavated for a surprise attack on Narnia. Rilian receives his father's blessing just before the old man dies. The final episode contains a poignant description of Caspian's resurrection (on Aslan's Mountain) and his joyful reunion with Eustace. One of the most delightful and interesting characters of Lewis's chronicles is Puddleglum, the eternal pessimist. His tendency always to find the worst in each situation might not seem funny, but under Lewis's witty and clever treatment Puddleglum's lines and actions become some of

the funniest in the cycle. The Underworld scenes, which are vividly described, will remind many readers of the Earldelving scenes in Garner's *The Weirdstone of Brisingamen,* although Garner's treatment is probably more detailed and horrific than Lewis's. Pictures adapted from illustrations by Pauline Baynes.

Lewis, C. S. *The Horse and His Boy.* London: Bles, 1954. New York: Collier, 1970 (paper).

Shasta is the hero of Book V of the Chronicles of Narnia, this "adventure that happened in Narnia and Calormen and the lands between, in the Golden Age when Peter was High King in Narnia and his brother and his two sisters were King and Queens under him." An orphan who leads a dull life with Arsheesh, an insensitive fisherman of Calormen, Shasta decides to run away after he discovers that a Tarkaan (great lord) plans to buy him and make him a slave. His escape is made good through the help of the Tarkaan's mount, a proud and conceited Narnian talking horse named Breehy-hinny-brinny-hoohy-hah, or Bree for short. On their way to Narnia they meet and join two other emigrés: Aravis, an aristocratic young girl whose father wants her to marry a wealthy but repulsive old man; and Hwin, another Narnian talking horse. Their journey nearly comes to an end in Tashbaan, the great Calormene city: Shasta is forced to join King Edmund, Queen Susan, and their party of Narnians for a time because he is mistaken for his look-alike, Prince Corin of Archenland; and Aravis is recognized by, and subsequently compelled to endure the hospitality of, her empty-headed friend, Lasaraleen. When the four companions are finally reunited outside the city gates they bring with them the terrible secret knowledge that Prince Rabadash (who has been jilted by Queen Susan) plans an attack on Archenland and Narnia as part of a plan to abduct Queen Susan. They race across the desert to warn the Archenlanders and Narnians, and with Aslan's help they succeed. This is Shasta's big day, for not only has he become a hero, but King Lune of Archenland has joyously claimed him as his long-lost son (the twin brother of Corin) and the next heir to the throne. *Horse* does not seem to fit into the cycle as smoothly as the other books. Calormen, with its distinctive Middle-Eastern flavor, seems more appropriate as a Dunsany backdrop than a Lewis setting, and King Edmund and Queen Susan seem out of place in Tashbaan and in the book as a whole. Furthermore, the narrative is not as sprightly and cohesive as most of the others, and there is not nearly as much good humor as in its companion volumes (the Lasaraleen episode is the main exception). The relationship between Shasta and Bree, however, is very nicely drawn. At first the excessively vain horse looks upon Shasta as an inferior ("the horse and his boy"), but as Shasta gains experience, poise, and courage, and as the horse begins to see his own shortcomings, the tables turn. Further adventures of the two would most probably have to be entitled "The Man and His Horse." Pictures adapted from illustrations by Pauline Baynes.

Lewis, C. S. *The Magician's Nephew.* London: Lane, 1955. New York: Collier, 1970 (paper).

Book VI in the Chronicles of Narnia is a key volume in the Narnian cycle not only because it "shows how all the comings and goings between our world and the land of Narnia first began," but also because it describes in an unforgettable manner the actual creation of Narnia by the Great Lion, Aslan. A prequel to the other six volumes, *Nephew* features young Digory Kirke (the old professor of Book I) and his neighbor Polly Plummer, who are given passage to a number of other worlds through the power of some magic rings constructed by Digory's Uncle Andrew. In one of these worlds the children awaken Queen Jadis (the White Witch of Book I) from an enchanted sleep. She follows them back to London where, as might be expected, she creates quite a stir. Once again with the aid of the magic rings, Digory and Polly whisk her from London into another world, but they also accidentally take along Uncle Andrew, a good-hearted London cabby named Frank, and his horse, Strawberry. This new world is an "empty land" until, before their very eyes, Aslan fills it with life—he creates Narnia. The rest of the novel is a loose retelling of the Book of Genesis, complete with a tree of knowledge and an evil tempter (Jadis). At the conclusion, Frank and his wife Nellie are left behind as king and queen of Narnia, and Digory, Polly, and Uncle Andrew return to Earth. Perhaps the most strongly Christian and Biblical of the chronicles, this poignant novel explains many of the references and events of the first five books, including the origin of the lamp-post that Lucy first sees when she gets to Narnia and the reason for the magical properties of the wardrobe in Professor Kirke's home. Furthermore, the reader can now comprehend why the old professor is so understanding and wise in his dealings with the Pevensie children in *The Lion, the Witch and the Wardrobe.* Pictures adapted from illustrations by Pauline Baynes.

Lewis, C. S. *The Last Battle.* London: Lane, 1956. New York: Collier, 1970 (paper).

The seventh and final book in the Chronicles of Narnia concerns Shift, a lazy and avaricious but clever ape, who dresses his docile friend Puzzle (a donkey) in a lionskin and then, using the specious argument that once everyone obeys them they will be able to "set everything right in Narnia," convinces him to pretend that he is the Great Lion, Aslan. Puzzle is uncomfortable with the plan, but he reluctantly agrees to go along with it. Little does he realize that he is becoming a major participant in an action that marks the beginning of the end for all Narnia. Oppression reigns as the power-hungry Shift calls in Rishda Tarkaan and his Calormene soldiers and gradually turns Narnia into a slave state. To make matters worse, many Narnians begin to lose faith in Aslan and what he stands for. King Tirian of Narnia, Eustace Scrubb, Jill Pole, and a small band of loyal Narnians wage a valiant struggle against the forces of tyranny, and in the end, with some unexpected help from

Tash the Calormene monster/god, Shift and Rishda are killed. The saving of Narnia, however, is not meant to be. Aslan has decided that it is time for Narnia to come to an end. Tirian, his loyal band of Narnians, and the "seven friends of Narnia" (Digory Kirke, Polly Plummer, Peter, Edmund and Lucy Pevensie—Susan no longer believes in Narnia—Eustace, and Jill) sadly witness the destruction of "old" Narnia, but their mood changes to one of joy when they discover that the "real" Narnia and the other "real" worlds (Plato's "shadow" principle) still exist. With jubilant cries of "Further up and further in!" they pass through "great golden gates" into a beautiful garden and there meet Reepicheep and many others of their "dead" friends and loved ones. "But for them it was only the beginning of the real story. All their life in this world and all their adventures in Narnia had only been the cover and title page: now at last they were beginning Chapter One of the Great Story, which no one on earth has read: which goes on forever: in which every chapter is better than the one before." With these lines *The Last Battle* and the Chronicles of Narnia end, and, since one of the most distinctive features of this magnificent cycle is the strong undercurrent of Christian doctrine with its convincing articulation of the theme of redemption through Christ, it is only appropriate that it should end on this joyously high note of eucatastrophe. Recipient in 1957 of the Carnegie medal for the best children's book published in the British Empire. Pictures adapted from illustrations by Pauline Baynes.

Lewis, C. S. *Till We Have Faces: A Myth Retold.* London: Bles, 1956. New York: Harcourt, 1957. Grand Rapids, MI: Eerdmans, 1964 (paper).

Lewis has sometimes been criticized for being too specifically Christian, or exclusively Christian, in his writings, both fiction and nonfiction. *Till We Have Faces,* an adaptation of the Cupid and Psyche myth, gives evidence of Lewis's broader religious sympathies. Lewis uses the ancient myth involving an invisible god–lover–husband to examine human frustration in attempting to understand or even believe in a god. Queen Orual of Glome, an Eastern kingdom in ancient times, is the writer–narrator of the book. It is her "Complaint Against the Gods" for the shabby treatment she has received from them. First, they made her so ugly that she constantly wears a veil. Then they stole her sister, Istra (Psyche in Greek), from her through their trickery and riddles. Part I concludes with a condemnation of the gods. In Part II, however, Orual updates her complaint, describing the visions she has had that have enabled her to truly understand herself and to realize why the gods remain hidden from us. They let us babble on and complain until we understand ourselves—that is, until we have faces. Then they show themselves. *Till We Have Faces* seems at first glimpse to be the rationalization of a myth. Actually, Lewis does this deliberately to put the readers off guard so that they enter into the story. Once he has them involved, Lewis reveals the true beauty as well as the tragedy of the myth. He most effectively describes the scene in which Psyche lights the lamp against the gods' commands, with such terrible consequences. The atmosphere of this book is markedly different from that of any of his other fiction works. *Till We Have Faces* is deeper, more philosophical, and more universal than any of his other books; yet it has memorable scenes of action as well, such as Queen Orual's duel for the throne.

Lindsay, David. *A Voyage to Arcturus.* London: Methuen, 1920. Boston: Gregg, 1977. New York: Ballantine, 1977 (paper).

A reading of Lindsay's *Voyage* calls to mind two other authors, Walter Pater and C. S. Lewis, though Lindsay is less accomplished than either of them. Walter Pater's novel *Marius the Epicurean* describes the religious and philosophical quest for meaning by Marius, a Roman in early Christian times who meets and questions representatives from every major religious and philosophical persuasion. This is similar to Maskull's quest in *Voyage,* except that Maskull's journey takes him to Tormance, a distant planet, and over its varied and unusual landscapes. But like Marius's quest, Maskull's ends on, at best, a note of ambivalence. C. S. Lewis's Outer Space trilogy, especially *Out of the Silent Planet* and *Perelandra,* suggests that Lewis drew upon Lindsay's model for his own space fantasies. One reads of such particulars as transportation on floating islands and lush landscapes of unearthly colors in Lewis, and recognizes their prototypes in Lindsay. The great difference between the two, of course, is that Lewis's universe has a definite hierarchy and attainable ethical and religious truths, while Lindsay's universe is singularly devoid of them. The structure of *Voyage* is that of a journey or quest and is actually quite simple, though it might not appear so to the reader, who listens to Maskull engaging the different beings he encounters in confused and confusing religio-philosophical discussions. Maskull, drawn by his own heart's desire for adventure, travels to Tormance, the planet satellite of the twin suns of Arcturus. Once there he journeys ever northward, keeping himself open to all experiences and ideas and in readiness to respond to some being or object in which he can put his faith. The succession of vividly described landscapes is the principal charm of the book. Scorched deserts, floating islands, precipitous mountains are dipped in the hitherto unknown colors of "ulfire" and "jale." Some of the unusual characters that Maskull encounters are also memorable. Leehallfae is a third sex—not a hermaphrodite, but a harmonious blending of male and female into something that differs from both. Lindsay cleverly constructs a complete pronoun declension for Leehallfae (ae, aer, aerself). *A Voyage to Arcturus* has numerous defects, yet the scenery and characters that inspired C. S. Lewis will captivate most readers.

Lindsay, David. *Devil's Tor.* London: Putnam, 1932. New York: Arno, 1978.

This work gives the lasting impression of being serious. Its sustained concern with the impact of the occult on individuals is combined with an attempt to see behind human mythologies; the effect is rather like reading a Charles Williams novel—written by Henry James. It is a difficult book, detailing rather than dramatizing the perceptions of the characters who are visited by the otherworld. The setting is modern England, yet as in Williams's works otherworldly occurrences challenge rational assumptions, stretching the boundaries of the primary world. A potent talisman, broken in the ancient past and fated to be rejoined in the present, is the focus of the work. Half of the talisman is retrieved from a tomb beneath Devil's Tor, while the other half travels from Tibet. The unknowing agents of the talisman are fated to participate in its rejoining, and the event irrevocably alters their views of the universe. The talisman is associated with absolute reality and calls forth the Ancient Mother—a deity who embodies the creative power of the Real. A man and a woman, Henry Saltfleet and Ingred Fleming, witness the rejoining and participate in its effects: they learn the mode of creation and recognize the paradigm in the details of the world about them. It is suggested that they are to begin a newly sensitized race. The work benefits from Lindsay's fascinating understanding of various mythologies—Nordic, Christian, Cretan, and Greek—and it presents a remarkable synthesis of them all. In fact, it presents Lindsay's own mythology, one that explains the others without explaining them away, expressing humanity's place as a participant in myth rather than a fabricator of it.

Linklater, Eric. *God Likes Them Plain.* London: Cape, 1935.
Linklater's fiction is quite popular in Great Britain, but very little attention has been paid to it on this side of the Atlantic. This is a sad situation indeed, since he is an absolutely superb prose stylist whose short stories and novels are not only delightfully entertaining but thematically substantive as well. An excellent sampler of Linklater's short fiction, *God Likes Them Plain* contains 16 selections: "The Dancers," "Thieves," "God Likes Them Plain," "Wineland," "The Duke," "Country-born," "The Crusader's Key," "The Prison of Cooch Parwanee," "Kind Kitty," "The Wrong Story," "The Abominable Imprecation," "Pathans," "The Redundant Miracle," "Mr. Timrod's Adventure," "The Revolution," and "His Majesty the Dentist." Although many of these stories contain fantastic elements, only four are pure fantasy—"Dancers," "God," "Kitty," and "Imprecation." These are of such high quality, however, that the volume is worth purchasing for them alone. Especially charming and unique is "Imprecation," which tells the story of Perigot, a handsome young musician, who, as a punishment for causing the death of a beautiful river-nymph, suffers the Curse of Shepherd Alken: "If you're a man, become a woman. If you're a woman, become a man." In his characteristically droll fashion, Linklater describes the embarrassing and frustrating events that befall the hapless Perigot once the curse takes effect, and how he finally neutralizes this "Abominable Imprecation." Perhaps Linklater's most distinctive trait is his delicious sense

of humor. At times it is sly and subtle; at times it is wild and capricious—but it is always effective. Linklater is addictive, so be prepared to devote some time to other of his works once you have sampled the literary fare of this fine collection.

Linklater, Eric. *A Spell for Old Bones.* London: Cape, 1949. New York: Arno, 1978.
This is a reprint of Linklater's 1949 novel in which he focuses on his favorite subjects, Scotland and history, in a witty, urbane, but ultimately serious work of fantasy. The story begins in Scotland "a little while before the Romans came." Two plots intertwine. One is the attractive but not overly romanticized love story of the clever, roguish poet Albyn and Princess Liss, wise daughter of the king of Galloway. The other is the comical but destructive conflict between two giants, Furbister and Od McGammon, tyrants who are envious and fearful of each other. Albyn is the central figure and, as court poet to Furbister and his ambassador to Od McGammon, links the contrasting plots of love and hate. The plots intersect in a magical climax. After the battle in which the giants and their armies totally annihilate each other, Liss restores Albyn to life with her tears. Albyn emerges from a two-day entombment in the earth, saying that he has composed three lines to a poem, a spell that will restore the dead of both armies (but not the giants) if he can only get the fourth line. Liss supplies the fourth line (which has to do with love), the scattered bones that had been picked clean by carrion reform and the armies return to life and to love. The story does not end here, however. The Romans are conquering Britain, and Albyn joins the conflict against the invader—he "never loved squares." It seems that while love can heal and govern, it is still vulnerable to aggression and must be defended. While Linklater's careful interweaving of plots is impressive, what principally sets the book apart is the style. Linklater is one of a few—George MacDonald and, more recently, Peter S. Beagle are others—who have the ability to successfully combine humor and high seriousness without one jarring the other. Another characteristic of Linklater's fantasy is the occasional erotic scene, which he depicts in a sensuous and lyrical fashion. Thus one of the book's most memorable scenes shows one of the giants, who cannot understand love, viewing Liss and Albyn lying in each other's arms. He wonders how they can form "a pattern so conformable to mutual desire, and pleasing to the aesthetic eye!"

Lovecraft, H[oward] P[hillips]. *The Dream-Quest of Unknown Kadath.* Buffalo, NY: Shroud, 1955. New York: Ballantine, 1976 (paper).
Underlying each of the tales in this collection are the notions that the waking world is mundane and that dreamworld visions are the stuff of excitement. The reader travels with the major protagonist, Randolph Carter, to realms that his imagination has conjured, finding beauty and horror, indescribable

splendors and nameless terrors. The title story of the volume, actually a novella, follows Carter's pursuit of Unknown Kadath, the ideal of his dreams. It is a city that he has dreamed of and lost; he attempts to find the Great Ones of his dreams in hope of regaining admission. His journey through Dream is filled with tortuous windings and the Gothic products of his imagination—ghouls and ghosts, faceless monsters and their ichorous spawn. But these are not only imagined, for at some point dream and waking are indistinguishable; in all six of the stories, dream and waking are both fully real. There is a good bit of Dunsany here—the dreamworld frame and a rolling, Biblical style. Yet Dunsany is less tempted by Gothic trappings. And Lovecraft certainly is tempted. We get little characterization and a great deal of detailed descriptions, much of it repellent and some laughable. But unlike many of Lovecraft's works, this is not simply low Gothic fantasy; the dreamworld becomes a full-fledged otherworld, and we submit to the laws of this world, however irrational. We accept the rules of Dream, learning to expect the unexpected and to tolerate the misshapen. If Lovecraft is a pulp fantasy writer, this is some of the very best of his pulp, a must for the fan of the bizarre. In addition to "Dream-Quest," this volume contains "Celephais," "The Silver Key," "Through the Gates of the Silver Key," "The White Ship," and "The Strange High House in the Mist."

Lupoff, Richard A. *Sword of the Demon.* New York: Harper, 1977. New York: Avon, 1978 (paper).

Fantasy literature has its fair share of look-alikes: novels that share certain common features, such as pseudomedieval settings, questing heroes, evil sorcerers, and gold-hoarding dragons. Lupoff enriches the genre with this refreshingly original fantasy creation. *Demon*'s primary plot line is typical enough: Kishimo (a kind of female samurai), Aizen (a demigod in league with the shikome, powerful demon warriors), the Miroku (the shape-shifting infant king, "bearer of salvation to the land of Tsunu"), and Okinu-nushi the Spirit Master undertake a quest to regain the land of Tsunu, a kingdom once ruled by the Miroku. Beyond this rather traditional quest motif, however, there are few similarities between *Demon* and the majority of high fantasy novels. To begin with, *Demon*'s setting is atypical. Although there are notable exceptions, the secondary worlds of most works of high fantasy are occidental or Middle Eastern in flavor and tradition. *Demon,* on the other hand, is distinctly Oriental in character—more specifically, Japanese. This is a world of samurai, geishas, *naga-suyari* spears, *kabuto* battle helmets, graceful wooden ships "with tall masts and slatted bamboo sails square-rigged to capture a following breeze," pastel lanterns, and hot saki. It is an exotic and sensual world characterized by highly ritualized actions and polite formality, but also by passion and violence; it haunts the reader's memory long after the book has been shelved. Also rather atypical is Lupoff's treatment of good and evil. The lines between the two are not so clearly drawn as in many other fantasies. Aizen, for example, is a highly ambivalent character. Although some of his actions are courageous and even admirable, his relationship with the horrible shikome and his selfish motivations and questionable intentions not only make it difficult to categorize him, but even to accurately assess our feelings toward him. Perhaps the most unusual aspect of *Demon* is its style. Using a poetic prose rich in imagery and evocative descriptions, Lupoff creates a series of surreal verbal color prints that sometimes assault and sometimes gently massage the senses. Although the reader is treated to a goodly number of exciting episodes—the horrific battle between the shikome and kappa ("the sea-sprites of infamous repute") on the mysterious Sea of Mists; the perilous journey through the "chill-water-dripping" Forest of Ice; the duel between Susano-wu (chamberlain of Ryujin the Dragon King of the Sea) and the fearful Lord Serpent of the river Hi—the exotic descriptions, and not the events themselves, are what most impress and ultimately remain with the reader. The extraordinary qualities of a book like *Sword of the Demon* cannot be adequately described or assessed in an annotation of this type. Only a reading will fully reveal the riches that lie within.

MacDonald, George. *Phantastes: A Faerie Romance for Men and Women.* London: Smith, Elder, 1858. Reprinted in *Phantastes and Lilith.* Grand Rapids, MI: Eerdmans, 1964 (paper).

In his introduction to *Phantastes,* C. S. Lewis claims that the work converted and baptized his imagination. It is a work of the most vivid imaginative power, serving as a—perhaps *the*—seminal work of modern fantasy. The tale presents an archetypal view of faeryland, where those who enter "must go on, and go through it." It is a nonrational world, occupied with animate trees and faery castles, a land where song is salvific and nearly everything is other than it seems. The traveler of the tale, Anodos, enters faërie through one of the most remarkable portals in all of fantasy, and his adventures lead him to an astonishing array of creatures and places. He meets Perceval and visits the House of the Four Doors (a series of portals within portals); he discovers his own shadow (perhaps the source for one of the central devices in the first volume of Le Guin's Earthsea trilogy), and he descends to the land of the goblins; he reads tales into which he enters and dies a faery death. Embedded in the accounts is one of MacDonald's finer pieces of short fantasy: one of the tales Anodos reads is the tale of Cosmo, which has been printed separately as "The Woman in the Mirror." Throughout his travels, Anodos is aware of the presence of forces that influence him and the world about him; a sort of pantheism pervades the work, a pantheism that asks us to believe in the grandeur of experience and the depth of living. MacDonald employs a richness of imagery that welds the senses and supports and broadens the thematic concern with the limitations of appearances. All the necessary qualities of high fantasy are here, many of them in nearly pure form: the secondary world, magic, adventure, inherent morality, even Tolkien's eucatastrophe, are present. MacDonald's place at the fountain-head of fantasy is not due solely to this work, but even if this were all that we had of him, it would assure him of a place among the great fantasists. His impact on Lewis is immeasurable (he is Lewis's guide through afterlife in *The Great Divorce*) and his influence on Carroll, Dunsany, Lindsay, Tolkien, Le Guin, and many, many more makes him a must for all readers of fantasy.

MacDonald, George. *At the Back of the North Wind.* London: Strahan, 1871. New York: Schocken, 1978 (paper).

The plot and setting of this novel are in some ways akin to those found in Charles Dickens's realistic novels of sentiment and social commentary on London life among the poor in the mid- to late nineteenth century. Little Diamond is a small boy living with his parents in rooms over a stable. His father is coachman to the wealthy Mr. Coleman, and life is rather pleasant. Mr. Coleman, however, becomes financially ruined and Diamond and his parents must exchange their view of a pleasant garden for one of a dirty courtyard, where Diamond's father works for a meager living as a cabman. Diamond is a winsome and courageous (albeit sickly) lad, and becomes a successful cabman though still very young. He has adventures with drunken cabmen, London policemen, and a little street sweeper, Nanny, who lives with Dirty Old Sal. He impresses the wealthy Mr. Raymond with his good-ness and his genius. Eventually, after Mr. Raymond is sure of his opinion of Diamond and his family, he asks Diamond to be a sort of page and Diamond's father to be his coachman in his beautiful country estate in Kent (which was originally built for Queen Elizabeth). All very Dickensian, from the vivid description of the London streets to the happy pastoral ending. Almost. The one huge difference is that shortly after the move to Kent, Diamond goes permanently to the back of the North Wind. MacDonald adds throughout his book a whole second dimension, call it dream vision, meta-physics or—most properly—faery tale, to the otherwise Dickensian story. This combination makes for a truly remarkable book. The character of the North Wind is both charming and philosophical-theological. The "back" of the North Wind is analogous to a paradise that must be gained through a combination of goodness, suffering, and faith. *At the Back of the North Wind* is a paradox in that MacDonald obviously wrote it for younger chil-dren, and yet it is more haunting and complex than his short faery tales or his Curdie books, which he wrote for older children and adults. At the same time, unlike the Curdie books, it suffers from too much detail and excessive direct moralizing. Nonetheless it will continue to be read by precocious children (like Diamond himself), and by other children when they are grown up enough to understand and more fully appreciate its achievements: the marvelous merging of the real and the supernatural (not in the formal religious sense); the numinous moments captured, such as Diamond's approach to the back of the North Wind; and the genuine insight into a cosmic plan that is beyond normal comprehension.

MacDonald, George. *The Princess and the Goblin.* London: [Strahan], 1872. New York: Puffin, 1964 (paper).

This, the first of MacDonald's two deservedly famous Curdie books, appeared in 1872 and continues today, over one hundred years later, to warm both children and adults. Many famous people have acknowledged the influence of these books, including C. S. Lewis, W. H. Auden, and J. R. R. Tolkien. Tolkien in fact didn't like faery tales as a youth, except for the Curdie books. One of the attractions of *The Princess and the Goblin* is that it completely absorbs the reader's attention. Contrary to what one might expect of a Victorian writer, the work is neither ponderous nor moralistic, but is filled with good humor and natural goodness that rise out of the story and characters. Eight-year-old Princess Irene is the unsuspecting object of a goblin plot, but she is aided by her own courage and by Curdie, the young miner who laughs at the goblins and wards them off with songs (they can't stand rhymes because they can't make them). Guiding and aiding both Irene and Curdie is the mysterious lady who lives in a forgotten part of the palace and calls herself Queen Irene, the great-great-grandmother of the princess. This lady is one of MacDonald's most wonderful characters; she is central to both Curdie books as a motivating and resuscitating force, a faery godmother indeed, but much closer to her mythical precursors than the traditional faery godmother. With her help and their own courage, Curdie and Irene thwart the selfish and evil designs of the goblins. Courage overcoming fear is the book's main theme. The narrator, who early in the book is too much of the grown-up speaking to children, fortunately lets the story tell itself for the most part. The style is cautious MacDonald—figurative but restrained, and somewhat simpler than in the second Curdie book. Still, there are flashes of the richer style, one of which is particularly memorable: Princess Irene, sitting with the bearded king on his horse, is described as sunlight shining through a gray cloud.

MacDonald, George. *The Princess and Curdie.* London: Chatto & Windus, 1883. New York: Puffin, 1966 (paper).

The second of the Curdie books, *The Princess and Curdie* was published in 1883, 11 years after *The Princess and the Goblin.* While both books are excellent for young and adult readers, *The Princess and Curdie* is, from a literary standpoint, the superior work. It also avoids the grown-up-speaking-to-child tone that occasionally grates on the reader in the earlier book. Without losing its appeal to children as well as adults, it is a more sophisticated book all round. Curdie, after the princess has left, has begun to lose his sense of wonder and is growing less and less humanly aware, and thus more and more animallike spiritually. This very Wordsworthian and Platonic theme is at the heart of the book. A Mysterious Lady, the princess's great-great-grandmother, in time pulls Curdie back from his growing callousness and purifies him in the fire of flaming roses. Not only does this marvelous fire burn away Curdie's dross, it also gives him the power to discern the inner hand or inner being of anyone with whom he shakes hands. Armed with this power and accompanied by a most unusual beast called Lina, Curdie travels through a wasteland to the royal city of Gwyntystorm and there helps Princess Irene to foil a plot against herself and the king. In this book, the Mysterious Lady is clearly the mother goddess of mythology, something only hinted at in the first Curdie book. The dialogue and descriptions are more typical MacDonald, less restrained, more in the high style, and rich in image and metaphor, not so simple as in *The Princess and the Goblin*. Words like "homeopathically" and others give most readers a moment's pause, whatever their ages. Pervading the book is an unmistakable note, at once sad and threatening, of humanity's spiritual forgetfulness. This note gives the ending an unusual twist. At the same time, the book contains MacDonald's irrepressible humor and some of the most memorable scenes and creatures in all of MacDonald's works. The best illustrations are those by Helen Stratton (Puffin Books).

MacDonald, George. *Lilith.* London: Chatto & Windus, 1895. Reprinted in *Phantastes and Lilith.* Grand Rapids, MI: Eerdmans, 1964 (paper).
Lilith is a superior work of theological fantasy. The moral and metaphysical journey of the major character, Mr. Vane, is both semi-allegorical and intensely literal. Led by the mystical Mr. Raven (who later turns out to be Adam), Vane leaves his comfortable library and, at first unwillingly, confronts his moral limitations and the paradoxes of metaphysics. Through his encounters he gains the spiritual fiber that allows him to accept himself and the mysteries of Being. The plot of the work is more associative than rational as Vane fades in and out of various states of dream and reality. He meets the delightful (though sometimes insipid) Little People; he observes the macabre dance of the Faceless Dead (perhaps the source for C. S. Lewis's *Till We Have Faces*); he passes through the Valley of Horrors. The central focus of the story is Vane's series of encounters with Lilith, the mythical first wife of Adam. Lilith, an early type of the witch-queen, personifies moral depravity in the guise of beauty. Vane must learn to look, first, beyond her beauty to her moral state; and later, even further to her intrinsic worth as a creature of God. Lilith, like Vane, discovers herself through the sustained intervention of Adam, Eve, and the sensitively portrayed Mara, the Lady of Sorrows. The strength of the work is the abandon with which it welds fantasy and theology, dream and reality, act and potency. Like MacDonald's other works, it had great impact on Lewis and David Lindsay, and the tough intellectualism here anticipates the works of Charles Williams.

MacDonald, George. *The Gifts of the Child Christ: Fairy Tales and Stories for the Childlike.* Ed. Glenn Edward Sadler. 2 vols. Grand Rapids, MI: Eerdmans, 1973 (paper).

Volume I contains 10 of MacDonald's finest stories and faery tales: "The Gifts of the Child Christ," "The History of Photogen and Nycteris," "The Shadows," "Little Daylight," "The Golden Key," "Cross Purposes," "The Wise Woman, or the Lost Princess: A Double Story," "The Castle: A Parable," "Port in a Storm," and "Papa's Story (A Scot's Christmas Story)." Perhaps the most popular of all these delightful MacDonald creations is "The Golden Key." Strongly informed with the author's distinct brand of Christian allegory, it is a poignant and moving account of Everyman's quest for spiritual meaning and fulfillment. Another tale worthy of special note is "Cross Purposes," which features the antics of Toadstool, one of the most delightfully capricious and uniquely molelike goblins of all faërie. Besides the stories, the reader will find an informative introductory essay by Glenn Edward Sadler and MacDonald's classic essay on the faery tale, "The Fantastic Imagination." Volume II contains two MacDonald poems— "The Girl That Lost Things" and "That Holy Thing"—and 10 faery tales and stories: "The Light Princess," "The Giant's Heart," "The Carasoyn," "The Gray Wolf," "The Cruel Painter," "The Broken Swords," "The Wow O' Rivven (The Bell)," "Uncle Cornelius, His Story," "The Butcher's Bills," and "Birth, Dreaming, Death (The Schoolmaster's Story)." Of all the stories contained in these two volumes there is probably none finer than "The Light Princess." Full of surprising events and clever contrivances, this exquisite tale of a princess who loses her "gravity" is one of the most charming and inventive short fantasy works of the nineteenth century. And as in most MacDonald creations, the reader can expect to find a good measure of the author's biting satire. Especially memorable are the episodes involving the two court Metaphysicals—Hum-Drum the Materialist and Kopy-Keck the Spiritualist. In his essay "The Fantastic Imagination," MacDonald writes: "For my part, I do not write for children, but for the childlike, whether of five, or fifty, or seventy-five." These two volumes are enthusiastically recommended for the "childlike" of all ages. Another good collection has been edited, with an introduction, by Roger Lancelyn Green: *The Complete Fairy Tales of George MacDonald* (New York: Schocken Books, 1977). Arthur Hughes's original woodcut illustrations are included in both the Sadler and Green editions.

McKillip, Patricia A. *The Throme of the Erril of Sherill.* New York: Atheneum, 1973.

The Cnite Caerles, in love with Damsen, the beautiful daughter of Magnus Thrall, King of Everywhere, asks for her hand in marriage; but the king, intent on possessing the Throme of the Erril of Sherill, refuses to grant permission until the Cnite succeeds in bringing to him that fabled epic of "singular and unsurpassed beauty." The determined Caerles sets out on his perilous quest, encountering along the way many strange and wonderful adventures. Since the Throme never existed, Caerles, of course, fails to meet the king's condition. But all is not lost, since genuine love has a way of overcoming even the most powerful obstacles. This brief but beautifully written story displays all the requisite ingredients of high fantasy: magical causality; a vividly described secondary world replete with a generous number of imposing figures; archetypal themes and motifs; and an elevated style. The last feature is perhaps the most remarkable. McKillip's use of evocative words and names (Mirk-Well of Morg, Dracoberus, Dolorous House of the dead Doleman) and exquisite imagery ("The Erle Merle was a tall, thin wraith of bones and pale skin and hair like the spun gossamer of spider's web") has rarely been equaled by other contemporary fantasists. Contains a number of fine illustrations by Julie Noonan.

McKillip, Patricia A. *The Forgotten Beasts of Eld.* New York: Atheneum, 1974. New York: Avon, 1975 (paper).

Patricia McKillip is among the most talented contemporary writers of high fantasy, as *The Forgotten Beasts of Eld* attests. As Tolkien has indicated, one of the great desires that fantasy satisfies is to communicate with creatures other than humans. Such communication and how it occurs are largely responsible for the attraction of this book. The young female wizard Sybel lives atop Eld Mountain with her magnificent beasts: Ter the Falcon, Cyrin the Boar, Moriah the Cat, Gules the Lion, the Black Swan of Tirlith, and Gyld the Dragon. These beasts have become but dim legends; Sybel's own existence is only a rumor to most people. She is content with her isolation, the animals she controls and with whom she communicates telepathically, and her search for the fabled White Bird named Liralen. The world of humans intrudes when Coren, a Lord of Sirle, brings her a baby to raise and protect in the aftermath of a battle disastrous to Sirle. Sybel, unacquainted with human emotions until then, raises the boy Tamlorn (who is actually the son of King Drede, who had defeated Sirle) for 12 happy years. Inevitably, Lords of Sirle and King Drede seek both Tamlorn and Sybel—Tamlorn because he is the rightful heir to Eldewold, Sybel because of her power. Sybel, though she falls in love with Coren of Sirle, resists becoming a pawn in a power struggle until Drede employs a wizard against her in a fearful manner. She then vows vengeance against Drede (the sort of vengeance that Coren had given up for love of her) even though she stands to lose the love of both Tamlorn and, even more painfully, of Coren (who she must manipulate to achieve her revenge). Only on the eve of battle does she abandon her plan, after a confrontation with the eerie, mysterious creature called the Blamoor. She abruptly relinquishes her passion for revenge, frees her beasts, and returns, emptied, to her mountain where she at last finds her deepest hope fulfilled when she discovers the nature of the Liralen. The plot is intricate, embracing the power struggle between the Lords of Sirle and King Drede, the personal conflict of Sybel, and her quest for the Liralen. Sybel, the wizard—Coren's "Ice-White Lady"—strongly engages our sympathies as she struggles between love and revenge. It is the Beasts of Eld themselves, however, that give the book its greatest power and originality. Readers familiar with Peter S. Beagle's *Last Unicorn* will recognize the central love-versus-fear motif, symbolized in both cases by legendary creatures who are, paradoxically, opposed to, yet dependent on, one another.

McKillip, Patricia A. *The Riddle-Master of Hed.* New York: Atheneum, 1976. New York: Del Rey, 1978 (paper).

This polished and substantive high fantasy novel recounts the quest of Morgon, Prince of Hed, to determine the significance of the three stars on his forehead (he is called the Star-Bearer) and to ascertain the nature of his destiny. Although Morgon is content leading the life of a farmer while ruling the small, peaceful land of Hed, fate seems to have other things in store for him. Complications begin to arise when he wins a riddle-game with the wraith of Peven, Lord of Aum, thereby unknowingly winning the hand of Raederle, daughter of the king of An. Accompanied by Deth, Harpist of the High One, Morgon sets out for An, but his ship is mysteriously wrecked. From this point on, Morgon finds himself pursued by an evil force, which manifests itself primarily in the form of dead shape changers that seem intent on taking his life. Believing that only the High One can now answer the serious questions he has about his obviously unique and special destiny, and about those who seem opposed to the fulfillment of that destiny, Star-Bearer slowly makes his way to Erlenstar Mountain, the High One's domain, encountering deadly opposition from the shape changers nearly every step of the way. He finally does reach Erlenstar, but discovers to his surprise and horror that the person who identifies himself as the High One is none other than Ghisteslwchlohm, founder of the school of wizards at Lungold, and a man of questionable actions and motives. *Riddle-Master* moves rather slowly at first while McKillip develops her characters and creates a detailed and believable secondary world, but the pace quickens in the second half of the novel when the focus is almost solely upon Morgon and his perilous journey to Erlenstar. Perhaps the most unique and memorable episode in the entire novel is Morgon's encounter and subsequent friendship with Har, the Wolf-King of Osterland. McKillip's descriptions of Har (in the form of a reindeer-like creature called a vesta) rescuing Morgon from a fierce blizzard, and Morgon's subsequent transformation into a vesta under the careful tutelage of Har, are brilliantly handled. The book contains a map of the secondary world (drawn by Kathy McKillip) and a very helpful glossary of people and places. *Riddle-Master* "is the first of three books about Morgon, Raederle, the world they live in and the end of an age."

McKillip, Patricia A. *Heir of Sea and Fire.* New York: Atheneum, 1977. New York: Del Rey, 1978 (paper).

In the second book in the projected Riddle-Master trilogy, a year has passed since Morgon, Prince of Hed (the Star-Bearer), disappeared on his journey to the High One. There have been reports of his death but no sure evidence to bear them out. This uncertainty, coupled with the mystery surrounding his disappearance, prompts Raederle (his bride-to-be), Lyra (the Morgol's daughter and land-heir), and Tristan (Morgon's young sister) to go in search of him. They discover that he is still alive after having barely survived a prolonged, nightmarish encounter with Ghisteslwchlohm (a Master-Riddler "dispensing justice in the name of the High One"), but all is not well, since he is still being pursued by the grisly shape changers. To complicate matters, Morgon is bent on tracking down and gaining revenge on Deth, the High One's harpist, who deceived and betrayed Morgon by failing to warn him about the real identity of the High One. Most of the complications remain unresolved at the end of this book (the reader will have to wait for the next installment), but at least Raederle and Morgon have been united and can now share the burden of the many riddles and problems that still remain unsolved. Whereas the focus in *Riddle-Master* was primarily upon Morgon and his search for identity and the nature of his destiny, this second volume primarily concerns itself with Raederle's gradual discovery of her identity and magical powers (she is the "Heir of Sea and Fire"). McKillip seems incapable of writing a poor novel, but *Heir* does not seem to possess the power and energy of some of her other works. Perhaps the fundamental problem here is that there is too much dialogue and description and not enough action. *Riddle-Master* gets off to a slow start, but gains good momentum about half-way through the narrative; *Heir*'s pace remains rather sluggish until the very last episode, which features the dramatic confrontation between the ghostly King Farr and Raederle. Despite the talkiness and slow pace, however, this novel will stand its ground against just about any other work of contemporary fantasy. McKillip is a rare talent: she knows how to create believable secondary worlds; she understands the nature of magic; she presents us with richly delineated and memorable characters; she invests her novels with substantive thematic import; and she has a smooth and polished writing style. Like the first book in the series, this edition contains Kathy McKillip's map of the Riddle-Master world and a glossary of people and places.

Martí-Ibáñez, Félix. *All the Wonders We Seek: Thirteen Tales of Surprise and Prodigy.* New York: Potter, 1963.

This is an absolutely delightful collection of fantasy stories containing "The Sleeping Bell," "The Star Hunt," "A Tomb in Malacor," "Niña Sol," "The Seekers of Dreams," "The Buried Paradise," "Between Two Dreams," "Amigo Heliotropo," "The Song without Words," "The Threshold of the

Door," "Havana: 60° Longitude West, 70° Latitude South," "Senhor Zumbeira's Leg," and "Riquiqui, I Love You!" All of the stories have Latin American settings, and draw heavily upon the myths, legends, and folklore of this exotic part of the world. "Niña Sol," for example, tells the poignant tale of a painter of landscapes who is irresistibly attracted to a mysterious Sun Girl straight out of Quechuan myth; "The Sleeping Bell" features one of the "living golden Venuses of the Colombian jungle"; "Seekers of Dreams" proves the truth of the legend that "a colony of fairies" exists in the forest of Paraguay; and "Amigo Heliotropo" retells, in a charming and unforgettable fashion, the legend of San Miguel. Martí-Ibáñez seems to do most things well: his characters are carefully and believably delineated; his settings are described with an admirable authenticity; his plot lines are streamlined and fast-moving; and his style is polished and elegant. Especially noteworthy is his brilliant use of imagery, evident in this brief passage from "Threshold": "The June air, with fingers as soft as perfumed silk, caressed my cheeks. The narrow street, drenched in sun, glowed with the same golden yellow that came out of Van Gogh's passionate brush. I had the impression that the houses were cooking to a golden brown in the sun, like doughnuts in a frying pan." In short, this is a collection of fine fantasy stories that will compare favorably with the best of the past century and a half.

Mayne, William. *Earthfasts.* New York: Dutton, 1967.
The time setting for *Earthfasts* is the present day, but the place, rural England, is an area with flavorful names like Garebrough, Haw Bank, and High Keld, reminiscent of the past history, legendary and true, of the country. This past history starts to come magically alive when two teenage English boys observe a drummer boy, clad in an eighteenth-century uniform, emerge from a hillside holding a lighted candle in one hand and tapping on a drum with the other. In their concern for the young drummer (Nellie Jack John of nearby Low Eskeleth in Arkingathdale) the boys fail to notice the unusual nature of the candle, which they throw away. They have, after all, their flash-light instead. David and Keith go to considerable personal sacrifice to ease Nellie Jack John's shock. David, the more studious of the two, is in fact acquainted with the legend of a young drummer boy who in 1742 went under the local castle to search for the treasure of King Arthur who, again according to legend, rested there with his men until the time appointed for his return. They fail to orient Nellie Jack John to the twentieth century, and he reenters the hillside and disappears. After this the boys suddenly remember the burning candle. They find it and it is still lighted—in fact it can't be extinguished, at least not in this world. Now all sorts of phenomena occur. Stone monoliths turn into giants; boggarts start exercising their mischief; and David disappears suddenly. Keith begins to have visions that turn out to be real and rather threatening, until he learns that the candle must be returned to whence it had been mistakenly brought—back under the

castle where it will mark the passage of time until the king returns. The book contains a number of memorable scenes, but perhaps none is more delightful than the inquest following David's disappearance, at which various characters attest to the activities of the boggart, much to the magistrate's discomfort. The characterization of the two boys presents a nice contrast between the more venturesome David, who is a budding scientist, and the steady, patient Keith, who is the follower until thrust into another role. The book concludes that not everything can be resolved scientifically, unless one is well intentioned, patient, and courageous.

Merritt, A[braham]. *The Ship of Ishtar.* New York: Putnam, 1926. Los Angeles: Borden, 1949.

One of Merritt's best and most popular novels, *The Ship of Ishtar* provides the reader with a heady mixture of romance, swashbuckling adventure, magic, and titillating eroticism. Couched in the author's inimitable brand of ornate poetic prose, this fantasy relates the fantastic exploits of John Kenton, an American scholar and adventurer who enters a secondary world through the magic of an ancient stone block that "Forsyth, the old archaeologist, had sent him from the sand shrouds of ages-dead Babylon." The vehicle for Kenton's journeys into this strange world is a miniature ship with toylike figures that he discovers when he breaks open the Babylonian relic. While on this Ship of Ishtar Kenton falls in love with Sharane, a beautiful princess/priestess of ancient Babylon, and then takes her side in the mortal struggle for the ship between her forces of love and life (i.e., those of Ishtar, Bestower of Life) and those of Nergal, Ruler of the Dead. With the help of their allies Gigi the drummer, Sigurd the Norseman, and Zubran the Persian, the lovers finally defeat the forces of death, but only at the cost of their own lives. This work is especially noteworthy for Merritt's deft and ingenious handling of Kenton's many passages from the primary world of his home in New York to the secondary world of the Ship of Ishtar. If the work has any faults they are the episodic nature of the narrative and the length of some of the descriptive passages. These are minor criticisms, however, and although some of Merritt's prose is a trifle purple, most of it is exquisitely beautiful, as evidenced by the memorable descriptions of Emakhtila, or Sorcerers' Isle, the sensuous "bubble women" of chapter 13, and the "golden isle" of chapter 10, of which the following is a partial description: "It was a sun yellow isle, high and rounded, and splashed with craters of color like nests of rainbows. Save for these pansied dapplings, the island curved all glowing topaz, from its base in the opalescent shallows of the azure sea to its crest, where feathered trees drooped branches like immense panaches of ostrich plumes dyed golden amber. Over and about the golden isle shot flashes of iridescences from what seemed luminous flying flowers."

Merritt, A. *The Fox Woman and Other Stories.* New York: Avon, 1949 (paper). New York: Arno, 1978.

This complete collection of stories and novelettes by one of America's finest contemporary fantasists contains "The Fox Woman" (a novelette), "The People of the Pit," "Through the Dragon Glass," "The Drone," "The Last Poet and the Robots," "Three Lines of Old French," "The White Road," "When Old Gods Wake," and "The Women of the Wood." Two of these selections, it should be noted, are fragments. As editor Wollheim explains: "When A. Merritt passed away in 1943, he left several unfinished projects on his desk. . . . It is believed that 'The White Road' was to have been a novel based on the theme of 'Through the Dragon Glass,' and 'When Old Gods Wake' . . . was to be a sequel to his novel *The Face in the Abyss*." Both fragments appear destined to have become opening chapters. Although each story in this collection can boast its own particular strengths ("Three Lines," for example, is as poignant a romance as you will find in this genre), the pièce de résistance is "The Women of the Wood." It is one of the author's most popular stories, and as Sam Moskowitz points out in *Explorers of the Infinite,* it is "the only story [Merritt] was completely satisfied with upon completion." A hauntingly beautiful story about the primeval conflict between humankind and nature, it displays a tightly woven narrative thread, evocative descriptions replete with an abundance of strong visual imagery, subtle characterization, believable dialogue, appropriate setting and atmosphere, and strong thematic import. These traits, by the way, are exhibited in most of Merritt's stories.

Mirrlees, Hope. *Lud-in-the-Mist.* London: Collins, 1926. New York: Del Rey, 1977 (paper).

Dorimare, a thriving seaport, is bordered by mountains to the north and east and by the sea to the south. To the west are the Debatable Hills, but no one goes there because beyond them lies Fairyland. The capital city is Lud-in-the-Mist, where a wealthy merchant class carries on a thriving, far-reaching trade, and, incidentally, rules the country. No excitement has disturbed the quiet industriousness of the Ludites since their forefathers overthrew the ruling monarch, Duke Aubrey, and got rid of his priests and churches (one inevitably thinks of the defeat of the monarchy at the hands of the Puritans in seventeenth-century England, a comparison that fits several other aspects of the novel as well). Nor is the proximity of Fairyland a challenge to the sober, even temper of Lud-in-the-Mist, at least not until someone begins to smuggle fairy fruit into the country, and Master Nathaniel Chanticleer, the mayor, sheepishly admits the inclination of his own fancy toward the mysterious Hills of the Elfin Marches. From this point on the book takes on the aspect of a good mystery story, with Master Chanticleer attempting to discover the smuggler's identity and actually discovering a great deal more. In several ways *Lud-in-the-Mist* resembles Lord Dunsany's fantasies about the otherworld, particularly *The King of Elfland's Daughter*. Like Dunsany, Mirrlees envisions faeries as ambivalent in their relationship to humanity. Faeries are older, more subtle creatures, who operate according to a different ethical code. Interestingly, however, the otherworld in both works is governed by definite laws; law, in fact, becomes one of the chief centers of focus in Mirrlees's book. Again, like Dunsany, Mirrlees is a conscious stylist in both dialogue and description. Some might find this tiresome, but those who have the time and inclination will relish such passages as this description of Master Chanticleer: "Rotund, rubicund, red-haired, with hazel eyes in which the jokes, before he uttered them, twinkled like trout in a burn."

Moore, C[atherine] L[ucile]. *Shambleau and Others.* New York: Gnome, 1953.

This is a fine collection of seven of Moore's stories: "Black God's Kiss," "Shambleau," "Black God's Shadow," "Black Thirst," "The Tree of Life," "Jirel Meets Magic," and "Scarlet Dream." Moore's most popular stories are those featuring Northwest Smith or Jirel of Joiry; all of the tales in this collection provide a showcase for one or the other of these characters. "Black God's Kiss," "Black God's Shadow," and "Jirel Meets Magic" are all lively sword and sinew fantasies that recount the adventures of the warrior-queen, Jirel. "Kiss" and "Shadow" tell of her relationship with Guillaume, a charismatic warrior who, after defeating her in battle, becomes her temporary captor. After escaping from Guillaume, she journeys to a hell-like domain in search of a weapon to subdue him. She finds it in the form of a deadly kiss transmitted from the Black God to Guillaume by her own lips. After he is dead, however, she sadly discovers that she actually loved the man. In "Shadow," a kind of sequel, Jirel returns to the Black God's domain in an attempt to save the soul of Guillaume from eternal torment in the Black God's kingdom. "Jirel Meets Magic" features a remarkable emotional and psychological conflict between Jirel and the faery queen Jarisme. In the story, Jirel passes through an enchanted casement into an eerie faeryland, and it is the description of this fantastic secondary world that gives the story its particular character. Of the three Northwest Smith stories the best is "Shambleau," a fascinating retelling of the Medusa story. Although most of the Smith stories take place on other planets and have some paraphernalia commonly associated with science fiction, they are essentially fantasy works in spirit and tone. Moore is a fine stylist, although she does tend to overburden her stories with extraordinarily long (but evocative) descriptions—frequently at the expense of characterization and action. All in all, a good sampler of Moore's short fantasy fiction.

Morris, Kenneth. *The Fates of the Princes of Dyfed.* Point Loma, CA: Theosophical Univ. Press, 1913. North Hollywood, CA: Newcastle, 1978 (paper).

More than 60 years after its first (but all too brief) appearance, this exceptional work of fantasy is once again available. In *The Fates,* Kenneth Morris, a

Welshman transplanted to Southern California, retells the first three parts
or branches of the great Welsh book of mythology, the *Mabinogion.* Sixteen years later, Morris saw his version of the fourth and final branch
published, the *Book of the Three Dragons.* Unlike Lloyd Alexander, who
uses the *Mabinogion* as an inspirational backdrop for the five books of
his Prydain cycle, Morris adheres closely to the style and story line of the
original, while adding his own insights and clarifications. More important,
as he states in his preface, Morris reinvests the gods with the divinity that
had been masked by time, when the *Mabinogion* was finally written down
from oral tradition in the thirteenth century. In so closely following its source,
Morris's version is akin to Evangeline Walton's modern version (in four
novels); Morris, however, is more concerned than is Walton with recapturing
the original style, the magical Welshness, of the *Mabinogion.* In this he
succeeds, and the matchless style of his work transports the reader to the
Island of the Mighty more readily than could the most potent of spells. The
principal setting for the book is ancient Britain (the Island of the Mighty),
but more particularly Dyfed (in Wales), Annwn (the Kingdom of the Dead),
and Wyddfa Mountain (home of the gods of the Cymry). The three branches
that Morris reconstructs here are Pwyll, king of Dyfed, in Annwn in the
service of Arawn, prince of the Underworld; the marriage of Pwyll to the
goddess Rhiannon, which concludes with Pwyll's downfall and Rhiannon's
disgrace; and the coming of age of Pryderi and his rescue of his mother
Rhiannon. This outline, of course, is broad and cannot hope to recreate the
intricacy of the overall structure nor the tone that modulates from scene to
scene in rich variety. Ultimately, the work is a Welsh *Divine Comedy,* with
the human heroes struggling through their infirmities to a godlike immortality. As they follow the quest of the heroes, readers will marvel at their
deeds and at many other wonders, such as the life-giving Cauldron of
Ceridwen, the ring to cure blindness, and the crown of youth. The book is
nicely illustrated and contains a helpful glossary and pronunciation guide.
Dainis Bisenieks has written a valuable introduction for the Newcastle
edition.

Morris, Kenneth. *Book of the Three Dragons.* London: Longmans, 1930.
   New York: Arno, 1978.
This is the sequel to Morris's earlier *Fates of the Princes of Dyfed* and completes the retelling of the four branches of the Welsh *Mabinogion.* It can,
however, be read independently. Morris incorporates whatever background
is required from the earlier parts and produces a work that is more tightly
knit and easier to follow than *The Fates.* Readers can thus more readily
savor Morris's incantatory prose, rich in imagery, figurative language, and
colorful adjectives. The story line is equally fascinating. In *Book of the
Three Dragons,* Pwyll, having fallen from greatness because of his own
human weaknesses, has wandered for many years throughout the world as

Dienw'r Anffodin, or the Nameless One with the Misfortunes. Having purged himself, the hero is permitted by the gods to be reborn as Manawyddan. He becomes an immortal but refuses a place in Wyddfa, home of the gods, to better serve his people, the Cymry, and the gods themselves. Misfortune has fallen on Wyddfa and the Island of the Mighty because the harp and the breastplate of two of the gods have been stolen. Manawyddan recovers both after many adventures, the last of which is his release of the spirits from hell with the music of the divine harp of Alawn. The most memorable episode is Manawyddan's pursuit of the sly, elusive Gwiawn Sea-Thief, Archfilcher. Gwiawn is a humorous spirit reminiscent of the Icelandic Loki. To catch this thief Manawyddan needs all the help he can muster: shoes that enable him to jump from one mountaintop to another; a sword that is so sharp it draws blood from the wind and can shave a gnat; a shield that outshines the moon. The entire tale is an affirmation of the majesty and compassion of the gods and of their reliance on humans to cooperate in the ceaseless struggle against evil. It is, moreover, this struggle that enables humanity, through duty, to achieve glory and immortality. *Book of the Three Dragons* is a masterpiece of style and imagination, a book that awakens in readers a sense of the majesty of divinity and at the same time permits them to smile at the frailty of humanity. Readers should take advantage of Morris's explanations of pronunciation to experience the magical sounds of the Welsh names.

Morris, Kenneth. *The Secret Mountain and Other Tales.* London: Faber & Gwyer, 1926.

The 10 tales in this fine collection are religious fantasies—religious, happily, in the most universal and unparochial sense. In 10 different ways, Morris traces the quest of the human spirit for beauty, truth, and goodness in and beyond this mortal life. And he does so with an elegant style and lucid, finely wrought stories. Several of the pieces are based on specific myths of various countries: "Red-Peach-Blossom Inlet" (Chinese); "Sion ap Siencyn" (Welsh); "The Rose and the Cup" (Persian); "The King and the Three Ascetics" (Indian); "The Apples of Knowledge" (Biblical). In two cases, Morris extrapolates from great humanistic and religious works of literature: "The Last Adventure of Don Quixote" and "The Divina Commedia of Evan Leyshon." In these two pieces, Morris exhibits a close knowledge of both the text and the spirit of his sources. He does take a few liberties with Dante when he has his derelict hero seeking out his proper place in hell, only to walk right through it because someone with the divine spark can never be satisfied there. In "Daffodil," Morris creates his own Pantheon or Olympus, but it consists largely of nature deities, one of whom, the Lady Daffodil, decides to come to earth to alleviate its hapless, squalid condition. In both "The Secret Mountain" and "The Saint and the Forest-Gods," Morris shows the continuity or unity of world mythologies. These two stories feature the "Old

Road," an ancient thoroughfare bridging Camelot and Babylon, the chief centers of Western and Eastern idealism and mythic splendor. Morris's principal themes in these works are the sameness of divinity whatever its name or guise, and the capability of humanity to regain the lost knowledge of its divine origin and nature. But important as themes are to Morris, he doesn't force them upon his readers. He dramatizes them through carefully constructed plots, tangible and discernible images and symbols, and a truly high style, both in description and dialogue. Though two of the stories ("Red-Peach-Blossom-Inlet" and "The Last Adventure of Don Quixote") have recently appeared in fantasy anthologies—*The Fantastic Imagination*, Volume II and *Dreamer of Dreams: An Anthology of Fantasy,* respectively (see Anthologies section)—one hopes that the entire volume, too long out of print, will soon be republished.

Morris, William. *The Story of the Glittering Plain.* Hammersmith, UK: Kelmscott, 1891. Reprinted as *The Glittering Plain.* North Hollywood, CA: Newcastle, 1973 (paper).
The brevity and tone of this work set it apart from the rest of Morris's fantasies; it is, unlike his other works, as much influenced by the folk tale as by the romance. Its plot is strikingly simple, without degenerating to mere formula, and yet it lacks the descriptive embellishment that is important to his later works. The tone is nicely balanced between parable and pure comedy, without the nuances of the full-blown romance. The tale follows the exploits of Hallblithe while he searches for his lover, who has been kidnapped by the men of the Isle of Ransom. The lover is simply and tellingly named the Hostage. Hallblithe eventually discovers the Hostage on Ransom, but only after he has been tricked into traveling to the Glittering Plain (the Undying Land) by the machinations of one of the Hostage's abductors, the Puny Fox. It is tempting to interpret Hallblithe's journey as an Orphean descent, but neither his quest nor the Undying Land is altered by his visit. There is little characterization here, although the Puny Fox is an interesting portrait of the compulsive liar who becomes a faithful and truthful retainer. The island of the Undying Land itself is marvelously well sketched: it is a haven of rejuvenation and bliss that admits newcomers only very selectively. Hallblithe's rejection of his admission is a statement of his love for the Hostage. Dreams are very important in the work; they anticipate the future and provide Hallblithe with directions for accomplishing his quest. Likewise, a book that is owned by the daughter of the king of the Glittering Plain is a type of far-seeing device; its pictures reflect the emotional state of its reader.

Morris, William. *The Wood beyond the World.* Hammersmith, UK: Kelmscott, 1894. New York: Dover, 1972 (paper).
This work combines magic and medievalism and employs the quest pattern. The pattern is familiar enough in fantasy, yet an undercurrent of tasteful

sexuality is also noticeable. The hero, Walter, journeys over sea and land to escape an unhappy marriage, and later, while pursuing a recurring vision of a Lady, a Maiden, and a Dwarf, is drawn beyond the world of his home. The Lady is a witch-queen who seduces Walter; the virtuous Maiden, something of an enchantress herself, accomplishes his escape and her own by shadowing, in Walter's form, a former lover of the Lady. The two females come to represent sensuality and chasity respectively, and when the Maiden kills the Lady, chastity symbolically destroys sensuality, enabling Walter to happily marry the Maiden. It would be unfair, however, to read the work only on this allegorical level. The plot is truly engaging, moving from Walter's home to the Wood and back. Along the way readers pass through medieval merchant life, a lonely hermitage, and the land of the awesome but innocent Bear-folk. The portrait of the Lady's dwarf—mindless evil personified—is superior. Morris's use of archaic language is at its best here, and there is more magic than in many of his other works. The vision that draws Walter beyond the world—his recurring vision of the trio—is a particularly notable and effective portal between two worlds. Notable, too, is the beautiful edition that Dover has produced. It is a facsimile of Morris's own Kelmscott edition, preserving the superb typescript and the ornamentation of the original.

Morris, William. *The Well at the World's End.* Hammersmith, UK: Kelmscott, 1896. New York: Ballantine, 1978 (paper).
Morris can probably be described as the father of modern high fantasy and this work is his most significant. It is his longest work of fantasy and his most impressive display of imaginative power. Essentially episodic, and closely akin to the medieval romance, the plot follows a quest pattern and allows for a dazzling array of adventures. Ralph, the hero of the work, leaves his home in the Upmeads in search of adventure and takes on a worthy task—to find the well at the world's end. His quest takes him through such a variety of conflicts and passions that a list would be unwieldy, yet some idea of the marvels can be indicated from a few names: Utterbol (the land of the wicked lord), the Wood Perilous, the Burg of the Four Friths, the Castle of Abundance. The work is a great deal more than a clothesline plot and a series of adventures; it is a tale of the growth of a boy to a man. By the time Ralph does reach the well, accompanied by his lover Ursula, he has passed through an initiation process that justifies the longevity and heightened talents that are the gifts of the well. Other than the virtues of the well's water, there is little here that qualifies as magic, yet the very atmosphere of the world is that of faërie, and this atmosphere is the strength of the work. Morris's deft handling of archaic language, medieval setting, and rich detail creates a magnificent map of Ralph's psyche as well as of his travels. Morris stands at the vanguard of modern fantasy, having had great influence on Dunsany, Cabell, Tolkien, Lewis, and many more. The contribution of this work is its broad sweep and its atmosphere, qualities readers have come to expect from the great works of fantasy.

Morris, William. *The Water of the Wondrous Isles.* Hammersmith, UK: Kelmscott, 1897.

Perhaps the most unusual aspect of this work is that its major character is a female who pursues a quest. Called Birdalone, her name typifies her solo wanderings on and among the Wondrous Isles. Stolen from her mother in infancy, Birdalone is raised by a witch who intends the girl to become the bane of men through her beauty. She escapes from the witch only to encounter, among other adventures, the Isle of Increase Unsought—the realm of the wood-witch's sister. Here she meets with Viridis, Aurea, and Atra, three women separated from their lovers and compelled to serve the wicked but forgetful queen. Birdalone eventually aids the three, but not before she and Atra's lover, the Black Squire, fall in love. The resolution of this confused friendship controls the rest of the tale. The most striking character of the work is Habundia, a wood-faery who is Birdalone's guardian and confidante. The faery works little magic, but her counsel and wisdom are the backdrop for Birdalone's development, and they contrast nicely with the small-mindedness of the witch sisters. Of the magic in the work, the most interesting examples are the Water of Might, an elixir whereby the witch-queen maintains her isle, and the Sending Boat, Birdalone's vehicle among the Wondrous Isles. The boat is a particularly eerie touch since it requires a blood offering (usually a pricked forearm) before it responds to command. The tale has many elements of the traditional romance—disguisings, multiple marriages, episodic plot—while the descriptions of Birdalone's emotions are fairly typical examples of Pre-Raphaelite excess. Yet a number of individual scenes are very fine and the quasi-medieval setting is maintained successfully throughout. Among the finest scenes is Birdalone's excursion to the Land of the Greywethers, a troll-like folk who grant wishes if the wisher can endure their horrible presence.

Morris, William. *The Sundering Flood.* Hammersmith, UK: Kelmscott, 1898.

Morris's last and most charming fantasy lacks the sweep of *The Well at the World's End* and the depth of *The Wood beyond the World,* but it benefits from superb characterization and a strong story. Osberne and Elfhild, the lovers of the tale, know each other only at a distance since they are separated by the waters of the Sundering Flood. Osberne, aided by the blessing of strength and an enchanted sword, Broadcleaver, seeks passage across the Flood; the tale follows his adventures. The lad's mystical guardian, Steelhead, and Stephen the Eater, his servant and steward, aid him along the way, but it is Osberne's own talent and innate good fortune that enable him to accomplish his goal. Steelhead is a wonderfully conceived character— a parahuman warrior reminiscent of Tolkien's Elven-kind. Stephen is a type of the loyal retainer who has more mettle about him than his looks betray. If there is a weakness here, it is the recounting of Elfhild's adventures near the end of the book. Her adventures are not as engaging as Osberne's and they are presented in retrospect and rather hurriedly—Morris finished the work only 25 days before his death. Otherwise, the integration of plot and subplot is well executed, and the opening sections of the book—the animated description of the tale's geography and the truly enchanting telling of Osberne's childhood encounter with a dwarf—are among Morris's very best.

Nichols, Ruth. *The Marrow of the World.* New York: Atheneum, 1972.
Linda has unsettling dreams or memories; she is restless, sometimes thoughtless, and quite unpredictable. Philip is just the opposite, considerate and placid; he loves Linda and defends her. Philip's Aunt Margaret has adopted Linda, who was discovered abandoned as a babe. No inquiries could discover her origins. Linda and Philip finally discover them, but only after they are drawn back to the otherworld from which Linda had been sent. Linda, it turns out, is the daughter of the evil witch Morgan, but her father was human. Morgan is dead, executed by the great wizard-ruler, Kyril; and it is Ygerna, Linda's half-sister and a full witch, who has made the spell to draw Linda back. Ygerna's purpose is to send Linda to get the marrow of the world. Ygerna plans first to restore herself with this magical substance whose properties give her near-immortality, and then to gain vengeance on Kyril. Linda has no choice but to comply, since only Ygerna, she thinks, can return her and Philip to their own world. Ygerna and Philip clash over Linda, the one claiming her for a witch, the other determined to bring her back, whatever the cost, to the world they had left. Linda is herself in great conflict, wanting to be human but somehow feeling fated to be a witch. In the end it is Philip who bests Ygerna, while Linda's human side triumphs— all with the advice of the wizard Kyril, who also goes under the name of Leo. The basic plot is an interesting one. The underwater motif offers something different and it has thematic significance. The name Morgan, after all, applies to a sea monster, and water is the elemental opposite to the fire that the witch most fears. The characterization of Linda and her inner conflict adds a pleasing tension. The themes—that a higher power is a help but not a substitute for individual courage, and that one must accept death— are important and effectively dramatized. Unfortunately, however, the book is simply too short. Economy of detail is gained at the expense of atmosphere. For instance, when Linda and the dwarf arrive at the source of the marrow of the world, it is a magical moment, but so brief that its effect is nearly lost while we are hurried on to the next adventure. Nichols, interestingly, has preceded Joyce Gregorian *(The Broken Citadel)* in the motif of a character from the otherworld growing up in this world, ignorant of her origins until something draws her back. On the other hand, Nichols follows C. S. Lewis's Narnian tales. Kyril-Leo (Kyril means lord, Leo means lion), the great wizard who has defeated the witch Morgan, becomes Philip and Linda's counsellor. He says he goes by many names, and he has the

power to return Linda and Philip to their own world, which he does, after placing his mark on them and telling them that they might return. Surely this is Lewis's Aslan. Nichols's earlier book, *A Walk out of the World,* is very similar to *The Marrow,* but not as mature a work in conception or execution.

Norton, Andre. *Witch World.* New York: Ace, 1963 (paper). Boston: Gregg, 1977.

This is Volume I of the Witch World novels. Since 1963, when her first Witch World book appeared, Norton has been adding numerous short stories and novels to the series. All the works are connected by their common setting in an alternate universe, the Witch World, a secondary world where magic thrives in a medieval atmosphere. The geography and history of this world are extensive, however, and some of the novels and stories retain only the slightest of ties to the places and events of the earlier core works of the series. For those who are intent upon piecing together the puzzle of how all the works are interrelated, Sandra Miesel, in Volume I of the Gregg Press edition, provides an introductory essay and a chart of time and geographical relationships. Gregg Press has published seven of the novels in the series, Volumes I-V of which constitute the most tightly knit segment, the Simon Tregarth sequence. The Simon Tregarth tales of the Witch World series are Norton's earliest ventures into her world of magic, where an ancient race of hereditary witches strives against extinction. The tales are concerned primarily with love, magic, and battle. What keeps the tales a cut above most sword and sinew works is a consistent, underlying morality and Norton's preference for pathos rather than bloodshed. Freedom is the essence of Norton's morality and it recurs as a theme throughout the five books. The books are potent, gripping in their movement, and sensitive in their presentation of human motives. The account is of a post-World War II fugitive, Simon Tregarth, who escapes his pursuers through a dimension portal—the Siege Perilous of Arthurian Britain. Tregarth emerges in the Witch World where the witch race (the Estcarpians) are beset simultaneously by marauding savages (the races of Alizon and Karsten) and a cruel, inhuman race of invaders from another dimension (the Kolder). At the outset, the Kolder present the most imminent danger since their major weapon, a technologically amplified form of psychic control, is at least as potent as the magical power of the Estcarpian witches. As the witches seek to maintain their freedom from the Kolder, the savages harass the boundaries of Estcarp. Simon, his witch-wife Jaelithe, and their children and allies confront and defeat the Kolder only to face continued danger from the savages and new enemies from other realms. In addition to the main idea of freedom, other themes holding the five books together are the love of Simon and Jaelithe and the various experiences of their children, who share a magical cohesion. Each of the volumes has an independent plot and each benefits from Norton's fast-paced style of narrative and her ability to capture a sense of reality in descriptive detail. Norton's imagination produces a series of memorable settings and characters that, unfortunately, tend to become formulaic. *Witch World* details Simon Tregarth's entry into the Witch World and the initial defeat of the Kolder. Readers find here the beginning of the love between Simon and Jaelithe and the development of their friendship with Koris, the vigorous wielder of the legendary ax of Volt. The discovery of this weapon is among the best scenes of the work. Unfortunately, the tale is flawed. As the first of Norton's series, it lacks a sense of history and tradition. Perhaps Norton was unsure of her genre as she tried to mix science fantasy and a touch of Mickey Spillane with less than complete success.

Norton, Andre. *Web of the Witch World.* New York: Ace, 1964 (paper). Boston: Gregg, 1977.
Volume II of the Witch World novels describes the freeing of the Witch World from the grip of the Kolder and the liberation of Simon and Jaelithe from the tyranny of Jaelithe's witch-training. As a witch, Jaelithe is barred from love, but she and Simon find greater power than the witches' in their mutual affection. The Kolder's desire for control moves the narrative and leads Simon to their hidden fastness. Jaelithe follows, linked to her husband by a power that combines love and magic. Between them, they unleash a race from beyond the realm of the Witch World, a race of Gothic horror that revenges itself on the Kolder for past wrongs.

Norton, Andre. *Three against the Witch World.* New York: Ace, 1965 (paper). Boston: Gregg, 1977.
In Volume III of the Witch World novels, readers meet the children of Simon and Jaelithe. The tale is told by the eldest, Kyllan the warrior, who recounts the trials of the triplets as they attempt to evade their heritage. The parents have disappeared, disapproved of by the witches of Estcarp. Kyllan and his brother, Kemoc, must rescue their sister, Kaththea, from the witches' keep, where she is being indoctrinated into the way of Power. The finest device of the story is the introduction of Escore, the hidden land of the Old Ones where the legends and myths of Estcarp are discovered to be realities. It is here that the triplets escape the pursuit of the witches and find freedom and danger in the land of legend.

Norton, Andre. *Warlock of the Witch World.* New York: Ace, 1967 (paper). Boston: Gregg, 1977.
Volume IV of the Witch World novels is perhaps the best of the Tregarth tales. Kemoc tells of his barely successful rescue of Kaththea from the seduction of Dark Power. The book gives greater depth to the sketch of Escore found in *Three against the Witch World* and, in particular, details the various races of this exotic realm. A broad variety of races is seen—the

birdlike Flannen, the delightful Mosswives, and the amphibious Krogen, to name only a few. One of the Krogen, Orsya, accompanies Kemoc on his quest, and through her own brand of magic, aids him as no one else could. The descriptive detail of the work is superb, and though the action is a bit too quick at times, the plot is tightly woven. Notable is Norton's successful representation of the "inside" of magic: near the end of the work Kemoc is ensorcelled and the reader shares this weird experience.

Norton, Andre. *Sorceress of the Witch World.* New York: Ace, 1968 (paper). Boston: Gregg, 1977.
In Volume V of the Witch World novels, after being rescued by Kemoc, Kaththea sets out to regain the magic she lost in her brush with the Dark Power. She becomes a spell-caster for a band of nomads, and, subsequently, discovers one of the portals that are gateways to and from the Witch World. On the Otherside, she finds a Kolderlike society, controlled by machines rather than magic. Also, she finds her long-sought parents and a potent warlock, Hilarion. The four of them combine their powers to return to the Witch World and rejoin the Escorians.

Norton, Andre. *Year of the Unicorn.* New York: Ace, 1965 (paper). Boston: Gregg, 1977.
Although this Volume VI of the Witch World novels was written before two of the Simon Tregarth tales, it breaks away from that group and moves to a different Witch World setting inhabited by other races. The protagonist, Gillan, is the bridge linking this book to the others in the series. Without at first knowing it herself, she is of the blood of the witches of Estcarp. As a child she had apparently been captured by the Hounds of Alizon and then shipwrecked on the coast of High Hallack. *Year of the Unicorn* begins in Norstead Abbey in High Hallack, where Gillan has for 10 years (she is now 20) been a ward of the religious sisterhood. It is on the eve of the Year of the Unicorn, when High Hallack must deliver twelve plus one brides to their allies, the Were Riders of the waste. Gillan, knowing she's different from the others and not willing to spend her life in the convent, manages to substitute herself for one of the chosen brides, and so begins an adventure that is a journey not only to the strange land of the Were Riders but to her innermost self as well. The Were Riders are a race of warrior-sorcerers. They are shape shifters and are also adept at casting spells of illusion. When Gillan selects Herrel to be her husband, the Were Riders immediately suspect her, because Herrel, dubbed Wronghanded, is considered to be inferior by his "pack" of fellows. When they discover that Gillan has the true sight and can see through their illusions, they attempt to control her by separating her strong-willed wraith from her body. The rest of the story concerns Gillan's struggle, with Herrel's assistance, literally to find herself, and in doing so she finds both where and who Gillan truly is. The illusions, the shape shiftings, and the

passages through gates that are dimension portals are all here, but they are much less interesting than Gillan's attempt to discover and control her inner magical powers, a task that becomes one with her struggle to find and understand herself. The book is sometimes melodramatic, and occasionally Norton uses lengthy dialogues between Gillan and Herrel to explain the complexities of the existing two (and more) Gillans. Readers will not long be bothered by these distractions, however, and on finishing the book they will once again be impressed with the inventiveness of which a gifted sub-creator is capable.

Norton, Andre. *Steel Magic.* Cleveland: Collins-World, 1965. New York: Archway, 1978 (paper).

Storytelling is Andre Norton's forte, as she ably demonstrates in the engrossing narrative of *Steel Magic,* an all-ages high fantasy. Three children—Greg, Eric, and Sara—enter Avalon through a door in an old crumbling wall, part of an estate previously owned by a Mr. Brosius (Merlinus Ambrosius in Avalon). They have been mysteriously summoned and accept their missions to restore the three talismans needed to oppose the Enemy. Greg goes after Excalibur, Eric after Huon's Horn, Sara after Merlin's Ring. Each child must overcome numerous magical obstacles, but Norton adds depth to the plot and the characters by adding a personal conflict for each child. Greg must overcome his fear of the dark, Sara her fear of spiders, and Eric his impatience. The children retrieve the talismans and Avalon—and our world—are safe again for a time. Critics can easily find fault with this book. It is an adventure story with little more in the way of theme than courage. The external obstacles that the children confront are little more than straw men. The internal conflicts hardly last long enough to be noticed. And there are several inconsistencies. But after making these criticisms most critics will conclude by saying, "But it's a fascinating tale."

Norton, Andre. *The Crystal Gryphon.* New York: Atheneum, 1972. New York: DAW, 1973 (paper).

The setting and language, especially the names of people and places, give a definite early Scandinavian flavor to this book. The country is one of rugged coasts and inland dales with names like Ulmsdale, Norsdale, and Norstead, inhabited by people called Nalda, Kerovan, and Ingilda. Also present are the magic and, to a lesser extent, the myth of the Icelandic Eddas and sagas. Before the dalesmen came, the land had been inhabited by the Old Ones, who had great powers and are now deities or demigods; Gunnora, the harvest goddess, is most prominent. Yet a new worship has mingled with and almost supplanted the old, a cult of the Cleansing Flame, whose worship includes Abbeys, holy women, and prayer beads. This is the world into which Kerovan, Lord-Heir in Ulmsdale, is born. He is like other men in appearance, except for his amber eyes and cloven feet. His father, however, proclaims Kerovan his heir, despite the rumors that Kerovan is a monster rejected by his own mother. To insure his son's position the Lord of Ulm affiances Kerovan to Joisan of Ithkrypt, a neighboring hold, when the two are still children. The two remain apart, however, since they are not of age. Both are students whose interests lead them to explore the ways of the Old Ones. The stage is now set for the central action. Joisan's part is twofold: remaining faithful to a marriage promise to a man she has never seen but about whom she has heard ugly rumors, and guarding the crystal gryphon, a thing of power. Kerovan's task is to accept his apparent deformities and to discover his kinship with the Old Ones and his share in their power. The two become the agents of the power in combatting the Dark Power of Kerovan's human kinsmen, a conflict which draws to a dramatic climax at the book's end. Norton's setting, story, and abundant use of magic are entertaining, but her most impressive achievement is her device of an alternating first-person point of view. Kerovan and Joisan share in this function, each taking a chapter in turn. The effect is to heighten the romantic connection between the two and to provide a revealing double perspective. Joisan emerges with honor for her fidelity to Kerovan; Kerovan overcomes his self-doubts, accepts himself, and patiently learns how to properly use the power. His opponents are destroyed because they don't really understand the Dark Power they conjure. This treatment of the nature of magic is very similar to Ursula Le Guin's in her Earthsea trilogy. *The Crystal Gryphon* is one of the best of several stories and novels that Norton has located on the broad map of the Witch World, but that have no direct connection with (and can be read independently of) the Simon Tregarth tales that form the original core of the Witch World series.

Pain, Barry. *Collected Tales, Volume One.* London: Secker, 1916.
Barry Pain is difficult to classify. His controlled urbane prose reminds one at times of his English countryman John Buchan; at other times his occasional whimsy recalls the style of the American Frank Stockton, though it is never quite so lighthearted. A sampling of tales from his first volume of *Collected Tales* shows that it contains some fine high fantasy. "Exchange" exhibits Pain's lightly macabre humor: "But the other day the only man of the world with whom I am acquainted accused the major of a want of taste, and based his accusation on the fact that he took the liberty of dying in the country-house of a friend, not having been invited for that purpose." "Exchange," involving a scarlet-clad witch from the real world of the Yorkshire Hills, falls somewhere between high and low fantasy. More solidly in the category of high fantasy is "The Glass of Supreme Moments." Lucas Morne, sitting in his college rooms surrounded by the leftovers of afternoon tea, suddenly notices that where his fireplace had been a stairway now rises, a portal into the otherworld. Morne there finds and peers into a magical glass under the direction of a mysterious veiled lady who turns out to be a

seductive figure of death. Pain's style moves from commonplace to elevated as the protagonist leaves behind his dingy room to ascend the stairs of silver and crystal. "The Moon-Slave" is a hauntingly memorable tale of myth fantasy. Princess Viola, fittingly named because of her love for music and dance, makes a rash promise to a full moon one evening, after discovering an open space in the midst of "an old forsaken maze." She subsequently finds herself drawn there and compelled to dance each month at the full moon. The concluding scene is a chiller, as Viola finds herself dancing with a cloven-hoofed god. The style in this, one of Pain's later works, is sensuous and uniformly elevated, but not excessive, rising as the action does to a climactic crescendo. These three stories display some of the variety of fantasy elements and the remarkable control of style in Pain's writing. The other 10 stories included are "The Celestial Grocery," "Zero," "Wilmay," "The Doll," "Ellen Rider," "Sparkling Burgundy," "Too Soon and Too Late," "The Night of Glory," "The Diary of a God," and "The Undying Thing." It is to be hoped that Pain's works, available in only a few libraries and from some used-book dealers, will once again be made more generally available, as they well deserve to be.

Pratt, Fletcher. *The Well of the Unicorn.* New York: Sloane, 1948. New
   York: Ballantine, 1976 (paper).
Before writing his own fantasy, Fletcher Pratt collaborated with L. Sprague de Camp in writing a series of novelettes centered around the humorous, somewhat bumbling hero, Harold Shea, in a variety of improbable escapades. In *Well of the Unicorn,* writing solo, Pratt is much more serious and less fanciful, but he does retain a more human type of hero, one who, like Harold Shea, bears no relationship to the thick-thewed, thin-brained barbarians of Robert E. Howard. In *Well of the Unicorn,* Airar Alvarson becomes a hero and a leader by means of his keen-sightedness, his knowledge of gramarye, and his wise and compassionate judgments, not by feats of arms. He is not irresistible to women, even those few to whom he himself is attracted. He is also refreshingly unsure of the correctness of his political views—he is a democrat in a feudal world. This world seems to be derived (at several removes) from Northern Europe of the middle ages. The focus of most of the action is Dalarna, whose Dalecarles are in revolt against the Vulking invaders. As the story opens, Airar Alvarson has just been turned out of his home, Trangsted in Varstmansted. He somehow is drawn into league with the rebels of the Iron Ring, and ultimately finds himself at their head, asking himself, "Why me?" The book quickly moves through a succession of strategic confrontations between the Dalecarles and the Vulkings. Underlying the military conflict is the more basic political struggle of democracy versus totalitarianism, with various in-between factions also vying for adherence. Magic in the work is principally a negative force, although there is some ambivalence here. The Well, symbol of religion, is opposed to all magic, but Airar's magic is always beneficial, as when he

exorcises the sea monsters from the fleet of the free-fishers. Pratt's style is deliberately archaic, and though it seems awkward at times, it adds an appropriate flavor to the book.

Rayner, William. *Stag Boy.* London: Collins, 1972. New York: Harcourt, 1973.

With its rolling limestone hills, heather-clad moors, quaint villages, bountiful apple orchards, and luxuriant forests inhabited by noble stags, Somersetshire is one of the most beautiful sections of England. It is in this scenic region, rich in history and legend, that *Stag Boy* is set, and it is from this distinctive setting that Rayner's novel derives much of its uniqueness and atmospheric beauty. The central character is Jim Hooper, a sensitive and rather frail (he suffers from asthma) young man whose life changes abruptly after he finds a strange horned helmet in an ancient burial mound. Once Jim places the helmet on his head he is able to project his own consciousness into the body of a huge black Exmoor stag. As time passes, he finds it easier and easier to enter the stag's mind, even without the helmet. Jim's secret is shared by Mary Rawle, his childhood sweetheart, and some of the most poignant and memorable scenes describe the midnight meetings between the stag and the 15-year-old girl. As the narrative progresses the symbiosis becomes stronger: the stag becomes more dependent upon Jim's guidance and Jim begins to feel the stag's drives and feelings. In a powerful climactic scene the magnificent stag is killed by hunters, thus freeing Jim from the symbiotic relationship, but the reader is left wondering when, where, and in what form the mysterious forces of humanity's dark past will again manifest themselves. Rayner, like Alan Garner *(The Owl Service, Red Shift),* very effectively demonstrates how the forces of magic impinge upon everyday life. Also like Garner, Rayner displays his profound love of nature and dramatizes the necessity for a more harmonious relationship between humans and their environment. All in all, this is a thoughtful, imaginative, and well-written fantasy novel.

Ruskin, John. *The King of the Golden River, or the Black Brothers.* London: Smith, Elder, 1863. New York: Dover, 1974 (paper). New York: Greenwillow, 1978.

This is an excellent faery tale. It follows the traditional pattern that rewards virtue and punishes greed and selfishness, and it does so without insipidity. The language of the piece is adult, the sentiment consistent, and the morality humane. Gluck, the younger of the Black Brothers, Schwartz and Hans, encounters the King of the Golden River and offers him kindness—even though he appears as a wanderer to the boy. The Black Brothers punish Gluck for his generosity, and through a series of events they in turn are punished by being transformed into black stones. The magic of the work is essentially animistic; the king is much like the kobolds and undines of

German Romanticism. The tradition of Hoffman and Tieck is strong here. Nature is alive and involved with humanity's morality; it seems intentionally to test humans and to accept only the worthy. An ideal land is the brothers' goal, and it is Gluck's reward at the end. A particularly fine scene finds Gluck talking to his favorite drinking mug, which his brothers have told him to melt. As Gluck watches it collapse in the heat, he finds that his mug, too, was a residence of the King of the Golden River.

Sherrell, Carl. *Raum.* New York: Avon, 1977 (paper).
Through a potent incantation, Jord, seer of Iceland, summons Asteroth, a high lord of the Underworld; but in his place comes Raum, "Earl of Netherworld, Vassal of Lucifer." Discontented because he believes that "there is much that has been withheld from us of Netherworld by our Lord Lucifer," Raum has come to the world of humans with the hope of getting answers to his questions from Merlin, the greatest of wizards. His search for the sage takes him to many lands and involves him in bloody battles with the Fins, the Vikings, and even some of King Arthur's knights. With the help of the sorceress, Morgan Le Fay, Raum finally finds Merlin in his sacred cave, but the wizard's words only reinforce Raum's growing awareness that he himself must find the answers to his questions, and that if he is to find happiness and contentment he must continue his "struggle to excel and attain a place far above his present level of being." And indeed Raum's struggle has resulted in a perceptible change in his character. His contact with human love, loyalty, courage, and tenderness has gradually made him more human and less demonic. His transformation continues after his discussion with Merlin, and the tears Raum sheds at the loss of Merlin's beloved Viviene provide convincing evidence of the humanizing effect of Raum's earthly sojourn. This is an energetic and fast-paced novel that holds the reader's interest, but it is seriously flawed: the dialogue is generally wooden and unconvincing, some of the characters do not come to life, and the author's attempts to create a high style are not always successful. The primary strength of the work lies in the delineation of Raum. The whole concept of the humanizing of a demon is intriguing, and the author convincingly describes his gradual change. Then, too, the novel has an emotional tone that many similar sword and sinew works lack. There is a tragic quality about the tormented half-human, half-demon protagonist that continues to haunt the reader's imagination after the last page of the novel has been turned. Fine illustrations by Stephen Fabian.

Simak, Clifford D. *Enchanted Pilgrimage.* New York: Putnam, 1975.
The year is 1975, but the time setting is the twelfth century, the place a university town, or the Borderland, or the Wasteland. Parallel universes, of course, but with a difference: in *Enchanted Pilgrimage,* there are three parallel universes. There is the chief setting of the book, just described;

there is the readers' universe, represented in the novel by Alexander Jones on his motorcycle; and there is one that is only alluded to, the one from which Mary the scullery maid discovers she and her parents came. Add to this a hidden university where resides a Caretaker who comes from another planet entirely and who hopes somehow to unite the best elements from the three parallel universes—magic, technology, and a higher humanism. This is the grand design of the book, but the 1975 medieval universe is the actual setting. The book's major heroes, with the exception of Mary, belong to that universe: Oliver the rafter goblin, Gib the marshman, Snively the gnome, and Hall of the Hollow Tree. And most important, magic is a reality in that universe: a flaming sword, a unicorn horn. Despite the jarring appearance of a man on a motorcycle in the midst of hellhounds, witches, and ogres, magic is what makes the book a work of fantasy. Magic and science coexist, with a clear preference for the former and a regret for the loss of magic in Jones's world. The ideal, however, is the illusive third universe, which is barely glimpsed, but from which the characters in the book will, one hopes, profit. The book is enjoyable science fantasy. The conception is intriguing, though what will spring from the amalgam of magic, technology, and humanism remains vague. While the human characters have scant attraction, the reader will enjoy many of the nonhumans, particularly Oliver the rafter goblin of Wyalusing University. The plot is carefully constructed, if at times slightly contrived. Simak succeeds in joining the two genres of science fiction and fantasy without undermining either—certainly not the fantasy. And while the work falls short of Poul Anderson's books in the same vein, it is superior to most other science fantasies.

Smith, Clark Ashton. *The Abominations of Yondo.* Sauk City, WI: Arkham House, 1960.

Even though many of Smith's tales are examples of realistic weird fiction, many others are fine examples of fantasy. His horrific descriptions are only part of the effect, for his story lines are unusually imaginative, rarely imitating traditional motifs or patterns. His contribution to Lovecraft's Cthulhu mythos ("The Nameless Offspring") captures the effect of the original, and his continuation of Beckford's *Vathek* ("The Third Episode of Vathek") duplicates the brittle Eastern atmosphere of the earlier tale. But it is in his own tales that Smith shines—in tales such as "The Ice Demon" and "The White Sybil," where the desolate isolation of the Arctic region is represented. When he combines this originality with the elements of fantasy, he produces some truly memorable tales. The best of this collection are perhaps "The Enchantress of Sylaire" and "The Witchcraft of Ulua"—two tales of young men beset by magical feminine wiles. The two tales end very differently, but both rely on subtle grotesquerie as well as magic. The entrance to Sylaire is a superior example of a portal to an otherworld—a haunting passage through a free-standing dolmen. And the figure of the wizard in "Ulua" is strangely disturbing. The ending of "Enchantress" is an unexpected reversal, one that (like many of Smith's techniques) can hardly be anticipated. His ability to surprise is one of his strengths.

Stewart, Mary. *The Crystal Cave.* New York: Morrow, 1970. New York: Fawcett, 1978 (paper). *The Hollow Hills.* New York: Morrow, 1973. New York: Fawcett, 1978 (paper).

These two books actually constitute a single epic work about Myrddin Emrys (Welsh) or Merlinus Ambrosius (Roman), better known as Merlin the Enchanter. *The Crystal Cave* begins with the conceiving of Merlin, follows his career for about 20 years, and concludes with the conceiving, under Merlin's management, of Arthur. *The Hollow Hills* begins, as though it were the next chapter of the previous book, with Merlin's dismissal by Uther, Arthur's father, who has nonetheless promised to deliver the babe, when born, to Merlin's care. The book traces Merlin's travels to the east, during which time he monitors, through his second sight, Arthur's growth in Brittany and in England. Merlin returns to finish Arthur's education, and the book concludes with Arthur being proclaimed king. With this Merlin epic Mary Stewart has rightly won an honorable place among the modern writers of Arthurian legend. In her use of Arthurian materials she falls somewhere between historical novelists such as Rosemary Sutcliffe, Anya Seton, and (most recently) Douglas Carmichael, and fantasists such as T. H. White, C. S. Lewis, and (most recently) Sanders Anne Laubenthal and Vera Chapman. That is, she bases her story on the (specious) history of Geoffrey of Monmouth *(Historia Regum Britanniae),* provides rational explanations of Geoffrey's fancies, and tempers his excesses; yet while she avoids the more usual paraphernalia of magic, she retains and even elaborates on Merlin's second sight and the oracular and prophetic abilities that flow from it. Taking a cue from Geoffrey, Stewart portrays Merlin much like an Old Testament prophet, an agent of the gods—or God (Merlin is not quite certain which). Thus in a sense this epic, like its source, is a blend of history and fantasy, and of myth and faery tale. Stewart's contribution to the Arthurian tradition is, of course, her superb and original depiction of Merlin. Extrapolating from her sources, Stewart makes Merlin the bastard son of Ambrosius Aurelianus, the first High King of Britain; thus he is the nephew of Uther Pendragon and cousin to Arthur. He is a Romano-British prince with scholarly rather than military tastes, called by some controlling power of divinity to fulfill the noble destiny of preparing the way for the greatest of the kings of Britain. This destiny controls his morality, which is more like the Old Testament code than the New. Thus, for instance, to ensure Arthur's birth, he helps Uther to an adulterous affair with the Lady Ygraine, and is forced to kill two soldiers who threaten to interfere. This causes him great anguish and a temporary loss of his powers. Stewart handles such complications skillfully, neither exonerating nor condemning Merlin, but presenting him as a man upon whom is thrust the burden of a prophet. As Merlin states, he took his power "not where I could find it; where it was given." It is, as has been mentioned, Merlin's second sight that provides the fantasy dimension to the story. On several occasions, the readers enter into the otherworld through Merlin's visions—his vision of the god Mithras fighting a bull, his vision of Macsen (Magnus Maximus) directing him to find his sword. The appeal of Stewart's epic work is broad, attracting readers whose interests range from history to Arthurian legend to fantasy. And despite some long and superfluous descriptive passages, the books will appeal to anyone who enjoys a story well told.

Stockton, Frank R. *The Story Teller's Pack: A Frank R. Stockton Reader.* New York: Scribner, 1897; 1968.
This handsome, well-edited volume contains 17 of Stockton's finest stories: "The Bishop's Ghost and the Printer's Baby"; "The Bee-Man of Orn"; "The Queen's Museum"; "Prince Hassak's March"; "The Banished King"; "The Griffin and the Minor Canon"; "The Accommodating Circumstance"; "Old Pipes and the Dryad"; "'The Philosophy of Relative Existences'"; "The Transferred Ghost"; "Our Story"; "The Lady or the Tiger?"; "'His Wife's Deceased Sister'"; "A Tale of Negative Gravity"; "The Remarkable Wreck of the Thomas Hyke"; "The Water-Devil"; and "The Casting Away of Mrs. Lecks and Mrs. Aleshine." Although not all of these selections are pure fantasy, the majority are, and those selected for inclusion are some of Stockton's very best. Worthy of special attention are "Bee-Man," "Banished King," "Minor Canon," "Circumstance," and "Old Pipes." All of these excellent fantasy tales exhibit Stockton's sly and whimsical humor, his penchant for irony and satire, and his extraordinarily fluent prose style. One of Stockton's hallmarks is his ability to develop a satiric reversal of situation and perspective, and this he does in an especially memorable fashion in "Circumstance," which features a rather curious and unusual School for Men, where the students (full-grown men, of course) are taught the proper treatment of boys—by schoolmasters who are boys. The selections are preceded by a substantive introduction that provides both biographical material on Stockton and astute critical commentary on a number of his works. Following the selections is a brief but helpful selective bibliography. The delightful illustrations by Bernarda Bryson beautifully capture the distinctive flavor of Stockton's witty and wonderfully imaginative tales.

Swann, Thomas Burnett. *Day of the Minotaur.* New York: Ace, 1966 (paper).
Purportedly "an authentic record of several months in the late Minoan period soon after the year 1500 B.C., when the forests of Crete were luxuriant with oak and cedars and ruled by a race who called themselves the Beasts,"

Swann's energetic narrative focuses on three characters: the Princess Thea, 16-year-old niece of King Minos; her 15-year-old brother, Icarus; and Eunostos, the Minotaur, fabled "bull that walks like a man." Captured by a raiding party of Achaeans led by the coarse Ajax, Thea and Icarus are sent as sacrifices to the cave of the Minotaur. Once there, however, they encounter a creature pleasantly different from the horrific monster they expect to find. Gentle and friendly, Eunostos is anxious to make a good impression on his aristocratic visitors. After befriending Eunostos and the other fantastic denizens of the Country of the Beasts, Thea and Icarus aid them in their attempts to turn back the Achaean invasion of the Beasts' homeland. Terrible losses are suffered by both sides, but the Achaeans are finally defeated, and the novel ends on a note of romance and hope, with Thea, Eunostos, and Icarus sailing for the Isles of the Blest. Perhaps the most interesting aspect of the novel is the portrayal of Eunostos. Granted, Swann's Minotaur is a powerful and awesome warrior whose fierce bellow strikes terror into the hearts of his foes, but he would much rather be cultivating his garden or quaffing some brew with his friends Zoe the Dryad and Moschus the Centaur than doing battle. The novel is good fun, and has the added benefit of introducing the reader to some fascinating creatures of Greek mythology. A slightly different version of this work was serialized in *Science Fantasy* under the title *The Blue Monkeys*. Swann's *Cry Silver Bells* also features the fantastic inhabitants of the Country of the Beasts. In this work, which is even more playful and erotic than *Minotaur*, Eunostos appears as an eight-year-old child. Zoe and Moschus are here too, and in remarkably fine fettle.

Swann, Thomas Burnett. *Lady of the Bees.* New York: Ace, 1976 (paper). An imaginative retelling of the Romulus and Remus legend, the narrative begins with a poignant description of the live burial of Rhea Silva, the ill-fated mother of the twins, and then proceeds to chronicle the lives of the legendary founders of Rome through their 18th year. Reared by Luperca, the she-wolf, and Mellonia, the tree-dryad, the brothers plot to restore the throne of Alba Longa to its rightful possessor, their grandfather Numitor. Years before, this gentle astronomer had lost his power to his ambitious brother, Amulius. With the help of Mellonia and the Forest Folk, the twins restore Numitor to the throne and then decide to build their own city on the banks of the Tiber. The fast-paced narrative ends on a sorrowful note as a result of a tragic misunderstanding between the brothers. Instead of using an omniscient narrator, Swann has chosen to tell the story from two different first-person points of view; approximately half the episodes are seen through the eyes of the Lady of the Bees, Mellonia, while the others are narrated by Sylvan, a young faun captured by Romulus in a raid and later befriended by Remus. From these two perspectives we gain an intimate understanding of the gentle, loving, and compassionate Remus, but only a more general and superficial impression of the ambitious and wolflike Romulus. A highlight of the novel is the memorable description of the idyllic Valley of the Blue Monkeys, reminiscent of James Hilton's Valley of the Blue Moon *(Lost Horizon)*. Segments of this novel initially appeared under the title of "Where Is the Bird of Fire?" in a collection of novelettes published by Ace Books in 1970, *Where Is the Bird of Fire? Green Phoenix* (1972) is another Swann novel that features Mellonia, Lady of the Bees. In this earlier work she is portrayed as a naive 17-year-old who falls in love with the Trojan hero Aeneas. In addition, *Queens Walk in the Dusk* (1977) tells the story of Dido, queen of Carthage, Aeneas, and Ascanius and thereby forms the first part of a loosely connected trilogy.

Thurber, James. *The White Deer.* New York: Harcourt, 1945; 1968 (paper). Readers who enjoy Thurber's brand of wit and high comedy—and this includes almost everyone—will take great pleasure in this delicate and whimsical fantasy romance. It is set in medieval times in a kingdom next to the enchanted forest that lies between the Moonstone Mines and Centaurs Mountain. King Clode and his three sons pursue a noble white deer in the enchanted woods, but when they bring it to bay it turns into a beautiful princess who cannot remember her name or even if she is truly a princess or a deer. Believing her to be a princess, King Clode decrees that she set a task for each of his three sons; the first to return victorious will wed the princess. All three succeed in their quests and return simultaneously to declare their love. But now comes the true test. The princess admits that she now believes her true form to be that of a deer, but if someone professes to love her anyway, she will retain her princess shape. Prince Thag and Prince Gallow both turn away, but Prince Jorn, the youngest, proclaims his enduring love. On his quest he had learned humility and genuine love. At his declaration, the enchantment is lifted from the authentic Princess Rosanore. This recounting of the tale does little justice to the book, which is a parody of romances and faery tales and at the same time a genuine and meaningful fantasy. The style glitters as it moves from witty wordplay to alliterative, rhyming prose to elegant courtly speech. In addition to being both a genuine fantasy and a parody of fantasies, it is a stylistic tour de force. And for added entertainment, it has a number of Thurber's incomparable cartoons.

Thurber, James. *The 13 Clocks.* New York: Simon & Schuster, 1950. New York: Fireside, 1977 (paper).
The 13 Clocks is an absolutely delightful comic fantasy that abundantly displays the wit and wordplay (puns, allusions, and coinings) so characteristic of Thurber's style. It is a slender volume guaranteed to provide pleasant diversion for readers of all ages. The plot is simple. The wicked duke of Coffin Castle proposes impossible feats for the suitors of his beautiful charge, Princess Saralinda, so that he will not have to give her hand in mar-

riage (he has designs of his own). However, even the most impossible of demands is met by Zorn of Zorna, who happily sails off into the sunset with the fair Saralinda. The story is not as important as Thurber's ingenious handling of character, language, and situation (time remains frozen in the duke's castle until Zorn completes his task). Note, for example, this initial description of the villainous duke: "He was six feet four, and forty-six, and even colder than he thought he was. One eye wore a velvet patch; the other glittered through a monocle, which made half his body seem closer to you than the other half. He had lost one eye when he was twelve, for he was fond of peering into nests and lairs in search of birds and animals to maul. One afternoon, a mother shrike had mauled him first. His nights were spent in evil dreams, and his days were given to wicked schemes." The duke is just one of the work's humorously bizarre characters; also featured are Whisper, the duke's spy-in-chief, who slinks through the night clothed in "velvet mask and hood"; the Golux, a clever and magical helpmate to Zorn who had "high hopes of being Evil when [he] was two," but is now "on the side of Good"; and the Todal, "a blob of glup" that "makes a sound like rabbits screaming, and smells of old, unopened rooms." Like George MacDonald's "The Light Princess," *Clocks* maintains its integrity as a faery tale even while Thurber, like MacDonald, parodies many of the stock ingredients of the genre. This is vintage Thurber. Illustrated by Marc Simont. Also see Thurber's *The Wonderful O* (New York: Simon & Schuster, 1957), a delightfully whimsical story overflowing with Thurberesque wordplay.

Tolkien, J[ohn] R[onald] R[euel]. *The Hobbit; or, There and Back Again.* London: Allen & Unwin, 1937. Boston: Houghton Mifflin, 1938. New York: Ballantine, 1976 (paper).

When it first appeared in 1937, *The Hobbit* was a modest success, so Stanley Unwin, Tolkien's publisher, asked him for a sequel. The sequel is now known as *The Lord of the Rings*. Rather than *LOTR* being considered a sequel, however, *The Hobbit* has been dubbed a prelude to the longer and more complex tale. Yet *The Hobbit* is, in its own right, outstanding both as literature and as fantasy. It has rightly become recognized as a classic in the faery-tale genre. The plot itself is fairly simple. Bilbo Baggins is hired as a burglar by 12 dwarfs, Thorin and Company, who seek to regain the riches of their ancestors now being hoarded by the dragon Smaug. (Hobbits make good burglars because they move quietly—perhaps because they grow four feet tall and go barefooted—and they have sharp eyes.) Actually, Bilbo is selected by Gandalf, the wizard, who recognizes his hidden potential for heroism. The story then describes the series of adventures, some magical and enchanting, some nearly disastrous, that the companions experience on their quest. But it would be misleading to describe the book as simply a sequence of adventures. The television version (1978) failed precisely because it made this mistake. The book is about Bilbo's development from a timid, insular Shire dweller to a courageous, self-sacrificing individual. Bilbo grows with each new experience and discovers new resources within himself with each new trial. Thus, in the best tradition of the quest motif, the real object of the quest is spiritual and personal rather than material. Another important theme that gives further unity to the work is the destructiveness of greed. And a less prominent but still important lesson is to beware of conformity. The interweaving of these adventures and themes with Bilbo's development makes *The Hobbit* an enriching experience for readers—or listeners—from age seven on. Readers of every age will sense the wonder of the work whether or not they can identify the archetype that elicits it. And all readers will respond to Tolkien's craftsmanship with language, noticeable in his descriptions and dialogue, but most prominent in his handling of names. Finally, readers of *The Hobbit* will be reminded that tragedy occurs in the secondary as well as the primary world, but they will be consoled by the fact that tragedy, even death, is not necessarily final. Tolkien refers to this view of tragedy as eucatastrophe.

Tolkien, J. R. R. *The Lord of the Rings*. 3 vols. *The Fellowship of the Ring*. London: Allen & Unwin, 1954. Boston: Houghton Mifflin, 1954. New York: Ballantine, 1965 (paper). *The Two Towers*. London: Allen & Unwin, 1955. Boston: Houghton Mifflin, 1956. New York: Ballantine, 1965 (paper). *The Return of the King*. London: Allen & Unwin, 1955. Boston: Houghton Mifflin, 1956. New York: Ballantine, 1965 (paper).
Tolkien and Stanley Unwin first discussed the possibility of a sequel to *The Hobbit* just weeks after that book appeared in 1937. *The Lord of the Rings,* the eventual result of this discussion, is much more than a sequel. It is the main work, to which *The Hobbit* is the preface. *LOTR* is a massive chronicle of the chief events of the Third Age of Middle Earth. Tolkien worked on it with a fair degree of consistency for 12 years before he completed the initial manuscript in 1950. Length of time in the making is not necessarily a reflection of the quality of a work, but in the case of *LOTR,* it is. Simply expressed, *LOTR* has become the norm according to which all other fantasy works must now be judged. It is common to speak of *LOTR* as a trilogy. Dividing the work into three volumes and publishing each one separately with an individual title was an editorial decision based on practical rather than literary considerations. It was a decision to which Tolkien agreed only reluctantly, since he had composed a single work divided into six parts or books. However, little or no real confusion has occurred because of the trilogy misnomer. The nature of the work speaks for itself, requiring that each volume be read in proper sequence. And those who become involved with the story will hardly be able to put the book down after the first volume. W. H. Auden expressed this nicely when he commented on the "cruelty"

of having to wait several months for each of the two subsequent volumes. The three-part division also has a fortunate logic, with each part containing two books of equal length according to Tolkien's original division. Indeed, the grouping has thematic justification, as we shall see.

The Fellowship of the Rings (Books I and II) appeared in the summer of 1954. Book I begins with a tone similar to that found in *The Hobbit*, making a transition from a more lighthearted to the more serious note that characterizes *LOTR* generally. Bilbo passes the ring on to his nephew and adopted heir, Frodo, significantly on the latter's 33rd birthday, the year of coming of age for hobbits.When Frodo discovers from Gandalf the nature and origins of the One Ring, Isildur's Bane, the Ring of Power, he decides to leave the Shire. He wants to protect the Shire and also to elude Sauron, the enemy who, if he should possess the ring, would enslave all of Middle Earth. Frodo is joined by Samwise, his servant, and two of his cousins, Pippin and Merry. As Book I closes, the group meets Strider, who turns out to be Aragorn, the traditional hero-type of the work. Book II principally concerns the Council of Elrond, at which the history of the ring is rehearsed and a plan formulated for its destruction (since no one can wield it without becoming tainted). Frodo recognizes and voluntarily accepts his destiny—"doom" in the Old English sense—and becomes the Ring Bearer. He must journey to the fortress of the enemy, for only there where it was forged can the ring be destroyed. To accompany him Elrond appoints eight representatives of various races and nations of Middle Earth. Book II then records the first steps of the Fellowship on their journey through the underground darkness of Moria to the green beauty of the forest of Lothlorien. The conclusion of Book II paints one of the bleaker scenes of the entire work, with the breaking up of the Fellowship. Some perish by drowning (or appear to); others are captured by Orc soldiers of Sauron, and Frodo and Sam set off by boat, little knowing where they are or what their direction should be.

The second volume, aptly entitled *The Two Towers* (Books III and IV, published in November 1954), follows the separate paths of the divided Fellowship. The two towers referred to in the title are both centers of evil: Orthanc, Saruman's monolithic headquarters in Isengard; and Cirith Ungol, the Dark Tower of Sauron, Lord of Mordor. Book III deals with Saruman in his tower in Isengard. Saruman, formerly called The White, had been the foremost wizard in the Council of the Wise, but fell victim of his own pride and the evil lure of Sauron. In the attack on Orthanc, Aragorn leads one remnant of the Fellowship, Gandalf another. Joining them is Theoden, King of the Mark of Rohan, who leads his horsemen (or Rohirrim), men of Middle Earth, against Saruman's armies. The events chronicled in Book III occur simultaneously with those in Book III. In Book IV, Frodo and Sam make quite a different type of assault on the second tower, the Dark Tower of Sauron. Frodo's will and Sam's loyalty, rather than any physical kind of strength, are challenged here. They are not alone, of course, for it is the extensive marshaling of forces at Isengard that attracts the eye of Sauron and allows the two hobbits and Gollum to approach the gates of Mordor unnoticed. The juxtaposition of events in Books III and IV suggests that while military strength is necessary, moral stamina is much more important in the conflict against the enemy.

The last volume, *The Return of the King* (Books V and VI), was published in October 1955, relieving the suspense of many anxious readers. In Book V, the action shifts once again to the part of the Fellowship that continues, ironically but designedly, to draw the attention of Sauron away from the Ring Bearer. Gandalf and Aragorn now establish an alliance of the men of Rohan and Gondor, drawing the Dark Lord to commit part of his forces in an assault against them. Book V, describing these events, offers a panorama of battle and scenes of heroic deeds. In Book VI Tolkien magnificently meets the challenge of how to satisfactorily conclude this epic. He provides a surprising but fitting climax and resolution to the entire work. At the moment when Aragorn and Gandalf are desperately attempting to rally their forces against Sauron's armies, Frodo, with some additional unexpected help, achieves his quest. After nearly four books, the Fellowship is finally reunited in triumph—a triumph that is not, however, unalloyed.

According to Tolkien, his "prime motive was the desire of a story teller to try his hand at a really long story that would hold the attention of readers, amuse them, delight them, and at times maybe excite them or deeply move them" (from the foreword to the 1965 edition). His story has accomplished this objective for countless readers—more readers than of any other fantasy work of the century. But it is not just the story that accounts for the work's unparalleled and continued success; it has wide thematic appeal as well. It examines issues that transcend boundaries of time and geography, issues such as destiny and free will, human corruptibility, and responsibility to society and to nature. No less appealing are the unique characters that have sprung from Tolkien's imagination: the familiar yet mysterious Tom Bombadil; the self-tormenting, pitiable Gollum; Treebeard, the leader of the Ents; Galadriel, the Elven Queen. Most significant among the characters is the hero of the epic, Frodo, the halfling from the Shire, the little person who the great ones overlook—to their own peril. However, the deepest and most lasting impression produced by *LOTR* is very likely due to the language. Tolkien employs language that ranges from the elegance of the Elven tongue to the guttural harshness of the Orcs' speech, and he sounds all the tones in between. He flavors the text with runes and letters in the flowing script of the Eldar.

Finally, in his greatest linguistic achievement, Tolkien formulates names which, as in only the very best fantasies, somehow capture the essence of what is named. Place names such as Lothlorien and Mordor and names of beings such as Galadriel and Lugburz remain with the reader, having bestirred some archetypal memories of good or evil. It is fitting that the bestowal of names should be Tolkien's greatest talent, otherwise the world that he "subcreated" (his term) would not seem as authentic as it is.

Tolkien, J. R. R. *Farmer Giles of Ham.* London: Allen & Unwin, 1949. Boston: Houghton Mifflin, 1949. *Smith of Wootton Major.* London: Allen & Unwin, 1967. Boston: Houghton Mifflin, 1967. Reprinted in one volume as *Smith of Wootton Major and Farmer Giles of Ham.* New York: Ballantine, 1975 (paper).

"Smith of Wootton Major" is the last story that Tolkien wrote, and therefore, as his swan song, it holds a very special place in the hearts of Tolkien enthusiasts. It is pure faery tale, focusing on the poignant adventures of Smith of Wootton Major, who unknowingly swallows a "fay-star" and subsequently is permitted to enter the magical land of faërie. Smith enjoys his acquaintance with the Perilous Realm for many years, even meeting the queen and king of Fairyland, but then is instructed by the latter to return the fay-star so that a new owner might have the opportunity to experience the joy and magical adventures encountered by Smith. Humphrey Carpenter, in *Tolkien: A Biography,* points out that unlike most of Tolkien's writings, this one contains many personal echoes. "Farmer Giles of Ham," the longer of the two selections, is an absolutely delightful mock-heroic tale that recounts "The Rise and Wonderful Adventures of Farmer Giles, Lord of Tame, Count of Worminghall and King of the Little Kingdom." After accidentally shooting a marauding giant with his blunderbuss (actually, he only wounds the leviathan in the nose), Farmer Giles quickly attains the stature of hero in his small village. At first he is rather confused by the whole turn of events, but as his fame spreads he warms to his prestigious status. He feels himself a hero of epic proportions indeed when the king sends a testimonial and a gift, a long sword that is later identified as the magical dragon-killer, Tailbiter. The good farmer's perspective on his newly acquired status changes, though, when a dragon, Chrysophylax Dives, invades the countryside and Giles is automatically expected to challenge the worm. Giles not only challenges him, but subdues him, and in a matter of time ends up king of his own "Little Kingdom." This story is a perfect showcase for Tolkien's wit and elfish sense of humor. It is a work that will make any gray day a good bit brighter. Both stories are sprinkled with delightful pen-and-ink sketches by Pauline Baynes. The only regret one might voice about this volume is that it does not contain "Leaf by Niggle," Tolkien's other fantasy short story, which brilliantly combines faery tale and religious allegory. But then those who have enjoyed the present volume will want to seek out *The Tolkien Reader,* where they will discover, in addition to other treasures, "Leaf by Niggle."

Tolkien, J. R. R. *The Father Christmas Letters.* Boston: Houghton Mifflin, 1976.

This slim but extremely handsome volume contains a fine sampling of the letters and drawings that Tolkien sent his children each Christmas for roughly 20 years. The family tradition began in 1920 when Tolkien's eldest son, John, was three years old, and continued through the childhoods of the three other children, Michael, Chistopher, and Priscilla. Most of the letters were ostensibly written by Father Christmas himself, but a few were composed by his chief assistant, the lovable but bumbling Polar Bear, and by his secretary, Ilbereth, an elf with "spidery" script. The missives were put into decorated envelopes complete with North Pole postage stamps designed and painted by Tolkien, and either hand-delivered by him or brought by a postman who was in on the game. The letters are delightful. They describe Father Christmas's house and his preparations for Christmas Eve, the hilarious adventures of Polar Bear, and the exciting battles waged against the malicious Goblins, who persistently raid Father Christmas's house and store-cellars. Baille Tolkien, J. R. R. Tolkien's daughter-in-law, has done a commendable editing job. Not only has she chosen 16 of the most delightful and representative letters (including the first and last), but she has also made certain that almost all of Tolkien's playful drawings and paintings were included. Furthermore, there are some examples of Father Christmas's shaky handwriting and of the unique postage stamps and envelopes. Preceding the letters is an all-too-brief but still enlightening introduction by the editor, and following them is an appendix containing an alphabet that Polar Bear invented from marks he found in the Goblin caves. This work provides further insight into the personality and artistry of the most popular fantasist of our time.

Tolkien, J. R. R. *The Silmarillion.* Boston: Houghton Mifflin, 1977. New York: Ballantine, 1979 (paper).

The Silmarillion serves as a "prequel" (Tolkien's own word) to *The Hobbit* and *The Lord of the Rings,* greatly enriching these other works. For if the others are tales of Middle Earth, *The Silmarillion* is its Bible—the mythopoeic account of the creation of Tolkien's land and the compendium of its cosmology and history. Five accounts make up the work: Ainulindalë (of creation), Valaquenta (of the Gods), Quenta Silmarillion (of the Elves), Akallabêth (of the Numenorean kings), and a shortened account of *LOTR,* "Of the Rings of Power and the Third Age." Each section benefits from the power and boldness of Tolkien's imaginative genius and from his brilliant style. If the "organ tones" of Ainulindalë are impressive, they are no more so than the deceptive ease of the catalog of gods or the grand Story of the Elven tragedy. Each combines precise detail of action with clear-cut motivation, defining what may be called the "inner consistency of reality." This inner consistency, though, is only one of the grand virtues of the work. En-chanting names, unbreakable oaths, magical boundaries, half-glimpsed races—all the aspects of high fantasy permeate the work. Yet the crowning achievement of the volume is to be found behind the myth and behind the fantasy, in the ethos that Tolkien has created. This ethos, combining touches of Nordic and Christian principles, breathes life into Tolkien's Elven race, which is the major focus of this work. The Elves learn it from the immortal Valar, and they pass on what they can to the other races of Middle Earth. Only the Elves, though, with their peculiar capacity for immortality, can participate fully in this ethos. It asks for undying commitment to a cause that can fail; it asks that they serve the cause of change when they are, finally, incapable of it. This for the Elves is eucatastrophe: a tragedy, but a tragedy that affirms their greatness. Hints of this ethos can be found in *The Lord of the Rings,* but *The Silmarillion* articulates it fully, defining its tender pathos; this is the work's great contribution to imaginative literature. The fantasy fan will also find here the full tales of Beren and Lúthien, of Eärendil's heroic voyage beyond the seas, of Feanor's fateful oath. Here, the careful reader can discover Gandalf's true nature. Christopher Tolkien is to be commended for his careful editing of a vast collection of material.

Vance, Jack. *The Dying Earth.* New York: Hillman, 1950. New York: Pocket Books, 1977 (paper).

"Once [Earth] was a tall world of cloudy mountains and bright rivers, and the sun was a white blazing ball. Ages of rain and wind have beaten and rounded the granite, and the sun is feeble and red. The continents have sunk and risen. A million cities have lifted towers, have fallen to dust. In place of the old peoples a few thousand strange souls live. There is evil on Earth, evil distilled by time. . . ." It is this setting—a dying earth, inhabited by incredible beings, where magic has replaced science—that forms the eerie backdrop for the six stories that compose *The Dying Earth.* Although a few characters appear in more than one story (Turjan of Miir and T'sais, for example) and some stories are loosely related ("Turjan of Miir," "Mazirian the Magician," and "T'sais"), each story is complete and can be read independent of the others. *The Dying Earth* is usually classified as science fantasy, and this is probably the most technically correct designation. Few of the stories, how-ever, have much to do with science, machinery, or technology ("Guyal of Sfere" is an exception). Magic prevails in this twilight world, and Vance's narratives contain an abundance—perhaps an overabundance—of elixirs, amulets, spells, runes, incantations, hissing alembics, crystals, and eternal lamps. It is this emphasis upon things magical and exotic that makes *The Dying Earth* so unique and memorable. For sheer imaginative power, few contemporary fantasists can equal Vance. Just when the reader thinks that Vance's repertoire of weird creatures (Twk-men, deodands, the pelgrane, the prowling erbs, the gids) has been exhausted, he brings out even stranger ones from his incredible menagerie. There are some similarities between

Vance and Clark Ashton Smith in terms of adjectival style and exotic/erotic descriptions, but generally speaking Vance stands alone in the world of fantasy literature.

Vance, Jack. *The Eyes of the Overworld.* New York: Ace, 1966 (paper). Boston: Gregg, 1977. New York: Pocket Books, 1977 (paper).

It is difficult, perhaps impossible, to name a contemporary fantasist with a creative imagination more fertile than that possessed by Jack Vance. His supply of bizarre characters and creatures, exotic settings, and ingenious plot devices is truly remarkable for its depth and diversity, and *Overworld* serves as a superlative vehicle for the display of this cornucopialike repertoire. Although a highly episodic work (six of the seven chapters appeared as individual stories in *The Magazine of Fantasy and Science Fiction*), *Overworld* is given unity through its picaresque hero, Cugel the Clever, who is the central character in all of the episodes. Caught in the act of burglarizing the manse of Iucounu the Laughing Magician, Cugel grudgingly agrees (actually he has little choice), as a kind of "requital" for his crime, to seek out the mate of a magic cusp possessed by Iucounu. To ensure Cugel's "expeditious discharge of his duties" the Laughing Magician takes Firx, "a small white creature, all claws, prongs, barbs, and hooks," and thrusts it against Cugel's abdomen, where it merges with his viscera and takes up a "vigilant post clasped around Cugel's liver." The remainder of the novel recounts Cugel's quest for the magic cusp, his attaining of it, and his long and hazardous journey back to the Laughing Magician's manse. This return trip takes Cugel through a number of exotic "Dying Earth" lands (see *The Dying Earth* annotation) where magic rules supreme, and brings him into contact with many weird beings including ghouls, demons, leucomorphs, erbs, deodands, and grues. Perhaps the best episode is the first, "The Overworld." It is distinguished by Vance's ingenious central device of the magic cusps of illusion, which allow the wearers to "look from this to the Overworld, which is the quintessence of human hope, visionary longing, and beatific dream." Also noteworthy is "The Cave in the Forest," which features the sorcerer Zaraides who finally removes Firx from Cugel's abdomen, and the repulsive rat-folk who have engineered an ingenious scheme for enticing their victims into their subterranean lair. All in all, this is a fine work of high fantasy.

Walton, Evangeline [pseud. of Evangeline Ensley]. *The Prince of Annwn.* New York: Ballantine, 1974 (paper). New York: Del Rey, 1978 (paper).

Three of our finest contemporary fantasists—Kenneth Morris, Lloyd Alexander, and Evangeline Walton—have repeatedly turned to the *Mabinogion,* that wonderfully vast repository of Welsh myth and legend, for both inspiration and materials. The resultant literary creations have been superlative: Morris's *The Fates of the Princes of Dyfed* and *Book of the Three Dragons* are, at long last, being reprinted and recognized as true works of genius; Alexander's Prydain books are the recipients of prestigious writing awards and have earned the love and respect of countless fantasy readers of all ages; and Walton's Mabinogion tetralogy—*The Prince of Annwn, The Children of Llyr, The Song of Rhiannon,* and *The Island of the Mighty*—has established itself as a contemporary classic. *Annwn,* the last of the four to be written, but the first in the series in that it retells the first branch of the *Mabinogion,* is the least complex but perhaps the most dramatic novel in the tetralogy. It is divided into two books: "Descent into the Abyss" and "Rhiannon of the Birds." The first opens as Pwyll, Prince of Dyfed, meets with Arawn, Prince of Annwn (death), in the woods of Glen Cuch. Under the terms of a pact he makes with Arawn, Pwyll must journey to the kingdom of Annwn to do battle with Havgan, a ruler of the Eastern World of Annwn, whose ambitions threaten both Annwn and the world of humankind. After encountering a number of trials and temptations devised to strengthen and temper his character, Pwyll confronts and defeats Havgan. The young champion's return to his own land is followed by three winters and three summers of happiness and plenty, but the "fourth winter [comes] howling like a wolf" and it is at this juncture, the beginning of grave troubles for Pwyll and his people, that Book II begins. Pwyll is confronted by the High Druid, who tells him that the suffering in the kingdom is a result of the young ruler's failure to marry and provide an heir. Pwyll's adventures on the "dread mound" of Gorsedd Arbeth and his journeys into the Bright World in search of a bride make up the rest of the novel. After barely escaping death on Gorsedd Arbeth, he returns triumphant with Rhiannon of the Birds as his bride. In this and the other Mabinogion books Walton practices a certain amount of artistic license in the handling of her source materials; she makes additions, deletions, and modifications in order to make her narrative more dramatically effective. She points out in a brief afterword, for example, that in *Annwn* she has "remodeled" certain scenes (for example, the combat between Pwyll and Havgan), and has added others (Pwyll's encounters with the three-jawed monster and the Bird of Death). The final effect is a lucid, dramatic, and powerful narrative. Although the shortest of the series, *Annwn* is rich in theme. Especially important are the themes of appearance versus reality, the importance of humanity living in harmony with nature, and the constant conflict between the old and the new. The writing of *Annwn* is of consistently high quality, and the description of the meeting of Pwyll with the Grey Man of Annwn in the opening chapter is exceptionally fine.

Walton, Evangeline. *The Children of Llyr.* New York: Ballantine, 1971 (paper). New York: Del Rey, 1978 (paper).
This is Walton's retelling of the second branch of the *Mabinogion.* As the title suggests, the novel focuses upon the lives of the five children of Llyr: Bran the Blessed, "kind and just" king over all the Island of the Mighty;

Manawyddan, his loyal and sensitive younger brother; their sister, Branwen, only daughter of Llyr and, for a brief period, the wife of Matholuch the High-King of Ireland; and the two half-brothers, Nissyen and Evnissyen, progeny of the forced union between Llyr's wife, Penardim, and the hateful Eurosswydd. Only Manawyddan remains alive at the end of this tragic history; the others die either during or shortly after the Great War between the Irish and the host of the Island of the Mighty. This is a novel permeated with raw emotion, brute violence, and human savagery. It lays bare the evil in humanity—its envy, its malice, its hate, its deceit and treachery. It is not reading matter for those with queasy stomachs. Perhaps the most grisly scenes are those that describe the horrific creations of the Cauldron of Rebirth. But there are also exquisitely poignant and tender episodes. Branwen's training of the starling and its determined flight to Bran bearing the message of his sister's ill-treatment by Matholuch, for example, is a segment both moving and powerful. It is, of course, Walton's vivid descriptions that bring these and other scenes to life. Some idea of her superb descriptive powers is suggested by this description of Matholuch, as he and his men first step onto the shore of the Island of the Mighty: "He was tall and comely, Matholuch; indeed, no man with any blemish might be High-King in Tara. His silky hair and beard were almost red, but in the dying sunlight they shone with a glitter that was golden. His keen eyes were almost blue, yet too pale for blueness; no young comely woman ever looked into them without dreaming of being the sunrise that would warm them."

Walton, Evangeline. *The Song of Rhiannon.* New York: Ballantine, 1972 (paper). New York: Del Rey, 1979 (paper).

Rhiannon, Walton's retelling of the third branch of the *Mabinogion,* serves as an excellent foil to *The Children of Llyr. Llyr* is a novel of bloody battles, deadly political intrigue, and far-reaching tragedy; *Rhiannon* is an essentially tranquil and nonviolent work that describes the great love between Manawyddan and Rhiannon and between Pryderi and Kigva. This is not to say that all is happiness; the characters do suffer defeats, and at times feel great sadness—but always only temporarily. The Land of Dyfed is "blasted" and turned into a "desert" for seven long years, and Rhiannon and Pryderi are kidnapped by the forces of the Bright World, but the wisdom and tenacity of Manawyddan prove strong enough to force the Grey Man to return the two prisoners and restore Dyfed to its proper prosperity. The conclusion, unlike that of *Llyr,* is joyous and optimistic. *Rhiannon,* like the other volumes in the tetralogy, is essentially serious, but it is not without humor. Indeed, Walton's "bogey," a mischievous, gnomelike creature who decides to haunt the castle of Manawyddan and Kigva, not only provides good comic relief, but actually plays an important role in the rescue of Rhiannon and Pryderi. Kigva does not appreciate his antics in the least, but Walton's readers surely will. Another especially memorable segment is the old woman's narration of the story of Pryderi's disappearance and sub-sequent return to Pwyll and Rhiannon (chapters 2 and 3). It is through this episode that the reader first learns that Pryderi is really the son of Mana-wyddan, not of Pwyll.

Walton, Evangeline. *The Virgin and the Swine.* Chicago: Willett, Clark, 1936. Reprinted as *The Island of the Mighty.* New York: Ballantine, 1970 (paper). New York: Del Rey, 1979 (paper).

This retelling of the fourth branch of the *Mabinogion* is the longest, most brilliantly polished, most intricately plotted, and most substantive of Walton's Mabinogion books. The central character and primary unifying force is Gwydion, eldest son of Dôn, but the narrative focus differs in each of the three books that compose this volume. In Book I, "The Pigs of Pryderi," the focus is upon Gwydion and his brother Gilvaethwy. Readers witness their short-lived triumphs (such as the acquisition—through the magic of illusion—of 12 of Pryderi's pigs, and the seduction of Goewyn), and their long-term punishments (they are transformed into three different kinds of beasts over a three-year period by Mâth the Ancient, King of Gwynedd). Book II, "Llew," recounts the birth and early years of Llew, son of Arianrhod. Book III, "The Loves of Blodeuwedd," tells the tragic story of Blodeuwedd, the exquisitely beautiful woman who is created out of flowers by Gwydion and Mâth so that Llew can take her as a wife and thus circumvent Arianrhod's curse: "Never shall his [Llew's] side touch a woman's of the race that now dwells upon this earth." (See Alan Garner's treatment of this legend in *The Owl Service.*) All three stories are masterfully told, and are characterized by an elevated style befitting the dignity of the original legends. *Island* has an epic sweep and grandeur that set it apart from the other volumes of the tetralogy. Walton's Mabinogion books have received a great deal of critical acclaim, and it is easy to see why: her secondary worlds are well defined and credible; her characters, whether human or supernatural, are carefully delineated and believable; her style is energetic, lucid, and polished; and her narratives are skillfully plotted. Furthermore, Walton, like the Welsh bards who first told these stories, recognizes the importance of combining instruction with entertainment. The Mabinogion books are smashing adventure stories, but they are also rich in thematic import. Walton's Mabinogion tetralogy is a bona fide masterpiece of myth fantasy.

Warner, Sylvia Townsend. *Kingdoms of Elfin.* New York: Viking, 1977. New York: Delta, 1978 (paper).

This collection contains 16 fantasy stories: "The One and the Other," "The Five Black Swans," "Elphenor and Weasel," "The Blameless Triangle," "The Revolt at Brocéliande," "The Mortal Milk," "Beliard," "Visitors to a Castle," "The Power of Cookery," "Winged Creatures," "The Search for an Ancestress," "The Climate of Exile," "The Late Sir Glamie," "Castor and Pollux," "The Occupation," and "Foxcastle." Except for "The Climate of Exile" and "The Late Sir Glamie," all of the above appeared originally in *The New Yorker,* and display the kind of urbane wit and subtle satire generally associated with that magazine. Although difficult to single out favorites from a collection of such high and even quality, "Beliard," "Castor and Pollux," and "Elphenor and Weasel" are especially memorable. "Elphenor," one of Warner's personal favorites, provides convincing evidence, if such is needed, that fantasy can instruct as well as entertain. The reader of this poignant tale will find no better statement on the destructive potential of bias and prejudice. This outstanding collection nicely displays the wide variety of settings, characters, and motifs that exist within the genre of high fantasy; it also provides a splendid showcase for Warner's energetic prose style, sprightly wit, and wry humor. Particularly remarkable is the large number of different kingdoms of faërie depicted in the stories. These diverse kingdoms of Elfin not only add to the variety alluded to above, but also provide fascinating studies of how the secondary and primary worlds relate.

White, T[erence] H[anbury]. *Mistress Masham's Repose.* New York: Putnam, 1946.

Terence Hanbury White ought to be recognized as a leader of children's rights; *Mistress Masham's Repose* is the charming novel that forcefully makes this point. If *The Once and Future King* is White's grand portrait on the subject of right versus might, *Mistress* is his flawless miniature on the same subject. The heroine of *Mistress* is a 10-year-old orphan, Maria, who lives on her estate of Malplaquet under the guardianship of Miss Brown and the Vicar, Mr. Hater, who bully her and intend to swindle her out of her inheritance. Malplaquet is a huge estate—it is, in fact, modeled on the Churchill-Marlborough estate of Blenheim. While exploring an island, the Island of Repose, Maria discovers a colony of Lilliputians who had been exploited by a Captain Biddell; he had exhibited them as side-show freaks after hearing about them from Gulliver. Maria impetuously treats the Lilliputians as her playthings until, with the help of the wise old professor, she realizes that she has been discourteous and even tyrannical, treating them as something subhuman just as her guardians had treated her because of her size. She matures greatly from her experiences and joins forces with the little people against Brown and Hater (Braun and Hitler?) who have by this time discovered the little people and connived to use them for their own gain. The plot of the book is effectively constructed to present the theme of both conscious and unconscious tyranny based on force and an inability to see the world from someone else's perspective. But White also develops the theme of old-fashioned manners or courtesy, using the eighteenth-century manners still retained by the Lilliputians as his norm. The entire work sparkles with White's satiric wit and polished prose. He employs the cul-

tured language of the eighteenth century to underscore the vulgarity of the
current state of the language. Younger readers may find the various styles
heavy going at times unless the work is read aloud to them, although the
speech of the Lilliputian schoolmaster (he is their spokesman) is written in
capital letters to accentuate the elevated tone. But all readers will enjoy
White's descriptive details of the life-style of little people, such as their boots
made from the tanned hides of mice or their handkerchiefs woven from
cobweb. And if the readers ever visit Blenheim Palace, they need only ask
their guide who the historical Mistress Masham was to discover the authentic detail that went into the composition of this deceptively unpretentious book.

White, T. H. *The Once and Future King*. London: Collins, 1958. New York:
    Putnam, 1958. New York: Berkley, 1966 (paper).
This singular classic of Arthurian fantasy is the epitome of the vast Arthurian tradition as it comes down to the twentieth century. If the work is not
true to every detail of its primary source (Malory), the accuracy of its tone
and atmosphere more than compensates. It starts at the court of Sir Ector
when Arthur is yet a boy—a foster child affectionately known as Wart.
Merlyn the magician tutors Wart and his imperious foster-brother, Kay.
Through Merlyn's magic, the boys (especially Wart) are given a remarkable
education. Wart learns by doing as well as by studying. He becomes a falcon
to learn respect for the military code; as a fish, he learns the meaning of
personal danger. In a particularly good section, Wart and Kay join Robin
Wood's [*sic*] band and defeat an army of griffins to gain access to a faery
castle. Arthur's youth is typified by wonder and carefree laughter, and,
throughout the book, regardless of the splendor of his Table Round or the
glory of the Holy Grail, these early days under Merlyn's tutelage are his
best. For it is Merlyn who embodies wonder and humor for Arthur—as he
signals them for the reader. The ancient wizard lives backward in time, re-
membering the twentieth century as the past and constantly confusing it
with his present. He is a bit of a bumbler, but his moral judgments are always exact and his lessons beneficial. Yet Merlyn cannot counsel Arthur
throughout the life of the king. Arthur is left to rule his young realm without Merlyn, and he valiantly attempts to modify the might makes right
ethos—first through chivalry and later through the quest for the Holy Grail.
Both attempts are successful for a long time, but neither circumvents the
final tragedy. Arthur's illegitimate birth, his bastard son, and the love of
Guenivere and Lancelot combine to manifest this tragedy—the fall of the
court of Arthur. The descriptive power of the work is undeniable; White
evokes a range of emotions rarely found, from the joy of a boy's carefree
energy to the massive sorrow of a thwarted ideal. The fantasy of the work
is delightful, the style is superior, and the story has "nor youth nor age."

Williams, Charles. *War in Heaven*. London: Gollancz, 1930. Grand Rapids, MI: Eerdmans, 1965 (paper).

Mystical, religious, theological, specifically Christian: the first three terms are generally considered more or less synonymous, but the nuances of meaning of all four terms are necessary if one is to categorize the fantasy novels of Charles Williams without giving the wrong impression. Williams is concerned with every manifestation of the spirit world, with demons as well as with angels. He has written brilliantly and authoritatively in numerous essays on topics such as witchcraft and Dante's divine Beatrice. The spirit world, good and bad, is the secondary world of all of Williams's fantasy novels. It varies from novel to novel, but its basic features are recognizable in each. Williams's spiritual secondary world is not the weird one of the typical ghost story, nor is it the traditional heaven and hell sort of spirit world. In fact, Williams's spirit world embraces both of these. It is simply a world with no dimensions in our sense of the word. Yet it exists "next to" the world in which we live, and the two worlds at times intersect. *War in Heaven,* because the amount of adventure far outweighs the amount of metaphysics, is a good place to start reading Charles Williams. The first line of the book is a classic: "The telephone bell was ringing wildly, but without result, since there was no-one in the room but the corpse." With this line begins the detective-story plot, one of the novel's three interconnecting plots. Gregory Persimmons, who perceives the achievement of the greatest possible evil as his greatest personal good or joy, is at the center of all three. He is responsible for the corpse, but, more important, he is addicting two unwitting victims to evil, because he needs suitable sacrifices for his Black Mass or Witches' Sabbath. An even more important element for his occult activities is a talisman of great power; in this case it is the Holy Grail. Persimmons's attempts to acquire and hold onto the Grail against strong opponents is the third and most important plot line in the novel. His chief opponent in the fight over the Grail is Julian Davenant, Archdeacon of Fardles (or, to use its earlier name, Castra Parvulorum—the Camp of the Children). Without realizing it, the Archdeacon has, in fact, been using the Grail at Mass for years. The three plots come together in a memorable climax in which the Archdeacon, with his companions, confronts Persimmons and his allies. They engage in a spiritual duel over the Grail, calling upon their masters and becoming channels for much higher powers than themselves. The Archdeacon triumphs, though he is mortally wounded in the process, and rescues both the Grail and Persimmons's human sacrifices. The climactic scene just described is one of three secondary world scenes, where the setting shifts from our time and space to a spiritual or supernatural world that occupies no time or place at all. The other two secondary world scenes are Persimmons's Black Mass and the Archdeacon's final High Mass, the powerfully moving conclusion to the book. These two scenes dramatize the theme of the book, the difference between absolute negation and absolute affirmation.

Williams, Charles. *Many Dimensions.* London: Gollancz, 1931. Grand
   Rapids, MI: Eerdmans, 1965 (paper).
The vehicle of power in this work is a Stone from the ancient crown of Suleiman ben Daood (Solomon). A piece of primal matter that responds to the will of the holder, the Stone is capable of traveling through time and space and of healing the sick. Although infinitely divisible, it loses none of its mass or potency. Possession of the Stone and its Types (duplications of the Stone) is the goal of various factions—the Persian Embassy, the British government, an American transport firm, and a number of individuals. These factions all have their particular reasons for wanting the Stone, and it is as the object of their desire that the Stone is the thematic focus of the work. Religious fanaticism, political control, mercenary gain, inhumane scientism—all are reasons for pursuing the talisman, but none are appropriate. Lord Arglay, Chief Justice of England, and his secretary, Chloe Burnett, represent proper regard for the Stone—acceptance and submission. Together the two manifest the power of the Stone and remove it from the reach of the others. Like Williams's other "supernatural thrillers," the work balances intrigue with mysticism, suspense with spirituality. Some interesting intellectual puzzles are posed as well. Cycles of time are discussed in light of the Stone's power to interrupt the past and the future. The nature of law is investigated by Lord Arglay and his aide. In effect, the work conflates spiritual fantasy and intellectuality, leaving the reader the distinct impression that the two are by nature inseparable.

Williams, Charles. *The Place of the Lion.* London: Gollancz, 1931. Grand
   Rapids, MI: Eerdmans, 1965 (paper).
The extended trance of an English mystic opens a door to an otherworld, a world of Platonic ideas, where natures are unadulterated, where strength is untempered by gentleness, subtlety by bravado. These pure natures enter our world in the forms of huge animals—the lion and the lamb, the snake and the phoenix—and challenge humanity's dominion over the earth. Humankind alone is no match for these principles, but by associating itself with high wisdom—with the eagle—it can establish the balance that should reign. Anthony Durrant, an intense and holy young man, hazards the place of the eagle for the sake of his love, Damaris Tighe, and his friend, Quentin Sabot, both of whom are directly challenged by the awesome power of the ideas. Through wisdom, Durrant recognizes the rightful nature of humanity's dominion over the earth. He accepts the role of Adam and reenacts the Edenic naming of the beasts, reasserting his spiritual authority over the animals. This is an erudite work, the product of careful and specific knowledge of Platonic philosophy, Biblical exegesis, and a variety of Neoplatonic

thinkers (especially Peter Abelard). If readers approach the work with care and attention, it will reward them with some genuine philosophy and some startlingly fresh speculation. Moreover, a number of the individual scenes of the work are thoroughly cinematic. Durrant's visions and the final naming scene challenge the reader's imagination with a montage of superb images. The work is one of Williams's best, and therefore among the finest of speculative fantasy.

Williams, Charles. *The Greater Trumps.* London: Gollancz, 1932. Grand Rapids, MI: Eerdmans, 1976 (paper).
Williams's talent is his ability to evoke awe and respect from his readers—awe at the fantastic possibilities of the universe and respect for those who accept these possibilities. In this work, he opens the door to the possibility that the Tarot deck is a potent mystical vehicle. The original deck of Tarot is sought after and finally used by contemporary members of an ancient Gypsy family whose aim is perfect prophecy. This prophecy is not simple fortune-telling; it is manipulation of the elemental forces of the moral universe. In conjunction with an ever-moving set of figurines, the Tarot deck is capable of disrupting the Dance that coordinates time, space, love, and intellect. The Gypsies—Henry, Aaron, and Joanna Lee—mistakenly seek to control the Dance; they seek to go where humans should fear to tread. Their efforts unleash a primal storm that unhinges the Dance, distorting the proper balance between matter and spirit and provoking chaos. In the face of the storm stand Sybil Coningsby and her niece, Nancy. With their relatives Lothair and Ralph, the two face irrational destruction; they face a power that hardly seems possible. Yet Sybil's serene awareness of the ultimate beneficence of the universe makes her a potent adversary of the storm, and Nancy, by the power of her own hands, finds a way to quell it. Williams's descriptions make his ranging concepts credible and this credibility is heightened by his talent for posing correspondences. The figures of the Tarot symbolize universal principles, and these very symbols come alive in the fiction. If the work does not convince one that symbols can come alive, it does convince one that principles can.

Williams, Charles. *Shadows of Ecstasy.* London: Gollancz, 1933. Grand Rapids, MI: Eerdmans, 1965 (paper).
Williams's ability to interwine the remarkable and the mundane produces another excellent work here. His topic is ecstasy and it is seen in a broad variety of forms: love, poetry, kingship, religion. Ecstasy is common to all of these and it gives tangible power to them all. Love is religion and kingship is poetry. They all are nonrational, they all are potent; and when they are channeled, they enable their advocates to transcend physical laws. Nigel Considine lives without aging, and by the power of his ecstasy he bends others to his will. His goal (the goal of ecstasy in the work) is not only deathless-

ness, but return from death. He seeks to escape mortality and very nearly succeeds. The setting is twentieth-century England and the characters are fantastic only in a mystical way: they thrust aside the normal and embrace the ecstatic. Yet the primary world is so thoroughly saturated with the power of ecstasy that it becomes an otherworld, one that lacks swordplay and talking trees, but where music is entirely palpable, where things spiritual, emotional, and intellectual are more real than physical ones.

Williams, Charles. *Descent into Hell.* London: Faber, 1937. Grand Rapids, MI: Eerdmans, 1965 (paper).
This is one of those books that is so impressive that, having read it once, every reader will want to own a personal copy for the second and subsequent readings. In soaring yet simple prose, the book is a celebration of genuine love and of the freedom and joy that accompany it. As in Williams's other works, but even more successfully, *Descent into Hell* integrates spirituality or metaphysics with a lively plot to produce a spiritual adventure. The setting is a new post-World War II suburb of London named Battle Hill, the site in earlier days of numerous bloody battles and of at least one martyrdom during Mary Tudor's reign. As is usual in a Williams novel, the primary or physical setting coexists with a secondary or spirit world. But, of course, this is from the materialist perspective; to those who inhabit the spirit world, the material world is itself spectral. As Williams points out, the term spirit is misleading in any case. "Nonhuman" more nearly describes this world inhabited by the dead who have not accepted their death and by the living who are spiritually dead—or by the living who are spiritually alive enough to enter it without fear and as an act of love. Two of these types come together in the brilliant climax to the novel. From her deathbed, Margaret Anstruther sends her grand-daughter, Pauline, to give solace to a dead man who has been wandering about the Hill ever since his suicide several years before. Margaret Anstruther's acceptance of death makes a similar acceptance possible for the suicide. When Pauline wishes him "peace," he finds redemption. Simultaneously, Pauline has a vision of her imprisoned ancestor, martyred 400 years ago. Pauline willingly shares her ancestor's fear and thus enables him to remain steadfast and accept his death. The theme thus dramatized is "substitution" or "substituted love," that is, taking on or sharing another's burden. This climactic scene is one of several moments in the book where the human and nonhuman worlds intersect, but it is the most numinous of such interactions in *Descent into Hell* and, perhaps, in all of Williams's fiction. Nowhere in literature will one find a more moving example of John Donne's well-known line, "No man is an island sufficient unto himself."

Williams, Charles. *All Hallows' Eve.* London: Faber, 1945. New York: Noonday, 1963 (paper).
In *All Hallows' Eve,* Williams's last and one of his more intricate and meta-

physical novels, the secondary world comes close to the Christian notion of Purgatory. In the novel it is called the City or the spiritual City; it is in a way spiritually superimposed on the city of London. The time is just after the physically and spiritually jarring events of World War II, a time propitious for the two cities, London and the City, to intersect, which they do in the lives of a group of people, some of whom are living, others dead. The two most important are Lester, who has recently died in a plane crash, and Betty, who is being victimized by Father Simon, a sorcerer who sends her into the spirit world to bring him back messages. Father Simon intends to send her spirit permanently to the otherworld, but as he attempts this operation, Lester intervenes and accepts for herself the curse intended for Betty. This chapter, entitled "The Magical Sacrifice," which takes place on the vigil of All Hallows (Halloween in America), is the turning point in the novel. Lester, because of her act of selfless love, begins to understand the mysteries of the City, which will lead to her redemption, and Simon begins to lose his power and face damnation. As one would expect, Williams's style is highly figurative, operating primarily through comparison and imagery both complex and sensory. For the reader who cannot live by metaphysics alone, in *All Hallows' Eve* (as in his other novels) Williams interweaves concrete, highly dramatic scenes of physical action with more exalted spiritual activities.

Wrightson, Patricia. *The Nargun and the Stars.* New York: Atheneum, 1974.

When young Simon Brent, an orphan, first arrives at Wongadilla, a sprawling 5,000-acre Australian sheep-run owned by Charlie Waters and his sister Edie (his mother's cousins), he doesn't quite know what to expect. At first, the natural inhabitants of the place—possums, wallabies, kookaburras—seem strange and exciting to him, but he soon discovers even more exotic creatures: the Potkoorok, a golden-eyed, green-skinned swamp creature who prides himself on being a consummate trickster; the Turongs, spindly tree spirits with "long straggling beards"; the Nyols, small, powerful cave dwellers who love to wrestle; and the Nargun, an ancient stone creature as old as the Earth itself ("Earth is its self and its being"). It is the danger that the Nargun poses to the home of Charlie and Edie that serves as the catalyst bringing the boy and his guardians together. At the conclusion of this fast-paced novel the Nargun is imprisoned in the bowels of a mountain and Jim and the Waterses seem destined to spend some happy years together. Wrightson's novel is filled with exceptionally vivid descriptive passages; especially fine is her opening description of the Nargun's epic 800-mile journey to Wongadilla. Equally memorable is her description of the mischievous Potkoorok: "The Potkoorok rose up slowly, water sliding off its green skin while it watched the boy. It stood about two feet tall with its webbed feet hidden in the swamp and its legs bent at the knee. Its golden eyes were old like the eyes of lizards, and its froglike face was sad for the dead frog. Because it was the face of a joker, it looked comical with its wide mouth turned down." It is a well-written novel unique in both its setting and its delineation of the various elf spirits of Wongadilla. Wrightson's *An Older Kind of Magic* (1972) also features the fascinating creatures of aboriginal legend: the Potkoorok, the Turongs, Net-Nets, Nyols, and Bitarrs. Although well written, this earlier novel doesn't possess the all-ages appeal of *Nargun;* it seems to have been written for a younger audience. However, those who enjoy *Nargun* will probably want to peruse *Magic.*

Yolen, Jane. *The Magic Three of Solatia.* New York: Crowell, 1974.
One wonders why this book did not win a Newbery award, except that it might be considered to be for an older audience. The novel is nicely structured, with four sections or books of approximately equal length, each beginning with an impressive illustration that ingeniously manages to capture the tone and central action of that book. This structure is most suited to the recurring theme, that one should remember that magic has consequences that may be greater than the doer of magic can bear. Actions, for instance, that occur in Book I are, by Book III, still finding their consequences and reflexes, both bad and good. Another theme also supported by the structure is that the good can, if allowed, somehow offset the evil consequences of an action. While the four books are nicely interwoven through characters, events, and themes, each book describes a self-contained story, giving four variations on a theme. Book I is about Sianna of the Song: how she is washed out to sea and spends a year on the Outermost Isle in the company of a witch-mermaid, Dread Mary, exchanging songs for spells, and about how she happens to own the three magic buttons. Book II pits Sianna against King Blaggard, a wizard who is corrupted by his irresponsible practice of magic. Book III shifts attention from Sianna to the quest of her son Lann, also a singer, who is named after the Gard-lann or golden bird. Though Sianna gives Lann the last remaining button (of the Magic Three), he does not use it. Book IV brings Lann to such a precarious position that he must use this most powerful magic and suffer the consequences. These consequences show that even in faery tales someone must pay—in fact all bear the burden—for the happy-ever-after ending. The style of the book is direct and relatively unadorned and should be suitable for both younger and older readers. All but the youngest reader, however, might occasionally object to the author's practice of needlessly repeating or belaboring a point. Older readers will relish a number of puns. All will welcome the book's healthy, appreciative attitude toward sexuality. Of Yolen's numerous works of fiction, this is so far the only one that fits into the all-ages category; the others are exclusively children's works.

Zelazny, Roger. *Nine Princes in Amber.* New York: Doubleday, 1970. New York: Avon, 1977 (paper).

This is the first book in the Amber series, five closely related novels which, while of uneven quality (the middle three are the best), are on the whole excellent, both for their unusually original fantasy elements and for their literary qualities. Readers should be cautioned at the outset that the series must be read in the proper sequence to gain the full (or in some of the novels *any*) understanding of the world of Amber, one of the more ingeniously conceived secondary worlds in fantasy literature. Amber is a royal country, indeed, *the* royal country, the center, cause, and sustainer of the universe. It is the place of the primal pattern of order. Zelazny does not reveal until the final volume that Oberon, the architect of Amber and the primal pattern, is a rebel from the Courts of Chaos. Chaos, however, now needs the order-chaos balance provided by Amber to insure its own existence. The royal family of Amber, Oberon's children, by "walking the pattern" gain a measure of Oberon's almost divinely creative powers. Thereafter they can (and frequently do) create other worlds called Shadow Earths simply by manipulating some formless matter (shadow) into whatever their imaginations conceive. This, of course, gives Zelazny endless possibilities for the series and he takes full advantage. Another of Zelazny's key inventions is the Trumps. Each member of the royal family (initially Oberon and his nine sons and four daughters) has a pack of Trumps, 10 cards, each one depicting one member of the family. Any member of the family can communicate with another by concentrating on the pertinent Trump. They can even be transported to wherever the person on the Trump is at the time, if that person cooperates. The series starts out like many standard sword and sinew works but develops rapidly in literary quality. Characterization improves; style becomes more polished; and philosophical complexities emerge. But even in the first book, such a secondary world as Amber is enough to draw the reader into the rest of the series. *Nine Princes in Amber* introduces readers to the princes and princesses of Amber, Oberon's nine sons and three of his four daughters: Corwin, Random, Eric, Bleys, Caine, Julian, Benedict, Gerard, Brand, Flora, Dierdre, and Llewella. Fiona, the fourth daughter, appears in the third book. Corwin is the narrator and central character throughout all the books. In this first one Corwin is living on our earth, his favorite Shadow Earth, as Carl Corey. He is in a sanitarium suffering from amnesia due to an accident caused by one of his brothers, who is trying to stop him from getting back to Amber to claim the throne in Oberon's extended absence. The Byzantine courtly intrigue within the royal family is a source of considerable suspense throughout the series. Corwin, with the help of Random, the playboy of the family, succeeds in returning to Amber and regaining his identity. Corwin's amnesia and cure initiate a gradual change in his character. He had hitherto been a venturesome, cruel, and self-serving soldier of fortune. Even while he resumes many of his old ways, he begins to question them. He even undergoes a symbolic death and resurrection when Eric, who has grasped the throne, imprisons him in the dungeons, and Corwin escapes. (Before Eric imprisoned him, however, Corwin uttered a dreadful curse—another family heirloom—an action that plays an important part in the next book.) Despite Zelazny's inventiveness, *Nine Princes in Amber* is the weakest book of the series, and could turn readers away from the others. The book features quantities of gratuitous sex and countless unnecessary throat-cuttings and blood-spurtings. The style features a crude, supposedly swagger-style modern idiom that is jarring. It is not until the second book that readers who are stalwart enough to persevere will discover that these negative features have a literary function.

Zelazny, Roger. *The Guns of Avalon.* New York: Doubleday, 1972. New York: Avon, 1974 (paper).

Far superior to *Nine Princes in Amber, The Guns of Avalon* (Book II of the Amber series) makes clear the rich complexity of Zelazny's design, which will carry through the remaining books. At the outset Corwin, still under the influence of past habits, feels he must avenge himself on his brother Eric and take the throne for himself. He postpones his revenge, however, when he witnesses the effects of the curse he had uttered when Eric blinded and imprisoned him. Manticoras, goat men, and other nightmarish creatures are terrorizing the Shadow Earths. Abashed by what he has wrought, Corwin joins the forces of Avalon—not King Arthur's, but a Shadow variety of it; for the first time in his career he is fighting not as a mercenary, but simply to defend the innocent. After hurling back the creatures from the Dark Circle in Titan-like fashion, Corwin pursues his revenge and his claim to the throne and the famous Jewel of Judgement that goes with it. As he is about to accomplish both, however, his anger against Eric dissipates in the face of Amber's need for defense and a unified front against a mysterious threat. The change in Corwin, the principal focus of this book, is carefully developed and convincing. Two new characters of importance enter the series at this point: Ganelon (not the betrayer of Roland) becomes Corwin's companion in arms, and Dara becomes his companion in love. Zelazny employs an effective elliptical style in describing the creation of new Shadow Earths.

Zelazny, Roger. *Sign of the Unicorn.* New York: Doubleday, 1975. New York: Avon, 1976 (paper).

In Book III of the Amber series, the politics of Amber, with plots and counterplots, creates considerable interest and suspense. It became clear at the conclusion of *The Guns of Avalon,* which settled the Eric–Corwin conflict, that a plot was being mounted against Amber that threatened its existence, and that the enemy was a traitor in the midst of the Royal Family. Corwin is now the heir apparent, but refuses to take the throne officially until the danger is past. He calls the family together and attempts to uncover the traitor. Unable to do so, Corwin hides the Jewel of Judgement, a powerful talisman, on our Shadow Earth. At the conclusion of the novel, the unicorn (the emblem of the Royal Family) appears and is taken as a sign of hope that Amber will survive. One of the attractions of this third book is the most effective shadow-shifting episode in the series. Prince Random (he is well named because of his erratic behavior) turns up to save Corwin from some subhuman pursuers. While fleeing on a glider-kite, Random shifts the Shadow Lands, earth and sky, to confuse the attackers, creating a fascinating kaleidescopic sequence of scenes.

Zelazny, Roger. *The Hand of Oberon.* New York: Doubleday, 1976. New York: Avon, 1977 (paper).
Many readers will probably find Book IV, *The Hand of Oberon,* the best of the five novels in the Amber series. Zelazny shelves sex and bloodletting almost completely, in favor of the attractions of a dramatic, suspenseful plot and an array of magical happenings. Brand turns out to be the traitor striving for Amber's ruin. He has damaged the primal pattern of the "real" Amber, causing reflexive darkness in the inhabited Amber. He attempts to destroy the pattern completely, but Corwin, with the help of Ganelon, confronts and apparently kills him by manipulating the artificial limb of their brother Benedict (Brand could not be killed in a normal duel). The most startling occurrence in the book is the return of Oberon, father of the Royal Family. He had disguised himself as Ganelon. The theme of duty over personal gain emerges most clearly in this book. Random even marries and brings order to his life. Corwin forgets numerous personal wrongs committed against him, unifies the Royal Family, and attends to the good of Amber as a proper ruler ought. His change, begun late in Book I of the series, could easily end here. The only question that remains is whether the primal pattern will be repaired, or chaos will eventually overwhelm the ordered world of Amber.

Zelazny, Roger. *Courts of Chaos.* New York: Doubleday, 1978.
The blurb on the jacket claims that "all your questions are answered" in this Book V, the conclusion of the Amber series. Actually, only one question is answered, but it is the most important one. Amber does triumph over the Courts of Chaos and over the mysterious apocalyptic storm that threatens to neutralize the victory. *Courts of Chaos* also makes explicit the theme of balance in the universe between chaos and order, a fruitful and dynamic relationship between creativity and discipline or matter and form or whatever similar pairings pertain. Another theme or lesson is the attainment of self-realization by striving even when success seems impossible. The opposite point of view is voiced by a bird named Hugi who perches on Corwin's shoulder and preaches surrender to the Absolute. *Courts of Chaos* also reminds the readers that Corwin, however noble he has become, has not be-

come a Galahad. When he is challenged by the Champion of Chaos, he runs away and then ambushes his would-be courtly opponent and "skewers" him when he is down, saying that this is war, not the Olympics. Aside from letting the reader know who wins, making some thematic statements, and shading in a corner of Corwin's character, *Courts of Chaos* achieves little and requires considerable padding to reach novel length. Still, it serves the function of summarizing a long story and thereby extending the reader's enjoyment. If it rests on the laurels of its predecessors, it does so with considerable justification. It also leaves a few doors open in case Zelazny wants to resurrect the series.

Zelazny, Roger. *Jack of Shadows.* New York: Walker, 1971.
Shadows is a fast-paced and highly imaginative novel that has as its setting an Earth that no longer rotates—an Earth half in darkness, half in light. Magic rules the lives of the Darksiders, science the lives of the Lightsiders. The picaresque hero, a Darksider called Jack of Shadows (he magically derives power from shadows), has acquired a legendary reputation for his skill as a thief, but when he attempts to steal the Hellflame (a "fist-sized ruby") he is apprehended and summarily executed. All Darksiders, however, have more than one life, and after his resurrection Jack sets out to gain revenge on those responsible for the taking of his life: the Lord of Bats and his cohorts Smage and Quazer; Benoni, Master of the Hellgames; and Blite, the executioner. After many years of waiting and planning, Jack finally gains his revenge by snuffing out their lives, and eventually becomes master of Darkside. Not content with mere power, he desires to destroy the light-dark polarity of his world. Thus he enters the fabled passageway that leads to the "heart of the world" in search of the "Great Machine which maintained the world as it was." He finds the machine, destroys it, and then witnesses the dawn's return to the darkside of the Earth. Although a unique work, in some respects *Shadows* is similar to Jack Vance's *The Eyes of the Overworld*. Both novels feature a central character who is a thieving rogue with considerable magical powers, along with a large supporting cast of remarkably weird creatures (for example, the Borshin in *Shadows*); both novels are highly episodic; both are extraordinarily inventive and imaginative; both have exotic, vividly described settings (witness *Shadows'* Dung Pits of Glyve and High Dudgeon); and both are characterized by an abundance of Dunsanian names. Unlike *Overworld*, however, *Shadows* adds to the story line, or literal level, a distinctly allegorical level of meaning, and thus *Shadows* has a somewhat greater sophistication of plot and theme. The allegory in *Shadows* arises from its treatment of Jack's running battle with his "Soul"—Everyman's quest for spiritual meaning and fulfillment; and in its depiction of Man's dichotomous nature—the emotional/magical (dark) side versus the intellectual/scientific (light) side. Although *Shadows* has plenty of swashbuckling action, Zelazny avoids the heavy emphasis on blood and gore found in the first two books of the Amber series.

Anthologies

Boyer, Robert H., and Zahorski, Kenneth J., eds. *The Fantastic Imagination: An Anthology of High Fantasy.* Vol. I. New York: Avon, 1977 (paper).

This is a unique anthology in that it consists exclusively of high fantasy stories. The 16 selections include Johann Ludwig Tieck's "Elves," Lord Dunsany's "Sword of Welleran," George MacDonald's "Light Princess," John Buchan's "Grove of Ashtaroth," J. B. Cabell's "Music from behind the Moon," Frank R. Stockton's "Accommodating Circumstance," H. E. Bates's "Peach Tree," Alexander Grin's "Loquacious Goblin," J. R. R. Tolkien's "Riddles in the Dark," C. S. Lewis's "Magician's Book" and "The Dufflepuds Made Happy," Mark Van Doren's "Tall One," Lloyd Alexander's "Foundling," Peter S. Beagle's "Come Lady Death," Ursula K. Le Guin's "Rule of Names," and Sylvia Townsend Warner's "Beliard." Each selection is preceded by a headnote containing biographical information on the author and succinct critical commentary on the story. A wide range of representative authors, covering a considerable period of time, provides a variety of settings, characters, motifs, and themes. Represented are English, American, and two Continental authors. The earliest piece is Tieck's "Elves" (1811) and the latest is Warner's "Beliard" (1974). A succinct but valuable introduction provides a definition of fantasy in general and high fantasy in particular. The book has received a very positive response from instructors who have adopted it for use in the classroom. A companion volume to *The Fantastic Imagination* (Volume II) and *Dark Imaginings*.

Boyer, Robert H., and Zahorski, Kenneth J., eds. *The Fantastic Imagination: An Anthology of High Fantasy.* Vol. II. New York: Avon, 1978 (paper).

This anthology is a companion volume to *The Fantastic Imagination: An Anthology of High Fantasy* (Volume I), and like its predecessor it consists solely of works of high fantasy. Of the 16 authors presented here, only six appear in Volume I, and two of the stories—Evangeline Walton's "Above Ker-Is" and Vera Chapman's "Crusader Damosel"—have never before been published. The other 14 selections are George MacDonald's "Golden Key," Barry Pain's "Glass of Supreme Moments," Frank R. Stockton's "Old Pipes and the Dryad," Lord Dunsany's "Kith of the Elf-Folk," Kenneth Morris's "Red-Peach-Blossom Inlet," Selma Lagerlöf's "Legend of the Christmas Rose," Eric Linklater's "Abominable Imprecation," C. L. Moore's "Jirel Meets Magic," David H. Keller's "Thirty and One," Ursula K. Le Guin's "April in Paris," Joan Aiken's "Harp of Fishbones," Lloyd Alexander's "The Smith, the Weaver, and the Harper," Sylvia Townsend Warner's "Elphenor and Weasel," and a cutting from Patricia McKillip's *Throme of the Erril of Sherill.* Three of the stories are myth fantasy (those by Alexander, Morris, and Walton), and the rest are faery tales. Approximately a century of literary endeavor in the area of fantasy literature is represented here; the oldest piece is MacDonald's "Golden Key" (1867) and the most recent is Chapman's "Crusader" (1977). Included along with the more readily encountered fantasy works are some that are relatively inaccessible, such as those by Morris, Linklater, and Pain. An introductory essay defines high fantasy and comments upon some of the unique traits of the selections. Headnotes containing biographical and critical materials precede the selections.

Boyer, Robert H., and Zahorski, Kenneth J., eds. *Dark Imaginings: A Collection of Gothic Fantasy.* New York: Dell, 1978 (paper).
In this collection of eight Gothic high fantasy and eight Gothic low fantasy stories, the editors have selected a wide range of representative authors covering a broad span of time. The earliest work included in George MacDonald's "Cross Purposes" (1867), and the most recent is Peter S. Beagle's "Lila the Werewolf" (1974). Besides MacDonald's story, the Gothic high fantasy section contains A. Merritt's "Women of the Wood," C. A. Smith's "Enchantress of Sylaire," Fritz Leiber's "Unholy Grail," Ursula K. Le Guin's "Darkness Box," and a self-contained chapter from Poul Anderson's *Three Hearts and Three Lions.* In addition to Beagle's story, the Gothic low fantasy section contains Arthur Conan Doyle's "Brown Hand," W. H. Hodgson's "Habitants of Middle Islet," H. Rider Haggard's "Smith and the Pharaohs," Algernon Blackwood's "Dance of Death," H. P. Lovecraft's "Haunter of the Dark," T. H. White's "Troll," and Ray Bradbury's "Crowd." Each selection is preceded by a headnote containing biographical and critical materials, and a concise introductory essay supplies a concrete definition of fantasy literature in general and Gothic fantasy in particular. Special attention is given to making a clear distinction between high and low Gothic fantasy, and to showing how Gothic fantasy relates to the Gothic tradition in general. In addition, the volume contains 17 original pen-and-ink illustrations by James Cagle. This handsome text includes some of the best-known American fantasists of the past century and a half. A companion volume to *The Fantastic Imagination*, Volumes I and II.

Carter, Lin, ed. *Dragons, Elves, and Heroes.* New York: Ballantine, 1969 (paper).
An entertaining and instructive anthology containing examples of fantasy from *Beowulf* to Tennyson's "Horns of Elfland." The selections include "The Ogre" from *Beowulf* (the first half of the poem, translated by Norma Lorre Goodrich); "The High History of the Sword Gram" from *The Volsunga Saga* (translated by William Morris); "Manawyddan Son of the Boundless" from the *Mabinogion* (the Kenneth Morris version); Rudyard Kipling's "Puck's Song" from *Puck of Pook's Hill;* "Barrow-Wright" from *The Grettir Saga* (S. Baring-Gould's prose version); James MacPherson's "Fingal at the Siege of Carric-Thura" from *The Poems of Ossian;* Sir Thomas

Malory's "The Sword of Avalon" from *Le Morte d'Arthur;* "Tom O'Bed-
lam's Song" (an anonymous English ballad of the Elizabethan period); "The
Last Giant of the Elder Age" from *The Kiev Cycle* (translated by Isabel
Florence Hapgood); "The Lost Words of Power" from *The Kalevala* (trans-
lated by John Martin Crawford); "Wonderful Things beyond Cathay" from
The Voyages and Travels of Sir John de Mandeville (edited by Arthur Lay-
ard); William Shakespeare's "Prospero Evokes the Air Spirits" from *The
Tempest;* Edmund Spenser's "Lords of Faerie" from *The Faerie Queene;*
"Tales of the Wisdom of the Ancients" from the *Gesta Romanorum* (trans-
lated by Charles Swan and revised by Wynnard Hooper); Francisco De
Moraes's "Magical Palace of Darkness" from *Palmerin of England;* "Rus-
tum against the City of Demons" from *The Shah-Namah of Firdausi* (Lin
Carter's version); Robert Browning's "Childe Roland to the Dark Tower
Came"; Voltaire's *Princess of Babylon;* and Alfred Lord Tennyson's
"Horns of Elfland." Most of Carter's selections are very short excerpts
taken from much longer works; a few, such as "Puck's Song," "Fingal,"
"Tom O'Bedlam," and "Horns of Elfland" are short poems; and at least
one, Voltaire's *Princess of Babylon,* is a substantive, full-length work. Carter
has compiled a fantasy sampler designed not only to entertain, but to illustrate the rich tradition from which all contemporary fantasists can draw.
It is an important volume because it introduces the reader to some of the
primary sources of contemporary fantasy—the myths, legends, epics, sagas,
romances, and poems of earlier times. Each selection is preceded by a headnote containing biographical and critical materials. These headnotes are
written in Carter's characteristically informal, nonscholarly style, and are
interesting and informative. The volume also contains a brief introduction
by Carter. The companion volume to this anthology is *The Young Magicians.*

Carter, Lin, ed. *The Young Magicians.* New York: Ballantine, 1969 (paper).
In this companion volume to *Dragons, Elves, and Heroes* devoted to those
fantasy writers "who derive from the William Morris tradition," the selections include William Morris's "Rapunzel" (a "fairy-tale retold in the form of
a verse-play"); Lord Dunsany's "Sword of Welleran"; E. R. Eddison's "In
Valhalla" from *Styrbiorn the Strong;* James Branch Cabell's "Way of Ecben" from *The Witch Woman;* H. P. Lovecraft's "Quest of Iranon" and
"Cats of Ulthar"; Clark Ashton Smith's "Maze of Maal Dweb" (part of
the Xiccarph cycle); Lin Carter's "Whelming of Oom"; A. Merritt's "Through
the Dragon Glass"; Robert E. Howard's "Valley of the Worm"; L. Sprague
de Camp's "Heldendämmerung" (a very short poem) and "Ka the Appall-
ing"; Henry Kuttner's "Cursed Be the City"; Jack Vance's "Turjan of Miir"
from *The Dying Earth;* C. S. Lewis's "Narnian Suite" (a brief poem that
appeared in *Punch,* November 4, 1953); J. R. R. Tolkien's "Once upon a
Time" and "The Dragon's Visit" (two Bombadil poems); and Lin Carter's
"Azlon" from *Khymyrium.* This is an entertaining sample of contemporary

fantasy, but overall the selections do not exhibit the high quality of those in the companion volume. There are several reasons for .this, but perhaps the most important is the editor's emphasis upon the sword and sinew school. How truly representative of modern fantasy Carter's selections are is questionable. Headnotes containing biographical and critical materials precede the selections. The volume also contains a brief introduction by the editor, and a "Basic Reading List of Modern Heroic Fantasy."

Carter, Lin, ed. *Golden Cities, Far.* New York: Ballantine, 1970 (paper).
Lin Carter is indeed omnivorous, if eclectic, in his own reading of fantasy and in his editing of it. In *Golden Cities, Far,* a companion volume to the earlier *Dragons, Elves, and Heroes,* he introduces readers to samples of early fantasy. In 7 of the 13 tales, the term "early" refers to both contents and date of composition. These include "How Nefer-ka-ptah Found the Book of Thoth" (Egyptian, sixteenth century B.C.); "Wars of the Giants of Albion" (Anglo-Latin, twelfth century); "Arcalaus the Enchanter" and "The Isle of Wonder" (Portuguese, thirteenth or fourteenth century); "The Palace of Illusions" (the most famous piece, from *Orlando Furioso,* Italian, sixteenth century); "The Yellow Dwarf" (French, seventeenth century); and "The White Bull" (from Voltaire's *Romances,* French, eighteenth century). For the lover or prospective reader of the predecessors of modern fantasy (though it must be remembered that something like the "Book of Thoth" was certainly not considered fantasy when written) these works will hold the greatest interest. The other six works are modern, modified versions or imitations of earlier works, or simply modern works on early subjects. Among these six, the most popular will probably be "Prince Ahmed and the Fairy Paribanou," a tale in the style of, and possibly even from, *A Thousand and One Nights* (or *The Arabian Nights*). Readers of exotic fantasy and readers of early literatures are indebted to Carter for making the works in *Golden Cities, Far* more accessible, and for the encouragement and stimulation he provides for further reading in the sources he uses.

Carter, Lin, ed. *New Worlds for Old.* New York: Ballantine, 1971 (paper).
In his introduction, Carter states the basic criterion for the selection of stories in this anthology. In a previous anthology *(Golden Cities, Far)* readers had, he says, "voyaged through . . . elder lands of legend; now, in *New Worlds for Old,* let us explore some of the more recent wonder-worlds of modern fantasy." Accordingly, he includes the following 12 short stories or excerpts and three poems: "Zulkais and Kalilah," a chapter written by William Beckford for his *Vathek,* but not included therein; "Silence: A Fable" by Edgar Allan Poe; "The Romance of Photogen and Nycteris" (also known as "The Day Boy and the Night Girl") by George MacDonald; "The Sphinx," a poem by Oscar Wilde; "The Fall of Babbulkund" by Lord Dunsany; "The Green Meadow" by H. P. Lovecraft; "The Feast in the House of the Worm"

by Gary Myers; "Zingazar" by Lin Carter; "A Wine of Wizardry," a poem by George Sterling; "The Garden of Fear" by Robert E. Howard; "Jirel Meets Magic" by C. L. Moore; "Duar the Accursed" by Clifford Ball; "The Hashish-Eater" by Clark Ashton Smith; "The Party at Lady Cusp-Canine's," a chapter intended by Mervyn Peake for *Titus Alone* but never included; "The Sword of Power" by Lin Carter. Of all these selections, readers will be most pleased to have the Beckford and Peake selections. Carter has done a service by making accessible these hitherto unavailable works, which are interesting both in themselves and in relationship to the novels for which they were intended. Carter has clearly intended to achieve a measure of comprehensiveness by editing *New Worlds for Old* to complement his other volume of modern fantasists, *The Young Magicians.* He is, however, limited by his predilection here for a Dunsany-Lovecraft-Howard type of story with a characteristically dreamy tone and creepy contents. Thus Carter omits works by authors like Barry Pain or Eric Linklater that merit recognition as much as or more than writers like Clifford Ball. And how, it might be asked, does an editor justify including two of his own works if he is attempting to be at all comprehensive? Carter's general introduction and his brief introductions to each selection are, as usual, interesting and informative.

Carter, Lin, ed. *Discoveries in Fantasy.* New York: Ballantine, 1972 (paper). In this volume, Carter makes an admirable attempt to resurrect four fantasy authors from an undeserved obscurity. The four writers included composed their works in the late nineteenth or early twentieth century, a time before Tolkien's immense success, when adult fantasy such as they wrote had a limited and short-lived appeal. The four writers—Ernest Bramah, Richard Garnett, Donald Corley, and Eden Phillpotts—represent an important chapter in the history of fantasy and, more important, their fantasies—primarily of the myth-based variety—are entertaining and well-written works. From Ernest Bramah's Kai Ling books Carter includes two selections, "The Vision of Yin" and "The Dragon of Chang Tao." Both are views of ancient China through the eyes of a Victorian Englishman. Though not authentic Chinese stories, they are witty, urbane fantasies characterized by a pithy, aphoristic humor. From Garnett's *Twilight of the Gods,* Carter selects two stories. "The Poet of Panopolis" describes the plight of the Greek gods in the early Christian era, while "The City of Philosophers" is a historical allegory of Rome at the beginning of the same Christian era. In both cases, Garnett satirizes Christianity—humorously, but with a serious undertone. From Donald Corley's numerous short stories, Carter offers two selections, "The Bird with the Golden Beak" and "The Song of Tombelaine." The former is in the style of an Eastern legend, while the latter is a medieval tale of love and violence. Both, if one wishes to be technical, are rationalized legend rather than fantasy. Corley, an American, apparently shared his countrymen's wariness of the magic of fantasy. From Eden Phillpotts, Carter includes one long, satirical, and slightly philosophical story, "The Miniature." The title refers to one of Zeus's entertaining creatures, man. The Olympian gods observe and comment upon the evolution and dissolution of humanity. What chiefly interests the gods is the succession of deities, including Jaweh, that humankind worships. Carter has compiled a valuable anthology, and while none of the authors he includes is likely to capture a large audience (even in the Tolkien era), they are certainly entertaining and worthy of remembrance.

Carter, Lin, ed. *Great Short Novels of Adult Fantasy.* Vol. I. New York: Ballantine, 1972 (paper).

This excellent anthology contains four novellas from considerably diverse authors of high fantasy, and the range of approaches demonstrates the variety possible within the genre. Fletcher Pratt and L. Sprague de Camp's "Wall of Serpents" is earthy and humorous to the point of slapstick; Anatole France's "Kingdom of the Dwarfs" is delicate and moralistic but not overly so; R. W. Chambers's "Maker of Moons" is Gothic and mysterious; and William Morris's "Hollow Land" is philosophical and of a high seriousness. "Wall of Serpents" belongs to a series of stories written by Pratt and de Camp over a period of years, featuring the comical and unlikely hero Harold Shea. In the different tales of the series, Shea visits various literary otherworlds by means of symbolic logic, including those of *The Faerie Queene* and *Orlando Furioso.* In "Wall of Serpents," he invades the world of the Finnish epic, the *Kalevala,* in order to find a magician great enough to extricate a number of people whom Shea had accidentally sent to several otherworlds. Despite the humor of the story, magic is a serious and an exacting task, and, in the world of the *Kalevala,* a task that requires poetic skill. France's "Kingdom of the Dwarfs" is a classic faery tale involving the initiation of George and Honey-Bee into responsible adulthood and love. While George is trapped by nixies, Honey-Bee is held as an honored captive by the king of the dwarfs. Innocent love, however, triumphs. The descriptions of the otherworlds of the nixies and dwarfs, even in translation, show the abilities that won Anatole France a Nobel Prize for literature. "The Maker of Moons" by R. W. Chambers is primarily a mystery story. It includes secret service men in search of someone who is making pure gold, but it also includes the Kuen-Yuin, sinister Oriental sorcerers of Yian, an otherworld "across seven oceans and the great river which is longer than from the earth to the moon." "The Hollow Land" is an early William Morris medieval fantasy romance. It describes the odyssey of Florian de Liliis, a young knight anxious for battle, into the otherworld of the Hollow Land and, through a process of purification, to a higher kind of existence. The tale is highly symbolic and intricate, but it never loses its plot line. All four novellas, different as they are, are successful high fantasies. Carter has collected four tales that are difficult to find; unfortunately, this volume is now itself quite rare, but it is well worth the search.

Carter, Lin, ed. *Great Short Novels of Adult Fantasy*. Vol. II. New York: Ballantine, 1973 (paper).

The title notwithstanding, this volume contains two short stories and two short novels. The first selection, "Woman in the Mirror," is one of a very few short faery tales written by George MacDonald for adults. MacDonald frequently salted short stories within a full-length fiction, and "Woman in the Mirror" is one of these, though Carter does not acknowledge the exact source. The story is set in a medieval German university town. The central magical device is an ancient mirror in which a beautiful lady is imprisoned. A young student falls in love with her, but is willing to release her (despite the fact that he might never see her again) by breaking the mirror, thus saving his own mind and soul, which are otherwise in peril. MacDonald's elegant style makes the story work, but it lacks the author's usual sparkling wit. The second story is "The Repairer of Reputations," a chapter from R. W. Chambers's *King in Yellow*. This is a weird tale of insanity and Gothic horror; the insanity, at least technically, makes it a realistic tale rather than a fantasy. "The Transmutation of Ling" is the first of the two novelettes in the anthology. It is one of Ernest Bramah's droll tales from the Kai Lung books that record the supposed narratives of a Chinese wanderer. This is a rambling (and unnecessarily long) story of thievery and corruption, with Ling as the victim—until, that is, he marries Mian, who gives him a philtre containing a liquid with a strange property. After he drinks from the philtre, whatever part of Ling's body is severed from the main part and dies (fortunately Ling discovers this from his barber) turns into pure gold. This creates many humorous turns of events, some unfortunate, others fortunate. The last and longest piece in the collection is Eden Phillpotts's novelette "The Lavender Dragon." Like the preceding tale, this one is enjoyable despite its unwarranted length. The Lavender Dragon reminds one of Kenneth Grahame's "Reluctant Dragon," who wanted to discuss ideas with people but whose intentions were always misunderstood. Phillpotts's dragon actually founds a commune called Dragonsville, a communistic society where religion is benevolently tolerated for those who need it. And all this right in the same country as Pongley-in-the-Marsh!

Carter, Lin, ed. *The Year's Best Fantasy Stories*. 4 vols. New York: DAW, 1975–1978 (paper).

This annual anthology series was inaugurated by Donald A. Wollheim in 1975 to provide a yearly "pick of the best of fantasy fiction." While most of the works are of good quality, there is a very real question about how well they represent the entire spectrum of contemporary fantasy, since so many of them are sword and sinew tales. Furthermore, not all of the selections were written, at least not in their entirety, during the year each volume is supposed to represent. The Clark Ashton Smith stories, for instance, are "posthumous collaborations"—that is, stories left unfinished at the time of Smith's death, but since completed by the editor, Lin Carter (with the exception of the very brief "Prince Alcouz and the Magicians"). Carter explains in his headnote to "The Double Tower": "Like his friend Robert E. Howard, the late Clark Ashton Smith also left among his papers the manuscripts of unpublished or unfinished stories, and notes and titles and outlines for many tales which he did not live to write. I have obtained permission from his Estate to complete several of these, and to turn some of Smith's notes and outlines into finished tales." In addition, approximately a half dozen of the stories appear "for the first time by arrangements with the authors." In other words, the sole test of their quality (that is, their being the "best" of the year) was the editor's decision to publish them. All in all, though, these are entertaining and lively stories that nicely illustrate the kind of energy and imaginative flair works of fantasy can possess. Besides the selections, each volume contains a brief introduction ("The Year in Fantasy") which serves to highlight some of the past year's most important publications and happenings in the world of fantasy, and even briefer but still helpful annotated bibliographies of "The Year's Best Fantasy Books," "Fantasy Art," "Important Reprints," and "Non-Fiction and Related." Compare Terry Carr's *Year's Finest Fantasy* (New York: Berkley Publishing Corp., 1978), which seems to be closely modeled on the Carter series.

The Year's Best Fantasy Stories. DAW, 1975.
Contents: Marion Zimmer Bradley, "The Jewel of Arwen"; Lloyd Alexander, "The Sword Dyrnwyn"; Robert E. Howard, "The Temple of Abomination"; Clark Ashton Smith, "The Double Tower"; Fritz Leiber, "Trapped in the Shadowland"; Lin Carter, "Black Hawk of Valkarth"; Hannes Bok, "Jewel Quest"; L. Sprague de Camp, "The Emperor's Fan"; Pat McIntosh, "Falcon's Mate"; Charles R. Saunders, "The City of Madness"; Jack Vance, "The Seventeen Virgins."

The Year's Best Fantasy Stories: 2. DAW, 1976.
Contents: Tanith Lee, "The Demoness"; Thomas Burnett Swann, "The Night of the Unicorn"; Pat McIntosh, "Cry Wolf"; Fritz Leiber, "Under the Thumbs of the Gods"; Paul Spencer, "The Guardian of the Vault"; L. Sprague de Camp, "The Lamp from Atlantis"; Gary Myers, "Xiurhn"; Lin Carter, "The City in the Jewel"; Walter C. DeBill, Jr., "In 'Ygiroth"; Clark Ashton Smith and Lin Carter, "The Scroll of Morloc"; C. A. Cador, "Payment in Kind"; Avram Davidson, "Milord Sir Smith, the English Wizard."

The Year's Best Fantasy Stories: 3. DAW, 1977.
Contents: L. Sprague de Camp, "Eudoric's Unicorn"; Gardner F. Fox, "Shadow of a Demon"; Pat McIntosh, "Ring of Black Stone"; George R. R. Martin, "The Lonely Songs of Laren Dorr"; Karl Edward Wagner, "Two Suns Setting"; Clark Ashton Smith, "The Stairs in the Crypt"; Raul Garcia Capella, "The Goblin Blade"; C. J. Cherryh, "The Dark King"; Lin Carter, "Black Moonlight"; Gary Myers, "The Snout in the Alcove"; Charles R. Saunders, "The Pool of the Moon."

The Year's Best Fantasy Stories: 4. DAW, 1978.
Contents: Poul Anderson, "The Tale of Hauk"; Grail Undwin, "A Farmer on the Clyde"; Clark Ashton Smith, "Prince Alcouz and the Magician"; Robert E. Howard and Andrew J. Offutt, "Nekht Semerkeht"; Lin Carter, "The Pillars of Hell"; Philip Coakley, "Lok the Depressor"; Avram Davidson, "Hark! Was That the Squeak of an Angry Throat?"; Pat McIntosh, "The Cloak of Dreams"; Phyllis Eisenstein, "The Land of Sorrow"; Tanith Lee, "Odds against the Gods"; Ramsey Campbell, "The Changer of Names."

Carter, Lin, ed. *Kingdoms of Sorcery.* New York: Doubleday, 1976.
This is a well-conceived and thoughtfully edited anthology that provides a good introduction to some of the world's most important writers of fantasy. The volume is divided into five sections: (1) "The Forerunners of Modern Fantasy"—Voltaire's "History of Babouc the Scythian"; William Beckford's "Palace of Subterranean Fire"; and George MacDonald's "Witch Woman"; (2) "Fantasy as Saga"—William Morris's "Folk of the Mountain Door"; E. R. Eddison's "Night-Piece on Ambremerine"; Fletcher Pratt's "Dr. Meliboë the Enchanter"; and Fritz Leiber's "Two Best Thieves in Lankhmar"; (3) "Fantasy as Parable"—Edgar Allan Poe's "Shadow" and "Silence"; Clark Ashton Smith's "Fables from the Edge of Night"; and Robert H. Barlow's "Tomb of the God"; (4) "Fantasy as (Humorous) Anecdote"—T. H. White's "Merlyn vs. Madame Mim"; L. Sprague de Camp's "Owl and the Ape"; and Lin Carter's "Twelve Wizards of Ong"; and (5) "Fantasy as Epic"—C. S. Lewis's "Deep Magic from the Dawn of Time"; J. R. R. Tolkien's "The Bridge of Khazad-Dûm"; and Richard Adams's "Story of the Blessing of El-Ahrairah." Almost all of the selections are excerpts from full-length works, and many have never before been anthologized. Each selection is preceded by a headnote containing biographical and critical materials. These headnotes are not scholarly, but they are helpful. An especially interesting selection is White's "Merlyn vs. Madame Mim." This "magic duel" scene appeared in the first edition of *The Sword in the Stone* but was left out of the revised version that was subsequently incorporated into *The Once and Future King* as Part 1. *Scorcery* also includes a very brief introduction by Carter and an appendix containing "Suggestions for Further Reading."

Carter, Lin, ed. *Realms of Wizardry.* New York: Doubleday, 1976.
This companion volume to *Kingdoms of Sorcery* contains 16 selections, which are grouped into five separate categories: (1) "Fantasy as Legend"—Lord Dunsany's "Hoard of the Gibbelins"; H. P. Lovecraft's "Doom That Came to Sarnath"; Robert Bloch's "Black Lotus"; and Gary Myers's "Gods of Earth"; (2) "Fantasy as Satire"—Richard Garnett's "City of Philosophers"; James Branch Cabell's "Some Ladies and Jurgen"; and Donald Corley's "Book of Lullûme"; (3) "Fantasy as Romance"—H. Rider Haggard's "Descent beneath Kôr"; A. Merritt's "Whelming of Cherkis"; and Hannes

Bok's "How Orcher Broke the Koph"; (4) "Fantasy as Adventure Story"—
Robert E. Howard's "Swords of the Purple Kingdom"; Clifford Ball's "Goddess Awakes"; and C. L. Moore and Henry Kuttner's "Quest of the Star-
stone"; and (5) "New Directions in Fantasy"—Jack Vance's "Liane the
Wayfarer"; Michael Moorcock's "Master of Chaos"; and Roger Zelazny's
"Thelinde's Song." Although *Wizardry* is a good sampler of certain types
of fantasy literature, in general the quality of the selections is not as high
as those in *Sorcery*. In a brief afterword, Carter states: "Taken together, as
the two halves of one huge book, the twin anthologies [i.e., *Sorcery* and *Wizardry*] indicate the broad spectrum of styles and narrative forms which
make up the world of modern fantasy." For the most part, editor Carter
makes good his claim. Of course, it is never possible to include all the writers who deserve representation in such anthologies, but one cannot help
but be disappointed by the omission of Ursula K. Le Guin, Peter S. Beagle,
Patricia McKillip, Alan Garner, Susan Cooper, Lloyd Alexander, Joy
Chant, and Evangeline Walton. Like its predecessor, *Wizardry* contains a
brief general introduction, critical/biographical headnotes, and "Suggestions for Further Reading."

Cott, Jonathan, ed. *Beyond the Looking Glass: Extraordinary Works of
Fairy Tale and Fantasy.* New York: Stonehill, 1973.
In his excellent introduction to this equally excellent anthology, Jonathan
Cott states that "from the 1840's–1890's, Victorian England witnessed
undoubtedly the greatest flowering of writing for children in the history of
literature." The reason for "the greatness of Victorian children's literature,"
Cott suggests, is that adults could examine "their senses of childhood without apologizing. . . ." Thus, these children's stories "are enjoyed and understood best by 'adults,' for the recovery of childhood. . . ." Most readers will
concur with Cott's judgment about both the quality and the universality of
the appeal in the following works that make up the anthology: John Ruskin's
"King of the Golden River or the Black Brothers"; Tom Hood's "Petsetilla's
Posy"; Mrs. Clifford's "Wooden Tony: An Anyhow Story"; Mary de Morgan's "Through the Fire" and "The Wanderings of Arasmon"; Maggie
Browne's "Wanted—A King"; Mark Lemon's "Tinykin's Transformations";
George MacDonald's "Golden Key" and "The Day Boy and the Night Girl"
(also called "The Romance of Photogen and Nycteris"); Christina Ros-
setti's "Goblin Market." The fact that George MacDonald and Mary de
Morgan are the only ones with two selections included is indicative of the
quality of these writers. MacDonald is the better known of the two and both
the stories selected by Cott have been recently anthologized elsewhere (see
Boyer and Zahorski, *The Fantastic Imagination*, Volume II, for "The Golden
Key," and Carter, *New Worlds for Old* for "The Day Boy and the Night
Girl"), and have, of course, appeared in the two recent editions of Mac-
Donald's children's stories. Mary de Morgan is less well known but de-

serves better. The two selections in the Cott volume demonstrate that her talent is on a par with MacDonald's. Both tales are notable for their treatment of the quest motif, tracing the remarkable and poignant journeys of protagonists with whom readers of all ages readily identify. Like MacDonald's, de Morgan's style is marked by control and refinement. The four tales by these two authors are the choicest selections, but the others are not far behind. The volume is attractively adorned with many of the stories' original illustrations. Readers will also profit from and enjoy Cott's introduction, "Notes on Fairy Faith and the Idea of Childhood."

Menville, Douglas, and Reginald, R., eds. *Dreamers of Dreams: An Anthology of Fantasy.* New York: Arno, 1978.

This is part of Arno's recent multivolume series, entitled *Lost Race and Adult Fantasy Fiction* and edited by Menville and Reginald. In *Dreamers of Dreams,* the editors have collected 13 shorter works of various types of fantasy, ranging from the horror story through the tale of reincarnation to pure faery tale and myth-based stories. Two of the longer pieces are lost-race rather than fantasy tales: Andrew Lang's "End of Phaeacia" (over one hundred pages) and Edward Everett Hale's "Queen of California" (45 pages). The 11 tales of fantasy are John Kendrick Bangs, "The Affliction of Baron Humpfelhimmel"; Laurence Housman, "The Blind God"; George Mac-Donald, "The Gray Wolf"; Bram Stoker, "The Invisible Giant"; Guy Boothby, "A Professor of Egyptology"; Kenneth Morris, "The Last Adventure of Don Quixote"; Mervyn Peake, "Same Time, Same Place"; John Ames Mitchell, "That First Affair"; Edwin Lester Arnold, "Rutherford the Twice-Born"; Lord Dunsany, "The Journey of the King"; and H. E. Bates, "The Seekers." Menville and Reginald clearly have selected these works on the basis of quality. Readers will choose favorites such as Housman's religious parable of an impersonal creator or Peake's nightmarish tale of horror or Bates's panoramic view of Fairyland, but all 13 are excellent finds. The further benefit of this volume is that, with the one exception of the MacDonald story, none of these fantasy or lost-race tales have hitherto been available outside of a few special library collections. The table of contents indicates the sources from which the stories are reprinted, but the reader who wants to know more about the authors or the backgrounds to the stories will be disappointed, since there is no introductory material at all.

Mobley, Jane, ed. *Phantasmagoria: Tales of Fantasy and the Supernatural.* Garden City, NY: Anchor, 1977 (paper).

This collection contains 18 selections, including both stories and excerpts from longer works. One story, "Arthur and Gorlagon," dates from the fourteenth century, but most of the selections are by well-known nineteenth- and twentieth-century fantasists. The anthology is divided into two sections: "The Wondrous Fair: Magical Fantasy" and "The Passing Strange: Supernatural Fiction." Included in the first and longer section are George Mac-Donald's "Golden Key," Lord Dunsany's "Fortress Unvanquishable Save the Sacnoth," Theodore Sturgeon's "Silken Swift," Robert Bloch's "Dark Isle," Jorge Luis Borges's "Rejected Sorcerer," Nicholas Stuart Gray's "According to Tradition," Andre Norton's "Gifts of Asti," Ursula K. Le Guin's "Rule of Names," Sylvia Townsend Warner's "Winged Creatures," and Peter S. Beagle's "Sia" (a chapter from a forthcoming novel). The second part contains J. Sheridan Le Fanu's "Account of Some Strange Disturbances in Aungier Street," Algernon Blackwood's "Confession," Oliver Onions's "Beckoning Fair One," M. R. James's "Oh, Whistle, and I'll Come to You, My Lad," Peter S. Beagle's "Come Lady Death," Elizabeth Jane Howard's "Three Miles Up," and Doris Betts's "Benson Watts Is Dead and in Virginia." Mobley does not provide headnotes to the stories (with the exception of a brief note preceding Beagle's "Sia"), but she does include two lucid and thoughtful essays, one on faery stories (high fantasy) and the other on supernatural fiction. Both essays provide concrete definitions of the two genres and helpful comments on several subgenres. A solid anthology edited by a knowledgeable critic of fantasy literature. At least one reviewer has suggested this as a companion volume to Boyer and Zahorski's two-volume work, *The Fantastic Imagination.*

II

Research
Aids

3

Fantasy Scholarship

The field of fantasy literature has begun to attract the attention of scholars and researchers who are publishing critical and reference works on the genre and its leading practitioners. The purpose of this bibliography is to acquaint the reader with some of the recently published materials that bear directly upon, or relate to, fantasy literature. The bibliography is divided into two sections, criticism and reference, each of which contains articles and books. For a comprehensive listing of doctoral dissertations, as well as numerous titles relating to fantasy art, film, and special motifs, see Marshall Tymn, et al., *A Research Guide to Science Fiction Studies* (Garland Publishing, 1977).

History, Criticism, and Author Studies

Alexander, Lloyd. "High Fantasy and Heroic Romance." *Horn Book Magazine* 47 (1971): 577–584. The one form of modern literature "that draws most directly from the fountainhead of mythology is the heroic romance, which is a form of high fantasy."

Amory, Mark. *Biography of Lord Dunsany*. London: Collins, 1972. Based in part upon Dunsany's autobiography, his letters, his wife's diary, and upon autobiographical passages in *The Curse of the Wise Woman*. Includes a bibliography of Dunsany's works.

Barbour, Douglas. "On Ursula Le Guin's *A Wizard of Earthsea*." *River-*

side Quarterly 6 (1974): 119–123. Argues that "all the important patterns of meaning that can be found in [Le Guin's] other novels are present here."

Batchelor, John. *Mervyn Peake: A Biographical and Critical Exploration.* London: Duckworth, 1974. An extended study in which Batchelor traces the multiple influences that enabled Peake to yield his best work.

Bergmann, Frank. "The Roots of Tolkien's Tree: The Influences of George MacDonald and German Romanticism upon Tolkien's Essay 'On Fairy-Stories.'" *Mosaic* 10 (1977): 1–14. A discussion of possible literary influences in Tolkien's essay.

Boies, J. J. "Existential Exchange in the Novels of Charles Williams." *Renascence* 26 (1974): 219–229. A study of existential themes in *Descent into Hell.*

Boyer, Robert H., and Zahorski, Kenneth J. "Science Fiction and Fantasy Literature: Clarification through Juxtaposition." *Wisconsin English Journal* 28 (1976): 2–8. Definitions of science fiction and fantasy, with application of their parallel elements in the classroom.

Brooks, Rick. "Andre Norton: Loss of Faith." In *The Many Worlds of Andre Norton,* edited by Roger Elwood. Radnor, PA: Chilton, 1974, pp. 178–200. Surveys the growing pessimism in Norton's novels, from *Star Man's Son* to *Exiles of the Stars.*

Callahan, Patrick J. "Animism & Magic in Tolkien's *The Lord of the Rings.*" *Riverside Quarterly* 4 (1971): 240–249. Maintains that the "forces of life and death [in Middle Earth] find their ultimate expression in those great archons of magical power, Mithrandir and Sauron, who more than any other agents control the destiny of their world."

Cameron, Eleanor. "High Fantasy: *A Wizard of Earthsea.*" *Horn Book Magazine* 47 (1971): 129–138. Le Guin's novel, an example of high fantasy, takes the reader "beyond magic to an understanding of truths which illuminate our difficulties in the world of reality."

Canary, Robert H. "Utopian and Fantastic Dualities in Robert Graves' *Watch the North Wind Rise.*" *Science-Fiction Studies* 1 (1974): 248–255. Surveys the elements of the fantastic in Graves's utopian novel.

Carpenter, Humphrey. *Tolkien: A Biography.* Boston: Houghton Mifflin, 1977. The "authorized" biography. The author was allowed access to family papers and includes personal reminiscences of Tolkien's children.

Carr, Marion. "Classic Hero in a New Mythology." *Horn Book Magazine* 47 (1971): 508–513. Outlines eight major motifs in Lloyd Alexander's Chronicles of Prydain in which Tarn, the hero, operates.

Carter, Lin. *Imaginary Worlds: The Art of Fantasy.* New York: Ballantine, 1973. An introduction to the important works and writers of fantasy fiction and their influence on the development of the genre. Contains three chapters on the techniques of writing fantasy.

Churchill, R. C. "The Man Who Was Sunday: G. K. Chesterton, 1874–1936." *Contemporary Review* 224 (1974): 12–15. A tribute to the literary achievement and influence of Chesterton, written on the one hundredth anniversary of his birth.

Clareson, Thomas D. "Lost Races, Lost Lands: A Pagan Princess of Their Very Own." *Journal of Popular Culture* 8 (1975): 714–723. An explanation of the characteristics of the nineteenth- and twentieth-century lost race novel, with particular attention to H. Rider Haggard and Edgar Rice Burroughs.

Clausen, Christopher. "'Lord of the Rings' and 'The Ballad of the White Horse.'" *South Atlantic Bulletin* 39 (1974): 10–16. Traces the literary influences of G. K. Chesterton's poem on Tolkien's trilogy.

Clipper, Lawrence J. *G. K. Chesterton*. New York: Twayne, 1974. A literary biography with information on Chesterton's works as well as his career as a man of letters and critic; includes a primary and secondary bibliography.

Copper, Susan. "Newbery Award Acceptance." *Horn Book Magazine* 52 (1976): 361–366. Acceptance speech for *The Grey King*, reflections on the nature of fantasy, and the intent of The Dark Is Rising series.

Corssley, Robert. "Education and Fantasy." *College English* 37 (1975): 281–293. A defense of the educative value of fantasy.

Cox, Harvey. *The Feast of Fools: A Theological Essay on Festivity and Fantasy*. Cambridge, MA: Harvard University Press, 1969. Contains important chapters on "Fantasy: The Ingredients" and "Fantasy and Utopia."

Crane, John. *T. H. White*. New York: Twayne, 1974. A biographical study of the author of *The Once and Future King*.

de Camp, L. Sprague. *Literary Swordsmen and Sorcerers: The Makers of Heroic Fantasy*. Sauk City, WI: Arkham House, 1976. A history of the heroic fantasy genre from its origins in prehistoric myths and legends. Contains biographic sketches of its leading practitioners and evaluations of classic works.

_____. *Lovecraft: A Biography*. Garden City, NY: Doubleday, 1975. A look at the Lovecraft legend and the bizarre life of the famous writer of horror tales; extensive secondary bibliography.

Eichner, Henry M. *Atlantean Chronicles*. Alhambra, CA: Fantasy Publishing Co., 1971. A critical account of lost continent literature with a fully annotated bibliography; best coverage of the field to date.

Emmons, Winifred S., Jr. "H. P. Lovecraft as a Mythmaker." *Extrapolation* 1 (1960): 35–37. A brief discussion of the Cthulhu mythos.

Floyd, Barbara. "A Critique of *The Once and Future King*. Part 1: Not Any Common Earth." *Riverside Quarterly* 1 (1965): 175–180. A discussion of the King Arthur motif in T. H. White's series. Begins with an analysis of *The Sword and the Stone.*

————. "A Critique of *The Once and Future. King.* Part 2: My Mother's Curse." *Riverside Quarterly* 2 (1966): 54–57. Continues the analysis with *The Queen of Air and Darkness.*

————. "A Critique of *The Once and Future King.* Part 3: The Tale of the Ill-Starred Knight." *Riverside Quarterly* 2 (1966): 127–133. Continues the analysis with *The Ill-Made Knight.*

————. "A Critique of *The Once and Future King.* Part 4: The Candle in the Wind." *Riverside Quarterly* 2 (1966): 210–213. Concludes the analysis with *The Candle in the Wind.*

Fredericks, S. C. "The Myth of Descent in Vincent King's *Light a Last Candle.*" *Riverside Quarterly* 6 (1973): 20–28. The mythological motif of descent exhibits an ironic framework in King's novel.

————. "Problems of Fantasy." *Science-Fiction Studies* 5 (1978): 33–44. Surveys the perspectives on fantasy common to the diverse theorists and suggests problem areas for future research in fantasy.

————. "Revivals of Ancient Mythologies in Current Science Fiction and Fantasy." In *Many Futures, Many Worlds: Theme and Form in Science Fiction,* edited by Thomas D. Clareson. Kent, OH: Kent State University Press, 1977, pp. 50–65. An examination of works by modern science fiction and fantasy writers who have consciously based their efforts on famous world myths.

Godshalk, William L. "Alfred Bester: Science Fiction or Fantasy?" *Extrapolation* 16 (1975): 149–155. Divides fantasy into four categories as a framework for discussion of *The Demolished Man.*

Green, Roger Lancelyn, and Hooper, Walter. *C. S. Lewis: A Biography.* London: Collins; New York: Harcourt Brace Jovanovich, 1974. The authorized biography.

Grotta, Daniel. *The Biography of J. R. R. Tolkien: Architect of Middle-Earth.* 2nd ed. Philadelphia: Running Press, 1978. A readable and fairly accurate biography, valuable for its account of Tolkien's literary reputation, the controversy surrounding the publication of *The Lord of the Rings* trilogy in America, and the growth of the Tolkien cult.

Hunter, Hollie. "One World." *Horn Book Magazine* 51 (1975): 557–563; "One World. Part Two." 52 (1976): 32–38. Examines the function of fantasy in children's literature.

Irwin, W. R. *The Game of the Impossible: A Rhetoric of Fantasy.* Urbana, IL: University of Illinois Press, 1976. An examination of the common characteristics of fantasies written between 1880 and 1957.

Jones, Robert Kenneth. *The Shudder Pulps: A History of the Weird Menace Magazines of the 1930's.* West Linn, OR: FAX Collector's Editions, 1975.

A fascinating study of this pulp genre containing much biographical material not easily located elsewhere.

Kennard, Jean E. *Number and Nightmare: Forms of Fantasy in Contemporary Fiction.* Hamden, CT: Archon Books, 1975. An examination of the fantasy techniques of Joseph Heller, John Barth, James Purdy, Kurt Vonnegut, Jr., Anthony Burgess, Iris Murdoch, and William Golding.

Kirchhoff, Frederick, ed. *Studies in the Late Prose Romances of William Morris: Papers Presented at the Annual Meeting of the Modern Language Association, December 1975.* New York: William Morris Society, 1976. A survey of Morris's fantasies.

Lanahan, William. "Slave Girls and Strategies: John Norman's Gor Series." *Algol* 12 (1974): 22–26. Attempts to establish more valid reasons than the sexual content for the popularity of the Gor series.

Le Guin, Ursula K. *Dreams Must Explain Themselves.* New York: Algol Press, 1975. Le Guin discusses her Earthsea trilogy in an informal essay; also included are her story "The Rule of Names," her National Book Award acceptance speech for *The Farthest Shore,* and an interview.

———. *From Elfland to Poughkeepsie.* Portland, OR: Pendragon Press, 1973. Text of a speech on the nature of fantasy delivered at the second annual Science Fiction Writer's Workshop at the University of Washington in 1972.

———. "Why Are Americans Afraid of Dragons?" *Pacific Northwest Library Association Quarterly* 38 (1974): 14–18. An explanation of why fantasy is kept from children, some discussion of fantasy as a force in maturation, and a justification of the necessity of fantasy for children.

Lewis, C. S. *Of Other Worlds: Essays and Stories.* Edited by Walter Hooper. New York: Harcourt, 1966. New York: Harvest Books, 1975 (paper). Several of Lewis's essays reveal his understanding of the nature of fantasy literature and its effects on readers; particularly important are "On Stories," "On Three Ways of Writing for Children," and "On Science Fiction."

Lovecraft, Howard Phillips. *Supernatural Horror in Literature.* New York: Ben Abramson, 1945. New York: Dover, 1973. A critical survey of the development of horror fiction from the Gothic school to its manifestation in recent American literature.

Lundwall, Sam J. "The Magic Unreality." In *Science Fiction: What It's All About.* New York: Ace, 1971. A well-rounded introduction to the fantasy genre, covering the important historical works and major writers.

Lupoff, Richard A. *Barsoom: Edgar Rice Burroughs and the Martian Vision.* Baltimore: Mirage Press, 1976. An entertaining study of the history, themes, and characters of the Mars series.

MacDonald, George. "The Fantastic Imagination." In *The Gifts of the Child Christ: Fairy Tales and Stories for the Childlike,* vol. 1, edited by Glenn Edward Sadler. Grand Rapids, MI: Eerdmans, 1974, pp. 23–28. A seminal work on the laws that govern the world of the faery tale by the father of English fantasy.

McGhan, Barry, "Andre Norton: Why Has She Been Neglected?" *Riverside Quarterly* 4 (1970): 128–131. Attributes the lack of critical attention to Norton's works to a shift in literary interest away from the adventure story in the 1950s and 1960s.

Mahon, Robert Lee. "Elegaic Elements in *The Lord of the Rings.*" *CEA Critic* 40 (1978): 33–36. Traces the elegaic elements in *LOTR* from three perspectives: background detail, social perspectives, and death.

Manlove, C. N. "Flight to Aleppo: T. H. White's *The Once and Future King.*" *Mosaic* 10 (1977): 65–83. A penetrating examination of character and theme in White's work.

————. *Modern Fantasy: Five Studies.* Cambridge: Cambridge University Press, 1975. A major literary analysis and evaluation of the achievement of five fantasy authors—Charles Kingsley, George MacDonald, C. S. Lewis, J. R. R. Tolkien, and Mervyn Peake—with an introduction discussing the nature and character of the genre.

Merla, Patrick. "'What Is Real?' Asked the Rabbit One Day." *Saturday Review of the Arts* 55 (November 1972): 43–50. Today's literary trends reveal a paradox: harsh realism in children's books, fantasy and escapism in adult books. Contains a brief bibliography of fantasy titles.

Mobley, Jane. "Toward a Definition of Fantasy Fiction." *Extrapolation* 15 (1974): 117–128. An attempt to separate fantasy fiction from the general area of speculative fiction on the basis of form and focus.

Moskowitz, Sam. *Explorers of the Infinite: Shapers of Science Fiction.* Cleveland: World, 1963. Westport, CT: Hyperion Press, 1974. Biographical essays on the early writers. Includes chapters on Edgar Allan Poe, Edgar Rice Burroughs, A. Merritt, and H. P. Lovecraft.

————. *Seekers of Tomorrow: Masters of Modern Science Fiction.* Cleveland: World, 1966. Westport, CT: Hyperion Press, 1974. A companion volume to *Explorers.* Includes chapters on L. Sprague de Camp, Fritz Leiber, and Robert Bloch.

Penzoldt, Peter. *The Supernatural in Fiction.* London: Peter Nevill, 1952. New York: Humanities Press, 1965. A study of the major motifs of the English short story of the supernatural.

Porges, Irwin. *Edgar Rice Burroughs: The Man Who Created Tarzan.* Provo, UT: Brigham Young University Press, 1975. The definitive work on Burroughs.

Rabkin, Eric S. *The Fantastic in Literature.* Princeton, NJ: Princeton University Press, 1976. A theoretical introduction to the nature of fantasy and its role in faery tales, Gothic fiction, utopian fiction, science fiction, religious allegory, and traditional literature.

———. "Fantasy Literature: Gut with a Backbone." *CEA Critic* 40 (1978): 6–11. A discussion of the possible contexts for a college fantasy course.

Reis, Richard H. *George MacDonald.* New York: Twayne, 1972. A study of MacDonald's life and place in literature.

Rome, Joy. "Twentieth-Century Gothic: Mervyn Peake's Gormenghast Trilogy." *Unisa English Studies* 12 (March 1974): 42–54. Compares Peake's trilogy to the eighteenth-century Gothic mode in setting and mood.

Rovin, Jeff. *The Fabulous Fantasy Films.* Cranbury, NJ: A. S. Barnes, 1977. A comprehensive study of over 600 fantasy films; contains a filmography.

St. Armand, Barton Levi. *The Roots of Horror in the Fiction of H. P. Lovecraft.* Elizabethtown, NY: Dragon Press, 1977. The first book-length study in English of the greatest writer of supernatural horror fiction of the twentieth century.

Scholes, Robert. "The Good Witch of the West." *Hollins Critic* 11 (April 1974): 1–12. A study of the Earthsea trilogy as a dynamically balanced system. Revised and included as a chapter in *Structural Fabulation* (University of Notre Dame Press, 1975).

Servotte, Herman. "A Miracle of Rare Device: Mervyn Peake's Gormenghast Trilogy." *Revue des Langues Vivantes* 40 (1974): 489–496. A brief biography of Peake followed by a discussion of setting, characterization, style, structure, and themes in the trilogy.

Shippey, T. A. "The Magic Art and the Evolution of Words: Ursula Le Guin's Earthsea Trilogy." *Mosaic* 10 (1977): 147–163. A discussion of semantic context in the trilogy.

Slate, Tom. "Edgar Rice Burroughs and the Heroic Epic." *Riverside Quarterly* 3 (1968): 118–124. The fiction of Burroughs shares the qualities of the heroic epic.

Slusser, George Edgar. *The Farthest Shores of Ursula K. Le Guin.* San Bernardino, CA: Borgo Press, 1976. A study of Le Guin's art, with major sections on the Hanish novels, *The Left Hand of Darkness,* the Earthsea trilogy, and *The Dispossessed.*

Smith, Clark Ashton. *Planets and Dimensions: Collected Essays of Clark Ashton Smith.* Edited by Charles K. Wolfe. Baltimore: Mirage Press, 1973. Reprints most of Smith's important nonfiction, including essays on horror, fantasy, Lovecraft, and William Hope Hodgson.

Stevenson, Lionel. "Purveyors of Myth and Magic." In *Yesterday and After: The History of the English Novel.* New York: Barnes & Noble, 1967, pp. 111–154. Discussions of Machen, Blackwood, M. R. James, Shiel, Eddison, and T. H. White.

Sullivan, Anita T. "Ray Bradbury and Fantasy." *English Journal* 61 (1972): 1309–1314. An analysis of Bradbury's transition from a writer of horror tales to a writer of fantasy.

Sullivan, John, ed. *G. K. Chesterton: A Centenary Appraisal.* New York: Barnes & Noble, 1974. A critical anthology of essays on Chesterton's reputation, ability, life, and influences.

Swanson, Donald R. "The Uses of Tradition: King Arthur in the Modern World." *CEA Critic* 36 (1974): 19–21. Uses the misinterpretation of *The Once and Future King* in the movie *Camelot* as a starting point for a discussion of the novel's thematic content.

Todorov, Tzvetan. *The Fantastic: A Structural Approach to a Literary Genre.* Translated by Richard Howard. Cleveland: Press of Case Western Reserve University, 1973. A detailed study of the fantastic and its place in the literary mainstream.

Tolkien, J. R. R. "On Fairy-Stories." In *Tree and Leaf.* Boston: Houghton Mifflin, 1965, pp. 3–84. Certainly the most venerable and oft-quoted statement on the nature and effects of the faery tale and its relationship to fantasy. An indispensable source of information, the essay is reprinted in *The Tolkien Reader* (Ballantine, 1966).

Ugolnik, Anthony. "*Wordhord Onleac:* The Medieval Sources of J. R. R. Tolkien's Linguistic Aesthetic." *Mosaic* 10 (1977): 15–31. Demonstrates how Tolkien's linguistic aesthetic defines the laws of language in his secondary world.

Van Ash, Cay, and Rohmer, Elizabeth Sax. *Master of Villainy: A Biography of Sax Rohmer.* Edited by Robert E. Briney. Bowling Green, OH: Bowling Green University Popular Press, 1972. An extended study of Rohmer's life and career which stresses people and events; notes and a primary bibliography by Briney.

Wagenknecht, Edward. "The Little Prince Rides the White Deer: Fantasy and Symbolism in Recent Literature." *College English* 7 (1946): 431–437. An important historical study of fantasy literature of the 1940s.

Walker, Paul. *Speaking of Science Fiction: The Paul Walker Interviews.* Oradell, NJ: Luna Publications, 1978. In-depth interviews reprinted from *Luna Monthly* and other fanzines; includes Le Guin, Leiber, Zelazny, Anderson, Moorcock, Norton, Henderson, Bloch, and others.

Warner, Sylvia Townsend. *T. H. White: A Biography.* London: Jonathan Cape, 1967. The indispensable life of White with emphasis on details of biography, not on a literary analysis of his work.

Wasson, Richard. "*The Green Child:* Herbert Reed's Ironic Fantasy."

PMLA 77 (1962): 645–651. An interpretation of form and content in Reed's fantasy.

Watney, John. *Mervyn Peake.* London: Michael Joseph; New York: St. Martin, 1976. A fascinating book about an intensely private and imaginative man whose artistic talent was widely recognized during his lifetime but whose novels have only achieved their remarkable success since his death.

Weinberg, Robert. *The Weird Tales Story.* West Linn, OR: FAX Collector's Editions, 1977. A history of the most important fantasy magazine of the twentieth century.

Wolfe, Gary K. "Symbolic Fantasy." *Genre* 8 (1975): 194–209. An examination of the critical appraisals of fantasy and a description of the genre's narrative, stylistic, structural, and mythical characteristics.

Wolff, Robert Lee. *The Golden Key: A Study of the Fiction of George MacDonald.* New Haven: Yale University Press, 1961. A literary analysis set in a historical framework.

Reference Works

Allen, Paul. "Forgotten Fantasy." *Science-Fiction Collector,* September 1977, pp. 23–24. A contents listing of the entire run (five issues) of *Forgotten Fantasy* magazine.

Ashley, Michael. *Who's Who in Horror and Fantasy Fiction.* London: Elm Tree Books, 1977. Bio-bibliographic sketches of writers and editors whose work was primarily in the genre or who exercised influence upon it from the early eighteenth century to the present.

Christensen, Bonniejean McGuire. "J. R. R. Tolkien: A Bibliography." *Bulletin of Bibliography & Magazine Notes* 27 (1970): 61–67. A record of all of Tolkien's published works and the relevant reviews and criticism.

Christopher, Joe R. "An Inklings Bibliography." *Mythlore* 4, no. 1 (1976): 33–38, 4, no. 2 (1976): 33–38; 4, no. 3 (1977): 33–38. An ongoing, annotated bibliography of current criticism on Tolkien, Lewis, and Williams.

Christopher, Joe R., and Ostling, Joan K. *C. S. Lewis: An Annotated Checklist of Writings about Him and His Works.* Kent, OH: Kent State University Press, 1973. The most complete listing of criticism on Lewis to date.

Davidson, Don Adrian. "Sword and Sorcery Fiction: An Annotated Book List." *English Journal* 61 (1972): 43–51. A selected, annotated bibliography of major sword and sorcery fantasy classified by appeal according to age, sex, grade level, and level of difficulty; omits publication dates.

Derleth, August. *Thirty Years of Arkham House 1939–1969: A History and Bibliography.* Sauk City, WI: Arkham House, 1970. Chronicles the history of this famous fantasy publishing house and lists all books and their contents published under the imprints of Arkham House, Mycroft & Moran, and Stanton & Lee.

Foster, Robert. *The Complete Guide to Middle-Earth: From The Hobbit to The Silmarillion.* New York: Del Rey, 1978. A revised, expanded, and updated concordance, based on the author's earlier *A Guide to Middle-Earth* (Mirage Press, 1971).

Glenn, Lois. *Charles W. S. Williams: A Checklist.* Kent, OH: Kent State University Press, 1975. An annotated checklist of Williams's published works with complete publishing history and about 100 items of criticism.

Hall, H. W. *Science Fiction Book Review Index 1923–73.* Detroit: Gale Research, 1975. A complete record of all books reviewed in the science fiction and fantasy magazines. Beginning in 1970, the coverage is expanded to include a number of general magazines, literary magazines, and fanzines. Continued in annual supplements.

Hammond, Wayne G. "Addenda to 'J. R. R. Tolkien: A Bibliography.'" *Bulletin of Bibliography & Magazine Notes* 34 (1977): 119–127. An addendum to the Christensen bibliography on Tolkien published in the *Bulletin of Bibliography* in 1970.

Heins, Henry Hardy. *A Golden Anniversary Bibliography of Edgar Rice Burroughs,* rev. ed. West Kingston, RI: Donald M. Grant, 1964. A complete bibliography of all editions of Burroughs's published works, exhaustively annotated and cross-indexed. The definitive Burroughs bibliography and a remarkable achievement.

Lee, Walt. *Reference Guide to Fantastic Films: Science Fiction, Fantasy, & Horror.* 3 vols. Los Angeles: Chelsea-Lee Books, 1972–1974. The single most valuable reference work on the fantastic cinema. Lists 20,000 films from 50 countries spanning a 75-year period.

Lewis, Naomi. *Fantasy Books for Children,* rev. ed. London: National Book League, 1977. An important and useful guide to children's fantasy literature with detailed critical annotations.

Lord, Glenn, ed. *The Last Celt: A Bio-Bibliography of Robert E. Howard.* West Kingston, RI: Donald M. Grant, 1976. The definitive reference tool for the study of Howard and his writings, divided into autobiography, biography, bibliography, and miscellaneous.

Norton, Andre. "Norton Bibliography." In *The Many Worlds of Andre Norton,* edited by Roger Elwood. Radnor, PA: Chilton, 1974, pp. 201–208. Lists Norton's books, collaborations, story collections, magazine fiction, edited anthologies, and nonfiction. Reprinted in *The Book of Andre Norton* (DAW, 1975).

Owings, Mark, with Chalker, Jack L. *The Revised H. P. Lovecraft Bibliog-*

raphy. Baltimore: Mirage Press, 1973. Includes Lovecraft's essays, verse, fiction, collections, translations, collaborations, and other material.

Post, J. B. *An Atlas of Fantasy.* Baltimore: Mirage Press, 1973. Maps of fantasy worlds from Burroughs and Tolkien to Al Capp, compiled by America's foremost map scholar and librarian.

Schlobin, Roger C. "An Annotated Bibliography of Fantasy Fiction." *CEA Critic* 40 (1978): 37–42. A selected reading list of novels and anthologies.

Shreffler, Philip A. *The H. P. Lovecraft Companion.* Westport, CT: Greenwood Press, 1977. An analysis and concordance to Lovecraft's weird fiction.

Stafford, Larry, and Wilson, Danny. *The Paperback Price Guide.* Dayton, OH: Wolfshead, 1976. A checklist of sword and sorcery fiction in paperback, arranged by author.

Tuck, Donald H. *Encyclopedia of Science Fiction and Fantasy through 1968.* Vol. I, Chicago: Advent, 1974. Vol. II, 1978. Contains biographical information on many authors, anthologists, editors, and prominent fans. Entries contain complete bibliographical information on hardcover, paperback, and series titles; the contents of collections and anthologies are listed.

Turner, David G. *The First Editions of Andre Norton.* Menlo Park, CA: David G. Turner, 1974. A chronological list of Norton's novels, magazine fiction, edited anthologies, and articles.

Tymn, Marshall B., and Schlobin, Roger C. *The Year's Scholarship in Science Fiction and Fantasy: 1972–1975.* Kent, OH: Kent State University Press, 1979. A hardcover cumulation of the field's only ongoing secondary bibliography. Contents appeared originally in the magazine *Extrapolation* (see chapter 4); the series continues in annual updates.

Tymn, Marshall B., Schlobin, Roger C., and Currey, L. W. *A Research Guide to Science Fiction Studies: An Annotated Checklist of Primary and Secondary Materials on Fantasy and Science Fiction.* New York: Garland, 1977. A bibliography of scholarly materials published in the United States and England. Spans the entire range of science fiction and fantasy scholarship from World War II to the present.

Waggoner, Diana. *The Hills of Faraway: A Guide to Fantasy.* New York: Atheneum, 1978. A discussion of the nature of fantasies followed by a partially annotated bibliography of nearly 1,000 titles.

Weinberg, Robert. *The Annotated Guide to Robert E. Howard's Sword & Sorcery.* West Linn, OR: Starmont House, 1976. Plot summaries of the sword and sorcery fiction with critical commentary.

Weinberg, Robert, and Berglund, E. P. *Reader's Guide to the Cthulhu Mythos,* rev. ed. Albuquerque: Silver Scarab Press, 1973. A comprehensive checklist of titles by H. P. Lovecraft and others working within or developing the well-known and influential mythos.

Wells, Stuart W., III. *The Science Fiction and Heroic Fantasy Author Index.* Duluth, MN: Purple Unicorn, 1978. A checklist of about 5,000 titles by some 1,000 authors published in hardcover and paperback in the United States from 1945 through mid-1978. Indispensable for the period 1969–1978.

4
Periodicals

Semi-professional and amateur fantasy magazines have been published in countless numbers by scores of fantasy clubs, organizations, and individuals for several decades and the phenomenon shows no sign of abating. Lately, the number of semi-professional publications in the fantasy genre has increased, reflecting the paucity of professional magazine markets for fantasy writers.

This section is a listing of the major fantasy fanzines, semi-prozines, and newsletters published in the United States, Canada, and the United Kingdom. They have endured the test of time and can be recommended for their overall fine quality and excellent coverage of the fantasy field.

Amon Hen. Newsletter of the Tolkien Society, 110 Breakspears Rd., London SE4 1UD, UK.

Amra: Swordplay & Sorcery. Box 8243, Philadelphia, PA 19101. Irregular; first issue, April 1956. *Amra* is the official publication of the Hyborean Legion, a society devoted to the study of Robert E. Howard and all heroic fantasy. Notable for its excellent artwork.

Anduril: Magazine of Fantasy. Ed. John Martin, 101 Eskdale, Tanhouse 5, Skelmersdale, Lancaster WN8 6EB, UK. Irregular. Winner of the British Fantasy Award in 1976, small press category, *Anduril* is a high-quality magazine containing articles, short fiction, book reviews, and artwork.

Ariel, the Book of Fantasy. Ed. Thomas Durwood, Suite 2406, Power & Light Bldg., Kansas City, MO 64105. Annual; first issue, September 1976. *Ariel* is a fantasy-science fiction anthology that showcases the most imaginative and exciting works by the best authors and illustrators in the field. Past contributors have been Ray Bradbury, Ursula Le Guin, Michael Moorcock, Roger Zelazny, Frank Frazetta, Richard Corben, and Tim Conrad.

British Fantasy Society Bulletin. Newsletter of the British Fantasy Society, 447a, Porter Ave., Dagenham, Essex RM9 4ND, UK.

CSL: The Bulletin of the New York C. S. Lewis Society. Ed. Eugene McGovern, 32 Park Dr., Ossining, NY 10562. Monthly; first issue, 1969. The official publication of the New York C. S. Lewis Society, *CSL* contains critical articles on the life and work of C. S. Lewis.

Chacal: The Magazine of Fantasy. Ed. Arnir Fenner, Box 186, Shawnee Mission, KS 66201. Irregular; first issue, 1976. Issued as a replacement for *REH: Lone Star Fictioneer,* this magazine is oriented toward sword and sorcery and features fiction, poetry, and fantasy art.

Cinefantastique. Ed. Frederick S. Clarke, Box 270, Oak Park, IL 60603. Quarterly; first issue, Fall 1970. A magazine devoted entirely to the science fiction, fantasy, and horror film. Features major articles on recent films and studies of the works of film directors. Additional content includes film reviews and previews and discussions of books on genre films. Superbly illustrated.

Count Dracula Society Quarterly. Newsletter of the Count Dracula Society, 334 West 54 St., Los Angeles, CA 90037.

Cricket: The Literary Magazine for Children. Ed. Marianne Carus, Open Court Publishing Co., Box 100, LaSalle, IL 61301. Monthly; first issue, 1973. This children's publication is an excellent source of fantasy articles, book reviews, and author profiles.

Cthulhu: Tales of the Cthulhu Mythos. Ed. Jon Harvey, Spectre Press, 18 Cefu Rd., Mynachdy, Cardiff CF4 3HS, Wales, UK. Irregular; first issue, July 1976. *Cthulhu* is a series of booklets featuring Lovecraftian fiction and art.

Dark Fantasy. Ed. Howard E. Day, 204 First St., Box 207, Gananoque, Ontario K7G 2T7, Canada. Quarterly; first issue, July 1973. Primarily a fiction and poetry magazine, *Dark Fantasy* publishes the work of new writers and artists.

Dark Horizons. Ed. Geoffrey N. Smith, 113a High St., Whitstable, Kent CT5 1AY, UK. Three times yearly; first issue, December 1971. Published by the British Fantasy Society, *Dark Horizons* contains fiction, poetry, articles, and interviews on all aspects of fantasy in literature.

August Derleth Society Newsletter. Published by the August Derleth Society, 418 East Main St., Sparta, WI 54656.

Eerie Country. Ed. W. Paul Ganley, Box 35, Amherst Branch, Buffalo, NY 14226. Irregular; first issue, July 1976. *Eerie Country,* the sister magazine of *Weirdbook,* contains weird/horror fiction and reviews originally intended for *Weirdbook.*

The Eildon Tree: A Quarterly Journal of Fantasy. Ed. Donald G. Keller, Box 24560, Los Angeles, CA 90024. Irregular (may have ceased publication); first issue, 1974. *The Eildon Tree,* the journal of the Fantasy Association, is primarily a magazine of serious commentary on high fantasy.

Eldritch Tales: A Magazine in the Weird Tales Tradition. Ed. Crispin Burnham, 1051 Wellington, Lawrence, KS 66044. Semi-annual; first issue, December 1975 as *Dark Messenger Reader. Eldritch Tales* contains mostly fiction, with some poetry and reviews, in the weird genre.

Extrapolation: A Journal of Science Fiction and Fantasy. Ed. Thomas D. Clareson, Box 3186, College of Wooster, Wooster, OH 44691. Quarterly; first issue, December 1959. The official journal of the Modern Language Association Seminar on Science Fiction, also serving the Science Fiction Research Association. The first academic journal for scholars and teachers in the science fiction and fantasy fields.

Fantasiae. Newsletter of the Fantasy Association, Box 24560, Los Angeles, CA 90024.

Fantasy Crossroads. Ed. Jonathan Bacon, 7613 Flint, No. A, Shawnee Mission, KS 66214. Quarterly; first issue, November 1974. Publishes new work (fiction and verse) by semi-professional and professional writers, and articles on heroic fantasy. It has a Robert E. Howard influence but continues to move away from that toward an emphasis on contemporary authors. *Fantasy Crossroads* illustrates most of its contents.

Fantasy Newsletter. Ed. Paul C. Allen, 1015 West 36 St., Loveland, CO 80537. Monthly; first issue, June 1978. The newsletter of the fantasy field. Reports on recent and forthcoming events and publications of interest to fantasy fans. Very thorough in its coverage, this attractively illustrated publication nicely complements the fantasy coverage in *Locus.*

Fantasy Tales: A Magazine of the Weird and Unusual. Ed. Stephen Jones and David Sutton, 33 Wren House, Tachbrook Estate, London SW1V 3QD, UK. Semi-annual; first issue, Summer 1977. Publishes fiction by established writers as well as newcomers to the horror/weird genre. *Fantasy Tales* received the British Fantasy Award in 1977 in the small press category.

Horn Book Magazine. Ed. Ethel L. Heins, 585 Boyleston St., Boston, MA 02116. Bimonthly; first issue 1924. Although devoted to children's literature, *Horn Book* has been a steady source of articles on both juvenile and adult fantasy; also publishes valuable book reviews.

Journal Fantome: A Review of the Macabre in the Arts & Letters. Ed. David A. McClintock, 720 North Park Ave., Warren, OH 44483. Quarterly; first issue, February, 1979. A promising new publication that reviews little-known or forgotten works of the macabre as well as recent criticism and films.

Kalkai: Studies in James Branch Cabell. Ed. Paul Spencer, 665 Lotus Ave., Oradell, NJ 07649. Irregular; first issue, 1965. The official publication of the James Branch Cabell Society, *Kalkai* contains critical, biographical, and bibliographical articles on Cabell and his work.

Locus: The Newspaper of the Science Fiction Field. Ed. Charles N. Brown, Box 3938, San Francisco, CA 94119. 15 per year; first issue, June 27, 1968. An indispensable publication for those who desire regular information on the current developments in the science fiction and fantasy scenes. Contains news items, forthcoming books, media notes, author notes, market reports, convention updates, book reviews, and articles.

Mallorn: The Journal of the Tolkien Society. Ed. Jonathan S. Simons, 11 Regal Way, Harrow, Middlesex HA3 0RZ, UK. Annual; first issue, 1970. Primarily a journal of critical studies focusing on the works of J. R. R. Tolkien, although other fantasy writers are represented.

Myrddin. Ed. Lawson Hill, 6633 N. Poncharttain, Chicago, IL 60646. Irregular; first issue, April 1975. A magazine of fiction, poetry, and articles on the fantasy genre. Each issue of *Myrddin* is published in a limited edition designed for collectors.

Mythlore: A Journal of J. R. R. Tolkien, C. S. Lewis, and Charles Williams. Ed. Glen Goodknight, Box 4671, Whittier, CA 90607. Quarterly. Published by the Mythopoeic Society, *Mythlore* contains articles, reviews, artwork, and an ongoing Inklings bibliography.

Mythprint. Newsletter of the Mythopoeic Society, Box 4671, Whittier, CA 90607.

Newsletter of the Mervyn Peake Society. Published by the Mervyn Peake Society, Central Library, Northgate St., Ipswich, Suffolk IP1 3DE, UK.

Nyctalops: A Journal of the Darkly Fantastic. Ed. Harry O. Morris, Jr., 500 Wellesley SE, Albuquerque, NM 87106. Irregular; first issue, May 1970. The major coverage of *Nyctalops* is on the darker side of fantasy and (to a lesser extent) the surreal. Nonfiction articles and essays on such authors as H. P. Lovecraft and C. A. Smith are the main content. Each issue features a large assortment of macabre artwork.

Mervyn Peake Review. Ed. G. Peter Winnington, University of Lausanne, Switzerland. Semi-annual. The journal of the Mervyn Peake Society; contains critical studies and commentary on the life and works of Peake.

Phantasy Digest. Ed. Wayne Warfield, Hall Publications, Box 326, Aberdeen, MD 21001. Contains fantasy fiction and criticism, Robert E. Howard reprints, news, booklists, and artwork.

The Romanticist. Ed. John C. Moran and Don Herron, 3610 Meadowbrook Ave., Nashville, TN 37205. Irregular; first issue, 1977. Published by the F. Marion Crawford Memorial Society, *The Romanticist* serves as a forum for studies about authors and artists representative of the romantic tradition in literature and the arts.

Saint Toad's Journal. Ed. Wolf Forrest, 919 Oak Hill Ave., Hagerstown, MD 21740. Quarterly; first issue, August 1976. *Saint Toad's* publishes *Weird Tales*-type fiction and poetry, emphasizing H. P. Lovecraft, Robert E. Howard, and Clark Ashton Smith.

Wark. Ed. Rosemary Pardoe, Flat 2, 38 Sandown Lane, Liverpool 15, UK. Three times yearly; first issue, 1974. *Wark* reviews fantasy fanzines, semiprozines, and other nonprofessional publications. Beginning in 1979 publication will be annual and *Wark* will be devoted only to fantasy magazines.

The Weird Tales Collector. Ed. Robert Weinberg, 10606 S. Central Park, Chicago, IL 60655. Quarterly; first issue, Summer 1977. *The Weird Tales Collector* is an article and checklist magazine on the weird and fantasy pulps, with its primary focus on *Weird Tales.* It was founded to supplement and add to the information presented in *The Weird Tales Story* (FAX Collector's Editions, 1977) by Robert Weinberg.

Weirdbook. Ed. W. Paul Ganley, Box 35, Amherst Branch, Buffalo, NY 14226. Semi-annual; first issue, April 1968. A magazine of pure fantasy, supernatural horror, sword and sorcery, and weird fantasy fiction, *Weirdbook* also publishes poetry and artwork and occasional special issues such as *The Gothic Horror and Other Weird Tales* and *Hollow Faces, Merciless Moons.*

Whispers. Ed. Stuart David Schiff, 5508 Dodge Dr., Fayetteville, NC 28303. Contains fiction, poetry, artwork, and research news for readers and buyers of fantasy and horror fiction. *Whispers* was the winner of the 1977 Howard Award (World Fantasy Convention). Doubleday has published an anthology of 20 stories from the magazine entitled *Whispers: An Anthology of Fantasy and Horror,* edited by Stuart David Schiff.

5

Fantasy Societies and Organizations

One of the distinguishing characteristics of the fantasy field is the tendency of its readers to organize themselves into special interest groups. Thousands of fans, writers, artists, collectors, and scholars attend fantasy-oriented conventions held each year; and many readers join clubs, societies, and organizations devoted to some phase of fantasy literature. The most active groups are in the United States and the United Kingdom.

Academy of Science Fiction, Fantasy and Horror Films. Founded in 1972, the academy is an organization devoted to presenting awards of merit and recognition for science fiction, fantasy, and horror films. Publication: *Popcorn* (house organ); awards: The Golden Scroll; information: 334 West 54 St., Los Angeles, CA 90037.

British Fantasy Society. Established in 1971, the British Fantasy Society is devoted to the study and discussion of all forms of fantasy in literature, films, and art. Publications: *British Fantasy Society Bulletin* (house organ) and *Dark Horizons*, a fantasy magazine; awards: British Fantasy Award; information: 447a, Porter Ave., Dagenham, Essex RM9 4ND, UK.

James Branch Cabell Society. Organized in 1965 to facilitate the exchange of ideas and information on the writings of James Branch Cabell. Publication: *Kalkai: Studies in James Branch Cabell*, a journal; awards: none; information: 665 Lotus Ave., Oradell, NJ 07649.

Count Dracula Society. Formed in 1962, the Count Dracula Society is devoted to the serious study of horror films and Gothic literature. Publication: *Count Dracula Society Quarterly* (house organ); awards: Ann Radcliffe Award; information: 334 West 54 St., Los Angeles, CA 90037.

F. Marion Crawford Memorial Society. Founded in 1975 to encourage the study and appreciation of modern manifestations of the romantic tradition in literature and art, with emphasis upon fantastic literature and the works of Francis Marion Crawford. Publication: *The Romanticist*, a journal; awards: none; information: Saracinesca House, 3610 Meadowbrook Ave., Nashville, TN 37205.

August Derleth Society. Organized in 1977 to bring together those persons interested in the works of August Derleth and his circle. Publication: *August Derleth Society Newsletter* (house organ); awards: none; information: 418 East Main St., Sparta, WI 54656.

Fantasy Association. Affiliated with the British Fantasy Society and the Mythopoeic Society, the Fantasy Association was founded in 1973 to foster communication and the serious exchange of ideas about fantasy literature. Publications: *Fantasiae* (house organ) and *The Eildon Tree*, a journal; awards: none; information: Box 24560, Los Angeles, CA 90024.

Hyborean Legion. Organized in 1956, the Hyborean Legion is devoted to the study of Conan, Robert E. Howard, and all heroic fantasy. Publications: *Sardonic Worlds*, a fanzine, and *Amra*, a fantasy magazine; awards: none; information: Box 8243, Philadelphia, PA 19101.

Mythopoeic Society. Formed in 1967, the society is devoted to the study of myth and fantasy literature, especially the works of J. R. R. Tolkien, C. S. Lewis, and Charles Williams. Publications: *Mythprint* (house organ) and *Mythlore*, a fantasy magazine; awards: none; information: Box 4671, Whittier, CA 90607.

National Fantasy Fan Federation. Established in 1941 for the purpose of disseminating information on fan activities and publications, NFFF provides needed services to those new to fandom through its information bureau and in-house publications, *The National Fantasy Fan* and *Tightbeam;* awards: none; information: Janie Lamb, Rte. 1, Box 364, Heiskell, TN 37754.

New York C. S. Lewis Society. Founded in 1969 "for the purpose of bringing together those who have a special enthusiasm for C. S. Lewis." Publication: *CSL: The Bulletin of the New York C. S. Lewis Society*, a journal; awards: none; information: 32 Park Dr., Ossining, NY 10562.

Mervyn Peake Society. Founded in 1975 "to promote Peake's work through the establishment of a responsible corpus of critical opinion." Publications: *Newsletter of the Mervyn Peake Society* (house organ) and *Mervyn Peake Review*, a journal; awards: none; information: Central Library, Northgate St., Ipswich, Suffolk IP1 3DE, UK.

Science Fiction Foundation. Founded in England in 1971 as a subject discipline within the North East London Polytechnic, the foundation promotes the use of science fiction and fantasy in education and has research facilities for scholars and students. Publication: *Foundation: The Review of Science Fiction*, a journal; awards: James Blish Award; information: North East London Polytechnic, Longbridge Rd., Dagenham, Essex RM8 2AS, UK.

Science Fiction Research Association. SFRA was founded in 1970 by Professor Thomas D. Clareson and a group of academics interested in promoting the study of science fiction and fantasy. Its programs seek to encourage and develop new scholarship in the field and to make both published and unpublished materials more widely available to students, teachers, and scholars. Publication: *SFRA Newsletter* (house organ); awards: Pilgrim Award; information: Marshall Tymn, English Dept., Eastern Michigan University, Ypsilanti, MI 48197.

The Tolkien Society. Formed in 1969 "to provide a focal point for the many people interested in the works of J. R. R. Tolkien." Publications: *Amon Hen* (house organ) and *Mallorn*, a fantasy magazine; awards: none; information: 110 Breakspears Rd., London SE4 1UD, UK.

6

Literary Awards

Although a number of lesser-known awards in the fantasy field exist, such as the Anne Radcliffe Award of the Count Dracula Society and the Fritz Leiber Award presented at the annual Fantasy Faire, there are only three major awards that were created especially for outstanding achievement in fantasy fiction. The number of these awards will undoubtedly increase as the popularity of the genre grows. Lately, in fact, special recognition has been accorded the fantastic film, criticism, and fan activity, reflecting a trend toward a more serious approach to the literature of fantasy and its study.

August Derleth Fantasy Award. Presented annually since 1972 by the British Fantasy Society for best novel, short story, film, and comic. Since 1977 the award has been restricted to the novel category, with the British Fantasy Award given for the other categories, including the addition of best artist.

1972 *The Knight of the Swords* by Michael Moorcock
1973 Novel: *The King of the Swords* by Michael Moorcock
     Story: "The Fallible Fiend" by L. Sprague de Camp
     Film: *Tales from the Crypt*
     Comic: *Conan* (Marvel)
1974 Novel: *Hrolf Kraki's Saga* by Poul Anderson
     Story: "The Jade Man's Eyes" by Michael Moorcock

Film: *The Legend of Hell House*
Comic: *Conan* (Marvel)
1975 Novel: *The Sword and the Stallion* by Michael Moorcock
Story: "Sticks" by Karl Edward Wagner
Film: *The Exorcist*
Comic: *Savage Sword of Conan* (Marvel)
1976 Novel: *The Hollow Lands* by Michael Moorcock
Story: *The Second Book of Fritz Leiber* (collection)
Film: *Monty Python and the Holy Grail*
Comic: *Savage Sword of Conan* (Marvel)
1977 Novel: *The Dragon and the George* by Gordon R. Dickson (ADFA)
Story: "Two Suns Setting" by Karl Edward Wagner (BFA)
Film: *The Omen* (BFA)
Artist: Mike Kaluta (BFA)
Small Press: *Fantasy Tales,* edited by Stephen Jones and David
Sutton (BFA)
1978 Novel: *The Chronicles of Thomas Covenant the Unbeliever (Lord
Foul's Bane; The Illearth War; The Power That Preserves)*
by Stephen R. Donaldson (ADFA)
Story: "Jeffty Is Five" by Harlan Ellison (BFA)
Film: *Close Encounters of the Third Kind* (BFA)
Comic: *Savage Sword of Conan* (Marvel) (BFA)
Artist: Boris Vallejo (BFA)
Small Press: *Fantasy Tales,* edited by Stephen Jones and David
Sutton (BFA)

Grand Master of Fantasy (Gandalf) Award. Presented annually since 1974 at the World Science Fiction Convention as part of the Hugo Award Ceremony for a writer who has devoted a major portion of his/her career advancing fantasy literature.

1974 J. R. R. Tolkien
1975 Fritz Leiber
1976 L. Sprague de Camp
1977 Andre Norton
1978 Poul Anderson

World Fantasy Awards. Presented annually since 1975 at the World Fantasy Convention for contributions to fantasy literature in the following categories: novel, short fiction, collection/anthology, artist, special award, and life achievement. The award, called the "Howard," is named after Howard Phillips Lovecraft and Robert E. Howard.

1975 Novel: *The Forgotten Beasts of Eld* by Patricia A. McKillip
Story: "Pages from a Young Girl's Diary" by Robert Aickman

Collection: *Worse Things Waiting* by Manly Wade Wellman
Artist: Lee Brown Coyle
Life achievement (for services to the genre): Robert Bloch

1976 Novel: *Bid Time Return* by Richard Matheson
Story: "Belsen Express" by Fritz Leiber
Artist: Frank Frazetta
Life achievement: Fritz Leiber

1977 Novel: *Doctor Rat* by William Kotzwinkle
Story: "There's a Long, Long Trail a'Winding" by Russell Kirk
Collection: *Frights,* ed. Kirby McCauley
Artist: Roger Dean
Special Award (nonprofessional): *Whispers,* ed. Stuart Schiff
Special award (professional): Alternate World Recordings
Life achievement: Ray Bradbury

1978 Novel: *Our Lady of Darkness* by Fritz Leiber
Story: "The Chimney" by Ramsey Campbell
Collection: *Murgunstrumm and Others* by Hugh B. Cave
Artist: Lee Brown Coyle
Special Award (nonprofessional): Robert Weinberg
Special award (professional): E. F. Bleiler
Life achievement: Frank Belknap Long

7
Fantasy Collections in U. S. and Canadian Libraries

The recent proliferation of fantasy and science fiction research activity and the popular interest in the field as a whole have promoted academic libraries to develop systematic collections of primary and secondary titles. The first attempt to compile a listing of such collections was Hal Hall's preliminary list in the April 1972 issue of the *SFRA Newsletter,* in which 35 American, 4 Canadian, and 2 British collections were identified. Hall updates this listing in his chapter on "Library Collections of Science Fiction and Fantasy" in *Anatomy of Wonder,* edited by Neil Barron (Bowker, 1976).

This listing of fantasy library collections is adapted from Elizabetn Cogell's chapter, "Science Fiction and Fantasy Collections in U.S. and Canadian Libraries," which will appear in *The Science Fiction Reference Book,* edited by Marshall B. Tymn (FAX, 1980). The Cogell inventory lists nearly 100 significant collections and is the most comprehensive listing of science fiction and fantasy library holdings compiled.

The largest collections remain in the hands of private individuals, although the number of these collections is dwindling as they are purchased by research libraries and science fiction book dealers. The world's most complete collection is owned by Forrest J. Ackerman, a noted science fiction fan, literary agent, film consultant, editor, and bookseller. His 200,000-piece collection is housed in a special Fantascience Museum in Hollywood, California.

California

Los Angeles Science Fantasy Society Library, 11360 Ventura Blvd., Studio City, CA 91604.
Founded in 1937 through donations by LASFS members, the library houses an extensive collection of 2,000 pulps and digest-sized professional magazines and about 900 fan magazines, including LASFS publications since 1938 *(Imagination, Vom, Shangri L'Affaires, Apa L)*. The library relies on donations to extend its collection and does not subscribe to current periodicals. Book holdings, approximately 2,000 volumes (80 percent are softcover), include autographed copies of books by Pournelle and Niven and other authors who are members of the society. Miscellaneous items include original magazine art and original manuscripts.

San Francisco Public Library, Civic Center, San Francisco, CA 94102.
The McComas Collection of Fantasy and Science Fiction began in the 1960s through the donation of a core collection by Frances McComas, founder and editor of *The Magazine of Fantasy and Science Fiction*. Through subsequent purchases the magazine collection has grown to massive proportions; it includes complete runs of 92 titles, beginning with *Amazing Science Fiction* in 1926, and is supplemented by subscriptions to nine leading fantasy/science fiction periodicals. The 1,300-volume book collection, which includes current works, is primarily hardcover.

University of California, Los Angeles, University Research Library, Los Angeles, CA 90024.
The Nitka Collection of Fantastic Fiction has added only a small amount of material since its founding in 1967. The collection consists primarily of about 6,500 magazines and 9,000 books, augmented by manuscripts, correspondence, and miscellaneous papers of Ray Bradbury, Clark Ashton Smith, L. Sprague de Camp, Fritz Leiber, and Lewis Padgett.

University of California, Riverside, University Library, Box 5900, Riverside, CA 92507.
Purchased in 1970 as a collection of 7,000 book titles from the widow of Dr. J. Lloyd Eaton, the Eaton Fantasy and Science Fiction Collection is especially strong in early and scarce items published from 1870 to 1930 by British and American authors. The collection includes works of fantasy, utopia, horror, occult, Gothic, speculative fiction, and science fiction, although volumes are not housed by these subject areas. Strong holdings exist for

Edgar Rice Burroughs, George Griffith, H. Rider Haggard, William F. Jenkins, David H. Keller, H. P. Lovecraft, A. Merritt, Talbot Mundy, E. E. Smith, Jules Verne, and S. Fowler Wright.

University of Southern California, University Library, University Park, Los Angeles, CA 90007.
The library's American Literature Collection contains the complete works of Ambrose Bierce, Edgar Rice Burroughs, August Derleth, Jack London, Ray Bradbury, and Kurt Vonnegut, and includes letters and correspondence of Bierce, Derleth, and London. The Cinema Library contains 25 volumes on the fantasy and science fiction film, published and unpublished screenplays, and 12 taped interviews with Ray Bradbury.

Illinois

Northern Illinois University Libraries, DeKalb, IL 60115.
The primary holdings consist of science fiction and fantasy magazines, about 2,000 issues (100 titles), dating from 1926. The library is currently in the process of acquiring an H. P. Lovecraft collection of first and early editions, including some manuscripts.

Wheaton College Library, 501 East Seminary Ave., Wheaton, IL 60187.
Established in 1965, the Marion E. Wade Collection houses an extensive number of fantasy periodicals, including *Mythlore, Mythprint, Unicorn,* and *Mallorn,* and a number of fantasy society bulletins. The collection also contains hundreds of early periodicals pertaining to G. K. Chesterton and books and articles by and about seven authors: Owen Barfield, G. K. Chesterton, C. S. Lewis, George MacDonald, Dorothy Sayers, J. R. R. Tolkien, and Charles Williams. It includes many first editions, as well as later editions, of Lewis, MacDonald, Tolkien, and Williams. Among the miscellaneous holdings are letters of the seven authors, including 1,115 original, unpublished letters by Lewis; 950 holograph letters by Williams; 96 theses and dissertations on the seven authors; and manuscripts by Lewis and Williams, including a first draft of Williams's *Descent into Hell.*

Indiana

Indiana University, Lilly Library, Bloomington, IN 47401.
Begun in 1972, the Lilly Library collection of science fiction and fantasy magazines, books, and manuscripts is one of the largest and fastest growing in the United States, housing a wealth of material for researchers in the field. The collection includes a comprehensive Arkham House run and complete first editions of H. G. Wells, Jules Verne, H. Rider Haggard, G. K.

Chesterton, August Derleth, and H. P. Lovecraft. The collection also contains complete or nearly complete runs of the major science fiction and fantasy magazines published during the 1930s and 1940s. Miscellaneous holdings include over 2,000 manuscript items by Derleth and papers of Anthony Boucher and Fritz Leiber. Much of the collection is still uncataloged.

Kansas

University of Kansas, Kenneth Spencer Research Library, Lawrence, KS 66045.
Established in 1965 as a bequest of James H. Stewart, the Stewart Fantasy Collection contains a long run of *Weird Tales* and about 470 books by H. P. Lovecraft, Arthur Machen, and Frank Belknap Long.

Kentucky

University of Louisville Library, Belknap Campus, Louisville, KY 40208.
To date, the library has acquired about 2,500 Edgar Rice Burroughs items, including first editions, reprints, magazines, and movie posters. The curator's goal is to make this the definite Burroughs collection. The library also has all but one of the regularly published Oz titles, most of L. Frank Baum's non-Oz fantasies, and many of his pseudonymous titles.

Pennsylvania

Pennsylvania State University, Pattee Library, University Park, PA 16801.
Started in 1973 for the Science Fiction Research Association annual meeting, the collection now contains about 4,000 magazine titles. Book holdings show a strong utopian emphasis and include a 59-volume run of Arkham House titles.

Rhode Island

Brown University Library, Box A, Providence, RI 02912.
The Howard Phillips Lovecraft Collection was founded in 1937 by Lovecraft's literary executor. Primary holdings include subscriptions to several fantasy periodicals and newsletters, including *H. P. Lovecraft Society Journal, Nyctalops, Weirdbook, Macabre,* and *Whispers;* numerous amateur journals from 1910 to 1940 relating to Lovecraft; and about 300 books containing Lovecraft material. Miscellaneous holdings extend to more than 4,000 Lovecraft items (1894–1960), including about 1,400 letters by Lovecraft and over 200 manuscripts of his essays, fiction, and poetry.

South Carolina

University of South Carolina, Thomas Cooper Library, Columbia, SC 29208.
The library collection contains a complete Arkham House run (130 volumes) and a medium-sized Lovecraft collection (44 primary works, including a virtually complete set of first editions, and 42 secondary works).

Virginia

University of Virginia, Alderman Library, Charlottesville, VA 22901.
The James Branch Cabell Collection contains about 2,000 original letters by Cabell and manuscripts for 38 books, including a first draft of *Jurgen,* several short stories, and articles.

Virginia Commonwealth University, James Branch Cabell Library, 901 Park Ave., Richmond, VA 23220.
The library holdings include 250 magazine articles and 142 books and pamphlets by and about Cabell, including first editions, revisions, and reprints, and 27 letters, dated 1921 to 1934.

Wisconsin

Marquette University, Memorial Library, 1415 West Wisconsin Ave., Milwaukee, WI 53233.
Established in 1957 when it was purchased from Tolkien, the John Reuel Tolkien Manuscripts house holographs, typescripts, and galleys with holograph corrections by Tolkien; some notes on *The Hobbit, Farmer Giles of Ham,* and *The Lord of the Rings;* and a holograph manuscript with colored pencil illustrations by the author for the unpublished "Mr. Bliss."

University of Wisconsin, La Crosse, Murphy Library, La Crosse, WI 54601.
The Paul W. Skeeters Collection, begun in 1971, contains over 1,000 first edition titles in horror, Gothic, fantasy, and science fiction literature dating from 1890 to the 1940s. The collection includes 125 Arkham House titles, many signed.

Canada

Queen's University, Douglas Library, Kingston, Ontario K7L 5C4, Canada.
The Gothic Fantasy Collection, established in 1968, is essentially a collection of eighteenth-, nineteenth-, and twentieth-century literature that shows the relationships between Gothic fiction, fantasy, and science fiction. It includes over 59 books by H. P. Lovecraft.

Core Collection Titles Available in the United Kingdom

The publication information provided in the following list of core collection titles available in the United Kingdom is based on *British Books in Print 1978*. Addresses for all British publishers and distributors listed here are included in the Directory of Publishers. Page numbers refer to the core collection annotations provided for each title in chapter 2.

Aiken, Joan. *A Harp of Fishbones*. London: Cape, 1972. Harmondsworth, Middlesex: Puffin, 1975 (paper). pp. 39–40.

Alexander, Lloyd. *The Black Cauldron*. London: Armada, 1973 (paper). pp. 40–41.

_____. *The Book of Three*. London: Armada, 1973 (paper). p. 40.

_____. *The Castle of Llyr*. London: Fontana, 1977 (paper). pp. 41–42.

Anderson, Poul. *Three Hearts and Three Lions*. London: Sphere, 1974 (paper). p. 45.

Babbitt, Natalie. *Tuck Everlasting*. London: Chatto, 1977. p. 48.

Baum, L. Frank. *The Wizard of Oz*. London: Dent, 1976 (paper). pp. 49–50.

Beagle, Peter S. *The Last Unicorn*. London: Bodley Head, 1968. pp. 50–51.

Blackwood, Algernon. *The Dance of Death.* London: Pan, 1973 (paper). p. 52.

Blish, James. *Black Easter; or, Faust Aleph-Null.* London: Faber, 1969. pp. 52–53.

————. *The Day after Judgement.* London: Faber, 1972. Harmondsworth, Middlesex: Penguin, 1975 (paper). pp. 53–54.

Brunner, John. *The Traveller in Black.* London: Severn House, 1977. pp. 55–56.

Carroll, Lewis. *Alice in Wonderland and Through the Looking Glass.* London: Macmillan, 1977; paper, n.d. pp. 60–61.

Chant, Joy. *The Grey Mane of Morning.* London: Allen & Unwin, 1977. pp. 62–63.

————. *Red Moon and Black Mountain.* London: Allen & Unwin, 1970. pp. 61–62.

Chapman, Vera. *The Green Knight.* London: Collings, 1975. p. 64.

————. *King Arthur's Daughter.* London: Collings, 1976. pp. 64–65.

————. *The King's Damosel.* London: Collings, 1976. pp. 63–64.

Cherryh, C. J. *Gate of Ivrel.* London: Futura, 1977 (paper). pp. 65–66.

Cooper, Susan. *The Dark Is Rising.* London: Chatto, 1973. Harmondsworth, Middlesex: Puffin, 1976 (paper). pp. 68–69.

————. *Greenwitch.* London: Chatto, 1974. Harmondsworth, Middlesex: Puffin, 1977 (paper). pp. 69–70.

————. *The Grey King.* London: Chatto, 1975. Harmondsworth, Middlesex: Puffin, 1977 (paper). pp. 70–71.

————. *Over Sea, under Stone.* London: Chatto, 1974. Harmondsworth, Middlesex: Puffin, 1968 (paper). pp. 67–68.

————. *Silver on the Tree.* London: Chatto, 1977. p. 71.

Cott, Jonathan, ed. *Beyond the Looking Glass.* St. Albans, Hertfordshire: Hart-Davis, 1974. p. 194.

Dickson, Gordon R. *The Dragon and the George.* New York: Ballantine (dist. London: Futura), 1977 (paper). p. 73.

Dunsany, Lord. *Gods, Men and Ghosts: The Best Supernatural Fiction of Lord Dunsany.* Ed. E. F. Bleiler. New York: Dover (dist. London: Constable), 1976 (paper). pp. 83–84.

————. *The King of Elfland's Daughter.* New York: Ballantine (dist. London: Pan), 1971 (paper). pp. 78–79.

Eddison, E. R. *The Worm Ouroboros.* London: Pan, 1973 (paper). p. 84.

Gardner, John. *Grendel.* London: Pan, 1973 (paper). p. 87.

Garner, Alan. *Elidor.* London: Collins, 1965. London: Armada (paper), n.d. p. 89.

_____. *The Moon of Gomrath.* London: Collins, 1963. London: Armada, 1972 (paper). pp. 88–89.

_____. *The Owl Service.* London: Collins, 1967. London: Armada, 1973 (paper). pp. 89–90.

_____. *Red Shift.* London: Collins, 1973. London: Armada, 1975 (paper). p. 90.

_____. *The Weirdstone of Brisingamen.* London: Collins, 1965. London: Armada, 1971 (paper). pp. 87–88.

Goldman, William. *The Princess Bride.* London: Macmillan, 1975. London: Pan, 1976 (paper). p. 91.

Haggard, H. Rider. *She.* London: Collins, 1974. London: Hodder, 1968 (paper). pp. 92–93.

Hales, E. E. Y. *Chariot of Fire.* London: Hodder, 1977. pp. 94–95.

Hoffmann, E. T. A. *Best Tales.* Ed. E. F. Bleiler. New York: Dover (dist. London: Constable), 1968 (paper). pp. 97–98.

Ingelow, Jean. *Mopsa the Fairy.* London: Dent, 1964. pp. 98–99.

Kendall, Carol. *The Minnipins* (American title: *The Gammage Cup*). Harmondsworth, Middlesex: Puffin, 1971 (paper). pp. 99–100.

Kurtz, Katherine. *Camber of Culdi.* New York: Ballantine (dist. London: Futura), 1977 (paper). p. 103.

La Motte Fouqué, Baron de. *Undine.* London: Calder, n.d. (paper). pp. 105–106.

Lee, Tanith. *Companions on the Road.* London: Macmillan, 1975. p. 108.

_____. *East of Midnight.* London: Macmillan, 1977. pp. 109–110.

_____. *The Winter Players.* London: Macmillan, 1976. pp. 107–108.

Le Guin, Ursula K. *The Farthest Shore.* London: Gollancz, 1973. Harmondsworth, Middlesex: Puffin, 1974 (paper). pp. 111–112.

_____. *The Tombs of Atuan.* London: Gollancz, 1972. Harmondsworth, Middlesex: Puffin, 1974 (paper). p. 111.

_____. *The Wind's Twelve Quarters.* London: Gollancz, 1976. St. Albans, Hertfordshire: Panther, 1978 (paper). p. 112–113.

_____. *A Wizard of Earthsea.* London: Gollancz, 1971. Harmondsworth, Middlesex: Puffin, 1971 (paper). p. 110.

Lewis, C. S. *The Horse and His Boy.* London: Collins, 1974. Harmondsworth, Middlesex: Puffin, 1970 (paper). p. 124.

_____. *The Last Battle.* London: Bodley Head, 1956. Harmondsworth, Middlesex: Puffin, 1970 (paper). pp. 125–126.

_____. *The Lion, the Witch and the Wardrobe.* London: Collins, 1974. Harmondsworth, Middlesex: Puffin, 1970 (paper). pp. 120–121.

————. *The Magician's Nephew.* London: Bodley Head, 1955. Harmondsworth, Middlesex: Puffin, 1970 (paper). p. 125.

————. *Out of the Silent Planet.* London: Bodley Head, 1945. London: Pan, 1968 (paper). pp. 118–119.

————. *Perelandra.* London: Bodley Head, 1943. p. 119.

————. *Prince Caspian.* London: Collins, 1974. Harmondsworth, Middlesex: Puffin, 1970 (paper). pp. 121–122.

————. *The Silver Chair.* London: Collins, 1974. Harmondsworth, Middlesex: Puffin, 1970 (paper). pp. 123–124.

————. *That Hideous Strength.* London: Bodley Head, 1945. London: Pan, 1968 (paper). p. 120.

————. *Till We Have Faces.* London: Collins, 1956. pp. 126–127.

————. *The Voyage of the "Dawn Treader."* London: Collins, 1974. Harmondsworth, Middlesex: Puffin, 1970 (paper). pp. 122–123.

MacDonald, George. *At the Back of the North Wind.* London: Dent, 1956. pp. 132–133.

————. *The Princess and Curdie.* London: Blackie, n.d. Harmondsworth, Middlesex: Puffin, 1970 (paper). pp. 133–134.

————. *The Princess and the Goblin.* London: Dent, 1949. Harmondsworth, Middlesex: Puffin, 1970 (paper). p. 133.

Mayne, William. *Earthfasts.* London: H. Hamilton, 1966. Harmondsworth, Middlesex: Penguin, 1969 (paper). pp. 139–140.

Mirrlees, Hope. *Lud-in-the-Mist.* New York: Ballantine (dist. London: Pan), 1972 (paper). pp. 141–142.

Morris, William. *The Sundering Flood.* Llanfynydd, Carmarthen: Unicorn Bookshop, 1973 (paper). pp. 147–148.

————. *The Wood beyond the World.* New York: Dover (dist. London: Constable), 1973 (paper). pp. 145–146.

Norton, Andre. *The Crystal Gryphon.* London: Gollancz, 1973. pp. 152–153.

————. *Sorceress of the Witch World.* London: G. Prior, 1977. p. 151.

————. *Steel Magic.* London: H. Hamilton, 1977. p. 152.

————. *Three against the Witch World.* London: G. Prior, 1977. p. 150.

————. *Warlock of the Witch World.* London: G. Prior, 1977. pp. 150–151.

————. *Web of the Witch World.* London: G. Prior, 1977. p. 150.

————. *Witch World.* London: G. Prior, 1977. pp. 149–150.

————. *Year of the Unicorn.* London: G. Prior, 1977. pp. 151–152.

Pratt, Fletcher. *The Well of the Unicorn.* New York: Ballantine (dist. London: Futura), 1977 (paper). pp. 154–155.

Rayner, William. *Stag Boy.* London: Collins, 1972. p. 155.

Ruskin, John. *King of the Golden River.* London: H. Hamilton, 1978. New York: Dover (dist. London: Constable), 1975 (paper). pp. 155–156.

Simak, Clifford D. *Enchanted Pilgrimage.* Harmondsworth, Middlesex: Fontana, 1977 (paper). pp. 156–157.

Smith, Clark Ashton. *The Abominations of Yondo.* Sudbury, Suffolk: Spearman, 1972. St. Albans, Hertfordshire: Panther, 1974 (paper). pp. 157–158.

Stewart, Mary. *The Hollow Hills.* London: Hodder, 1973. London: Coronet, 1974 (paper). pp. 158–159.

Swann, Thomas Burnett. *Day of the Minotaur.* St. Albans, Hertfordshire: Mayflower, 1975 (paper). pp. 159–160.

Thurber, James. *The 13 Clocks and The Wonderful 0.* London: H. Hamilton, 1966. Harmondsworth, Middlesex: Puffin, 1970 (paper). pp. 161–162.

———. *The White Deer.* Harmondsworth, Middlesex: Puffin, 1963 (paper). pp. 161–162.

Tolkien, J. R. R. *Farmer Giles of Ham.* London: Allen & Unwin, 1976. p. 166.

———. *The Father Christmas Letters.* London: Allen & Unwin, 1976. p. 167.

———. *The Lord of the Rings.* 3 vol. *The Fellowship of the Ring.* London: Allen & Unwin, 1966; paper, 1974. *The Two Towers.* London: Allen & Unwin, 1966; paper, 1974. *The Return of the King.* London: Allen & Unwin, 1966; paper, 1974. pp. 163–166.

———. *The Silmarillion.* London: Allen & Unwin, 1977. pp. 167–168.

———. *Smith of Wootton Major.* London: Allen & Unwin, 1975. p. 166.

Warner, Sylvia Townsend. *Kingdoms of Elfin.* London: Chatto, 1977. pp. 172–173.

White, T. H. *Mistress Masham's Repose.* London: Cape, 1947. pp. 173–174.

———. *The Once and Future King.* London: Collins, 1959. pp. 174–175.

Williams, Charles. *Shadows of Ecstasy.* London: Faber, 1965 (paper). pp. 177–178.

———. *War in Heaven.* London: Sphere, 1976 (paper). pp. 175–176.

Wrightson, Patricia. *The Nargun and the Stars.* London: Hutchinson, 1973. pp. 179–180.

Zelazny, Roger. *The Guns of Avalon.* London: Corgi, 1975 (paper). p. 182.

———. *The Hand of Oberon.* London: Faber, 1978. p. 183.

———. *Sign of the Unicorn.* London: Faber, 1977. pp. 182–183.

Directory of Publishers

The following is a comprehensive list of publishers of science fiction and fantasy literature in the United States and the United Kingdom. Included and indicated with an asterisk are the specialty presses that devote nearly all of their efforts to science fiction, fantasy, and the horror fields, many of whom cater almost exclusively to collectors, producing books in limited editions.

A&W Visual Library
  95 Madison Ave.
  New York, NY 10016

Abacus Books
  (see Sphere)

Abelard-Schuman
  (see Blackie)

Ace Books
  1120 Avenue of the Americas
  New York, NY 10036

*Advent Publishers
  Box A3228
  Chicago, IL 60690

*Algol Press
  Box 4175
  New York, NY 10017

George Allen & Unwin
  40 Museum St.
  London WC1A 1LU

Aladdin
  (see Atheneum)

W. H. Allen & Co.
  44 Hill St.
  London W1X 8LB

Allison & Busby
  6a Noel St.
  London W1V 3RB

Anchor Books
(see Doubleday)

*Apocalypse Press
Box 1821
Topeka, KS 66601

Archon Books
(see Shoe String)

Archway Paperbacks
(see Pocket Books)

*Arkham House
Sauk City, WI 53583

Arno Press
330 Madison Ave.
New York, NY 10017

Arrow Books
(see Hutchinson)

Atheneum Publishers
122 E. 42 St.
New York, NY 10017

Avon Books
959 Eighth Ave.
New York, NY 10019

Bailey Bros. & Swinfen
Warner House
Bowles Well Gardens
Folkestone, Kent CT19 6PH,
England

Ballantine Books
201 E. 50 St.
New York, NY 10022

Bantam Books
666 Fifth Ave.
New York, NY 10019

A. S. Barnes
Box 421
Cranbury, NJ 08512

Barnes & Noble
10 E. 53 St.
New York, NY 10022

Baronet Publishing Co.
509 Madison Ave.
New York, NY 10022

Berkley Publishing Corp.
200 Madison Ave.
New York, NY 10016

Blackie & Son
450 Edgware Rd.
London W2 1EG

*Blue Star
Box 14615
Hartford, CT 06114

The Bodley Head
9 Bow St.
London W2CE 7AL

Borden Publishing Co.
1855 W. Main St.
Alhambra, CA 91801

*Borgo Press
Box 2845
San Bernardino, CA 92406

R. R. Bowker Co.
1180 Avenue of the Americas
New York, NY 10036

R. R. Bowker Co. (U.K.)
Erasmus House
Epping, Essex CM16 4BU,
England

Bowling Green University Popular Press
101 University Hall
Bowling Green University
Bowling Green, OH 43403

*Bran's Head Books
91 Wimborne Ave.
Hayes, Middlesex,
England

Calder & Boyars
18 Brewer St.
London W1R 4AS

Jonathan Cape
30 Bedford Square
London WC1B 3EL

*Carcosa
  Box 1064
  Chapel Hill, NC 27514

Chatto & Windus
  40–42 William IV St.
  London WC2N 4DF

*Chelsea-Lee Books
  Box 66273
  Los Angeles, CA 90066

Chilton Book Co.
  201 King of Prussia Rd.
  Radnor, PA 19089

*Russ Cochran
  Box 437
  West Plains, MO 65775

College & University Press
  267 Chapel St.
  New Haven, CT 06513

Collier Books
  (see Macmillan)

Rex Collings
  69 Marylebone High St.
  London W1

William Collins (U.K.)
  14 St. James's Place
  London SW1A 1PS

Collins, William & World Pub. Co.
  2080 W. 117 St.
  Cleveland, OH 44111

Condor Publishing Co.
  521 Fifth Ave.
  New York, NY 10017

Constable & Co.
  10 Orange St.
  Leicester Square
  London WC2

Contemporary Books
  180 N. Michigan Ave.
  Chicago, IL 60601

Corgi Books
  Century House
  61/63 Uxbridge Rd.
  London W5 5SA

Coronet Books
  (see Hodder & Stoughton)

Coward, McCann & Geoghegan
  200 Madison Ave.
  New York, NY 10016

Thomas Y. Crowell
  10 E. 53 St.
  New York, NY 10022

Crown Publishers
  One Park Ave.
  New York, NY 10016

*Crystal Visions Press
  809 Cleermont Dr.
  Huntsville, AL 35801

DAW Books
  1301 Avenue of the Americas
  New York, NY 10019

*Gerry de la Ree
  7 Cedarwood Lane
  Saddle River, NJ 07458

*Del Rey Books
  (see Ballantine)

Dell Books
  One Dag Hammarskjold Plaza
  245 E. 47 St.
  New York, NY 10017

Delta Books
  (see Dell)

J. M. Dent & Sons
  26 Albemarle St.
  London W1X 4QY

Devin-Adair Co.
  143 S. Beach Ave.
  Old Greenwich, CT 06870

*Howard DeVore
  4705 Weddel St.
  Dearborn Heights, MI 48125

Dial Press
  One Dag Hammarskjold Plaza
  245 E. 47 St.
  New York, NY 10017

Dobson Books
  80 Kensington Church St.
  London W8 4BZ

The Donning Company
  253 W. Bute St.
  Norfolk, VA 23510

Doubleday & Co.
  245 Park Ave.
  New York, NY 10017

Dover Publications
  180 Varick St.
  New York, NY 10014

*Dragon Press
  Elizabethtown, NY 12932

E. P. Dutton & Co.
  201 Park Ave.
  New York, NY 10003

Eerdmans Publishing Co.
  255 Jefferson Ave. S.E.
  Grand Rapids, MI 49503

*Eidolon Press
  4608 Nazaire Rd.
  Pensacola, FL 32505

Faber & Faber
  3 Queens Square
  London WC1N 3AU

*Fantome Press
  720 N. Park Ave.
  Warren, OH 44483

Farrar, Straus & Giroux
  19 Union Square W.
  New York, NY 10003

Fawcett World Library
  1515 Broadway
  New York, NY 10036

*FAX Collector's Editions
  Box E
  West Linn, OR 97068

*Ferret Fantasy
  27 Beechcroft Rd.
  Upper Tooting
  London SW17

*Firebell Books
  Box 804
  Glen Rock, NJ 07452

Fireside Books
  (see Simon & Schuster)

Fontana Books
  (see Penguin, U.K.)

*Futura Publications
  110 Warner Rd.
  London SE5 7HQ

Gale Research Co.
  Book Tower
  Detroit, MI 48226

*W. Paul Ganley
  Box 35, Amherst Branch
  Buffalo, NY 14226

Garland Publishing
  545 Madison Ave.
  New York, NY 10022

Victor Gollancz
  14 Henrietta St.
  London WC2E 8QJ

Granada Publishing
  Box 9
  29 Frogmore St.
  St. Albans, Hertfordshire AL2 2NF,
  England

*Donald M. Grant
  West Kingston, RI 02892

Greenwillow Books
  105 Madison Ave.
  New York, NY 10016

Greenwood Press
  51 Riverside Ave.
  Westport, CT 06880

Gregg Press
  (see G. K. Hall)

Robert Hale
  Clerkenwell House
  45–47 Clerkenwell Green
  London EC1R 0HT

G. K. Hall & Co.
  70 Lincoln St.
  Boston, MA 02111

*Hall Publications
Box 326
Aberdeen, MD 21001

Hamish Hamilton
90 Great Russell St.
London WC1B 3PT

The Hamlyn Group
Astronaut House
Hounslow Rd.
Feltham, Middlesex TW14 9AR,
England

Harcourt Brace Jovanovich
757 Third Ave.
New York, NY 10017

Harmony Books
(see Crown)

Harper & Row
10 E. 53 St.
New York, NY 10022

Hart-Davis, MacGibbon
(see Granada)

*Heritage Press
Box 721
Forest Park, GA 30050

Hodder & Stoughton
47 Bedford Square
London WC1B 3DP

Holt, Rinehart & Winston
383 Madison Ave.
New York, NY 10017

Houghton Mifflin Co.
2 Park St.
Boston, MA 02107

Hutchinson Publishing Group
3 Fitzroy Square
London W1P 6JD

Hyperion Press
45 Riverside Ave.
Westport, CT 06880

*Institute for Specialized Literature
Box 4201
North Hollywood, CA 91607

Jove/HBJ Books
(see Harcourt)

Kennikat Press
90 South Bayles Ave.
Port Washington, NY 11050

Kent State University Press
Kent, OH 44240

Alfred A. Knopf
(see Random)

*Luna Publications
655 Orchard St.
Oradell, NJ 07649

Macmillan
866 Third Ave.
New York, NY 10022

Macmillan Publishers (U.K.)
Little Essex St.
London WC2R 3LF

Magnum Books
11 New Fetter Lane
London EC4P 4EE

Manor Books
432 Park Ave. S.
New York, NY 10016

Mayflower Books
(see Granada)

Mentor Books
(see New American Library)

Millington Books
109 Southhampton Row
London WC1B 4HH

*Mirage Press
Box 7887
Baltimore, MD 21207

*Morning Star Press
Box 6011
Leawood, KS 66206

William Morrow & Co.
105 Madison Ave.
New York, NY 10016

*Necronomicon Press
101 Lockwood St.
West Warwick, RI 02893

Thomas Nelson
30 E. 42 St.
New York, NY 10017

*NESFA Press
Box G, MIT Branch
Cambridge, MA 02139

New American Library
1301 Avenue of the Americas
New York, NY 10019

New English Library
Barnard's Inn, Holborn
London EC1N 2JR

*Newcastle Publishing Co.
13419 Saticoy St.
North Hollywood, CA 91605

Noonday Press
(see Farrar)

Octopus Books
59 Grosvenor St.
London W1X 9DA

*Owlswick Press
Box 8243
Philadelphia, PA 19101

Oxford University Press
200 Madison Ave.
New York, NY 10016

Pan Books
Cavaye Place
London SW10 9PG

Panther Books
(see Granada)

Parnassus Press
4080 Halleck St.
Emeryville, CA 94608

Peacock Press
(see Bantam)

*Pendragon Press
Box 14834
Portland, OR 97214

Penguin Books
(see Viking Penguin)

Penguin Books (U.K.)
Bath Rd.
Harmondsworth, Middlesex
UB7 0DA,
England

*Pennyfarthing Press
Box 7745
San Francisco, CA 94120

*Phantasia Press
13101 Lincoln
Huntington Woods, MI 48070

Pierrot Publishing
17 Oakley Rd.
London N1 3LL

Pinnacle Books
Box 13160, Sta. E
Oakland, CA 94661

Pocket Books
1230 Avenue of the Americas
New York, NY 10020

Popular Library
600 Third Ave.
New York, NY 10016

Clarkson N. Potter
(see Crown)

Prentice-Hall
Englewood Cliffs, NJ 07632

Princeton University Press
Princeton, NJ 08540

George Prior Associated Publishers
Rugby Chambers
2 Rugby St.
London WC1N 3QU

Puffin Books
(see Viking)

Puffin Books (U.K.)
(see Penguin, U.K.)

*Purple Mouth Press
713 Paul St.
Newport News, VA 23605

*Purple Unicorn Books
4532 London Rd.
Duluth, MN 55804

G. P. Putnam's Sons
200 Madison Ave.
New York, NY 10016

*Quantum Books
(see Dial)

Quick Fox Books
33 W. 60 St.
New York, NY 10023

*Randen
Box 3157
Culver City, CA 90230

Random House
201 E. 50 St.
New York, NY 10022

Robson Books
28 Poland St.
London W1V 3DB

Running Press
38 S. 19 St.
Philadelphia, PA 19103

St. Martin's Press
175 Fifth Ave.
New York, NY 10010

Scarecrow Press
52 Liberty St.
Box 656
Metuchen, NJ 08840

Schocken Books
200 Madison Ave.
New York, NY 10016

Scholarly Press
19722 E. Nine Mile Rd.
St. Clair Shores, MI 48080

*Science Fiction Book Club
(see Doubleday)

Charles Scribner's Sons
597 Fifth Ave.
New York, NY 10017

Seabury Press
815 Second Ave.
New York, NY 10017

Severn House Publishers
144–146 New Bond St.
London W1Y 9FD

Shoe String Press
995 Sherman Ave.
Box 4327
Hamden, CT 06514

Sidwick & Jackso..
One Tavistock Chambers
Bloomsbury Way
London WC1A 2SG

Signet Books
(see New American Library)

*Silver Scarab Press
500 Wellesley S.E.
Albuquerque, NM 87106

Simon & Schuster
1230 Avenue of the Americas
New York, NY 10020

Southern Illinois University Press
Box 3697
Carbondale, IL 62901

Neville Spearman
Priory Gate
57 Friars St.
Sudbury, Suffolk,
England

Sphere Books
30–32 Gray's Inn Rd.
London WC1X 8JL

*Roy A. Squires
1745 Kenneth Rd.
Glendale, CA 91201

Starblaze Editions
(see Donning)

*Starmont House
(see FAX)

Stonehill Publishing Co.
 10 E. 40 St.
 New York, NY 10016

*Tamberlane Press
 Box 5402
 San Francisco, CA 94101

Tandem Publishing
 (see Wyndham)

Taplinger Publishing Co.
 200 Park Ave. S.
 New York, NY 10003

Target Books
 (see W. H. Allen)

Times Books
 3 Park Ave.
 New York, NY 10016

Trophy Books
 (see Harper)

*Underwood/Miller
 239 N. Fourth St.
 Columbia, PA 17512

Unicorn Bookshop
 Nant-Gwilwu
 Llanfynydd,
 Carmarthen SA32 7TT,
 Wales

Viking Penguin
 625 Madison Ave.
 New York, NY 10022

Vintage Books
 (see Random House)

Voyager Books
 (see Harcourt)

Walker & Co.
 720 Fifth Ave.
 New York, NY 10019

Warner Books
 75 Rockefeller Plaza
 New York, NY 10019

Franklin Watts
 730 Fifth Ave.
 New York, NY 10019

Weidenfeld Publishers
 11 St. John's Hill
 London SW11 1XA

*Robert Weinberg
 10606 S. Central Park
 Chicago, IL 60655

*Whispers Press
 Box 1492-W
 Azalea St.
 Brown Mills, NJ 08015

Workman Publishing Co.
 One W. 39 St.
 New York, NY 10018

Wyndham Publications
 123 King St.
 Hammersmith, London W6 9JG

Zebra Books
 521 Fifth Ave.
 New York, NY 10017

Index